CAT

INTERACTIVE TEXT

Advanced
Paper 8

Implementing Audit Procedures

BPP is the **official provider** of training materials for the ACCA's CAT qualification. This Interactive Text forms part of a suite of learning tools, which also includes CD-ROMs for tuition and computer based assessment, and the innovative, internet-based 'virtual campus'.

This text has been specifically written to the **current syllabus** and Teaching Guide.

- Clear language and presentation
- Plenty of activities, examples and quizzes to demonstrate and practise techniques
- Syllabus and Teaching Guide
- A question and answer bank prepared by BPP authors

FOR DECEMBER 2005 AND JUNE 2006 EXAMS

BPP PROFESSIONAL EDUCATION

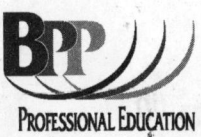

First edition August 2003
Fourth edition June 2005

ISBN 0 7517 2307 X (previous edition 0 7517 1654 5)

British Library Cataloguing-in-Publication Data
*A catalogue record for this book
is available from the British Library*

Published by

*BPP Professional Education
Aldine House, Aldine Place
London W12 8AW*

www.bpp.com

*Printed in Great Britain by W M Print
45-47 Frederick Street
Walsall
West Midlands
WS2 9NE*

All our rights reserved. No part of this publication may be reproduced, stored in a retrieval system or transmitted, in any form or by any means, electronic, mechanical, photocopying, recording or otherwise, without the prior written permission of BPP Professional Education.

We are grateful to the Association of Chartered Certified Accountants for permission to reproduce the syllabus, teaching guide, past examination questions and questions from the pilot paper of which the Association holds the copyright. The answers have been prepared by BPP Professional Education.

©

*BPP Professional Education
2005*

Contents

	Page
INTRODUCTION	
How to use this Interactive Text – Syllabus and study sessions – Approach to examining the syllabus	(iv)

PART A: BUSINESS AND AUDIT FRAMEWORK

1	Business environment	3
2	Auditors' responsibility	19
3	Audit regulation	29
4	Audit engagement	51

PART B: AUDIT PLANNING

5	Risk assessment	69
6	Audit planning	91

PART C: CONTROLS

7	Internal control evaluation	123
8	Tests of controls: income cycles	154
9	Tests of controls: asset cycles	174

PART D: SUBSTANTIVE PROCEDURES

10	Analytical procedures and estimates	191
11	Stocks and work in progress	207
12	Fixed assets	228
13	Debtors and cash	241
14	Liabilities	261

PART E: AUDIT COMPLETION

15	Forming an audit judgement	277
16	The external audit opinion	310

QUESTION BANK   327

ANSWER BANK   339

LIST OF KEY TERMS   379

INDEX   380

REVIEW FORM AND FREE PRIZE DRAW

ORDER FORM

How to use this Interactive Text

HOW TO USE THIS INTERACTIVE TEXT

Aim of this Interactive Text

> To provide the knowledge and practice to help you succeed in the examination for Paper 8 *Implementing Audit Procedures*

To pass the examination you need a thorough understanding in all areas covered by the syllabus and teaching guide.

Recommended approach

(a) To pass you need to be able to answer questions on **everything** specified by the syllabus and teaching guide. Read the text very carefully and do not skip any of it.

(b) Learning is an **active** process. Do **all** the activities as you work through the text so you can be sure you really understand what you have read.

(c) After you have covered the material in the Interactive Text, work through the **Question Bank**, checking your answers carefully against the **Answer Bank**.

(d) Before you take the exam, check that you still remember the material using the following quick revision plan.

    (i) Read through the **chapter topic list** at the beginning of each chapter. Are there any gaps in your knowledge? If so, study the section again.

    (ii) Read and learn the **key terms**.

    (iii) Look at the **exam alerts**. These show the ways in which topics might be examined.

    (iv) Read and learn the **key learning points**, which are a summary of each chapter.

    (v) Do the **quick quizzes** again. If you know what you're doing, they shouldn't take long.

This approach is only a suggestion. You or your college may well adapt it to suit your needs.

Remember this is a **practical** course.

(a) Try to relate the material to your experience in the workplace or any other work experience you may have had.

(b) Try to make as many links as you can from papers at the Introductory, Intermediate and Advanced levels.

SYLLABUS

Introduction

This booklet contains the Study Guide for Paper 8 (GBR): Implementing Audit Procedures.

The Study Guide is designed to help you plan your studies and to provide more detailed interpretation of the syllabus for ACCA's Certified Accounting Technician examinations. It contains both the Syllabus and the Study Sessions for the paper, which you can follow when preparing for the examination.

The Syllabus outlines the content of the paper and how that content is examined. The Study Sessions take the syllabus and expand it into teaching or study sessions of similar length. These sessions indicate what the examiner expects of candidates for each part of the syllabus, and therefore gives you guidance in the skills you are expected to demonstrate in the examinations. The time to complete each session will vary according to your individual capabilities and the time you have available to study. Tuition providers offering face-to-face tuition are recommended to design courses with a minimum of two hours tuition per study session. However, repeated coverage of the material is vital to ensure your understanding and recall of the subject. Be sure to practice past examination questions to consolidate your knowledge and read your *student accountant* magazine regularly.

If you have any queries concerning the study guide, please direct them to:

Education Department
ACCA 29 Lincoln's Inn Fields London WC2A 3EE United Kingdom
tel: +44 (0)20 7396 5891/2 fax: +44 (0)20 7396 5968
e-mail: info@accaglobal.com

Additional information can be accessed on the ACCA website at:
www.accaglobal.com

© The Association of Chartered Certified Accountants
May 2004

ABOUT ACCA
ACCA is the largest and fastest-growing international accounting body, with over 320,000 students and members in 160 countries. ACCA has an extensive network of 70 staffed offices and other centres around the world.

Syllabus

Implementing Audit Procedures (GBR)

AIMS
To develop knowledge and understanding of the audit process from the planning stage through to the reporting stage and the techniques used in the conduct of internal and external audits.

OBJECTIVES
On completion of this paper, candidates should be able to:

- explain the rules of professional conduct relating to the ethics of integrity, objectivity, independence and confidentiality and undertake audit procedures accordingly
- identify control objectives and weaknesses for an accounting system under review
- assess audit risks, produce an audit plan and design appropriate audit procedures
- carry out appropriate audit procedures in accordance with an audit plan on the basis of a validly selected sample
- draw valid conclusions from the results of audit tests
- prepare draft reports relating to an audit assignment.

POSITION OF THE PAPER IN THE OVERALL SYLLABUS
Paper 8 requires knowledge and understanding of Paper 1, *Recording Financial Transactions* and Paper 3, *Maintaining Financial Records*, to provide a basic understanding of the nature and objectives of an audit and general audit practice. Candidates will also be expected to be familiar with Paper 6, *Drafting Financial Statements*.

SYLLABUS CONTENT

1 **The business environment**
   - (a) The nature of accounting records, audit and the audit report
   - (b) Legal requirements for becoming an auditor
   - (c) Legal duties of an auditor
   - (d) Legal responsibilities of auditors
   - (e) Fraud and error
       - (i) liability to clients
       - (ii) liability to third parties

2 **The audit framework**
   - (a) External audit and internal audit
   - (b) Regulatory framework of auditing
       - (i) statutory legislation
       - (ii) auditing standards
       - (iii) requirements of professional bodies
   - (c) The audit engagement process

3 **Audit personnel**
   - (a) The audit team
   - (b) Liaison with client staff
   - (c) Liaison with third parties
       - (i) experts
       - (ii) internal audit

4 **Audit planning**
   - (a) The nature of an audit plan and programme
   - (b) Knowledge of the business
   - (c) Risk
   - (d) Materiality
   - (e) Documentation
   - (f) Audit planning meeting

5 **Accounting systems and controls**
   - (a) The nature of accounting systems
   - (b) General principles of control
   - (c) Techniques to record accounting systems
       - (i) narrative notes
       - (ii) flowcharts
   - (d) Techniques to evaluate accounting systems
       - (i) internal control questionnaires
       - (ii) internal control evaluation questionnaires
       - (iii) checklists
   - (e) Major control cycles (manual and computerised)
       - (i) income (sales)
       - (ii) expenditure (purchases / stock / fixed assets / payroll / expenses)
   - (f) Tests of control
   - (g) Reporting control weaknesses

6 **Audit evidence and sampling**
   - (a) Financial statement assertions
   - (b) Audit evidence and procedures
   - (c) Verification techniques – physical examination, reperformance, third party confirmation, documentary evidence, vouching and analytical review

Implementing Audit Procedures (GBR)

    (d) Audit sampling
    (e) Types of testing – tests of control and substantive testing
    (f) Computer-assisted audit techniques
    (g) Audit of balance sheet items – existence, completeness, ownership, valuation and disclosure

7 Audit completion
    (a) Audit review
        (i) post balance sheet events
        (ii) going concern
        (iii) opening balances and comparatives
    (b) Analytical procedures
    (c) Recording significant and material errors
    (d) Review by senior audit staff
    (e) Report of audit points arising (report to partner)
    (f) Letter of representation

8 Audit report
    (a) The standard audit report
    (b) Qualifications in audit reports

EXCLUDED TOPICS

The following topics are specifically excluded from Paper 8:
- group audits
- corporate governance
- detailed understanding of audit requirements relating to:
  - fraud
  - auditing standards on laws and regulations
  - quality control
  - related parties
  - service organisations
  - reports to those charged with governance
  - reporting to regulators in the financial sector

KEY AREAS OF THE SYLLABUS

The key topic areas are as follows:
- controls
- audit planning
- practical application of audit techniques
- preparing draft reports.

APPROACH TO EXAMINING THE SYLLABUS

The examination is a three-hour written paper. The paper consists of four compulsory questions.

ADDITIONAL INFORMATION

Accounting and auditing standards will not be examined until six months after they have been published. The cut off date for the June examination is 30 November preceding the June examination. The cut off date for the December examination is 31 May preceding the December examination.

Study sessions

Implementing Audit Procedures (GBR)

STUDY SESSIONS

1 **The purpose and scope of an external audit and the audit framework**
   (a) Explain the purpose and scope of an external audit
   (b) Outline the statutory requirements governing the appointment and removal of auditors
   (c) Outline the statutory duties and responsibilities of auditors
   (d) Explain the scope of Statements of Auditing Standards (International Standards on Auditing from December 2005)
   (e) Outline the fundamental principles of independent auditing

2 **Rules of professional conduct and professional ethics**
   (a) Discuss the fundamental principles of the Code of ethics within the Rules of Professional Conduct of ACCA
   (b) Discuss the detailed requirements of, and illustrate the application of professional ethics in the context of auditor independence, objectivity and integrity as set out in ACCA's Code of ethics
   (c) Describe the auditor's responsibility with regard to confidentiality as set out in ACCA's Code of ethics

3 **Internal audit**
   (a) Explain the purpose and scope of internal audit
   (b) Compare and contrast the roles of the internal audit function and the external audit function with regard to the detection of fraud and error
   (c) Identify the factors that external auditors should consider when evaluating the work of internal auditors

4 & 5 **True and fair view, materiality, the auditors' report**
   (a) Explain the concept of a true and fair view
   (b) Explain the concept of materiality and discuss the factors to be considered when making a judgement on whether an item is material
   (c) Provide and review an example of an auditors' report with an unqualified opinion on the financial statements of an incorporated company
   (d) Discuss the basic elements of the auditors' report
   (e) Discuss the concept of 'reasonable assurance'

6 **The audit engagement process**
   (a) Explain the purpose and content of client acceptance procedures comprising client screening, professional clearance and independence checks
   (b) Explain the purpose of an audit engagement letter
   (c) Examine and discuss the contents of an audit engagement letter

7, 8 & 9 **Planning the audit**
   (a) Distinguish between a systems approach to an audit and a direct verification approach
   (b) Explain the concept of audit risk, focusing in particular on inherent risk and control risk
   (c) Explain how auditors use knowledge of the business, in audit planning
   (d) Identify sources from which auditors may obtain knowledge of the business
   (e) Explain the role of audit programmes and summarise the advantages/disadvantages of using standard programmes
   (f) Outline planning issues with regard to audit planning meetings, the timing of audit work, staffing, training of the audit team, the use of suitable experts, and liaison with client staff including internal auditors
   (g) Explain how auditors may plan to use computer assisted audit techniques
   (h) Illustrate the use of an audit planning memorandum

10 **Documenting the audit**
   (a) Discuss the reasons for maintaining audit working papers
   (b) Explain the purpose of the current file and the permanent file
   (c) Describe the contents of a current file and a permanent file
   (d) Outline the quality control procedures that should exist over the review of audit working papers and in the reporting of important audit points to the audit engagement partner

Implementing Audit Procedures (GBR)

(e) Illustrate how information technology can be used in the documentation of audit work

11 Internal control I
 (a) Explain the following terms:
  (i) internal control system
  (ii) control environment
  (iii) control procedures
 (b) Describe the objectives of an internal control system
 (c) Discuss the different types of internal control
 (d) Describe and illustrate the inherent limitations of internal control systems
 (e) Discuss the importance of internal control to auditors

12, 13 & 14 Internal control II
 (a) Describe and illustrate control procedures to meet specified objectives for each of the following functional areas:
  (i) purchases and trade creditors
  (ii) sales and trade debtors
  (iii) wages and salaries
  (iv) tangible fixed assets
  (v) stock
  (vi) bank receipts and payments
  (vii) cash receipts and payments

15 Internal control III
 (a) Distinguish between application controls and general controls in computer-based systems and identify the objectives of each control type
 (b) Provide examples of specific general controls and application controls
 (c) Outline the typical control problems encountered in small computer-based systems

16 & 17 Internal control IV
 (a) Describe the techniques used by auditors to record and evaluate manual and computer-based accounting systems
 (b) Provide examples of, and explain the format and contents of internal control questionnaires (ICQ's) and internal control evaluation questionnaires (ICEQ's)

(c) Explain the purpose of tests of control
(d) Distinguish between tests of control and substantive procedures

18, 19 & 20 Audit testing of accounting systems controls
 (a) Explain the audit approach to testing accounting system controls over the following functional areas:
  (i) purchases and trade creditors
  (ii) sales and trade debtors
  (iii) wages and salaries
  (iv) tangible fixed assets
  (v) stock
  (vi) bank receipts and payments
  (vii) cash receipts and payments
 (b) Explain the purpose of a management letter, indicating when it should be issued
 (c) Provide information on an accounting system in a functional area and prepare points for inclusion in a management letter, in the following format:
  – description of weakness
  – implication of weakness
  – recommendation(s) to address weakness

21 Audit sampling
 (a) Explain the relevance of sampling to the auditor
 (b) Outline selection methods, including random selection, systematic selection and haphazard selection
 (c) Outline the main factors affecting sample size

22 Audit evidence I
 (a) Explain the importance of evidential material in the audit process
 (b) Identify the factors that influence the reliability of audit evidence
 (c) Describe and give examples of procedures used by auditors to obtain audit evidence, including the use of analytical procedures and computer assisted audit techniques

23 Audit evidence II
 (a) Explain the importance of financial statement assertions
 (b) For each area in the financial statements of an

Implementing Audit Procedures (GBR)

incorporated company, provide examples of the representations made by directors

(d) Explain the rationale for designing audit programmes by reference to audit objectives

(e) Outline the factors determining the nature, timing and extent of substantive procedures to be carried out on an audit

24 & 25 Audit evidence III

(a) Design audit programmes to meet specific audit objectives with regard to the following balance sheet items:
  (i) tangible fixed assets
  (ii) investments
  (iii) trade debtors
  (iv) prepayments
  (v) bank and cash
  (vi) trade creditors
  (vii) accruals
  (viii) provisions

26 & 27 Audit evidence IV

(a) Explain why the audit of stock is often an area of high audit risk

(b) Describe the audit procedures that should be undertaken before, during and after attending a stocktake

(c) Discuss the extent to which an auditor can rely on a system of continuous stocktaking

(d) Design an audit programme to meet specific audit objectives for the audit of stock

28 & 29 Audit completion

(a) Explain the purpose and nature of carrying out an overall review of the financial statements prior to expressing an audit opinion and outline the purpose and nature of:
  (i) the application of analytical procedures
  (ii) a review of opening balances and comparatives
  (iii) a review of post balance sheet events
  (iv) an evaluation of Going Concern

(b) Explain the purpose of a letter of representation

(c) Describe the contents of a letter of representation and provide examples of typical representations made in such a letter

30 Audit report

(a) Revise the form and content of an auditors report with an unqualified opinion on the financial statements of an incorporated company (see sessions 4 & 5)

(b) Outline the circumstances in which an auditor should issue a report with:
  (i) a qualified opinion
  (ii) an adverse opinion
  (iii) a disclaimer of opinion

31 & 32 Revision

APPROACH TO EXAMINING THE SYLLABUS

Paper 8 is a three-hour written paper.

It consists of:

	No of marks
4 compulsory written questions of 25 marks each	100
Total	100

Analysis of past papers

June 2005

1	Fixed assets: controls, fixed asset register, disposals and purchases	25
2	Stocktake, revaluation of stocks and cut-off	25
3	Audit planning and audit evidence	25
4	Going concern	25

December 2004

1	Wages: internal controls; internal control objectives	25
2	Appointment, inherent risk	25
3	Audit evidence, explanation of procedures	25
4	Internal audit, fraud, ACCA Code of Ethics	25

June 2004

1	Internal controls, purchase and creditors systems	25
2	Audit approach, audit of sales	25
3	Sampling and debtors	25
4	Independence and objectivity	25

Pilot paper

1	Stock control system, sales completeness	25
2	Stock: risk, cost v NRV	25
3	Fixed assets and debtors: controls, substantive tests	25
4	Engagement letter, knowledge of the business, internal auditors	25

Part A
Business and audit framework

Chapter 1   Business environment

Chapter topic list

1   Introduction
2   The company and the law
3   The audit
4   Internal control

The following study sessions are covered in this Chapter:

		Syllabus reference
1(a)	Explain the purpose and scope of external audit	1
1(b)	Outline the statutory requirements governing the appointment and removal of auditors	1
1(c)	Outline the statutory duties and responsibilities of auditors	1
4(a)	Explain the concept of a true and fair view	1
4(c)	Provide and review an example of an auditors' report with an unqualified opinion on the financial statements of an incorporated company	1
4(d)	Discuss the basic elements of an auditors' report	1
4(e)	Discuss the concept of reasonable assurance	1
3(a)	Explain the purpose and scope of internal audit	2

Part A: Business and audit framework

1 INTRODUCTION

The problem

1.1 Alex has **set up in business** selling flowers. For two years all goes well. The flowers sell steadily and Alex gets some income from the business.

1.2 Alex feels that the business could make more money if he invested in some new premises and if he employed an assistant. He needs more money to do this. **He decides to ask his rich friend Jane to invest** in the business.

1.3 Jane wants to invest but she does not wish to work for the business or take on any risk for the business debts.

1.4 **Jane suggests to Alex that** he converts the business into a **company**. This will mean that if the company becomes insolvent, she will only lose at maximum the amount she has invested in the company. Alex agrees. Jane buys 95% of the shares and Alex buys 5%. They both agree that Alex is to be paid a reasonable salary as managing director of the business.

1.5 At the end of the first year of trading as a limited company, **Jane receives a copy of the accounts. Profits are lower than she expected**. This means that her return from the company (in dividends) will not be as high as she had hoped.

1.6 Jane contacts Alex for an explanation. He tells her that the accounts are accurate. Jane knows that Alex gets paid a salary regardless of what the profits are. She is concerned that this means he is not as worried about profit levels as she is.

1.7 **Jane feels she needs further assurance on the accounts**, but she does not know a great deal about financial matters. How can she obtain the assurance she wants?

The solution

1.8 The assurance Jane is seeking can be given by an **audit** of the financial statements. An auditor can provide the two things Jane requires.

- A **knowledgeable review** of the company's business and of the accounts
- An **impartial view** since Alex's view may be partial

2 THE COMPANY AND THE LAW

The Companies Act 1985

2.1 Jane obtains certain benefits from investing in a company rather than a different form of business vehicle. The key **benefit** is that she will only ever be liable for the cost of her shares. **Creditors of the company** can **never sue Jane for any company debts**.

2.2 This **advantage is offset** by the fact that companies are required to conform to a number of **regulations**, some of which require companies to **publish information** about themselves for the benefit of the public and people who deal with the company, for example, suppliers, customers, lenders.

2.3 The key law for companies in the UK is the **Companies Act 1985** and the Companies Act 1989. We are going to look at what these Acts require companies to keep in relation to financial records and regulations in connection with audit and auditors.

Financial records

'Every company shall keep accounting records which are sufficient to show and explain the company's transactions and are such as to

(a) disclose with reasonable accuracy, at any time, the financial position of the company at that time, and

(b) enable the directors to ensure that any balance sheet and profit and loss account prepared under this Part complies with the requirements of this Act.'

Companies Act 1985

2.4 In other words, the records must be detailed enough that an accountant could walk in on any day and be able to prepare a balance sheet and profit and loss account.

2.5 The Act then gives details of what this means in practice. Accounting records must contain:

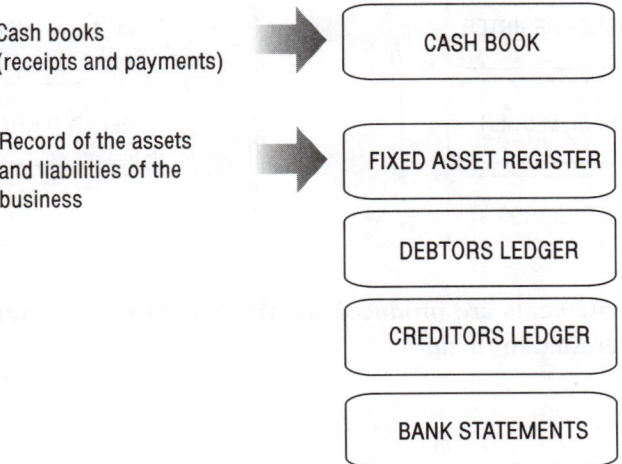

2.6 If the company deals in goods, they are also required to keep:

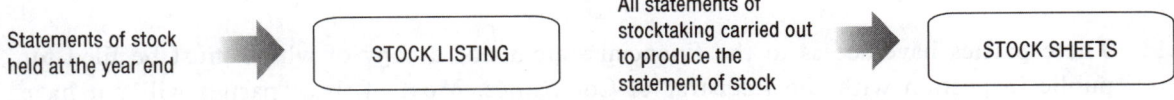

2.7 Where it is not a normal retail trade, statements of all goods sold and purchased showing enough details of the goods and buyers and sellers that they can all be identified, must be retained.

2.8 If the company does not keep these records, the directors and officers of the company may be found guilty of an offence and be imprisoned and/or fined. These records must be kept at the office registered with the Registrar of Companies (a government department) or somewhere else that the directors think is fit.

2.9 The law also requires that these accounting records are kept for a certain period of time:

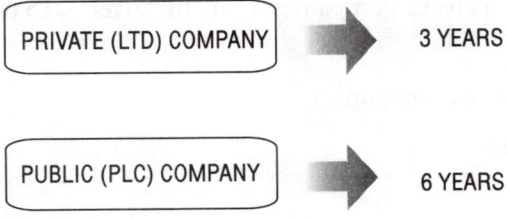

2.10 You should be aware from your other studies that in practice, the detail of the accounting records which a company keeps will vary according to the nature of the business. We can

Part A: Business and audit framework

see above that the law only requires a company to keep stock records if it has stock. Similarly, if it only makes cash sales, it will not need to keep debtors' records.

The financial statements

2.11 As you should be aware from your other studies, directors are required to produce financial statements every year.

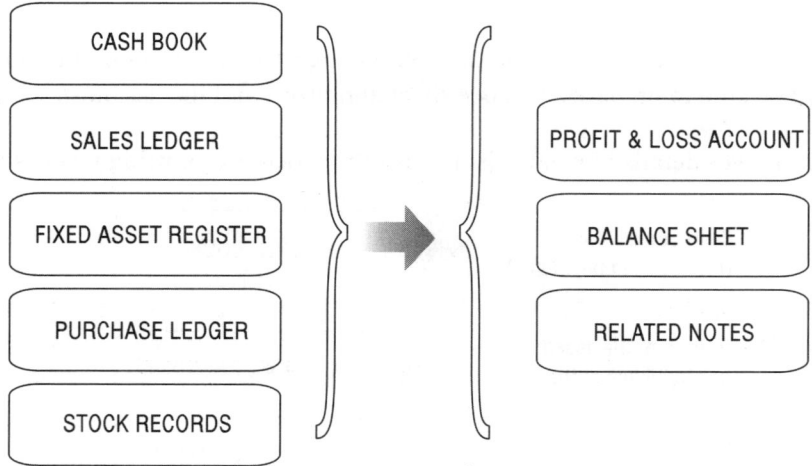

2.12 These financial statements are produced for the benefit of shareholders, but many other parties may be interested in them:

- The bank
- Suppliers
- Customers
- Employees
- Tax authorities

2.13 These parties have access to the financial statements, a copy of which must be filed for public inspection with the Registrar of Companies. **Most** of these parties will not have access to the underlying records.

Audit requirement and exemptions

2.14 The Companies Act 1985 **requires companies to have an audit**. Some other entities, such as building societies, trade unions, housing associations and large charities are also required to have audits under different laws.

2.15 Certain companies are allowed not to have an audit (they are exempt from the audit requirement):

- Small companies (private companies with turnover <£5.6m and balance sheet total <£2.4m)
- Small charities that are companies
- Dormant companies

Auditors

Appointment

2.16 Auditors should usually be appointed by shareholders at a shareholders' annual general meeting. In unusual circumstances they may be appointed by directors. Auditors are usually re-elected annually, but a private (Ltd) company may pass a resolution which deems that the existing auditors are automatically re-elected annually.

Report

2.17 The Companies Act requires auditors to produce a report for company members (shareholders). This should state whether the financial statements show a **true and fair view** of the **state of affairs** at the year end and the **profit and loss** for the year. They shall also consider whether the **report** which the **directors** make as part of the annual statement is **consistent** with the accounts.

2.18 As part of their audit, the auditors must check whether the company has **kept adequate accounting records** (as discussed above) and whether each geographical **branch** of the business has given **sufficient information** for the audit, and that the **underlying records match** the financial statements the directors have prepared.

2.19 The law **does not** state what form the report should take, but auditors usually use one like the one shown on pages 7 - 8, due to professional requirements. The law states that the report must give the auditors' name, the date of the report and their signature. This has been highlighted on the report overleaf.

2.20 There are several other things the Companies Act requires auditors to identify in their report, if relevant:

- Proper accounting records have not been kept
- Proper returns have not been received from branches
- The financial statements do not agree with underlying records
- Information and explanations required by the auditors have not been given by the company officials

2.21 Copies of the auditors' report must be:

- Circulated to members of the company (often at the annual general meeting)
- Sent to the Registrar of Companies

Independent auditors' report to the shareholders of XYZ Limited

We have audited the financial statements of (name of entity) for the year ended ... which comprise (state the primary financial statements such as the profit and loss account, the balance sheet, the cash flow statement, the statements of total recognised gains and losses) and the related notes. These financial statements have been prepared under the historical cost convention (as modified by the revaluation of certain fixed assets) and the accounting policies set out therein.

Respective responsibilities of directors and auditors

The director's responsibilities for preparing the annual report and the financial statements in accordance with applicable law and United Kingdom Accounting Standards are set out in the statement of director's responsibilities.

Our responsibility is to audit the financial statements in accordance with relevant legal and regulatory requirements and United Kingdom Auditing Standards.

Part A: Business and audit framework

properly prepared in accordance with the (Companies Act 1985). We also report to you if, in our opinion, the director's report is not consistent with the financial statements, if the company has not kept proper accounting records, if we have not received all the information and explanations we required for our audit, or if information specified by law regarding directors' remuneration and transactions with the company is not disclosed.

We read other information contained in the annual report and consider whether it is consistent with the audited financial statements. This other information comprises only (the Director's Report, the Chairman's Statement, the Operating and Financial Review). We consider the implications for our report if we become aware of any apparent misstatements or material inconsistencies with the financial statements. Our responsibilities do not extend to any other information.

Basis of audit opinion

We conducted our audit in accordance with United Kingdom Auditing Standards issued by the Auditing Practices Board. An audit includes examination, on a test basis, of evidence relevant to the amounts and disclosures in the financial statements. It also includes an assessment of the significant estimates and judgements made by the directors in the preparation of the financial statements, and of whether the accounting policies are appropriates to the company's circumstances, consistently applied and adequately disclosed.

We planned and performed out audit so as to obtain all the information and explanations which we considered necessary in order to provide us with sufficient evidence to give reasonable assurance that the financial statements are free from material misstatement, whether caused by fraud or other irregularity or error. In forming our opinion we also evaluated the overall adequacy of the presentation of information in the financial statements.

Opinion

In our opinion the financial statements give a true and fair view of the statement of the company's affairs as at ... and of its profit (loss) for the year then ended and have been properly prepared in accordance with the (Companies Act 1985).

Registered auditors   *Address*

Date

> **Point to Note**
>
> ISA 700 *The auditor's report on financial statements* states that illustrative examples of a UK audit report are to be issued in a Bulletin. At present this Bulletin is in draft form only and is therefore not examinable.
>
> The examiner has confirmed that the above format of the audit report (based on SAS 600) will be examinable for December 2005. If the Bulletin becomes examinable for June 2006 candidates it will be covered in the Practice and Revision Kit.

Rights

2.22 The Companies Act gives auditors certain rights, shown in the table.

s 389A(1)	*Access to records*	A right of access at all times to the books, accounts and vouchers of the company
s 389A(1)	*Information and explanations*	A right to require from the company's officers such information and explanations as they think necessary for the performance of their duties as auditors
s 390(1)(a) and (b)	*Attendance at/ notices of general meetings*	A right to attend any general meetings of the company and to receive all notices of and communications relating to such meetings which any member of the company is entitled to receive

1: Business environment

s 390(1)(c)	Right to speak at general meetings	A right to be heard at general meetings which they attend on any part of the business that concerns them as auditors
s 381B(2)-(4)	Rights in relation to written resolutions	A right to receive a copy of any written resolution proposed
s 253	Right to require laying of accounts	A right to give notice in writing requiring that a general meeting be held for the purpose of laying the accounts and reports before the company (if an elective resolution dispensing with laying of accounts is in force)

Resignation

2.23 The law is designed **to ensure** that **auditors do not resign without explaining why**. If auditors wish to resign part-way through their term of office they must:

Step 1. **Instigate resignation procedures**

Auditors deposit **written notice** together with **statement of circumstances** relevant to members/creditors or statement that no circumstances exist

Step 2. **Give notice of resignation**

Sent by **company** to Registrar of Companies within **14 days**

Step 3. **Provide a statement of circumstances**

Sent by:

(a) Auditors to Registrar of Companies within **28 days**

(b) Company to everyone entitled to receive a copy of accounts within **14 days** (unless company applies to court because statement of circumstances defamatory)

Step 4. **Convene a general meeting**

Auditors can **require directors** to call extraordinary general meeting to discuss circumstances of resignation

Directors must send out notice for meeting within **21 days** of having received requisition by auditors

Meeting must take place within **28 days** of **notice** of meeting being sent out

Step 5. **Give a statement prior to general meeting**

Auditors may require company to circulate (different) **statement of circumstances** to everyone entitled to notice of meeting

Step 6. **Other rights of auditors**

Can **receive all notices** that relate to:

(a) A general meeting at which their term of office would have expired
(b) A general meeting where casual vacancy caused by their resignation is to be filled

Can **speak** at these meetings on **any matter** which **concerns them as auditors**

Removal of an auditor

2.24 The auditors **cannot** be removed by board resolution. The right to remove the directors belongs to the shareholders.

2.25 The objects of these provisions are:

- To **preserve the right of the members** to appoint the auditors of their choice
- To **preserve the auditors' independence** of the directors by not permitting directors, who may be in disagreement with the auditors, to dismiss them

Step 1. **Notice of removal**

Either special notice (28 days) with copy sent to auditor
Or if elective resolution in place, **written resolution** to terminate auditors' appointment
Directors must convene meeting to take place within 28 days of notice

Step 2. **Representations**

Auditors can make **representations** on why they ought to stay in office and may require company to state in notice representations have been made and send copy to members

Step 3. **If resolution passed**

(a) Company must **notify registrar** within **14 days**

(b) Auditors must **deposit statement of circumstances** at company's registered office **within 14 days** of ceasing to hold office

(c) Statement must be sent to registrar within **28 days** of deposit

Step 4. **Auditor rights**

Can **receive notice** of and **speak** at:

(a) General meeting at which their term of office would have expired
(b) General meeting where casual vacancy caused by their removal to be filled

Exam alert

You may be asked to apply the statutory rules to a real-life situation, for example considering how the directors can try to have auditors they dislike removed.

3 THE AUDIT

3.1 Once auditors have been appointed for the year, they will carry out an audit at the appropriate time.

Definition of audit

KEY TERM

An **audit** is an exercise that auditors carry out in order to be able to give the legal opinion whether financial statements give a true and fair view.

3.2 An audit is a combination of tests and enquiries and judgements made by the auditors. We shall look at these elements in detail in Parts C and D of this Interactive Text. The purpose of the tests and enquiries and judgements is to give an opinion in a report, which we will look at in more detail in Part E of this Interactive Text.

1: Business environment

True and fair

3.3 The law requires auditors to give an opinion whether financial statements are **true and fair**. However, it does not say what 'true and fair' means. Auditors go by generally accepted meanings:

> **KEY TERMS**
>
> **True:** Information is factual and conforms with reality, not false. In addition the information conforms with required standards and law. The accounts have been correctly extracted from the books and records.
>
> **Fair:** Information is free from discrimination and bias and in compliance with expected standards and rules. The accounts should reflect the commercial substance of the company's underlying transactions.

3.4 EXAMPLE

Here is an example of how a section of a balance sheet can be true, but not fair.

BALANCE SHEET OF A LTD 31 DECEMBER 20X6

	20X6 £	20X5 £
Fixed assets	3,000	3,000
Current assets	800	800

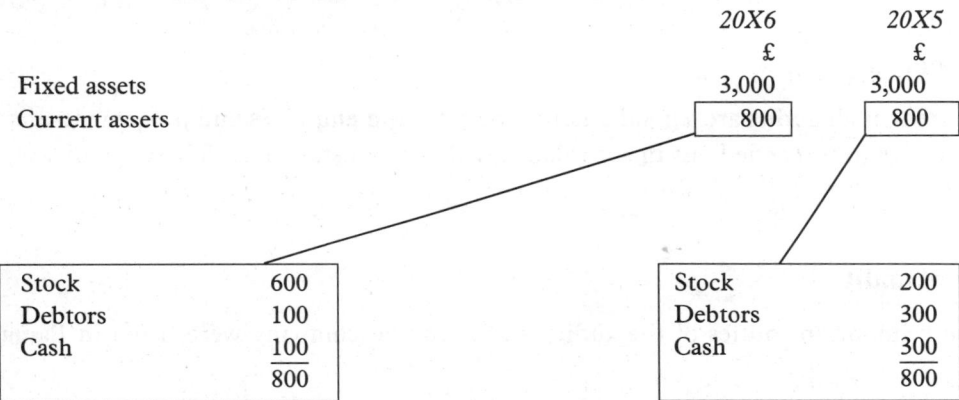

Stock	600		Stock	200
Debtors	100		Debtors	300
Cash	100		Cash	300
	800			800

When just the main headings of fixed and current assets are shown, the impression is given that nothing much has changed at the company from 20X5 to 20X6. However further analysis of the current assets shows that in fact, the situation has changed and the company now has a much less liquid balance sheet. The original information is true, but the information given in the boxes shows that it did not give an accurate impression – it was not fair.

3.5 It is important also to understand that true and fair **does not mean absolutely correct**. Auditors cannot say that financial statements are absolutely correct because:

- Financial statements are a combination of fact and **judgement**, which is subjective
- An audit also includes **judgements** made by the auditors
- Auditors do not test every transaction (or audits would be too expensive) so minor errors may exist
- Company management may hide fraud or make mistakes in drafting financial statements

3.6 An audit therefore gives what is called 'reasonable assurance', rather than **absolute** assurance.

This is defined in the Glossary of Terms as a high, but not absolute, level of assurance. To provide absolute assurance would be very difficult due to the following factors:

- The use of selective testing
- The inherent limitations of internal control
- The fact that much of the evidence available to the auditor is persuasive rather than conclusive
- The use of judgement in gathering and evaluating evidence and forming conclusions based on that evidence

In order to give reasonable assurance the auditor must obtain sufficient appropriate audit evidence enabling him to make a **positive** statement about the truth and fairness of the financial statements in the audit report.

Properly prepared

3.7 Auditors also state whether financial statements are properly prepared. This means prepared in accordance with law and accounting standards. You should know about these from your other studies.

Auditing standards

3.8 To ensure that all audits are a good quality, the tests and enquiries and judgements made by auditors have to be carried out in accordance with certain standards. These are discussed in Chapter 3.

Chronology of audit

3.9 The more important duties of the auditors of a limited company were listed in Paragraph 2.17.

3.10 Certain **common elements** form a major part of the auditors' work on any client.

- **Making tests** and enquiries to form an opinion as to the reliability of the accounting records
- **Checking** the **accounts** against the underlying records
- **Reviewing** the **accounts** for compliance with the law and standards

3.11 The main stages of an audit that are **normally** followed are outlined here.

Determine audit approach

Stage 1. The scope of the audit and the auditors' general approach should be determined.

A **letter of engagement** setting out the terms of the audit will be submitted or confirmed before the start of each annual audit. (See Chapter 4).

Auditors must prepare an **audit strategy** to be placed on the audit file. (See Chapter 6.) The planning aspects of an audit are very important.

1: Business environment

Understanding the entity (including documenting and confirming the accounting systems and internal control)

Stage 2. The objective here is to obtain information to enable the auditor to assess the risks of material misstatement in the financial statements. Procedures include inquiries of management, analytical procedures, observation and inspection and prior period knowledge.

Stage 3. The objective at this stage is to determine the **flow of documents** and **extent of controls** in existence. This is a fact-finding exercise. (See Chapter 7.)

Stage 4. The objective here is to prepare a **comprehensive record** for use in evaluation of the systems. (See Chapter 7.)

Stage 5. The auditors' objective here is to **confirm** that the **system recorded** is the same as that in **operation**. (See Chapter 7.) **Walkthrough** tests may be used.

Assess the risk of material misstatement

Stage 6 This includes **evaluating** the **systems** to assess their reliability and formulate a basis for testing their effectiveness in practice.

Select audit procedures to respond to risk of material misstatement

Stage 7. If the controls are assessed as effective in theory, tests should be performed to check that they do work in practice. These are called **tests of controls**.

Stage 7 should **only be carried out** if the controls are evaluated at Stage 6 as probably being effective.

If the auditors know that the controls are ineffective then there is no point in carrying out tests of controls which will merely confirm what is already known. Instead the auditors should go straight on to carry out full substantive procedures (Stage 9).

Stage 8. After evaluating the systems and carrying out tests of controls, auditors normally send management a **report to management** identifying weaknesses and recommending improvements.

Stages 9. The auditor must always carry out **substantive procedures** on material items. These tests are not concerned with the workings of the system. They are concerned with substantiating the figures in the **accounting records**, and eventually, in the final accounts themselves.

Review the financial statements

Stage 10. The aim of the overall review is to determine the **overall reliability** of the accounts by making a critical analysis of content and presentation.

Express an opinion

Stage 11. The **report to the members** (Auditors' report) is the end product of the audit in which the auditors express their opinion of the accounts. (See Chapter 16)

Stage 12. The **report to management** is an additional end product of the audit. Its purpose is to make further suggestions for improvements in the systems and to place on record specific points in connection with the audit and accounts.

3.12 All these matters will be looked at in the rest of this Interactive Text.

4 INTERNAL CONTROL

A different problem

4.1 Jane is happier about the financial statements that Alex has sent her now she knows that she can appoint someone to check that they are true and fair.

4.2 However, she is worried about some other things. For example, how does she know that the systems Alex has put in place to record transactions on a daily basis work properly? How does she know that Alex won't do business with people that defraud the company and waste her investment? In other words, how does she know that the company is operating efficiently and effectively?

The solution

4.3 In simple terms, there is no solution to this problem. Jane has invested in Alex's company. She should have considered whether Alex is a good manager before she made that investment, and now she has to **trust** that he will manage it well, as he has a legal duty to do.

However, two things could give her some assurance about this problem too.

Internal control

4.4 Directors set up internal control to mitigate against risks that the company faces. These systems can be wide-ranging. For example, management might institute controls such as:

- Credit sales will not be made to customers unless references about them have been obtained
- Two directors have to agree before the company buys fixed assets

4.5 We will look at internal control in more detail in Chapter 7. But if Jane knows there is a system in place, this may give her comfort about the business operating effectively.

Internal audit 12/04

4.6 Large companies may employ people who have auditing skills to oversee whether internal control systems operate effectively. These people are known as internal auditors, because they are employed by and are internal to the company.

4.7 Internal auditors are **very different** from external auditors, although they use similar skills. The key difference is that internal auditors report to directors, not shareholders. The differences are outlined in the following table.

DIFFERENCES BETWEEN EXTERNAL AND INTERNAL AUDITORS		
	External	Internal
Independence	Independent of organisation	Appointed by management
Responsibilities	Fixed by statute	Decided by management
Report to	Members	Management
Scope of work	Express an opinion on truth and fairness of accounts	Consider whatever financial and operational areas management determines

4.8 Alex's business is likely to be too small to be able to afford to employ an internal audit department. However, if in future the business were to grow, the directors could consider establishing one.

4.9 An internal audit department would benefit the company as a whole. It would have no direct benefit to Jane, but she could take comfort from the fact that she knew the internal control systems were being checked to ensure they were operating efficiently and effectively.

Activity 1.1

(a) What does an unqualified audit report imply?

(b) What, according to the suggested wording of the statement of directors' responsibilities, are directors required to do when preparing accounts?

Activity 1.2

Louie and Dewie were in business as a partnership manufacturing multi-coloured teddy bears. They have now decided to incorporate their business as Louie and Dewie Ltd, and have appointed your firm as auditors. They know that the company's accounts will have to show a true and fair view, but are not sure what the phrase 'true and fair view' means.

Required

Explain in a letter to Louie and Dewie what is meant by the term true and fair view and how it applies to accounts. Use terminology that they will understand.

Activity 1.3

Dan and Thomas are in partnership together. Thomas has always been responsible for the financial side of the partnership while Dan has been responsible for sales. Recently a customer has told Dan that there would be advantages for the partnership in having the accounts and accounting records audited. Dan has asked you if what the customer says is true.

Required

Explain to Dan what the advantages will be of having the partnership's accounts and records audited.

Part A: Business and audit framework

Key learning points

- Companies are subject to law, specifically the Companies Acts 1985 and 1989.
- The Companies Act 1985 requires companies to:
    - Keep accounting records
    - Have an annual audit for the benefit of shareholders
- The Companies Act 1985 requires auditors to:
    - Give an opinion as to whether the accounts give a true and fair view
    - Ensure the directors' report is consistent with the accounts
    - Be appointed by the shareholders
- The Act also gives auditors certain rights, such as to be given information. The auditors must report if information is not given or certain other matters are not complied with.
- The aim of an audit is for auditors to report on whether a true and fair view is shown by the accounts.
- The key stages of an audit are:
    - Understand the entity and assess risk of material misstatement
    - Carry out procedures to obtain sufficient appropriate audit evidence
    - Evaluate the presentation of accounts
    - Issue a report containing a clear expression of opinion.
- The key stages of the audit process are:
    - Determine audit approach
    - Understand the entity
    - Assess the risk of material misstatement
    - Select audit procedures to respond to risk of material misstatements
    - Review the financial statements
    - Express an opinion
- Internal auditors are employed as part of an organisation's internal control. Their responsibilities are determined by management and may be wide-ranging.

Quick quiz

1. Auditors normally report on whether accounts give a _____ and _____ view. Fill in the blanks.
2. What are the main sections in the current unqualified audit report?
3. What are some limitations on auditing?
4. Which statute principally governs the audit of limited companies?
5. What type of tests confirm auditors' understanding of an accounting system?
6. What areas of a company's business would tests of controls normally cover?
7. What type of procedures do auditors use to test the financial statements?
8. As well as reporting on the financial statements, what other type of report might auditors make at the end of the audit?

1: Business environment

Answers to quick quiz

1. Auditors normally report on whether accounts give a **true** and **fair** view.

2. The main sections of the audit report are:

   (a) The introduction identifying the financial statements audited
   (b) The respective responsibilities of directors and auditors
   (c) Scope paragraph (basis of opinion)
   (d) The opinion

3. Limitations on auditing include those resulting from:

   (a) The impracticality of examining all items within an account balance or class of transactions
   (b) The inherent limitations of any accounting and control system
   (c) The possibility of collusion or misrepresentation for fraudulent purposes
   (d) Most audit evidence being persuasive rather than conclusive.

4. The Companies Act 1985 governs the audit of limited companies.

5. Walk-through tests confirm auditors' understanding of an accounting system.

6. Tests of control normally cover only those areas subject to effective internal control.

7. Substantive procedures are used by auditors to test financial statements.

8. As well as issuing an audit report, auditors might also send a final report to management.

Answers to activities

Answer 1.1

(a) An unqualified audit report implies:

   (i) Proper accounting records have been kept and proper returns have been received from the branches not visited by the auditors.
   (ii) The accounts agree with the accounting records and returns.
   (iii) All necessary information and explanations have been received by the auditors.
   (iv) Details of directors' emoluments and other benefits have been correctly disclosed.
   (v) Details of loans and other transactions with directors and others have been correctly disclosed in the accounts.
   (vi) The information given in the directors' report is consistent with the accounts.

(b) When preparing accounts directors should:

   (i) Select suitable accounting policies and then apply them consistently
   (ii) Make judgements and estimates that are reasonable and prudent
   (iii) State whether applicable accounting standards have been followed (large companies)
   (iv) Prepare the accounts on the going concern basis unless inappropriate

Answer 1.2

Louie and Dewie Ltd
Paddington House
Teddy Road
Bear Cross BE1 1AR

22 October 20X7

Dear Mr Louie and Mr Dewie

Thank you for your letter of 18 October. As you stated we, as your auditors, are required to report on whether your accounts show a true and fair view. I set out below what these terms mean, and how they apply in the context of your accounts.

Part A: Business and audit framework

Truth

To be true, accounts should not contain false statements or material errors. An example of a false statement would be that the company had not paid any emoluments to you as directors when in fact emoluments had been paid. A material error is an error which could affect the views of the users of the accounts, including yourselves as directors and also the bank and the Inland Revenue. For example if stocks were overvalued by £20,000, this might mean that the bank took a more favourable view of your profitability and liquidity, and therefore be influenced in making a lending decision.

Fairness

Fairness means that the accounts should show an unbiased picture of the company's business and should be prepared using accounting policies that are appropriate to the business. Fairness also implies that the accounts should reflect the commercial substance of the company's transactions. For example a number of the assets you have leased will be included on the balance sheet as if you owned them, since you are receiving most of the benefits and are bearing most of the costs that arise during the assets' useful lives. Fairness also involves taking a prudent view of future events that affect the accounts, for example making provisions against debtors who are unlikely to pay what they owe you.

Truth and fairness in accounts

The Companies Act lays down a number of requirements with which accounts should comply. These include the requirement for accounts to contain a profit and loss account and balance sheet, requirements governing the formats these can take, and also the detailed information that should be contained in the profit and loss account, balance sheet or notes to the accounts. Compliance with the Companies Act requirements is normally necessary for the accounts to show a true and fair view; however if compliance with the Companies Act means that the accounts do not show a true and fair view in any respect, then the need to show a true and fair view overrides the detailed Companies Act requirements.

An additional source of guidance on what constitutes a true and fair view is given by accounting standards published by the Accounting Standards Board. These are known as Statements of Standard Accounting Practice (SSAPs) and Financial Reporting Standards (FRSs), and give guidance on subjects such as depreciation of fixed assets and accounting for stock. The Companies Act does gives statutory backing to these standards. Again however the need to show a true and fair view is paramount.

Finally I should mention that legal guidance states that what constitutes a true and fair view is not fixed but evolves over time, since the expectations of users change over time.

Please do not hesitate to contact me should you wish to discuss truth and fairness further.

Yours sincerely

A Partner

Answer 1.3

The partnership will gain the following advantages from having the books audited.

(a) Although Dan presumably has a good idea about the partnership's sales, he may not be aware of other financial transactions of the partnership. For Dan, an audit by someone who is objective and who can understand the accounting records will give reassurance that the partnership is producing the results claimed by Thomas.

(b) An audit may identify weaknesses in the accounting system of the business. The auditor may be able to suggest improvements which would save the partnership time and money.

(c) Arguments between the partners will be avoided if the accounts are checked by an independent auditor. This particularly applies to partner profit shares.

(d) The accounts will have greater credibility for other users if they are audited. For example a bank may make extra finance conditional on the partnership producing audited accounts.

Now try Question 1 in the Exam Question Bank

Chapter 2   Auditors' responsibility

Chapter topic list

1   Introduction
2   Statement of directors' responsibilities
3   Fraud and error
4   Contract law
5   Third parties

The following study sessions are covered in this Chapter:

Syllabus reference

1(c)   Outline the statutory duties and responsibilities of auditors   1

3(b)   Compare and contrast the roles of the internal audit function and the external
       audit function with regard to the detection of fraud and error   2

Part A: Business and audit framework

1 INTRODUCTION

1.1 In Chapter 1, we introduced the key statutory duty of the external auditor, which is to report to shareholders of the company on the truth and fairness of the financial statements. However, the auditors' responsibilities do not end there.

1.2 The **law** imposes other statutory duties on the auditor and these matters are reported on by implication in the audit report. We covered most of the issues in the diagram below in Chapter 1, but shall look particularly at the statement of directors' responsibilities here.

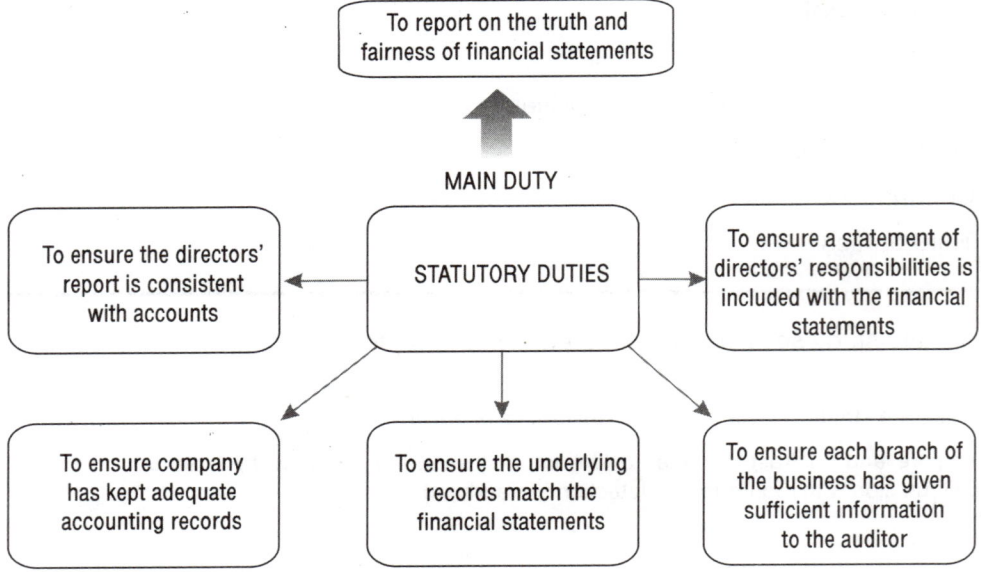

1.3 Auditing standards impose further **professional** responsibilities on the auditors in respect of fraud and error. We shall look at these, and compare them to the duties of internal auditors.

1.4 Lastly, as service providers, auditors also have a general legal duty to follow auditing standards as part of their statutory duty of care. We shall explore to whom auditors may have liability in the event of negligence.

1.5 The law gives certain parties some remedies in the event of the auditors making a mistake. However, available remedies fall into two categories, and a third party such as the bank is less likely to have a successful claim against the auditor. The key claimant is the company, with whom the auditors have a **contract**.

1.6 Note that in this context, the **company** means all the shareholders together.

1.7 Third parties, such as the bank or individual shareholders **may** have a claim against the auditors. As they have no contract with the auditors, this may be more difficult to prove.

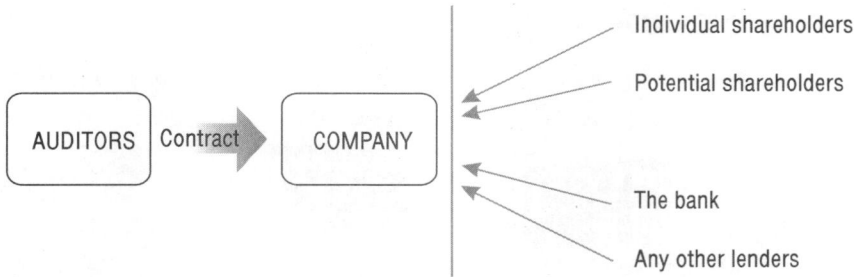

1.8 As the auditors have no direct contact with these third parties, the law states that they can only be liable to them if the auditors were aware that the third party **existed AND** that they were going to **rely** on the audited accounts. Even if both these factors are true, the auditor may not be liable to the third party.

1.9 In the case of **individual shareholders**, the **reliance** this refers to is **additional reliance** to the usual reliance of seeing how their existing investment has been maintained in the past year. In other words, individual shareholders could only have a case if the auditor was aware that they were using the audited accounts for an **additional purpose,** for example, buying new shares in the company.

2 STATEMENT OF DIRECTORS' RESPONSIBILITIES

2.1 As part of the report which they put together to accompany the financial statements, the directors of a company should include a statement of directors' responsibilities, such as:

> Company law requires the directors to prepare financial statements for each financial year which give a true and fair view of the state of affairs of the company and of the profit or loss of the company for that period. In preparing those financial statements, the directors are required to:
>
> (a) Select suitable accounting policies and then apply them consistently
>
> (b) Make judgements and estimates that are reasonable and prudent
>
> (c) State whether applicable accounting standards have been followed, subject to any material departures disclosed and explained in the financial statements (large companies only)
>
> (d) Prepare the financial statements on the going concern basis unless it is inappropriate to presume that the company will continue in business (if not a separate statement on going concern is made by the directors)
>
> The directors are responsible for keeping proper accounting records which disclose with reasonable accuracy at any time the financial position of the company and to enable them to ensure that the financial statements comply with the Companies Act 1985. They are also responsible for safeguarding the assets of the company and hence for taking reasonable steps for the prevention and detection of fraud and other irregularities.

2.2 This wording can be adapted to suit the specific situation.

Auditors' responsibility

2.3 If the directors do not include a section of this nature in their annual report, the auditors should include it in the audit report.

Part A: Business and audit framework

3 FRAUD AND ERROR

3.1 ISA 240 *The auditor's responsibility to consider fraud in an audit of financial statements* defines these terms as follows.

> **ISA 240.5/6**
>
> The term 'error' refers to an unintentional misstatement in financial statements, including the omission of an amount or a disclosure such as the following:
>
> - A mistake in gathering or processing data from which financial statements are prepared
> - An incorrect accounting estimate arising from oversight or misinterpretation of the facts
> - A mistake in the application of accounting principles relating to measurement, recognition, classification, presentation or disclosure
>
> The term fraud refers to an intentional act by one or more individuals among management, those charged with governance, employees or third parties involving the use of deception to obtain an unjust or illegal advantage.

As you can see from the above definitions, the critical decision is whether the action was **intentional** or **unintentional**.

3.2 Fraud and error, say in recording original transactions when they happen, may cause financial statements to not give a true and fair view. The **directors** have a **statutory duty** to protect the assets of the company, and this includes a duty to prevent and detect fraud and error. A major way directors try to do this is by having internal control and, sometimes, internal auditors, which we mentioned in Chapter 1.

External auditors

3.3 Auditing standards give guidance to auditors about detecting misstatements in financial statements. These misstatements may be caused by either fraud or error, although error is likely to be more common. We will focus heavily on the procedures to detect material misstatements due to error in Part B of this Text. Here, we shall look briefly at procedures relating to fraud, which you do not need to know in so much detail.

What is the auditors' responsibility for fraud?

3.4 This is set out in ISA 240 *The auditor's responsibility to consider fraud in an audit of financial statements*. This states that:

> **ISA 240.24/27**
>
> The auditors should maintain an attitude of professional scepticism throughout the audit, recognising the possibility that a material misstatement due to fraud could exist, notwithstanding the auditor's past experience with the entity about the honesty and integrity of management and those charged with governance.
>
> Members of the engagement team should discuss the susceptibility of the entity's financial statements to material misstatements due to fraud.

3.5 We will talk about **materiality** in Chapter 6. The key thing to note is that auditors must be **aware**. Whatever task they are carrying out on an audit, they should be aware that fraud might exist. If they are **put on enquiry** by certain factors they notice, they must satisfy

themselves as to what those factors indicate. In practical terms however the risk of not detecting material misstatement resulting from fraud is higher than the risk from error due to factors such as deliberate concealment and collusion.

What should auditors do if they think fraud exists?

Step 1. **Carry out extra or different procedures**

Step 2. **Document their findings**

Step 3. **Make appropriate reports**

Step 4. **Consider the impact on the rest of the audit**

3.6 The following factors indicate a possibility of fraud.

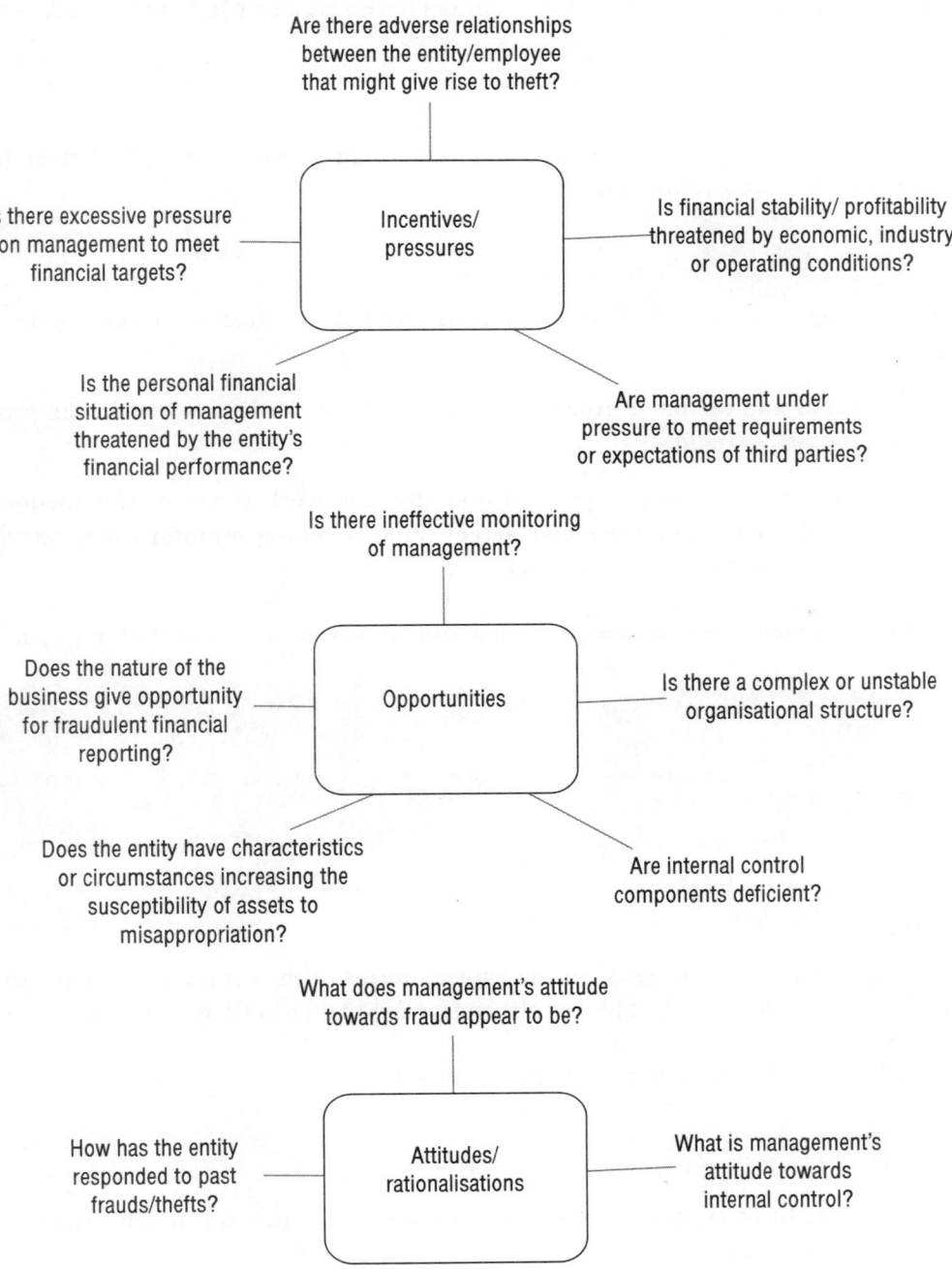

Part A: Business and audit framework

Reporting

3.7 There are three potential sets of people that the auditors could report to:

MANGEMENT	☑ If they actually discover fraud by employees
	☑ If they suspect fraud by employees
	☒ If they think the suspected fraud casts doubt on the integrity of the managers

| THOSE CHARGED WITH GOVERNANCE (DIRECTORS) | ☑ If they have identified fraud involving management |
| | ☑ If they have identified fraud involving employees who have significant roles in internal controls |

| THIRD PARTIES | ☑ If the auditors have a statutory duty to do so. |

Internal auditors

3.8 Remember that internal auditors are employed by the company as part of their internal control and business risk systems.

What is the internal auditors' responsibility for fraud?

3.9 Fraud is a **key business risk**. It is the responsibility of the directors to prevent and detect fraud.

3.10 As the **internal auditor has a role in risk management** he is involved in the process of managing the risk of fraud.

3.11 The internal auditor can help to **prevent** fraud by their work **assessing the adequacy and effectiveness of control systems** and **detect** fraud by **being mindful** when carrying out their work and **reporting any suspicions**.

3.12 The very **existence of an internal audit** department may act as a **deterrent** to fraud.

Exam alert
You could be asked to compare and contrast this aspect of internal and external auditors as part of a question.

4 CONTRACT LAW

4.1 The company and auditors agree on the **express terms** of the contract which are set out in an engagement letter. We shall look at the engagement letter in Chapter 4.

4.2 English law also imposes **implied terms** into contracts.

Implied terms

4.3 Law states that there are certain terms which **always** exist in a contract between the audit firm and the company:

- The auditors have a duty to exercise **reasonable care**.

2: Auditors' responsibility

- The auditors have a duty to carry out the work required with **reasonable expediency**.
- The auditors have a right to **reasonable remuneration**.

What does a duty of reasonable care mean?

4.4 There is not a list of things that an auditor must do/not do to prove he has exercised a duty of reasonable care. However, there are several guidelines.

- Auditors should use generally accepted auditing techniques (that is, adhere to auditing standards which we shall discuss in the next chapter)
- If auditors' suspicions are aroused, they must carry out investigations until they are satisfied (this is called being 'put on enquiry')
- Auditors must act honestly and carefully when making judgements

Negligence

4.5 If the auditors breach the terms of their contract the **company** will have a claim against them for damages.

4.6 If the auditors breach their **implied duty of care** under the contract, the company may be able to sue them for **negligence**.

4.7 Three things must exist for the company to bring a successful claim:

(a) **Duty of care**

There existed a duty of care enforceable at law. *(Under a **contract**, this is always the case.)*

(b) **Negligence**

In a situation where a duty of care existed, the auditors were negligent in the performance of that duty, judged by the accepted professional standards of the day.

(c) **Damages**

The client has suffered some monetary loss as a direct consequence of the negligence on the part of the auditors.

5 THIRD PARTIES

5.1 If the auditors have been negligent, it is possible that a third party may also have a claim against the auditors even though they do not have a contract with them.

Third party negligence claims

5.2 The three requirements for a third party negligence claim are the same as they are for the company:

(a) **Duty of care**

There existed a duty of care enforceable at law. *(Without a **contract**, this may not be the case.)*

(b) **Negligence**

In a situation where a duty of care existed, the auditors were negligent in the performance of that duty, judged by the accepted professional standards of the day.

Part A: Business and audit framework

(c) **Damages**

The client has suffered some monetary loss as a direct consequence of the negligence on the part of the auditors.

Duty of care

5.3 With third party negligence claims, the key issue is whether the auditor owed the third party a duty of care. The answer to this question can be seen to an extent in the cases that judges have considered in the past.

5.4 As a general rule (used in a case known as *Caparo*), it seems that judges **do not think** that **auditors owe third parties a duty of care**. It is only in **exceptional** circumstances that such a duty arises.

5.5 The exceptional circumstances which judges have referred to are when an auditor knows that a third party is relying on the audited accounts. For example, if a director tells the auditor that the bank will rely on the audited accounts, or if someone says to the auditor that he will purchase new shares on the strength of the audited accounts.

5.6 Remember that the auditor is entitled to try to **disclaim liability** to those people, for example, by writing to them and stating that the audit report is only for the purposes of the shareholders and that they do not admit legal liability to anyone else. If the third party tried to bring a negligence claim, a judge would have to determine whether such a letter had legal effect, given all the facts.

Activity 2.1

You are the auditor of Falmouth Ltd and are currently planning this year's audit. You have just had a planning meeting with the company's Managing Director, during which he has told you about two anonymous tip-offs he has received concerning frauds at the two largest of the company's five branches.

(a) He has been told at one branch that the manager has been submitting false claims for travel expenses and false invoices for non-existent purchases in order to fund his own tastes for expensive cars and his girlfriend's tastes for jewellery and foreign holidays.

(b) At another branch, the stores staff have been acting in collusion to steal significant quantities of stock. They have done this by claiming that certain stock is damaged or scrap, and has therefore been disposed of for nil value.

What actions will you take as auditor to investigate these allegations?

2: Auditors' responsibility

Key learning points

- Auditors have statutory duties and professional duties in respect of audits.
- The auditors must include a statement of directors' responsibilities in their report if the directors do not elsewhere.
- Auditors must be aware of the possibilities of misstatements in financial statements due to fraud or error.
- Auditors may have to report to various parties in the event that fraud, error or non-compliance with law is suspected.
- The law implies terms into the contract between the auditors and the company.
- A key implied term is that auditors will exercise reasonable care.
- If the auditors breach their duty of care and it causes loss to the company, the company may sue the audit firm for damages.
- Third parties (for example banks, individual shareholders) do not have a contract with the audit firm.
- Therefore, auditors do not automatically owe third parties a duty of care.
- Third parties may have a claim against auditors for negligence, if they were in a special relationship with the auditor:
  - If the auditor knows they exist
  - If the auditor knows they intend to rely on audited financial statements

Quick quiz

1. What should the auditors do if the directors have not included a statement of directors' responsibilities in their report?
2. How much assurance of detecting fraud and error should auditors seek to obtain from audit procedures?
3. When should auditors disclose suspicions of fraud to third parties?
4. What implied term is included in a contract between audit firm and audit client?
5. What must a client prove to bring a successful action against auditors in contract?
6. Why is the situation between auditors and third parties different from auditors and audit clients?

Answers to quick quiz

1. Include it in their audit report.
2. Auditors should have a **reasonable expectation** of detecting fraud and error.
3.
   - When the suspected fraud causes doubt on the integrity of management
   - If it is the public interest to make such a report and the directors refuse to do so.
4. A duty on the part of the auditors to exercise reasonable care.
5.
   - A duty of care, enforceable at law, existed
   - The auditors were negligent in performance of that duty (according to contemporary professional standards)
   - The client has suffered financial loss as a result of the auditors' negligence
6. Auditors automatically owe clients a duty of (reasonable) care under the terms of the contract between them. There is no such 'automatic' duty to third parties, who must prove such a duty exists.

Part A: Business and audit framework

Answer to activity

Answer 2.1

As auditor, I have a responsibility under ISA 240 to plan procedures that give reasonable assurance of detecting fraud that has a material effect on the company's financial statements. The indications are that the amounts involved are material, and I have also been warned by the managing director that there may be potential problems. I would therefore investigate the allegations as part of the audit.

I would discreetly try and check if the branch manager had a lifestyle that appeared to be unduly lavish. There may be legitimate reasons for expensive purchases, for example a legacy or lottery win.

I would also consider the general behaviour of the manager during the audit. Signs of particular concern would include a lack of co-operation, evidence that the branch's staff were cowed, and general evidence of limited central control of the branch, as well as lack of the specific controls outlined below.

Travel expenses

I would carry out analytical procedures on travel expenses to see how they compared with previous years and also with the levels of expenses at other branches. I would investigate significant variations, although there may be legitimate reasons for these, for example special sales promotions.

I would also consider the controls operated by head office over the expenses. Strong controls would include head office booking of tickets or hotel accommodation, and approval of other travel expenses.

I would also examine the documentation for individual expenses, considering whether the amounts claimed appeared reasonable, and checking with other evidence that the travel had been undertaken, for example evidence of sales arising

Purchases

I would also consider analytical evidence here. As well as comparing levels of purchases with previous years and other branches, I would also consider profit margins, and attempt to reconcile amounts purchased with amounts sold and in stock.

I would consider internal controls over purchases. I would assess the strength of the system, for example whether suppliers were chosen from an approved list, and whether payments to suppliers could be made without being supported by a valid purchase invoice or purchase order. I would also ascertain the degree of involvement of the branch manager in the purchasing process, whether he chose suppliers, or whether there were any suppliers that he handled directly outside the normal purchase system.

I would also scrutinise the records of suppliers to see if any appeared to have unusual addresses such as box numbers or an address which was the same as the home address of the branch manager. I would examine individual invoices to see if they had unusual features such as missing addresses or phone numbers, incomplete or inadequate product descriptions or were photocopies. I would also be alert for different suppliers with the same address or with similar business stationery.

I would scrutinise the records of stock written off and ascertain the reasons for write-off. If the company had a policy for scrapping stock, I would ascertain whether the write-offs fulfilled that policy. If stock had to be written off for reasons such as deterioration due to damp, I would check whether the problem had been remedied. I would also consider whether stock write-offs had to be authorised; I would gain comfort if write-offs had to be authorised by someone who was independent of stores.

I would also carry out analytical procedures on stock write-offs, considering the amounts written off and the proportion of stock held that was written off. I would compare these figures with write-offs for previous years and write-offs for other branches. I would also consider whether stock orders appeared to be in excess of requirements, as some stock might be ordered just to be stolen.

I would review the records of internal stock-takes carried out during the year. I would check whether they were carried out by staff who were independent of the stock section, and whether they identified particular problems at the branch with obsolete or slow-moving stock.

Lastly I would also attend the end of year stocktake. I would pay particular attention to the instructions for dealing with obsolete or slow-moving stock, and check at the stocktake that these instructions were being put into practice. I would also consider the condition of stock identified as damaged or obsolete to see if the assessment appeared reasonable.

Now try Question 2 in the Exam Question Bank

Chapter 3   Audit regulation

Chapter topic list

1. Introduction
2. Structure of the UK accounting and auditing profession
3. Auditing standards
4. APB Ethical Standards
5. ACCA Rules of Professional Conduct
6. Integrity, objectivity and independence
7. The professional duty of confidence

The following study sessions are covered in this Chapter:

Syllabus reference

1(d)	Explain the scope of Statements of Auditing Standards	2
1(e)	Outline the fundamental principles of independent auditing	2
2(a)	Discuss the fundamental principles of the Code of Ethics within the Rules of Professional Conduct of ACCA	2
2(b)	Discuss the detailed requirements of, and illustrate the application of, professional ethics in the context of auditor independence, objectivity and integrity as set out in ACCA's Code of Ethics	2
2(c)	Describe the auditor's responsibility with regard to confidentiality as set out in ACCA's Code of Ethics	2

Part A: Business and audit framework

1 INTRODUCTION

1.1 This chapter summarises the roles of the various authorities that make the rules that affect auditors in this country. The Companies Act 1989 set up a system of audit regulation, administered by a number of **Recognised Supervisory Bodies** (RSBs).

1.2 These bodies aim to ensure that audits are conducted competently, by auditors who are '**fit and proper**'. To this end each RSB operates a **monitoring regime**, which involves periodic visits to firms by inspectors.

1.3 All auditors must follow certain standards when carrying out an audit. The body that sets those standards is the **Auditing Practices Board**. The most important guidance the Board issues is **Statements of Auditing Standards**, which contain principles and procedures that all auditors are obliged to follow.

1.4 Auditors are also subject to the **ethical rules of their RSB**. Lastly in this chapter we shall look at the key **ethical guidance issued by ACCA**.

2 STRUCTURE OF THE UK ACCOUNTING AND AUDITING PROFESSION

2.1 In the UK there are a large number of different accountancy, or accountancy-related, institutes and associations such as the Association of Chartered Certified Accountants (ACCA) or Chartered Institute of Management Accountants (CIMA).

2.2 All these bodies vary from each other depending on the **nature of their aims** and the **specialisms** their members wish to attain. They are all, however, characterised by various attributes:

- Stringent entrance requirements (examinations and practical experience)
- Strict codes of ethics
- Technical updating of members.

2.3 The membership of all these bodies is scattered through practice, industry, government and public bodies.

Eligibility as an external auditor

2.4 **Membership** of a Recognised Supervisory Body is the **main criteria** for eligibility as an auditor. An audit firm may be a body corporate (such as a company), a partnership or a sole practitioner. There is no such requirement for internal auditors.

2.5 The Companies Act 1985 also requires an auditor to hold an '**appropriate qualification**'. A person holds an 'appropriate qualification' if he or she has gained one of the following.

- Acknowledgement that he or she has met the **criteria** for appointment as an auditor under CA 1985
- A **recognised qualification** obtained in the UK
- An **approved overseas qualification**

Ineligibility as auditor

2.6 Under the Companies Act 1985, a person is **ineligible** for appointment as a company auditor if he or she is any of the following.

3: Audit regulation

An **officer** or **employee** of the company
A **partner** or **employee** of such a person
A **partnership** in which such a person is a partner
Ineligible by the first three issues for appointment as auditor of any parent or subsidiary undertaking or a subsidiary undertaking of any parent undertaking of the company
There exists between him or her or any associate (of his or hers) and the company a **connection** of any description as may be specified in regulations laid down by Secretary of State

2.7 The legislation does **not** disqualify the following individuals from being an auditor of a limited company:

- A shareholder of the company
- A debtor or creditor of the company
- A close relative (such as a spouse or child) of an officer or employee of the company

2.8 However, the guidance of the accountancy bodies applying to their own members are stricter than statute in this respect.

2.9 Under s 389 CA 1985, if during his term of office a company auditor becomes ineligible for appointment to the office, he must vacate office and give notice in writing to the company.

Recognised Supervisory Bodies

2.10 The EU 8th Directive on company law requires that persons carrying out statutory audits must be approved by the authorities of EU member states.

2.11 The authority to give this approval in the UK is delegated to RSBs. Under the new Act, an auditor must be a member of an RSB and be eligible under its own rules. The ACCA is a RSB.

2.12 The RSBs are required to have rules to ensure that persons eligible for appointment as a company auditor are either (4(1), Sch 11, CA 1989):

- Individuals holding an appropriate qualification
- Firms controlled by qualified persons

2.13 Professional qualifications, which will be prerequisites for membership of an RSB, will be offered by Recognised Qualifying Bodies (RQBs) approved by the Secretary of State.

Supervisory and monitoring roles

2.14 RSBs must also implement procedures for inspecting their registered auditors on a regular basis. A **Monitoring Unit** was set up for this purpose by the ACCA.

2.15 The frequency of inspection will depend on the number of partners, number of offices and number of listed company audits (these factors are also reflected in the size of annual registration fees payable). The length of inspections depends on the size of the firm.

2.16 The following features should be apparent in each practice visited by the monitoring unit.

- A **properly structured audit approach**, suitable for the range of clients served and work undertaken by the practice
- Carefully instituted **quality control procedures**, revised and updated constantly, to which the practice as a whole is committed. This will include:
  - Staff recruitment
  - Staff training
  - Continuing professional development
  - Frequent quality control review

Part A: Business and audit framework

- **Commitment to ethical guidelines**, with an emphasis on independence issues
- An emphasis on **technical excellence**
- Adherence to the '**fit and proper**' criteria by checking personnel records and references
- Use of internal and, if necessary, external **peer reviews** and consultations
- **Appropriate fee** charging per audit assignment

Activity 3.1

Who is ineligible for appointment as a company auditor?

3 AUDITING STANDARDS

The Auditing Practices Board (APB)

3.1 The APB makes the following types of pronouncement:

- Ethical Standards
- Quality Control Standards
- International Standards on Auditing (UK and Ireland)
- Practice Notes
- Bulletins

3.2 In December 2004 the APB issued five **Ethical Standards** in accordance with UK government recommendations. We will look at these in Section 4.

3.3 **Quality Control Standards** aim to ensure that auditors conduct their work to the highest standards. To date only one has been issued: ISQC 1: *Quality control for firms that perform audits and reviews of historical financial information, and other assurance and related services engagements.*

International Standards on Auditing (ISAs)

3.4 In order to support the **international harmonisation** of auditing standards, in 2004 the APB decided to adopt **International Standards on Auditing** issued by the International Audit and Assurance Standards Board (IAASB) in place of its own Statements of Auditing Standards (SASs).

Strictly speaking the new standards should be referred to as International Standards on Auditing (UK and Ireland). Throughout this text we will simply refer to them as **ISAs**.

3.5 ISAs contain **basic principles** and **essential procedures** identified by bold type lettering.

This is supplemented by related guidance and explanatory material.

The basic principles and essential procedures are to be understood and applied in the context of the explanatory and other material. The APB therefore considers that it is necessary to consider the **whole text** of a Standard to understand and apply the basic principles and essential procedures.

3.6 The **authority** of ISAs is defined by the APB as follows.

> 'Apparent failures by auditors to comply with APB standards are liable to be investigated by the relevant accountancy body. Auditors who do not comply with auditing standards when performing company or other audits make themselves liable to regulatory action which may include the withdrawal of registration and hence of eligibility to perform company audits.'

3: Audit regulation

> **Exam alert**
>
> In this Interactive Text we will highlight statements of basic principles and essential procedures that are contained in bold print in ISAs. However you must remember that these statements are designed to be practical guidance and you must be able to **apply** the standards to practical situations.

3.7 **Practice Notes** are issued 'to assist auditors in applying Auditing Standards of general application to particular circumstances and industries'.

3.8 **Bulletins** are issued 'to provide auditors with timely guidance on new or emerging issues'.

3.9 Practice Notes and Bulletins are persuasive rather than prescriptive, but they indicate good practice and have a similar status to the explanatory material in ISAs. Both Practice Notes and Bulletins may be included in later ISAs.

3.10 The APB ISAs which you should be aware of are listed below.

Preface to ISAs and RSs
Glossary of Terms

International Standards on Auditing

No	Title
120	Framework of ISAs
200	Objective and general principles governing an audit of financial statements
210	Terms of audit engagement
220	Quality control for audits of historical financial information*
230	Documentation
240	The auditor's responsibility to consider fraud in an audit of financial statements*
250	Consideration of laws and regulations in an audit of financial statements*
260	Communication of audit matters with those charged with governance*
300 (R)	Planning
315	Understanding the entity and its environment and assessing the risks of material misstatements
320	Audit materiality
330	The auditor's procedures in response to assessed risks
401	Auditing in a computer information systems environment
402	Audit considerations relating to entities using service organisations
500 (R)	Audit evidence
501	Audit evidence - additional considerations for specific items
505	External confirmations
520	Analytical procedures
530	Audit sampling and other means of testing
540	Audit of accounting estimates
560	Subsequent events
570	Going concern
580	Management representations
610	Considering the work of internal audit
620	Using the work of an expert
700	The auditor's report on financial statements

Notes

1 Students should be aware of the nature and meaning of the audit report and should be able to discuss the content and wording of the report. Students would not be asked to reproduce the audit report in full in an exam question, but they may be requested to

Part A: Business and audit framework

prepare explanatory paragraphs for inclusion in the report particularly in situations leading to a modified report.

Activity 3.2

What types of guidance do International Standards on Auditing (ISAs) contain?

---

4 APB ETHICAL STANDARDS

The APB issues ethical standards also. Here is a summary of the ethical standards.

4.1 ES 1: Integrity, objectivity and independence

This standard outlines the general requirements with regard to these matters. It states that integrity, objectivity and confidentiality are fundamental ethical principles.

Integrity implies qualities of **confidentiality**.

Objectivity is a state of mind that excludes bias, prejudice and compromise. It requires that the auditors' judgement is not affected by conflicts of interest.

Independence is related to and underpins objectivity. However whereas objectivity is a personal behavioural characteristic concerning the auditors' state of mind, independence relates to the circumstances surrounding the audit.

In practical terms it states that firms should establish policies to ensure that the firm and everyone in a position to influence the conduct and the outcome of the audit act with integrity, objectivity and independence. An ethics partner should be designated to set and communicate these policies. For listed or public interest companies, an independent partner should review the conclusions drawn by the engagement partner as to the firm's independence.

As part of the general guidance in the standard it also outlines the types of threats to independence that the auditors face. These are as follows:

- **Self-interest threat**

    'This arises when auditors have financial or other interests which might cause them to be reluctant to take actions that would be adverse to the interests of the audit firm or any individual in a position to influence the outcome of the audit.'

    Example: Where they have an investment in the client, are seeking to provide additional services to the client or need to recover long-outstanding fees.

- **Self-review threat**

    'This arises when the results of a non-audit service performed by the auditors or by others within the audit firm are reflected in the amounts included or disclosed in the financial statements. In the course of the audit the auditors may need to re-evaluate the work performed in the non-audit service. As, by virtue of providing the non-audit service, the audit firm is associated with aspects of the preparation of the financial statements, it may be (or may be perceived to be) unable to take an impartial view of the relevant aspects of those financial statements.'

    Example: Where the audit firm has been involved in maintaining the accounting records, or undertaking valuations that are incorporated in the financial statements.

- **Management threat**

    'This arises where the audit firm undertakes work that involves making judgements and taking decisions, which are the responsibility of management. In such work, the audit firm may become closely aligned with the views and interests of management.'

    Example: Where it has been involved in the design, selection and implementation of financial information technology systems.

- **Advocacy threat**

    'This arises where the audit firm undertakes work that involves acting as an advocate for an audit client and supporting a position taken by management in an adversarial context'.

    Example: By acting as a legal advocate for the client in litigation.

- **Familiarity (or trust) threat**

    'This arises when the auditors are predisposed to accept or are insufficiently questioning of the client's point of view.'

    Example: Where they develop close personal relationships with client personnel through long association with the client.

- **Intimidation threat**

    'This arises where the auditors' conduct is influenced by fear or threats.'

    Example: Where they encounter an aggressive and dominating individual.

    These categories are not necessarily distinct. Certain circumstances may give rise to more than one type of threat. Where the audit engagement partner identifies threats to the auditors' objectivity safeguards should be applied. (ES 1 does not set out the detail of what the safeguards should include.)

4.2 ES 2: Financial, business, employment and personal relationships

Financial relationships

General considerations

'The audit firm, any partner in the audit firm, a person in a position to influence the conduct and outcome of the audit or an immediate family member of such a person should not hold:

(a) any direct financial interest in an audit client or an affiliate of an audit client; or

(b) any indirect financial interest in an audit client or an affiliate of an audit client, where the investment is material to the audit firm or the individual and to the intermediary; or

(c) any indirect financial interest in an audit client or an affiliate of an audit client where the person holding it has both:

  (i) the ability to influence the investment decisions of the intermediary; and
  (ii) actual knowledge of the existence of the underlying investment.

In the above cases the threats to the auditors' objectivity are such that no safeguards can eliminate them or reduce them to an acceptable level.

Where the financial interest is held by the audit firm, a partner or an immediate family member **the entire interest should be disposed of** (or a sufficient amount of an indirect interest is disposed of so that the remaining interest is no longer material) or **the firm should not accept or should withdraw from the audit**.

Where a financial interest is acquired **unintentionally**, for example through inheritance, the **disposal of the financial interest** is required immediately or as soon as possible. Where disposal does not take place immediately, the audit firm must adopt safeguards. These may include the temporary exclusion of the person in a position to influence the conduct and outcome of the audit.

Where a person in a position to influence the outcome of the audit or a partner in the audit firm becomes aware that a close family member holds a financial interest, it should be reported to the audit engagement partner. If there is any doubt as to the action to be taken the audit engagement partner should resolve the issue through **consultation with the ethics partner.**

Loans and guarantees

Audit firms, persons in a position to influence the conduct and outcome of the audit and immediate family members of such persons should not make a loan to/accept a loan from, or guarantee the borrowings of/have their borrowings guaranteed by, an audit client or its affiliates unless this represents a deposit made with a bank or similar deposit taking institution in the ordinary course of business and on normal business terms.

Business relationships

'Audit firms, persons in a position to influence the conduct and outcome of the audit and immediate family members of such persons should not enter into business relationships with an audit client or its affiliates except where they involve the purchase of goods and services from the audit firm or the audit client in the ordinary course of business and on an arm's length basis and the value involved is not material to either party.'

Where a business relationship has been entered into either the relationship is terminated or the firm does not accept (withdraws) from the engagement/or that person does not retain a position in which they exert such influence on the audit engagement.

Employment relationships

'An audit firm should not admit to the partnership or employ a person to undertake audit work if that person is also employed by the audit client or its affiliates ('dual employment').

A partner or employee of the audit firm should not accept appointment:

(a) to the board of directors

(b) to any subcommittee of that board

(c) to such a position in an entity which hold more than 20% of the voting rights in the audit client, or in which the audit client holds directly or indirectly more than 20% of the voting rights.

Loan staff assignments

'An audit client should not enter into an agreement with an audit client to provide a partner or employee to work for a temporary period as if that individual were an employee unless the audit client:

(a) agrees that the individual concerned will not hold a management position

(b) acknowledges its responsibility for directing and supervising the work to be performed.'

On completion of the loan staff assignment that individual should not be given any role on the audit involving any function or activity that they performed or supervised during that assignment.

Partners and engagement team members joining an audit client

Partners, senior members of the engagement team and other members of the engagement team should notify the firm of any situation involving their potential employment with an audit client. The individual should be removed from the team and any work performed by them on the most recent audit should be reviewed.

'Where a partner leaves the firm and is appointed as a director (including as a non-executive director) or to a key management position with an audit client, having acted as audit engagement partner at any time in the **two years** prior to his appointment, the firm should resign as auditors. The firm should not accept reappointment as auditors until a two-year period, commencing when the former partner ceased to act for the client, has elapsed or the former partner ceases employment with the former client, whichever is sooner.'

Where the above situation applies to a member of the engagement team the audit firm should consider whether the composition of the audit team is appropriate.

Directors and employees joining an audit firm

Where a director or a former employee joins an audit firm that individual should not be assigned to a position in which he or she is able to influence the conduct and outcome of the audit for a period of two years.

Family members employed by an audit client

As a general governance issue ES 2 states that the audit firm should have policies and procedures that require partners and professional staff to report family relationships involving audit clients.

Where a person in a position to influence the conduct and outcome of the audit, or a partner in the firm becomes aware that an immediate family member is employed by an audit client in a position to exercise influence on the accounting records or financial statements, that individual should cease to have any further role in the audit.

In the case of a close family member the matter should be reported to the audit engagement partner to take appropriate action.

4.3 **ES 3: Long association with the audit engagement**

General provisions

Where audit engagement partners, key audit partners and staff in senior positions have a long association with the audit safeguards should be applied. **Where they cannot be applied the audit firm should either resign or not stand for reappointment.**

Safeguards include:

- **Rotating the audit partner** and other senior members of the audit team after a pre-determined number of years
- Involving an **additional partner**
- Applying **independent internal quality reviews**

Once an audit partner has held the role for a continuous period of ten years careful consideration should be given to whether objectivity would have the appearance of being impaired.

Additional provisions for listed companies

The firm should establish policies to ensure that:

(a) no one should act as audit engagement partner or independent partner for a continuous period longer than **five years**

(b) they should not hold a position of responsibility regarding this audit client again until a further period of five years has elapsed

Where senior staff have been involved on an audit for a continuous period longer than seven years the audit engagement partner should review the safeguards put in place.

In addition, key audit partners (an audit partner other than the engagement partner who is involved at a *group* level) should not act for more than seven years. If the engagement partner becomes a key partner, the total for his combined roles must not exceed seven years.

4.4 ES 4: Fees, remuneration and evaluation policies, litigation, gifts and hospitality

Fees

An audit should not be undertaken on a **contingent fee** basis.

The audit fee should reflect the **time spent** and the **skills and experience** of the personnel performing the audit.

Where fees are **overdue** the auditor needs to consider whether the firm can continue as auditors.

Where it is expected that the fees for both audit and non-audit services receivable from a listed audit client and its subsidiaries will regularly exceed **10% of the annual fee income of the audit firm** (15% for non-listed), the firm should **not act as the auditors** and should either resign or not stand for reappointment.

Where the above fees will regularly exceed **5% of the annual fee income** the audit engagement partner should **disclose** this to the ethics partner and those charged with governance and consider whether safeguards should be applied.

New firms should not undertake any audits of listed companies, where fees would represent 10% or more of the annual fee income of the firm. In addition, for a period not exceeding two years, independent reviews should be performed on those audits of unlisted entities that represent more than 10% of the annual fee income.

Performance criteria and remuneration of staff should not depend on the selling of non-audit services.

Threatened and actual litigation

Where litigation between the audit client and the audit firm is already in progress or is probable, the audit firm should either not continue or should not accept the engagement.

Gifts and hospitality

The audit firm, those in a position to influence the conduct and outcome of the audit and immediate family members should **not accept gifts from the audit client**, unless the value is clearly insignificant.

Hospitality should not be accepted either, unless it is **reasonable** in terms of its frequency, nature and cost.

4.5 ES 5: Non-audit services provided to audit clients

This standard issues general guidance regarding the approach to non-audit services but also goes on to describe how these principles should be applied to specific non-audit services.

General approach

ES 5 does not prohibit the provision of other services. However, it requires the audit engagement partner to:

- Consider whether the objectives of the proposed engagement would be perceived to be inconsistent with the objectives of the audit
- Identify and assess the significance of any related threats to the auditors' objectivity
- Identify and assess the effectiveness of the available safeguards

Where the engagement partner considers it probable that the objectives of the two assignments are inconsistent, the audit firm should either not undertake the non-audit service or not accept/withdraw from the audit engagement.

Safeguards

Where there is a threat to the auditors' objectivity the audit engagement partner should assess whether there are safeguards that could be applied which would eliminate the threat or reduce it to an acceptable level. If safeguards can be applied the non-audit service can be provided. If safeguards cannot be applied, the audit firm should either not undertake the non-audit work, or not accept, or withdraw from, the audit engagement.

4.6 Application of general principles to specific non-audit services

These include the following:

Internal audit services

In general term this service can be provided assuming that adequate safeguards are in place.

Safeguards include:

- Using different staff for internal and external audit purposes
- Review of the audit of the financial statements performed by a partner who is not involved with the external audit.

However the firm should not undertake the engagement where the auditor will place significant reliance on internal audit as part of the audit of the financial statements or where the audit firm would be taking on a management role.

Information technology services

The audit firm should not undertake an engagement to design, provide or implement technology systems for an audit client where:

- The system concerned would be important to any significant part of the accounting system or to the production of the financial statements and the auditor would place significant reliance upon them as part of the audit of the financial statements; or
- The audit firm would undertake part of the role of management.

Valuation services

The audit firm should not provide a valuation to a client where the valuation would:

- Involve a significant degree of subjective judgement; and
- Have a material effect on the financial statements.

Actuarial valuation services

The audit firm should not provide actuarial valuation services to an audit client unless they are satisfied the significant judgements will be made by informed management or the valuation has no material effect on the financial statements.

Tax services

In general terms tax services may be provided although the auditor must assess the possible threats to objectivity.

Safeguards would include:

- Use of different staff
- Tax services reviewed by an independent tax partner
- External independent advice on tax work
- Tax computations prepared by the audit team are reviewed by a partner or senior staff member who is not a member of the audit team

Part A: Business and audit framework

The audit firm **should not** provide tax services:

- Where the fee for tax work is calculated on a contingent fee basis and the engagement fees are material to the audit firm
- Where the engagement would involve the audit firm undertaking a management role
- Where it would involve acting as an advocate for the client.

Litigation support or legal services

The audit client should not accept such work if relevant matters might have a material impact on financial statements.

Recruitment and remuneration services

The audit firm should not provide a service which would involve the firm taking responsibility for the appointment of any director or employee of the audit client.

For a **listed company** the audit firm should not provide a recruitment service in relation to a key management position.

Corporate finance

This term covers a range of activity but the key threat is that the auditor takes on the role of management. The engagement partner needs to ensure that appropriate safeguards are applied. For example:

- The use of different staff
- Advice is reviewed by an independent corporate finance partner.

There are certain circumstances where the corporate finance work should not be undertaken. These include:

- Where the engagement would involve the audit firm taking responsibility for dealing in, underwriting or promoting shares
- Where the partner doubts the appropriateness of an accounting treatment related to the advice provided
- The corporate finance fee is calculated on a contingent basis and is material to the audit firm.

Transaction related services

Such services should not be accepted if the audit engagement partner has (or ought to) doubt about the appropriateness of accounting treatments used, or there are contingent fees and the matter is material or is dependent on significant judgements in financial statements.

Accounting services

These should not be provided to any listed client or where it would involve the auditor taking management decisions.

Glossary of terms used in the Ethical Standards

Close family	A non-dependent parent, child or sibling
Immediate family	A spouse (or equivalent) or dependent
Person in a position to influence the conduct and outcome of the audit	Any person who is directly involved in the audit including the audit partners, audit managers, audit staff, professional personnel from other disciplines involved in the audit and those who provide quality control or direct oversight of the audit. It also includes any person who forms part of the chain of command for the audit within the firm or any person within the firm who may be in a position to exert influence.

5 ACCA RULES OF PROFESSIONAL CONDUCT 12/04

5.1 All members and students of the ACCA are subject to the *Rules of Professional Conduct* published by the ACCA. Within this is the Code of Ethics. Guidance is in the form of:

- Fundamental principles
- Specific guidance
- Explanatory notes

Where there is any **discrepancy** between the APB Ethical Standards and the ACCA's Code of Ethics the more **stringent** requirement should be applied.

The fundamental principles

5.2 Members should:

Behave with **integrity** in all professional, business and personal financial relationships. Integrity implies not merely **honesty** but **fair dealing** and **truthfulness**
Strive for **objectivity** in all professional and business judgements (Objectivity is the state of mind which has regard to all considerations relevant to the task in hand but no other. It is bound up with intellectual honesty.)
Not accept or perform work which they are not **competent** to undertake unless they obtain such advice and assistance as will enable them competently to carry out the work
Carry out their professional work with **due skill, care, diligence** and **expedition** and with proper regard for the **technical** and **professional standards** expected of them as members
Behave with **courtesy** and **consideration** towards all with whom they come into contact during the course of performing their work

5.3 Compliance with the fundamental principles may potentially be threatened by a broad range of circumstances.

The ACCA's Code of Ethics categorises these as follows:

(a) self-interest (eg. financial interests, concern over employment security)
(b) self-review (eg decisions made and reviewed by same person)
(c) advocacy (not improper provided it does not result in misleading information)
(d) familiarity (eg long association, acceptance of gifts)
(e) Intimidation (eg threat of dismissal)

5.4 Safeguards that may eliminate or reduce these threats to unacceptable levels include:

- Safeguards created by the profession, legislation or regulation (eg training, professional standards).
- Safeguards in the work environment (eg leadership, quality control policies)
- Safeguards created by the individual (eg CPD requirements)

6 INTEGRITY, OBJECTIVITY AND INDEPENDENCE

> **Code of Ethics**
> Independence requires
> (a) Independence of mind
> (b) Independence in appearance

Part A: Business and audit framework

6.1 In other words it is not sufficient for the auditor to be independent. He must be seen to be independent.

6.2 You will see that **some situations** will **constitute such a significant threat to independence** that an **audit practice should not act** as auditors if they arise.

Below is a list of circumstances in which independence may be threatened.

6.3 EXAMPLE

No loans or guarantees should be given to or obtained from a client other than a financial institution.

6.4 More often the risks described **constitute a less significant threat to independence**, and it is up to the **auditors** to **decide** whether the threat is sufficient to prevent them from acting, or what safeguards they can put in place to mitigate the threat.

> **Exam alert**
>
> If an ethical problem comes up in the exams, remember that the ACCA guidance may not always provide a clear-cut solution. You should
> (a) Always identify the potential threat to independence and
> (b) Consider whether it appears strong enough to prevent the auditors from continuing to act, or whether the auditors can continue to act with appropriate safeguards.

Undue dependence on an audit client

> **Code of Ethics**
>
> 'Objectivity may be threatened or appear to be threatened by undue dependence on any audit client or group of connected clients.'

6.5 The Code recommends that, in general, the recurring work paid by one client or group of connected clients should not exceed **15%** of the gross practice income. In the case of **listed** and other **public interest** companies, the figure should be **10%** of the gross practice income.

6.6 A review of the risk to independence should be instituted for all large fees, certainly **10%** (public interest **5%**) and greater of gross practice income.

6.7 The Code also suggests that non-recurring fees might affect independence if they are large enough.

6.8 EXAMPLE

Abacus Accountants & Co have a gross practice income of £750,000. Abacus are the auditors of Grey Ltd for which they charge a fee of £65,000. The directors have recently asked Abacus to take on regular tax work. The fee for this is likely to be in excess of £50,000.

Based on the current situation fees from Grey Ltd constitute 8.7% (65,000/750,000) of the gross practice income. This falls well below the 15% benchmark which applies to private companies.

If the tax work is accepted this fee will also need to be taken into account as it is a recurring fee rather than a one off assignment.

Based on the above total fees from Grey Ltd would then constitute 14.4% (115,000/800,000) of the gross practice income. Whilst it still remains below 15% of the gross practice income it does exceed 10%. As a result a review should be performed by Abacus Co to ensure that independence will be maintained in spite of the additional fees earned from Grey Ltd.

Overdue fees

> **Code of Ethics**
>
> 'The existence of significant overdue fees from an audit client or group of associated clients can be a threat or appear to be a threat to objectivity akin to that of a loan.'

6.9 Firms must therefore ensure that overdue fees, along with fees from current work, could not be construed as a loan.

Actual or threatened litigation

> **Code of Ethics**
>
> 'A firm's objectivity may be threatened or appear to be threatened when it is involved in, or even threatened with litigation in relation to a client.'

6.10 Litigation of certain sorts will represent a 'breakdown of the relationship of trust' between auditor and client. This would impair the independence of the auditor or cause the directors of the client to become unwilling to disclose information to the auditor. A dispute which is only in relation to audit fees may not cause such problems.

Associated firms; influences outside the practice

> **Code of Ethics**
>
> 'A firm's objectivity may be threatened or appear to be threatened as a result of pressures arising from associated practices or organisations, or from other external sources, such as bankers, solicitors, government or those introducing business.'

Family and other personal relationships

> **Code of Ethics**
>
> 'A member's objectivity may be threatened or appear to be threatened as a consequence of a family or other close personal or business relationship.'

6.11 Problems arise if an officer or senior employee of an audit client is **closely connected** with the partner or senior staff member responsible for the conduct of the audit.

6.12 In this context, closely connected people include (as well as the definition given below), adult children and their spouses, siblings and their spouses, any relative to whom regular financial assistance is given or who is indebted to the staff member or partner.

> **KEY TERM**
>
> The following people will normally be regarded as **closely connected** with a person.
>
> (a) His (or her) spouse or cohabitee other than a spouse from whom the person is separated, or, in the case of a shareholding, a spouse or cohabitee of whose financial affairs the person has been denied knowledge

> (b) His (or her) minor children, including stepchildren
>
> (c) A company in which he or she has a 20 per cent interest or more
>
> The following persons will normally be regarded as being closely connected with a practice.
>
> (a) A partner or, in the case of a corporate practice, a director or shareholder
>
> (b) A person closely connected with (a)
>
> (c) An employee of the practice
>
> *Note.* The categories in these paragraphs are not exhaustive of the relationships which might threaten independence.

6.13 Proximity needs to be taken into account, including whether the partner or staff member is involved in the audit and the position of the person in the client's office (the more junior, the less risk).

6.14 **EXAMPLE**

Abacus Co have been the auditors of Red Ltd for a number of years. Angela Moore has recently been appointed as the Finance director of Red Ltd. She is married to Andrew Moore who is an audit manager in Abacus Ltd.

In this case the personal relationship between Angela and Andrew Moore threatens objectivity. This is accentuated by the fact that Angela is in a senior position at Red Ltd and is in a position to influence the financial statements.

Andrew Moore as an audit manager is also in a position of influence. In this instance an appropriate solution would be to appoint another audit manager to this particular audit.

6.15 Problems can arise if partners or staff are involved on clients for too long.

Beneficial interests in shares and other investments

> **Code of Ethics**
>
> 'A member's objectivity may be threatened or appear to be threatened where he (or she) holds a beneficial interest in the shares or other forms of investment in a company upon which the practice reports.'

6.16 Staff and partners should not have shareholdings in client businesses. (This includes beneficial shareholdings held by a spouse or minor child.) Any share acquired involuntarily should be disposed of. If statute or articles require shareholding, the minimum required should be held.

> **Code of Ethics**
>
> 'Where a partner or staff member holds shares in any capacity in a company which is an audit client of the practice they should not be voted at any general meeting of the company in relation to the appointment, removal or remuneration of auditors.'

Beneficial interests in trusts and trustees investments

> **Code of Ethics**
>
> 'The objectivity of a practice may be threatened or appear to be threatened where a partner or a person closely connected with the partner has a beneficial interest in a trust having a shareholding in an audit client company.'

6.17 Having an interest in a trust which holds shares is similar to having shares above. If the partner is a trustee (he has control over the shareholding) **the firm should not act**. Alternatively, the partner could resign as trustee.

> **Code of Ethics**
>
> 'A member's objectivity may be threatened or appear to be threatened by trustee shareholdings and other trustee investments.'

Loans

> **Code of Ethics**
>
> 'Objectivity may be threatened or appear to be threatened by a loan to or from an audit client.'

6.18 No loans or guarantees should be undertaken unless they are with client financial institutions in the normal course of business (but the loan cannot be applied for partnership capital and the partner concerned must not be the engagement partner).

Goods and services; hospitality

> **Code of Ethics**
>
> 'Objectivity may be threatened or appear to be threatened by acceptance of goods, services or hospitality from an audit client.'
>
> Acceptance on normal commercial terms, or with only a modest benefit, is acceptable.

6.19 EXAMPLE

Fit Ltd, a health and fitness club has recently contacted Abacus Co with a view to appointing them as auditors.

Following a meeting between the board of Fit Ltd and the senior partner of Abacus Co, all of the firm's partners have received offers of free gym membership for a year worth £140 each.

If the partners were to accept this offer it is likely that their objectivity would be seen to be impaired. The value of the gift is considerable both in terms of the firm as a whole and the individual partners. The partners should not accept the gift if they wish to take on the audit.

Provision of other services to audit clients

> **Code of Ethics**
>
> 'There are occasions where objectivity may be threatened or appear to be threatened by the provision to an audit client of services other than the audit.'

Activity 3.3

List other services that auditors may provide to clients.

6.20 If auditors provide other services their independence may be threatened in a number of ways.
- Auditors can end up making **management decisions** for the company and this would definitely harm their independence.

Part A: Business and audit framework

- Some critics have suggested that auditors will be **unwilling to qualify** audit reports if as a result they risk not just losing the audit, but also lucrative non-audit work.

6.21 Many **small firms** aim to provide a complete service for their client - accountancy, taxation and general advice as well as audits. With these clients, it may be difficult to demonstrate that the firm has carried out an objective audit of accounts it has prepared.

Safeguards
The **engagement letter** should **separately identify** the **non-audit services** provided, make clear the limitations of the services, and stress directors' responsibilities (including responsibilities for preparing accounting records and prevention of fraud).
One way of countering this problem is to have **different staff** preparing the accounts and carrying out the audit.
If the same staff member prepares the accounts and carries out the audit, the audit work done must be carefully **planned** and **recorded**. In particular the file should show what audit assurance has been obtained through carrying out accountancy work.

6.22 An important rule affecting **large firms** is that auditors should not (except in an emergency) provide accountancy services for public companies. However large firms can provide consultancy services, corporate finance and taxation, often for very significant fees.

6.23 Many large firms have countered the threat to independence by the use of separate departments for each service (consultancy, audit, taxation and so on). **Chinese walls supposedly operate** between these departments; this means that no information **is passed between them**.

Review procedures

> **Code of Ethics**
>
> 'Every audit firm should establish adequate review machinery, including an annual review, in order to satisfy itself that each engagement may properly be accepted or be continued having regard to the guidance given in this statement, and to identify situations where independence may be at risk and where the appropriate safeguards should be applied.'

6.24 ISQC 1, which you do not need to know in detail, requires that firms have appropriate internal procedures to deal with potential independence problems, including:

Safeguards
Internal rules, that for example no partners or staff should have shares in audit clients
Client acceptance procedures (covered in Chapter 4)
An annual review of independence, both for the whole firm (circulation of a list of prohibited shareholdings) and for individual clients
Consultation procedures in cases of doubt

6.25 Any additional safeguards required should be assessed by an independent partner, and might include **second partner review** of certain clients, **rotation** of the engagement partner or rotation of senior audit staff. In such circumstances, sole practitioners should consult another member externally.

Activity 3.4

Consider whether providing the following additional services to audit clients may compromise your independence as an auditor. If they do, consider how the risk to your independence could be safeguarded.

3: Audit regulation

(a) Taxation, preparing a client's corporation tax computation and negotiating with the Inland Revenue.
(b) Preparing a client's annual accounts.
(c) Attending meetings of a client's board of directors.

7 THE PROFESSIONAL DUTY OF CONFIDENCE

7.1 Clients expect that their business affairs will be kept confidential by their accountants. However this expectation may cause accountants problems. Maintaining **client confidentiality** may mean that auditors cannot 'blow the whistle' on malpractices of the client, and hence such malpractices will be allowed to continue.

7.2 **Information acquired** in the course of professional work **should not be disclosed except where**

- **Consent has been obtained** from the client, employer or other proper source, **or**
- There is a **public duty** to disclose, or
- There is a **legal or professional right or duty** to disclose.

7.3 A member acquiring information in the course of professional work should neither use nor appear to use that information for his **personal advantage** or for the **advantage** of a **third party**.

7.4 In general, where there is a right (as opposed to a duty) to disclose information, a member should only make disclosure in pursuit of a **public duty** or **professional obligation**.

7.5 A member must make it clear to a client that he may only act for him if the client agrees to disclose in full to the member all information relevant to the engagement.

7.6 Where a member agrees to serve a client in a professional capacity both the member and the client should be aware that it is an implied term of that agreement that the member will not disclose the client's affairs to any other person save with the client's consent or within the terms of certain recognised exceptions.

7.7 The recognised exceptions are as follows.

Obligatory disclosure	Voluntary disclosure
If a member knows or suspects his client to have committed the offence of **treason** he is obliged to disclose all the information at his disposal to a competent authority. Suspicions of **terrorism** or **drug money laundering** also give rise to a duty to report.	**In certain cases voluntary disclosure may be made by the member where:** Disclosure is reasonably **necessary** to **protect** the **member's interests**, for example to enable him to sue for fees or defend an action for, say, negligence.
Under ISA 250 *Consideration of laws and regulations in an audit of financial statements* the auditor should consider whether **non-compliance with laws and regulations** affects the financial statements. Auditors may have to include in their audit report a statement that non-compliance has led to significant uncertainties, or non-compliance means that the auditors disagree with the way certain items have been treated in the accounts.	Disclosure is compelled by **process of law**, for example where in an action a member is required to give evidence or discovery of documents. There is a **public duty** to disclose, say where an offence has been committed which is contrary to the public interest.

7.8 **EXAMPLE**

If an ACCA member is requested to assist the police, the Inland Revenue or other authority by providing information about a client's affairs in connection with enquiries being made, he should first enquire under what statutory authority the information is demanded.

Part A: Business and audit framework

Unless he is satisfied that such statutory authority exists he should decline to give any information until he has obtained his client's authority. If the client's authority is not forthcoming and the demand for information is pressed the member should not accede unless so advised by his solicitor.

7.9 If a member knows or suspects that a client has committed a wrongful act he must give careful thought to his own position. He must ensure that he has not prejudiced himself by, for example, relying on information given by the client which subsequently proves to be incorrect.

7.10 It would be a criminal offence for a member to act positively, without lawful authority or reasonable excuse, in such a manner as to impede with intent the arrest or prosecution of a client whom he knows or believes to have committed an 'arrestable offence'.

Key learning points

- The Companies Act requires auditors to hold an **appropriate qualification** and to be a member of a **recognised supervisory body.**
- A person is **ineligible** to act as auditor if he is an **employee** or officer or has various other close connections with the company.
- Recognised supervisory bodies must follow a number of procedures to ensure their members are **fit** and **proper** and **competent** and that audit work is conducted **properly.**
- The Auditing Practices Board issues:
  - Ethical Standards
  - Quality Control Standards
  - ISAs
  - Practice Notes
  - Bulletins
- ISAs contain basic principles and procedures with which auditors must comply as well as other material designed to help auditors.
- The APB have issued five Ethical Standards.

  ES1 – Integrity, objectivity and independence
  ES2 – Financial, business, employment and personal relationships
  ES3 – Long association with the audit engagement
  ES4 – Fees, remuneration and evaluation, policies, litigation, gifts and hospitality
  ES5 – Non-audit services provided to audit clients

- The ACCA Code of Ethics imposes various obligations on auditors and other members.
- The Code contains guidance on maintenance of **objectivity** and **independence** by auditors.
- Potential threats to objectivity include:
  - Undue dependence on an audit client
  - Family and other personal relationships
  - Beneficial interests in shares
  - Acceptance of hospitality
  - Provision of other services
- Auditors have a professional duty of **confidentiality**. However they may be compelled by law or consider it desirable in the **public interest** to disclose details of clients' affairs to third parties.

Quick quiz

1. What does the term appropriate qualification mean?
2. Name the five categories of pronouncement issued by the Auditing Practices Board.
3. What is the principle of independence?

3: Audit regulation

4   What is the maximum fee income that should be received from one client?

5   How does legislation govern the appointment of auditors?

6   Describe the review machinery that firms should adopt to ensure that they have maintained independence.

7   Give examples of people who are closely connected:
    (a)   With a person
    (b)   With a practice

8   When is an ACCA member
    (a)   Obliged
    (b)   Allowed

    to make disclosure of clients' affairs to third parties?

Answers to quick quiz

1   A person holds an appropriate qualification if he or she has gained:

    (a)   Acknowledgement that he or she has satisfied existing criteria for appointment as an auditor under Companies Act 1985
    (b)   A recognised qualification obtained in the United Kingdom
    (c)   An approved overseas qualification

2   (a)   Ethical Standards   (d)   Practice Notes
    (b)   Quality control standards   (e)   Bulletins
    (c)   International Standards on Auditing

3   The description given of the principle of independence is:

    'A member's objectivity must be beyond question if he (or she) is to report as an auditor. That objectivity can only be assured if the member is, and is seen to be, independent.'

4   The maximum fee income receivable from one client is 15% of gross practice income, or 10% if the client is listed or public interest.

5   Company law prevents an officer or employee of a company (or their partner) from becoming the auditor of that company.

6   Firms should have review machinery, including an annual review to ensure they are acting as auditors in accordance with the Code of Ethics, to identify situations where independence may be at risk and where the appropriate safeguards should be applied.

7   (a)   People closely connected with a person include:

        (i)   Spouse or cohabitee
        (ii)   His or her minor children
        (iii) A company in which he or she has a 20% interest or more

    (b)   People closely connected with a practice include:

        (i)   A partner (or director or shareholder of a corporate practice)
        (ii)   A person closely connected with a partner/director/shareholder
        (iii) An employee of the practice

8   (a)   An ACCA member is obliged to disclose client's affairs to an appropriate authority if he knows or suspects treason, terrorism or drug money laundering.

    (b)   An ACCA member may disclose a client's affairs:

        (i)   To protect his interests
        (ii)   Where disclosure is compelled by process of law
        (iii) Where there is a public duty to disclose

Answers to activities

Answer 3.1

Under the Companies Act 1985, a person is *ineligible* for appointment as a company auditor if he or she is any of the following:

Part A: Business and audit framework

(a) An **officer** or **employee** of the company

(b) A **partner** or **employee** of such a person

(c) A **partnership** in which such a person is a partner

(d) **Ineligible** by virtue of (a), (b) or (c) for appointment as auditor of any parent or subsidiary undertaking or a subsidiary undertaking of any parent undertaking of the company

(e) There exists between him or her or any associate (of his or hers) and the company (or company as referred to in (d) above) a **connection** of any description as may be specified in regulations laid down by Secretary of State

Answer 3.2

ISAs contain the following types of guidance:

(a) Basic principles and essential procedures with which auditors must comply when carrying out an audit of financial statements

(b) Explanatory and other material designed to assist auditors in interpreting and applying the basic principles and essential procedures (ie the whole text of the standard must be considered).

Answer 3.3

Other services include:

(a) Writing up the client's books
(b) Preparing annual accounts
(c) Preparing management accounts
(d) Completion of tax returns and negotiations with the Inland Revenue
(e) Dealing with directors' tax affairs
(f) Investment business advice
(g) Systems advice
(h) Management consultancy
(i) Investigations

Answer 3.4

(a) Preparing a taxation computation is unlikely to impair auditor independence, since a company's tax liability would generally be checked as part of the audit. Routine negotiations with the Inland Revenue should not normally impair independence.

There may however be a problem if a significant tax liability is under dispute, since the auditor may believe the accounts should disclose details of the dispute, but the directors may disagree. In these circumstances the auditor may find it impossible to act as both auditor and tax advise.

(b) The major risk with the auditor preparing the accounts is that the auditor may not be detached when he reviews the accounts. In addition the audit files may not demonstrate sufficiently how the accountancy work has been used as a source of audit assurance.

The audit firm can counter the risk to independence by having different staff members prepare the accounts and audit them. Alternatively the work should be reviewed by someone unconnected with the preparation of the accounts. Audit firms' internal guidance can also help, by clearly demonstrating how much audit assurance can be gained from accounting work, and what extra work will be required to give sufficient audit assurance.

(c) Attendance of meetings of the board of directors imposes a clear threat to auditor independence as the auditor may become involved in management decisions on which he subsequently has to report. The Companies Act also regards as a director anyone who carries out the functions of a director; an auditor would be exposed to this provision if he regularly attended board meetings and hence would be ineligible under the Companies Act to act as auditor.

The best way to preserve auditor independence would be for an auditor only to attend the board meetings at which the annual accounts are discussed.

Now try Question 3 in the Exam Question Bank

Chapter 4 Audit engagement

Chapter topic list

1   Introduction
2   Appointment procedures
3   Client screening
4   The engagement letter

The following study sessions are covered in this Chapter:

		Syllabus reference
6(a)	Explain the purpose and content of client acceptance procedures comprising client screening, professional clearance and independence checks	2
6(b)	Explain the purpose of an engagement letter	2
6(c)	Examine and discuss the contents of an audit engagement letter	2

Part A: Business and audit framework

1 INTRODUCTION

1.1 We saw in the first chapter how the law impacts upon how companies change auditors. This chapter deals with **professional requirements** governing the appointment of new auditors.

1.2 The key requirement is for the current and proposed auditors to **communicate** about the client's affairs. One reason for this is to preserve the integrity of the auditors' position. Thus the current and proposed auditors must ask the client for permission to discuss his affairs, but if the client refuses, the proposed auditors should decline nomination.

1.3 A second reason for the two auditors communicating is to give the proposed auditors **information** which will help them decide whether to accept nomination. Hence also there is a professional requirement for the proposed auditors to seek references about the client.

1.4 Many firms have more stringent **screening procedures**, since auditors can suffer adverse publicity or be sued if their client has gone into insolvency or a major fraud has occurred. Client acceptance procedures aim to identify the **risks** associated with taking on the client and assess whether there are good **high level controls** such as management involvement and integrity.

1.5 Assuming appointment is accepted, it is then necessary for the terms of the engagement to be confirmed. This is done by means of an **engagement letter,** which sets out the respective responsibilities of the auditors and directors, and details the scope of the audit.

2 APPOINTMENT PROCEDURES   12/04

2.1 This section covers the procedures that the auditors must undertake to ensure that their appointment is valid and that they are clear to act. These matters are also covered in the ACCA's *Rules of Professional Conduct.*

Before accepting nomination

2.2 Before a new audit client is accepted, the auditors must ensure that there are **no independence** or **other ethical problems** likely to cause conflict with the ethical code. Furthermore, new auditors should ensure that they have been appointed in a proper and legal manner.

ACCEPTANCE PROCEDURES	
Ensure **professionally qualified** to act	Consider whether disqualified on legal or ethical grounds
Ensure **existing resources adequate**	Consider available time, staff and technical expertise
Obtain references	Make independent enquiries if directors not personally known (see Section 3 of this chapter)
Communicate with present auditors	Enquire whether there are reasons/circumstances behind the change which the new auditors ought to know, also courtesy
	See flowchart over page for process

4: Audit engagement

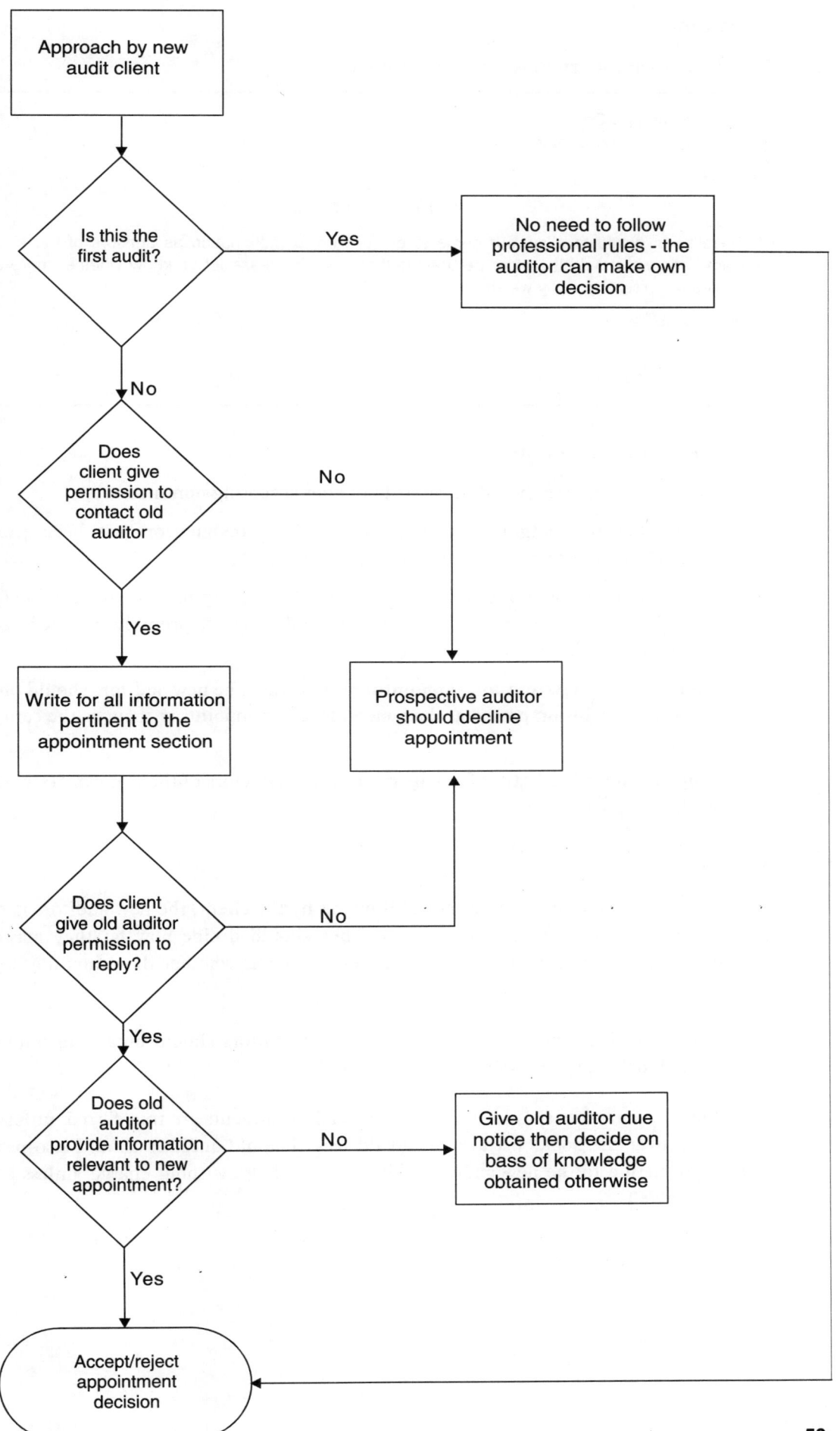

```
         Approach by new
         audit client
                │
                ▼
         ◇ Is this the first audit? ──Yes──▶ No need to follow professional rules - the auditor can make own decision
                │
                No
                ▼
         ◇ Does client give permission to contact old auditor ──No──▶ Prospective auditor should decline appointment
                │
                Yes
                ▼
         Write for all information pertinent to the appointment section
                │
                ▼
         ◇ Does client give old auditor permission to reply? ──No──▶ Prospective auditor should decline appointment
                │
                Yes
                ▼
         ◇ Does old auditor provide information relevant to new appointment? ──No──▶ Give old auditor due notice then decide on basis of knowledge obtained otherwise
                │
                Yes
                ▼
         ( Accept/reject appointment decision )
```

53

Example letters

2.3 This is an example of an initial communication.

> To: Retiring & Co
> Certified Accountants
>
> Dear Sirs
>
> Re: New Client Co Ltd
>
> We have been asked to allow our name to go forward for nomination as auditors of the above company, and we should therefore be grateful if you would please let us know whether there are any professional reasons why we should not accept nomination...... .
>
> Acquiring & Co
>
> Certified Accountants

Procedures after accepting nomination

2.4 The following procedures should be carried out after accepting nomination.

(a) **Ensure** that the **outgoing auditors' removal** or **resignation** has been **properly conducted** in accordance with the Companies Act 1985.

The new auditors should see a **valid notice** of the outgoing auditors' resignation (under s 392 CA 1985), or confirm that the outgoing auditors were properly removed (under s 391 CA 1985).

(b) **Ensure** that the **new auditors' appointment is valid**. The new auditors should obtain a copy of the resolution passed at the general meeting appointing them as the company's auditors.

(c) Set up and **submit a letter of engagement** to the directors of the company (see Section 4 of this chapter).

Other matters

2.5 Where the previous auditors have **fees still owing** by the client, the new auditors need not decline appointment solely for this reason. They should decide how far they may go in helping the former auditors to obtain their fees, as well as whether they should accept the appointment.

2.6 Once a new appointment has taken place, the new auditors should obtain **all books and papers** which belong to the client from the old auditors.

2.7 The former accountants should ensure that all such documents are transferred, **unless** they have a lien over the books because of unpaid fees. The old auditors should also pass any useful information to the new auditors if it will be of help, without charge, unless a lot of work is involved.

3 CLIENT SCREENING

3.1 As well as contacting previous auditors many firms, particularly larger firms, carry out other stringent checks on potential audit clients and their management. The procedures laid out here are tailored to the case of a large audit firm and a large (probably public) company audit, but the procedures may be adapted for smaller audit firms and smaller audits.

Factors for consideration

Management integrity

3.2 The integrity of those managing a company will be of great importance.

Risk

3.3 The following table contrasts low and high risk clients.

LOW RISK	HIGH RISK
Good long-term prospects	Poor recent or forecast performance
Well-financed	Likely lack of finance
Strong internal controls	Significant control weaknesses
Conservative, prudent accounting policies	Evidence of questionable integrity, doubtful accounting policies
Competent, honest management	Lack of finance director
Few unusual transactions	Significant related party or unexplained transactions

Engagement economics

3.4 Generally, the expected fees from a new client should reflect the **level of risk** expected. They should also offer the same sort of return expected of clients of this nature and reflect the overall financial strategy of the audit firm.

Relationship

3.5 The audit firm will generally want the relationship with a client to be long term. This is not only to enjoy receiving fees year after year; it is also to allow the audit work to be enhanced by better knowledge of the client and thereby offer a better service. **Conflict of interest** problems are significant here; the firm should establish that no existing clients will cause difficulties as competitors of the new client.

Ability to perform the work

3.6 The audit firm must have the resources to perform the work properly, as well as any relevant specialist knowledge or skills. The impact on existing engagements must be estimated, in terms of staff time and the timing of the audit.

Part A: Business and audit framework

SOURCES OF INFORMATION ABOUT NEW CLIENTS	
Enquiries of other sources	Bankers, solicitors
Review of **documents**	Most recent annual accounts, listing particulars, credit rating
Previous accountants/auditors	Previous auditors should disclose fully all relevant information
Review of **rules and standards**	Consider specific laws/standards that relate to industry

Approval

3.7 Once all the relevant procedures and information gathering has taken place, the company can be put forward for approval. The engagement partner will have completed a client acceptance form and this, along with any other relevant documentation, will be submitted to the managing partner, or whichever partner is in overall charge of accepting clients.

> **Exam alert**
>
> In the exam you may be given a 'real-life' client situation and asked what factors you would consider in deciding whether to accept appointment. The ethical considerations covered in Chapter 3 may be relevant.

Activity 4.1

The directors of Compton and Edrich Limited have invited your firm to act as auditors for the year ended 31 December 20X7. They are going to ask their current auditors to resign, since they are unhappy with the service they have been given.

Required

(a) Describe the matters you would consider and the investigations you would carry out before accepting appointment as auditors.

(b) Describe the statutory and ethical procedures that you should follow before and after accepting appointment.

4 THE ENGAGEMENT LETTER   Pilot paper

4.1 An engagement letter should:

- Define clearly the **extent** of the **auditors' responsibilities** and so minimise the possibility of any misunderstanding between the client and the auditors

- Provide **written confirmation** of the **auditors' acceptance** of the appointment, the scope of the audit, the form of their report and the scope of any non-audit services

4.2 If an engagement letter is not sent to clients, both new and existing, there is scope for argument about the precise extent of the respective obligations of the client and its directors and the auditors. The contents of an engagement letter should be discussed and agreed with management before it is sent.

4.3 Guidance is available in the form of ISA 210 *Terms of audit engagements*.

> **ISA 210.2**
> The auditor and the client should agree on the terms of the engagement.
>
> **ISA 210.2-1**
> The terms of the engagement should be recorded in writing.

Obviously the agreed terms should be in writing and the usual form would be a **letter of engagement**. Any other form of appropriate contract, however, may be used.

4.4 The ISA makes two further comments about the client/auditor agreement.

- The ISA applies to **audit engagements** only, although the guidance may be used for related services; a distinction should be made between audit and non-audit letters.

- Even in countries where the audit objectives and scope and the auditor's obligations are established by law, an **audit engagement letter** may be informative for clients.

Audit engagement letters

4.5 The auditors should send an engagement letter to all new clients soon after **their appointment** as auditors and, in any event, before the commencement of the first audit assignment. They should also consider sending an engagement letter to existing clients to whom no letter has previously been sent as soon as a suitable opportunity presents itself.

4.6 An example of a letter of engagement, given by ISA 210, is reproduced below. The form and content of audit engagement letters may vary for each client, but they would generally include reference to the following.

(a) The **objective** of the **audit** of financial statements

(b) **Management's responsibility** for the financial statements

(c) The **financial reporting framework** adopted by management in preparing the financial statements. (The applicable financial reporting framework).

(d) The **scope** of the audit, including reference to applicable legislation, regulations, or pronouncements of professional bodies to which the auditor adheres

(e) The **form of any reports** or other communication of results of the engagement

(f) The fact that because of the **test nature** and other **inherent limitations** of an audit, together with the inherent limitations of any accounting and internal control system, there is an unavoidable risk that even some material misstatement may remain undiscovered

(g) **Unrestricted access** to whatever records, documentation and other information requested in connection with the audit

4.7 The auditor may wish to include in the letter the following items.

- Arrangements regarding the **planning** of the audit

- Expectation of receiving from management **written confirmation** of **representations** made in connection with the audit

- Request for the client to **confirm the terms** of the engagement by acknowledging receipt of the engagement letter

- Description of any **other letters or reports** the auditor expects to issue to the client
- Any confidentiality of other letters or reports to be issued
- Basis on which **fees** are computed and any billing arrangements

4.8 When relevant, the following points could also be made.

- Arrangements concerning the involvement of **other auditors** and **experts** in some aspects of the audit
- Arrangements concerning the involvement of **internal auditors** and other client staff
- Arrangements to be made with the **predecessor auditor**, if any, in the case of an initial audit
- Any **restriction of the auditor's liability** when such possibility exists
- A reference to any **further agreements** between the auditor and the client

Recurring audits

> **ISA 210.16**
>
> On recurring audits, the auditor should consider whether circumstances require the terms of the engagement to be revised and whether there is a need to remind the client of the existing terms of the engagement.

4.9 Once it has been agreed by the client, an engagement letter will, if it so provides, remain effective from one audit appointment to another until it is replaced. However, the engagement letter should be **reviewed annually** to ensure that it continues to reflect the client's circumstances.

4.10 The ISA suggests that the following factors may make the agreement of a new letter appropriate.

- Any indication that the client **misunderstands** the objective and scope of the audit
- Any **revised** or **special terms** of the engagement
- A recent **change of senior management**, board of directors or ownership committee
- A **significant change** in the **nature or size** of the client's business
- **Legal requirements**
- A change in the **financial reporting framework** adopted by management in preparing the financial statements.

Acceptance of a change in engagement

> **ISA 210.18**
>
> An auditor who, before the completion of the engagement, is requested to change the engagement to one which provides a lower level of assurance, should consider the appropriateness of doing so.

4.11 In the case of a change in the terms of engagement prior to completion, this may result from:

(a) A **change in circumstances** affecting the need for the service

(b) A **misunderstanding** as to the nature of an audit or of the related service originally requested

(c) A **restriction on the scope** of the engagement, whether imposed by management or caused by circumstances

The auditors should consider such a request for change, and the reason for it, very seriously, particularly in terms of any restriction in the scope of the engagement.

4.12 In the case of (a) and (b) above, these would normally be acceptable reasons for requesting a change in the engagement. A change would not be considered reasonable, however, if it seemed to relate to information that is incorrect, incomplete or otherwise unsatisfactory.

4.13 In addition to the above, an auditor engaged to perform an audit in accordance with ISAs must consider **any legal** or **contractual implications** of **the change**.

4.14 The audit report issued after such a change has been agreed (and the relevant audit work carried out) should be appropriate to the revised terms of engagement. Such an audit report should *not* include reference to:

- The original engagement
- Any procedures performed under the original engagement

> **ISA 210.17-19**
>
> Where the terms of the engagement are changed, the auditor and the client should agree on the new terms.
>
> The auditor should not agree to a change of engagement where there is no reasonable justification for doing so.
>
> If the auditor is unable to agree to a change of the engagement and is not permitted to continue the original engagement, the auditor should withdraw and consider whether there is any obligation, either contractual or otherwise, to report to other parties, such as the board of directors or shareholders, the circumstances necessitating the withdrawal.

4.15 The standard gives an example of where an auditor should *not* agree to a change of engagement; where the auditor is unable to obtain sufficient appropriate audit evidence regarding debtors and the client asks for the engagement to be changed to a review engagement to avoid a qualified audit opinion or a disclaimer of opinion.

Example of an audit engagement letter

4.16 The following letter is for use as a guide in conjunction with the considerations outlined in this ISA and will need to be varied according to individual requirements and circumstances.

Part A: Business and audit framework

AN EXAMPLE OF AN ENGAGEMENT LETTER

To the directors of...

The purpose of this letter is to set out the basis on which we (are to) act as auditors of the company (and its subsidiaries) and the respective areas of responsibility of the directors and of ourselves.

Responsibility of directors and auditors

1. As directors of the above company, you are responsible for ensuring that the company maintains proper accounting records and for preparing financial statements which give a true and fair view and have been prepared in accordance with the Companies Act 1985. You are also responsible for making available to us, as and when required, all the company's accounting records and all other relevant records and related information, including minutes of all management and shareholders' meetings.

2. We have a statutory responsibility to report to the members whether in our opinion the financial statements give a true and fair view of the state of the company's affairs and of the profit or loss for the year and whether they have been properly prepared in accordance with the Companies Act 1985 (or other relevant legislation). In arriving at our opinion, we are required to consider the following matters, and to report on any in respect of which we are not satisfied:

    (a) whether proper accounting records have been kept by the company and proper returns adequate for our audit have been received from branches not visited by us;

    (b) whether the company's balance sheet and profit and loss account are in agreement with the accounting records and returns;

    (c) whether we have obtained all the information and explanations which we think necessary for the purposes of our audit; and

    (d) whether the information in the directors' report is consistent with the financial statements.

    In addition, there are certain other matters which, according to the circumstances, may need to be dealt with in our report. For example, where the financial statements do not give full details of directors' remuneration or of their transactions with the company, the Companies Act requires us to disclose such matters in our report.

3. We have a professional responsibility to report if the financial statements do not comply in any material respect with applicable accounting standards, unless in our opinion the non-compliance is justified in the circumstances. In determining whether the departure is justified we consider:

    (a) whether the departure is required in order for the financial statements to give a true and fair view; and

    (b) whether adequate disclosure has been made concerning the departure

    Our professional responsibilities also include:

    (a) including in our report a description of the directors' responsibilities for the financial statements where the financial statements or accompanying information do not include such a description; and

    (b) considering whether other information in documents containing audited financial statements is consistent with those financial statements.

4. Our audit will be conducted in accordance with the Auditing Standards issued by the Auditing Practices Board, and will include such tests of transactions and of the existence, ownership and valuation of assets and liabilities as we consider necessary. We shall obtain an understanding of the accounting and internal control systems in order to assess their adequacy as a basis for the preparation of the financial statements and to establish whether proper accounting records have been maintained by the company. We shall expect to obtain such appropriate evidence as we consider sufficient to enable us to draw reasonable conclusions therefrom

5   The nature and extent of our procedures will vary according to our assessment of the company's accounting system and, where we wish to place reliance on it, the internal control system, and may cover any aspect of the business's operations. Our audit is not designed to identify all significant weaknesses in the company's systems but, if such weaknesses come to our notice during the course of our audit which we think should be brought to your attention, we shall report them to you. Any such report may not be provided to third parties without our prior written consent. Such consent will be granted only on the basis that such reports are not prepared with the interests of anyone other than the company in mind and that we accept no duty or responsibility to any other party as concerns the reports.

6   As part of our normal audit procedures, we may request you to provide written confirmation of oral representations which we have received from you during the course of the audit on matters having a material effect on the financial statements. In connection with representations and the supply of information to us generally, we draw your attention to section 389A of the Companies Act 1985 under which it is an offence for an officer of the company to mislead the auditors.

7   In order to assist us with the examination of your financial statements, we shall request sight of all documents or statements, including the chairman's statement, operating and financial review and the directors' report, which are due to be issued with the financial statements. We are also entitled to attend all general meetings of the company and to receive notice of all such meetings.

8   The responsibility for safeguarding the assets of the company and for the prevention and detection of fraud, error and non-compliance with law or regulations rests with yourselves. However, we shall endeavour to plan our audit so that we have a reasonable expectation of detecting material misstatements in the financial statements or accounting records (including those resulting from fraud, error or non-compliance with law or regulations), but our examination should not be relied upon to disclose all such material misstatements or frauds, errors or instances of non-compliance as may exist.

9   (Where appropriate). We shall not be treated as having notice, for the purposes of our audit responsibilities, of information provided to members of our firm other than those engaged on the audit (for example information provided in connection with accounting, taxation and other services).

10   Once we have issued our report we have no further direct responsibility in relation to the financial statements for that financial year. However, we expect that you will inform us of any material event occurring between the date of our report and that of the Annual General Meeting which may affect the financial statements.

Other services

11   You have requested that we provide other services in respect of ... . The terms under which we provide these other services are dealt with in a separate letter. We will also agree in a separate letter of engagement the provision of any services relating to investment business advice as defined by the Financial Services Act 1986.

Fees

12   Our fees are computed on the basis of the time spent on your affairs by the partners and our staff and on the levels of skill and responsibility involved. Unless otherwise agreed, our fees will be billed at appropriate intervals during the course of the year and will be due on presentation.

Applicable law

13   This (engagement letter) shall be governed by, and construed in accordance with, (English) law. The Courts of (England) shall have exclusive jurisdiction relation to any claim, dispute or difference concerning the (engagement letter) and any matter arising from it. Each party irrevocably waives any right it may have to object to an action being brought in those Courts, to claim that the action has been brought in an inconvenient forum, or to claim that those Courts do not have jurisdiction.

Part A: Business and audit framework

> 14 Once it has been agreed, this letter will remain effective, from one audit appointment to another, until it is replaced. We shall be grateful if you could confirm in writing your agreement to these terms by signing and returning the enclosed copy of this letter, or let us know if they are not in accordance with your understanding of our terms of engagement.
>
> Yours faithfully
>
> Certified Accountants

Activity 4.2

(a) Explain why it is important for auditors to send a letter of engagement to a new client prior to undertaking an audit.

(b) Describe briefly the main contents of an engagement letter.

Key learning points

- The **present** and **proposed auditors** must **communicate** about the client.
- The client must be asked to give permission for this communication to occur. If the client **refuses** to give **permission,** the proposed auditors must **decline nomination**.
- The proposed auditors must also ensure they:
    - Are **professionally qualified** to act
    - Have **sufficient resources**
    - Seek **references**
- Most firms have **client acceptance procedures** reviewing the **management integrity** and **risk** of the prospective client, as well as the **likely profitability** of the engagement.
- **Investigations** may be carried out for high-risk clients.
- An engagement letter should be sent to all new clients. The letter should:
    - **Specify** the **respective responsibilities** of directors and the auditors
    - Lay down the **scope** of the **auditors'** work

Quick quiz

1. Why should proposed auditors communicate with the present auditors?
2. List factors that may indicate a new client is:
    (a) Low risk
    (b) High risk
3. What should new auditors do once they have accepted nomination?
4. To whom should an engagement letter be addressed?
5. When should auditors issue a new engagement letter?
6. What should auditors do if they are requested to change the terms of an engagement before an audit is completed?

4: Audit engagement

Answers to quick quiz

1 Proposed auditors should communicate with present auditors to ascertain whether there are any factors concerning the proposed change that they should consider, and also because of professional courtesy.

2 (a) A number of factors that indicate that a potential client is low risk:

 (i) The client has a stable business.
 (ii) The business is well-financed.
 (iii) Internal controls are strong.
 (iv) Accounting policies are conservative and prudent.
 (v) Management appears honest and competent.

 (b) A number of factors indicate that a potential client is high risk:

 (i) Audit reports on previous accounts were qualified.
 (ii) Internal controls are poor.
 (iii) The client lacks a finance director or company accountant.
 (iv) The accounting policies may lead to the accounts giving too favourable a picture.
 (v) There are significant related party transactions.

3 Once they have accepted nomination new auditors should:

 (a) Ensure that the outgoing auditors' departure from office has been conducted in accordance with the Companies Act.

 (b) Ensure their appointment is valid.

 (c) Send out an appropriate letter of engagement.

4 An engagement letter should be addressed to the directors of the client.

5 Auditors should issue a new engagement letter if:

 (a) The client misunderstands the objective and scope of the audit.

 (b) There has been a significant change in management and ownership, the nature and size of the client's business, or legal and professional requirements.

6 If asked to change the terms of an engagement, auditors should consider whether the change is appropriate. If they do feel it is appropriate, they should obtain written agreement to the revised terms.

Answers to activities

Answer 4.1

(a) We should consider the following matters before accepting appointment as auditors.

 Qualification to act
 We should ensure we are qualified to act as auditors and are not disqualified on any legal or professional grounds.

 Technical competence
 We should consider whether the firm has the necessary expertise to carry out an effective audit, particularly if the client is in a regulated or specialised industry.

 Resources
 Likewise, we should consider whether we have the resources to perform the work properly, bearing in mind other staff commitments when the audit is due to take place.

 Ethical matters
 We should ensure no partners or staff hold shares in the potential audit client or have any other relationship which could impair independence.

 We should consider whether the level of fees we are likely to obtain will compromise independence. Generally this will apply if audit fees (plus fees for other recurring work) exceed 15% of gross practice income.

 We should also consider whether taking on the audit will cause conflicts of interest with other clients. In particular we should be careful if we already audit competitors of Compton and Edrich Ltd.

Part A: Business and audit framework

Risk assessment

We should consider whether the risk associated with the audit of the client will pose a significant danger to our reputation as auditors. This involves considering a number of factors.

(i) The viability and stability of the client's business
(ii) The character and involvement of management
(iii) The system of internal controls, particularly the client's finance and accounting function
(iv) The accounting policies

Replacement of previous auditors

As well as considering the above, we should also consider why the previous auditors have been replaced. The directors may be unhappy with the service provided, but we should contact the other auditors to find out if there has been any disagreement with the directors over accounting matters.

Procedures for obtaining information

When considering accepting appointment we should obtain information from the following sources.

(i) Communication with the previous auditors
(ii) The client's most recent annual accounts
(iii) Other business publications of the client
(iv) Press reports on the client's activities
(v) Credit ratings from Dun and Bradstreet
(vi) References from existing clients

(b) *Before appointment*

(i) We should request the prospective client's permission to communicate with the auditors last appointed. If such permission is refused we should decline nomination.

(ii) On receipt of permission, we should request in writing of the auditors last appointed all information which ought to be made available to us to enable us to decide whether we are prepared to accept nomination. (Note. If no reply is received, a further letter may be sent which states that if no answer is received by a specified date, it will be assumed that there are no reasons not to accept nomination.)

(iii) If fees are owed to the previous auditors we may still accept nomination, although we may decide that the company will be slow to pay its bills and therefore decline nomination.

After appointment

(i) We should ensure that the outgoing auditors' removal or resignation has been properly conducted in accordance with the Companies Act 1985. We should see a valid notice of the outgoing auditors' resignation (under s 392 CA 1985), or confirm that the outgoing auditors were properly removed (under s 391 CA 1985).

(ii) We should ensure that our appointment is valid. We should obtain a copy of the resolution passed at the meeting appointing us as the company's auditors (special notice = 28 days, ordinary resolution = simple majority > 50%).

(iii) We should set up and submit a letter of engagement to the directors of the company.

Answer 4.2

(a) Auditors should send out an engagement letter for the following reasons.

Defining responsibilities

An engagement letter defines the extent of auditors' and directors' responsibilities.

For auditors, the engagement letter states that their duties are governed by the Companies Act, not the wishes of the directors. It should also state that auditors report to the members (not the directors). For directors, the engagement letter states they are responsible for safeguarding assets, maintaining a proper system of internal control and preventing fraud. The letter should thus minimise the possibility of misunderstanding between auditors and directors.

Documenting acceptance

The engagement letter also provides confirmation in writing of the auditors' acceptance of appointment, the objective and scope of the audit and the form of the audit report.

4: Audit engagement

Other matters

The letter should also lay out the basis on which fees are charged and hence minimise the possibility of arguments about fees.

The letter also sets down what the client should do if he is unhappy with the service he has been given.

(b) The main contents and form of the engagement letter will be as follows.

    (i) It will be addressed to the directors and on the audit firm's letterhead.

    (ii) It will lay out the responsibilities of the directors of the company.

        (1) Maintaining proper accounting records
        (2) Ensuring the accounts show a true and fair view
        (3) Accounts are prepared in accordance with CA 1985
        (4) Making all records/accounts available to the auditors

    (iii) It should also lay out the duties of the auditors, comprising mainly a statutory duty to report to the members their opinion on whether the accounts show a true and fair view and are prepared in accordance with CA 1985.

    (iv) It should state that the audit will be conducted according to auditing standards.

    (v) It should state that the accounts should normally comply with accounting standards (SSAPs and FRSs) and the auditors will report if they do not.

    (vi) It should state that it is the directors' responsibility to detect fraud and error, but that audit procedures are designed so that there is a reasonable expectation of detecting material misstatements.

Other matters which might be covered include the following.

    (i) Fees and billing arrangements
    (ii) Procedures where the client has a complaint about the service
    (iii) Arrangements to be made with the predecessor auditors, in the case of an initial audit
    (iv) A reference to any further agreements between the auditors and the client
    (v) A proposed timetable for the engagement
    (vi) Any agreement about further services (tax, preparing accounts etc)

The letter should end by stating that it will remain effective from one audit appointment to another, until it is replaced. The directors should confirm acceptance in writing.

Now try Question 4 in the Exam Question Bank

Part B
Audit planning

Chapter 5 Risk assessment

Chapter topic list

1 Introduction
2 Audit evidence
3 Materiality
4 Understanding the entity and its environment
5 Risk assessment
6 Responding to the risk assessment

The following study sessions are covered in this Chapter:

Syllabus reference

4(b)	Explain the concept of materiality and discuss the factors to be considered when making a judgement on whether an item is material	4
7(a)	Distinguish between a systems approach to an audit and a direct verification approach	4
7(b)	Explain the concept of audit risk focusing in particular on inherent risk and control risk	4
7(c)	Explain how auditors use knowledge of the business, in audit planning	4
7(d)	Identify sources from which auditors may obtain knowledge of the business	4
22(a)	Explain the importance of evidential material in the audit process	6
22(b)	Identify the factors that influence the reliability of audit evidence	6
22(c)	Describe and give examples of procedures used by the auditors to obtain audit evidence, including the use of computer assisted audit techniques	6
23(a)	Explain the importance of financial statement assertions	6
23(d)	Explain the rationale for designing audit programmes by reference to audit objectives	6
23(e)	Outline the factors determining the nature, timing and extent of substantive procedures to be carried out on an audit	6

Part B: Audit planning

1 INTRODUCTION

1.1 We have already mentioned in Chapter 2 that the auditor is required to obtain evidence about misstatements in financial statements usually caused by error but sometimes caused by fraud. In this chapter we shall look at how they start to do this.

1.2 First we address the question of **what evidence is**, and how auditors go about collecting it. It is important to understand that there are two types of test performed to collect evidence: **tests of controls** and **substantive procedures**.

1.3 Although we have referred to misstatements in general terms up to now auditing standards actually require auditors to be concerned with **material** misstatements. Here we will outline **what materiality is**, and how it helps auditors determine what to test.

1.4 Lastly, we shall look at the process by which auditors determine where material misstatements are most likely to arise and therefore how auditors determine the **nature**, **timing** and **extent** of their **testing**. The process is as follows:

- **Obtain an understanding** of the entity and its environment
- **Assess the risks** of material misstatements through the gained understanding
- **Respond to those risks**

1.5 The auditor's responses to the assessed risks will be formulated into the **audit strategy** (general approach) and the **audit plan** (detailed testing approach) that we shall look at in detail in the next chapter.

1.6 EXAMPLE

When considering some of the aspects of an audit, we shall use an example of a small audit firm, Taylor and Co, and one of its clients, Brown Ltd.

For the audit of Brown Ltd, the audit partner, Dougie Taylor has selected an audit senior, Jo Price, and an audit assistant, Jonathan Okacha. Jo Price will be responsible for putting together the audit strategy.

We will now look at some of the more technical areas of the audit plan and the steps Jo will take in respect of the Brown Ltd audit.

2 AUDIT EVIDENCE 12/04

> **KEY TERM**
>
> **Audit evidence** is all of the information used by the auditor in arriving at the conclusion on which the audit opinion is based. Audit evidence includes the information contained in the accounting records underlying the financial statements and other information.

2.1 In order to reach a position in which they can express a professional opinion, the auditors need to gather evidence from various sources. ISA 500 *Audit Evidence* covers this area.

> **ISA 500.2**
>
> The auditor should obtain sufficient appropriate audit evidence to be able to draw reasonable conclusions on which to base the audit opinion.

Sufficient appropriate audit evidence

2.2 'Sufficiency' and 'appropriateness' are interrelated.

- **Sufficiency** is the measure of the **quantity** of audit evidence.
- **Appropriateness** is the measure of the **quality** or **relevance** and **reliability** of the audit evidence.

2.3 Auditors are essentially looking for enough reliable audit evidence. Audit evidence usually indicates what is probable rather than what is definite (is usually persuasive rather then conclusive) so different sources are examined by the auditors. Not **all** sources of evidence will be examined because auditors can only give **reasonable assurance** that the financial statements are free from misstatement, for the following reasons:

(a) Auditors **do not check every item** in the accounting records. This would be too **time-consuming** and not effective in a **cost-benefit** sense. Instead for many tests they check a sample of items in the population being tested. We shall look at sampling in more detail in Chapter 6.

(b) The **limitations of accounting systems and internal control.** The auditors will be looking to rely on the accounting system, and may be looking to rely on internal control. The accounting records may not give the **level of detail** the auditors require, or the accounting systems may be operated by staff who do not have a **full understanding** of the system. We shall look at internal control in more detail in Chapter 7.

(c) The possibility that directors or staff may **not tell** the **truth** or **collude in fraud.**

(d) The fact that **audit evidence** indicates what is **probable** rather than what is **certain.** Auditors have to make judgements, based on the available evidence, on whether to include certain items in the accounts, for example provisions against specific debts. They will also have to decide in the **reasonableness of estimates.**

(e) Auditors will often not be qualified to make judgements themselves on certain audit evidence. They may need to call on expert assistance.

2.4 Auditors' judgement as to what is sufficient appropriate audit evidence is influenced by a number of factors.

- **Risk assessment**
- The **materiality** of the item being examined
- The **experience gained during previous audits**
- The **source** and **reliability of information** available

2.5 We shall go on to consider these matters in the rest of this chapter. The key issue for auditors is that if they are unable to obtain sufficient appropriate audit evidence, they may have to modify their audit report.

Audit approach

2.6 The auditors will determine an approach to the audit based on their risk assessment, as we shall see later. In general terms, there are two types of approach.

Part B: Audit planning

> **KEY TERMS**
>
> A **systems-based approach** is an approach to audit which seeks to place reliance on the accounting systems of an entity.
>
> A **direct verification approach** is an approach which does not place reliance on systems, where the auditor only verifies individual transactions and balances in the financial statements.

2.7 The systems approach is sometimes called a **combined approach**, because it will involve the auditor carrying out both tests of controls and substantive procedures.

2.8 The direct verification approach is sometimes called the **substantive approach** as it involves the auditors substantiating the financial statements by carrying out only substantive procedures.

Tests of controls

> **KEY TERM**
>
> **Tests of controls** are tests to obtain audit evidence about two aspects of the accounting systems and internal control:
>
> - **Design**. The accounting systems and internal control are capable of preventing or detecting material misstatements.
> - **Operation**. The systems exist and have operated effectively throughout the relevant period.

Substantive procedures

> **KEY TERM**
>
> **Substantive procedures** are tests to obtain audit evidence to detect material misstatements in the financial statements. They are generally of two types:
>
> - Analytical procedures, and
> - Other procedures such as tests of details of classes of transactions, account balances, and disclosures.

2.9 Substantive procedures are designed to **obtain evidence about the financial statement assertions** which are basically what the accounts say about the assets, liabilities and transactions of the client, and the events that affect the client's accounts.

5: Risk assessment

FINANCIAL STATEMENT ASSERTIONS	
Existence	Assets, liabilities and equity interests exist.
Rights and obligations	An asset or liability 'belongs' to the client
Occurrence	A transaction or event took place which relates to the client
Completeness and cut off	All relevant assets, liabilities, equity interests, transactions and events are recorded, and there are no undisclosed items. Transactions and events have been recorded in the correct accounting period.
Valuation (and allocation)	An asset or liability is recorded at an appropriate value
Measurement/accuracy	A transaction or event is measured at a proper amount
Presentation and disclosure	Financial information is appropriately presented and described and disclosures are clearly expressed.

ISA 500.16

The auditor should use assertions for **classes of transactions**, **account balances**, and **presentation and disclosures** in sufficient detail to form a basis for the assessment of risks of material misstatement and the design and performance of further audit procedures.

2.10 The ISA gives examples of assertions in these areas.

Assertions used by the auditor	
Assertions about **classes of transactions** and events for the period under audit	**Occurrence**: transactions and events that have been recorded have occurred and pertain to the entity.
	Completeness: all transactions and events that should have been recorded have been recorded.
	Accuracy: amounts and other data relating to recorded transactions and events have been recorded appropriately.
	Cutoff: transactions and events have been recorded in the correct accounting period (see measurement, above).
	Classification: transactions and events have been recorded in the proper accounts.
Assertions about **account balances** at the period end	**Existence**: assets, liabilities and equity interests exist.
	Rights and obligations: the entity holds or controls the rights to assets, and liabilities are the obligations of the entity.
	Completeness: all assets, liabilities and equity interests that should have been recorded have been recorded.
	Valuation and allocation: assets, liabilities, and equity interests are included in the financial statements at appropriate amounts and any resulting valuation or allocation adjustments are appropriately recorded.

Part B: Audit planning

Assertions used by the auditor	
Assertions about presentation and disclosure	**Occurrence and rights and obligations**: disclosed events, transactions and other matters have occurred and pertain to the entity.
	Completeness: all disclosures that should have been included in the financial statements have been included.
	Classification and understandability: financial information is appropriately presented and described, and disclosures are clearly expressed.
	Accuracy and valuation: financial and other information is disclosed fairly and at appropriate amounts.

2.11 Audit evidence is usually obtained to support each financial statement assertion and evidence from one does not compensate for failure to obtain evidence for another. However tests may provide audit evidence of more than one assertion.

2.12 In the case of **completeness** particularly, the auditors are heavily reliant on the effectiveness of the internal control system in ensuring that all data is satisfactorily captured in the accounting records. If internal control is very weak the auditors may not be able to obtain sufficient evidence as regards completeness, and hence may have to modify their audit report.

Activity 5.1

Can you state which of the following tests are tests of controls and which are substantive procedures?

(a) Checking that invoices have been approved by the managing director
(b) Attending the year-end stock count
(c) Reviewing accounting records after the year-end for events that affect this year's accounts
(d) Obtaining confirmation from the bank of balances held at the year-end
(e) Checking how unauthorised personnel are prevented from entering where stock is held
(f) Checking if references are sought for all new major customers

Reliability of evidence

2.13 The following generalisations may help in assessing the reliability of audit evidence.

- Audit evidence from **external sources** (eg confirmation received from a third party) is **more reliable** than that obtained from the **entity's records**.

- Audit evidence obtained from the **entity's records** is more reliable when the related accounting and internal **control system operates effectively**.

- Evidence obtained **directly by auditors** is **more reliable** than that obtained by or **from the entity**.

- Evidence in the **form of documents and written representations** is **more reliable** than **oral representations**.

- **Original documents** are **more reliable** than **photocopies, telexes or facsimiles**.

2.14 Consistency of audit evidence from different sources will have a corroborating effect, making the evidence more persuasive. Where such evidence is **inconsistent**, the auditors must determine what additional procedures are necessary to resolve the inconsistency. Auditors must consider the cost-benefit relationship of obtaining evidence *but* any difficulty or expense is not in itself a valid basis for omitting a necessary procedure.

5: Risk assessment

> **Exam alert**
>
> You may be asked to consider how strong certain evidence is from the auditor's viewpoint.

	PROCEDURES
Inspection of assets	Inspection of assets that are recorded in the accounting records confirms **existence,** gives evidence of **valuation** but does not confirm rights and obligations. Auditors may need the aid of experts
	Confirmation that assets seen are recorded in the accounting records gives evidence of **completeness**
Inspection of documentation	Confirmation to documentation of items recorded in the accounting records demonstrates that a transaction **occurred** or a balance **exists**
	Confirmation that items recorded in the supporting documentation are recorded in the accounting records tests **completeness**
	Cut-off can be verified by inspecting the reverse population, checking transactions recorded after the balance sheet date to supporting documentation to confirm that they occurred after the balance sheet date
	Inspection also provides evidence of **valuation** and **measurement, rights and obligations,** and the nature of items (**presentation and disclosure**). It can also be used to **compare** documents (and hence test **consistency** of audit evidence), and to **confirm authorisation**
Observation	Involves watching a procedure being performed (eg post opening, or inventory being counted)
	Of limited use when testing controls, as only confirms control procedure took place when auditor watching
Inquiries	Seeking information from **client staff** or **external sources** about **operation of controls** or how certain items have been treated in the accounting records e.g. how provisions have been calculated
	Strength of evidence depends on knowledge and integrity of source of information. It may be necessary to corroborate inquiries particularly those made of client's staff
Confirmation	Seeking confirmation from another source of details in client's accounting records e.g. confirmation from bank of **existence** and **rights and obligations** of bank balances
Computations	Checking arithmetic of client's records e.g. adding up ledger account. If a formula is involved, the auditors should also consider the reasonableness of the formula
Reconciliations	Checking the reconciliations of clients' control accounts provides evidence of **completeness**
Analytical procedures	See Chapter 10
Computer assisted audit techniques	- see below

Activity 5.2

List the financial statement assertions, and discuss the strength or weakness of the following sources of audit evidence, and the financial statement assertions to which they relate.

(a) Physical inspection of a fixed asset by an auditor

(b) Confirmation by a debtor of money owed

(c) Oral representations by management that all creditors owed money at the year-end have been included in the accounts

Part B: Audit planning

3 MATERIALITY

3.1 Materiality relates to the level of error that affects the decisions of users of the accounts. ISA 320 *Audit materiality* provides guidance.

> **KEY TERM**
>
> Information is **material** if its omission or misstatement could influence the economic decisions of users taken on the basis of the financial statements.
>
> Materiality depends on the size of the item or error judged in the particular circumstances of its omission or misstatement.
>
> Materiality provides a threshold or cut-off point rather than being a primary qualitative characteristic which information must have to be useful.

3.2 EXAMPLE

For example, if a company has a profit of £100,00 an error of £1,000 is unlikely to be significant. If a company has a profit of £10,000 an error of £1,000 will have a more significant impact on the readers of the accounts.

3.3 Some items such as directors' fees and equity capital are capable of exact definition. Readers would expect these figures to be accurate. Other balances such as provisions for obsolete inventories are an intelligent estimate and therefore greater latitude is allowed.

> **ISA 320.8**
>
> Materiality should be considered by the auditor when:
> (a) determining the nature, timing and extent of audit procedures; and
> (b) evaluating the effect of misstatements.

3.4 Materiality considerations during **audit planning** are extremely important. The assessment of materiality at this stage should be based on the most recent and reliable financial information and will help to determine an effective and efficient audit approach. Materiality assessment will help the auditors to decide:

- **How many** and **what items** to examine
- Whether to use **sampling techniques**
- What **level of error** is likely to lead to a modified audit opinion

3.5 The resulting combination of audit procedures should help to reduce detection risk to an appropriately low level.

Practical implications

3.6 Because many users of accounts are primarily interested in the **profitability** of the company, materiality is often thought of in terms of a value associated with the level of profit before tax. For example, if profit before tax was £40,000, auditors might consider that all matters in the financial statements equal to 5% of £40,000 (ie £2,000) will be important to users.

5: Risk assessment

3.7 However, auditors should beware thinking of materiality solely in these terms. For example some users might be more concerned with asset values or specific matters in the financial statement rather than 'value' at all, so auditors may have a monetary guide to what is important to users, but should also use their professional judgement at all times to consider what is important to users.

3.8 At the planning stage, auditors will set a 'value level' for planning materiality based on draft financial information available to them. However, this should be reviewed as the audit progresses and as any changes are made to the financial information.

3.9 In addition, certain types of error should be investigated even if they are small in monetary terms, because, as stated above, they are important for other reasons.

- **Recurring errors** as these may indicate weaknesses in the accounting system.
- **Errors** that would mean **breaches** of **statutory requirements**.
- **Critical point errors**, for example those that change a loss into profit
- **Conceptual errors**, errors that involve breaches in the accounting requirements.

3.10 EXAMPLE

Jo Price has made enquiries with the directors and has been told that draft profit before tax for Brown Ltd for the year is £100,000. She has therefore proposed that planning materiality is £5,000 (5%). She will use this figure to assist her in setting sample sizes and when drafting the detailed audit work to be carried out in the audit plan.

Activity 5.3

Which measures of a client's business is an auditor likely to use when setting a level of materiality:

(a) For a client that has a stable asset base, steady turnover over the last few years but has only made a small pre-tax profit this year owing to a large one-off expense?

(b) For a client where the outside shareholders have expressed concern over declining profits over the last few years?

---

4 UNDERSTANDING THE ENTITY AND ITS ENVIRONMENT

4.1 ISA 315 *Understanding the entity and its environment and assessing the risks of material misstatement* states that 'the auditor should **obtain an understanding** of the entity and its environment, including its internal control, sufficient to **identify and assess the risks of material misstatement** of the financial statements whether due to fraud or error, and sufficient to design and perform further audit procedures'.

4.2 The ISA gives guidance on obtaining this understanding. The table below summarises some of the key points.

Part B: Audit planning

	Summary: Obtaining an understanding of the entity and its environment
Why?	To identify and assess the risks of material misstatement in the financial statements
	To enable the auditor to design and perform further audit procedures
	To provide a frame of reference for exercising audit judgement, for example, when setting audit materiality
How?	Inquiries of management and others within the entity
	Analytical procedures
	Observation and inspection
	Prior period knowledge
	Discussion of the susceptibility of the financial statements to material misstatement among the engagement team
What?	Industry, regulatory and other external factors, including the reporting framework
	Nature of the entity, including selection and application of accounting policies
	Objectives and strategies and relating business risks that might cause material misstatement in the financial statements
	Measurement and review of the entity's financial performance
	Internal control (which we shall look at in detail in Chapter 7)

4.3 EXAMPLE

Jo Price will have to bear all of these key points in mind. She may need to visit the client during the course of her planning work to update her understanding of the client. If not, she will certainly need to telephone someone at the client to discuss developments since the previous audit. Alternatively the audit partner may have had meetings with Brown's directors and can pass on pertinent details to her.

Why?

4.4 As can be seen in the table above, the reasons the auditor is to obtain the understanding of the entity and its environment are very much bound up with assessing risks and exercising audit judgement. We shall look at these aspects more in the next two sections of this chapter.

How?

4.5 ISA 315 sets out the methods that the auditor **must** use to obtain the understanding. The auditor does not have to use all of these for each area, but a combination of these procedures should be used. These are:

- Inquiries of management and others within the entity
- Analytical procedures
- Observation and inspection

4.6 The **audit team** is also required by ISA 315 to **discuss the susceptibility of the financial statements to material misstatement.** Judgement must be exercised in determining which members of the team should be involved in which parts of the discussion, but all team

5: Risk assessment

members should be involved in the discussion relevant to the parts of the audit they will be involved in.

4.7 Lastly, if it is a recurring audit, the auditors may have obtained a great deal of knowledge about the entity and the environment in the course of prior year audits. The auditor is entitled to use this information in the current year audit, but he must make sure that he has determined whether any **changes** in the year have affected the relevance of information obtained in previous years.

Inquiries of management and others within the entity

4.8 The auditors will usually obtain most of the information they require from staff in the accounts department, but may also need to make enquiries of other personnel, for example, internal audit, production staff or those charged with governance.

4.9 EXAMPLES

Those charged with governance may give insight into the environment in which the financial statements are prepared. In-house legal counsel may help with understanding matters such as outstanding litigation, or compliance with laws and regulations. Sales and marketing personnel may give information about marketing strategies and sales trends.

Analytical procedures

4.10 Analytical procedures are a useful tool in risk assessment.

> **KEY TERM**
>
> **Analytical procedures** means evaluation of financial information made by a study of plausible relationships among both financial and non-financial data. Analytical procedures also encompass the investigation of identified fluctuations and relationships that are inconsistent with other relevant information or deviate significantly from predicted amounts.

> **Point to Note**
>
> We shall look at the mechanics of analytical procedures in Chapter 10.

Observation and inspection

4.11 These techniques are likely to confirm the answers made to inquiries made of management. They will include observing the normal operations of a company, reading documents or manuals relating to the client's operations or visiting premises and meeting staff.

What?

4.12 The ISA sets out a number of requirements about what the auditors must consider in relation to obtaining an understanding of the business. The general areas are shown in the following diagram.

Part B: Audit planning

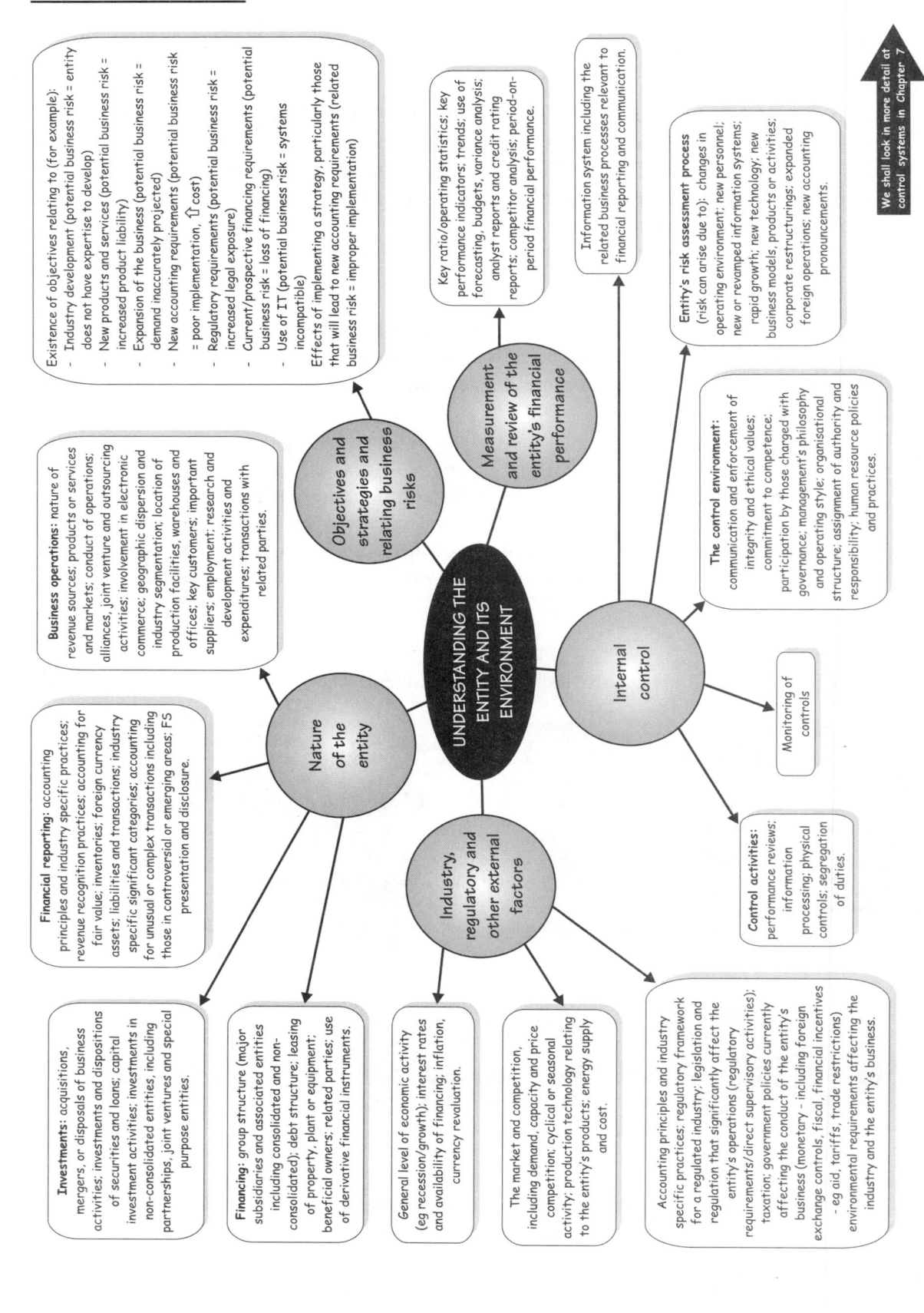

UNDERSTANDING THE ENTITY AND ITS ENVIRONMENT

Objectives and strategies and relating business risks

Existence of objectives relating to (for example):
- Industry development (potential business risk = entity does not have expertise to develop)
- New products and services (potential business risk = increased product liability)
- Expansion of the business (potential business risk = demand inaccurately projected)
- New accounting requirements (potential business risk = poor implementation, ⇧ cost)
- Regulatory requirements (potential business risk = increased legal exposure)
- Current/prospective financing requirements (potential business risk = loss of financing)
- Use of IT (potential business risk = systems incompatible)

Effects of implementing a strategy, particularly those that will lead to new accounting requirements (related business risk = improper implementation)

Measurement and review of the entity's financial performance

Key ratio/operating statistics; key performance indicators; trends; use of forecasting, budgets, variance analysis; analyst reports and credit rating reports; competitor analysis; period-on-period financial performance.

Internal control

Entity's risk assessment process (risk can arise due to): changes in operating environment; new personnel; new or revamped information systems; rapid growth; new technology; new business models, products or activities; corporate restructurings; expanded foreign operations; new accounting pronouncements.

Information system including the related business processes relevant to financial reporting and communication.

The control environment: communication and enforcement of integrity and ethical values; commitment to competence; participation by those charged with governance; management's philosophy and operating style; organisational structure; assignment of authority and responsibility; human resource policies and practices.

Monitoring of controls

Control activities: performance reviews; information processing; physical controls; segregation of duties.

We shall look in more detail at control systems in Chapter 7

Business operations
nature of revenue sources; products or services and markets; conduct of operations; alliances, joint venture and outsourcing activities; involvement in electronic commerce; geographic dispersion and industry segmentation; location of production facilities, warehouses and offices; key customers; important suppliers; employment; research and development activities and expenditures; transactions with related parties.

Nature of the entity

Financial reporting: accounting principles and industry specific practices; revenue recognition practices; accounting for fair value; inventories; foreign currency assets; liabilities and transactions; industry specific significant categories; accounting for unusual or complex transactions including those in controversial or emerging areas; FS presentation and disclosure.

Investments: acquisitions, mergers, or disposals of business activities; investments and dispositions of securities and loans; capital investment activities; investments in non-consolidated entities, including partnerships, joint ventures and special purpose entities.

Financing: group structure (major subsidiaries and associated entities including consolidated and non-consolidated); debt structure; leasing of property, plant or equipment; beneficial owners; related parties; use of derivative financial instruments.

Industry, regulatory and other external factors

General level of economic activity (eg recession/growth); interest rates and availability of financing; inflation, currency revaluation.

The market and competition, including demand, capacity and price competition; cyclical or seasonal activity; production technology relating to the entity's products; energy supply and cost.

Accounting principles and industry specific practices; regulatory framework for a regulated industry; legislation and regulation that significantly affect the entity's operations (regulatory requirements/direct supervisory activities); taxation; government policies currently affecting the conduct of the entity's business (monetary - including foreign exchange controls, fiscal, financial incentives - eg aid, tariffs, trade restrictions); environmental requirements affecting the industry and the entity's business.

5 RISK ASSESSMENT 12/04

Introduction to risk

5.1 Auditors follow a **risk-based approach** to auditing. In the risk-based approach, auditors analyse the risks associated with the client's business, transactions and systems, which could lead to misstatements in the financial statements, and direct their testing to risky areas.

5.2 They are therefore not concerned with individual routine transactions, although they will still be concerned with material, non-routine transactions.

> **KEY TERM**
>
> **Audit risk** is the risk that the auditors give an inappropriate audit opinion when the financial statements are materially misstated.

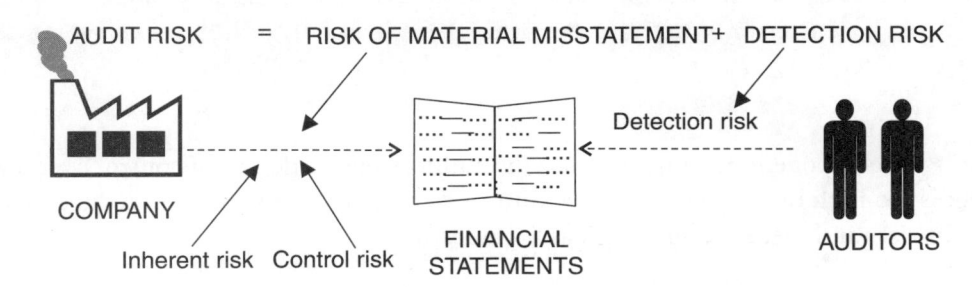

AUDIT RISK = RISK OF MATERIAL MISSTATEMENT + DETECTION RISK

COMPANY — Inherent risk, Control risk → FINANCIAL STATEMENTS ← Detection risk — AUDITORS

5.3 As you can see from the above diagram, audit risk has two major components. One is dependent on the entity, and is the risk of material misstatement arising in the financial statements. The other is dependent on the auditor, and is the risk that the auditor will not detect material misstatements in the financial statements.

Risk of material misstatement in the financial statements

5.4 Risk of material misstatement in the financial statements can be seen to fall into two general categories of risk, known as **inherent risk** and **control risk**. We shall explore both of these categories here.

> **KEY TERM**
>
> **Inherent risk** is the susceptibility of an assertion to a misstatement and that could be material individually or when aggregated with other misstatements, assuming that there were no related internal controls.

5.5 Inherent risk is the risk that items will be mis-stated due to characteristics of those items, such as the fact they are estimates or that they are important items in the accounts. The auditors must use their professional judgement and all available knowledge to assess inherent risk. If no such information or knowledge is available then the inherent risk is **high**.

5.6 Inherent risk is affected by the nature of the entity; for example, the industry it is in and the regulations it falls under, and also the nature of the strategies it adopts.

Part B: Audit planning

> **KEY TERM**
>
> **Control risk** is the risk that a misstatement that could occur in an assertion and that could be material, individually or when aggregated with other misstatements, will not be prevented or detected and corrected on a timely basis by the entity's internal control.

5.7 We shall look at control risk in more detail in Chapter 7.

Risk that the auditor will not detect a material misstatement in the financial statements

5.8 This aspect of audit risk is known as detection risk.

> **KEY TERM**
>
> **Detection risk** is the risk that the auditors' procedures will not detect a misstatement that exists in an assertions that could be material, individually or when aggregated with other misstatements.

5.9 This is the component of audit risk that the auditors have a degree of control over, because, if risk is too high to be tolerated, the auditors can carry out more work to reduce this aspect of audit risk, and therefore audit risk as a whole.

5.10 ISA 200 states that 'the auditor should plan and perform the audit to reduce audit risk to an acceptably low level that is consistent with the objective of the audit', that is, giving reasonable assurance on the truth and fairness of the financial statements.

Business risk

5.11 The other major category of risk which the auditor must be aware of is that of **business risk**. As you saw on page 80 and will see in more detail in Chapter 7, the auditor is required to consider the company's process of business risk management.

Assessing the risk of material misstatement

5.12 The ISA says that 'the auditor should **identify** and **assess the risks of material misstatement** at the **financial statement level**, and at the assertion level for classes of transactions, account balances and disclosures'. It requires the auditor to take the following steps:

Step 1. Identify risks throughout the process of obtaining an understanding of the entity

Step 2. Relate the risks to what can go wrong at the assertion level

Step 3. Consider whether the risks are of a magnitude that could result in a material misstatement

Step 4. Consider the likelihood of the risks causing a material misstatement

5.13 **EXAMPLE**

The audit team at Brown Ltd has been carrying out procedures to obtain an understanding of the entity. Brown Ltd is a manufacturing company. In the course of making inquiries, they have discovered that the company has had a stable sales ledger in the past and has a number of well established suppliers. In the last year it has been facing competition from a new company and it has lost one or two customers as a result of perceived quality issues. In addition the company regularly produces 10% more than current orders.

The knowledge above suggests two risks, one that the company may have value-effected even obsolete inventories, and another that if their production quality standards are insufficiently high, they could run the risk of losing custom.

We shall look at each of these risks in turn and relate them to the assertion level.

Stocks

If certain of the stocks are obsolete due to the fact that it has been produced in excess of the customer's requirement and there is no other available market for the stock, then there is a risk that stock as a whole in the financial statements will not be carried at the **appropriate value**. Given that stock is likely to be a material balance in the balance sheet of a manufacturing company, and the misstatement could be up to 10% of the total value, this has the capacity to be a material misstatement.

The factors that will contribute to the likelihood of these risks causing a misstatement are matters such as:

- Whether management regularly review stock levels and scrap items that are obsolete
- Whether such items are identified and scrapped at the stock count
- Whether such items can be put back into production and changed so that they are saleable

Losing custom

The long term risk of losing custom is a risk that in the future the company will not be able to operate (a going concern risk, which we shall look at in more detail in Chapter 15). It could have an impact on the financial statements, if sales were attributed to them that they dispute, sales and debtors could be overstated, that is, not carried at the correct **value**. However, it appears less likely that this would be a material problem in either area, as the problem is likely to be restricted to a few customers, and only a few sales to those customers.

Again, review of the company's controls over the recording of sales and the debt collection procedures of the company would indicate how likely these risks to the financial statements are to materialise.

Activity 5.4 : assessing the risks of material misstatement

You are involved with the audit of Tantpro Ltd, a small company. You have been carrying out procedures to gain an understanding of the entity. The following matters have come to your attention:

The company offers standard credit terms to its customers of 60 days from the date of invoice. Statements are sent to customers on a monthly basis. However, Tantpro Ltd does not employ a credit controller, and other than sending the statements on a monthly basis, it does not otherwise communicate with its customers on a systematic basis. On occasion, the sales ledger clerk may telephone a customer if the company has not received a payment for some time. Some customers pay regularly according to the credit terms offered to them, but others pay on a very haphazard basis and do not provide a remittance advice. Sales ledger receipts are entered onto the sales ledger but not matched to invoices remitted. The company does not produce an aged list of balances.

Part B: Audit planning

Required

From the above information, assess the risks of material misstatement arising at in the financial statements. Outline the potential materiality of the risks and discuss factors in the likelihood of the risks arising.

Significant risks

5.14 Some risks identified may be significant risks, in which case they present **special audit considerations** for the auditors. The following factors indicate that a risk might be a significant risk:

- Risk of fraud
- Its relationship with recent developments
- The degree of subjectivity in the financial information
- It is an unusual transaction
- It is a significant transaction with a related party
- The complexity of the transaction

5.15 Routine, non-complex transactions are less likely to give rise to significant risk than unusual transactions or matters of director judgement. This is because unusual transactions are likely to have more:

- Management intervention
- Complex accounting principles or calculations
- Manual intervention
- Opportunity for control procedures not to be followed

5.16 When the auditor identifies a significant risk, if he hasn't done so already, he must evaluate the design and implementation of the entity's controls in that area.

6 RESPONDING TO THE RISK ASSESSMENT

6.1 The main requirement of ISA 330 *The auditor's procedures in response to assessed risks* is 'in order to reduce audit risk to an acceptably low level, the auditor should determine overall responses to assessed risks at the financial statement level, and should design and perform further audit procedures to respond to assessed risks at the assertion level'.

6.2 In other words, having assessed the risks of material misstatements in the financial statements, the auditor has to **plan the work** that will be carried out **to ensure** that **he can give an opinion** that the financial statements give a true and fair view, that is, that any material misstatements have been identified and amended if necessary.

Overall responses

6.3 Overall responses to risks of material misstatement will be changes to the general audit strategy or re-affirmations to staff of the general audit strategy. For example:

- Emphasising to audit staff the need to maintain professional scepticism
- Assigning additional or more experienced staff to the audit team
- Using experts
- Providing more supervision on the audit
- Incorporating more unpredictability into the audit procedures

5: Risk assessment

6.4 EXAMPLE

As we have seen, stock at Brown Ltd has been identified as a risk area. This is typically the case due to the often subjective nature of stock valuation. Here risk is increased further by the quality issues Brown Ltd has experienced. When allocating work on the audit Jo would want to ensure that she is heavily involved in this aspect of the work. It would be inappropriate to delegate all aspects of this work to Jonathan although he may be able to assist in the collation of information on which her judgement will be based.

6.5 The evaluation of the control environment that will have taken place as part of the assessment of the client's internal control systems will help the auditor determine whether they are going to take a substantive approach (focusing mainly on substantive procedures) or a combined approach (tests of controls and substantive procedures).

Responses to the risks of material misstatement at the assertion level

6.6 The ISA says that 'the auditor should design and perform further audit procedures whose **nature, timing** and **extent** are responsive to the assessed risks of material misstatement at the assertion level'. Nature refers to the purpose and the type of test that is carried out.

Tests of controls

6.7 The ISA states that 'when the auditor's assessment of risks of material misstatement includes an expectation that controls are operating effectively, the auditor should perform tests of controls to obtain sufficient appropriate audit evidence that the controls were operating effectively at relevant times during the period under audit'. So, for example, if controls over sales and receivables were expected to operate effectively, auditors should test controls in that area.

6.8 It may also be necessary to undertake tests of controls when it will not be possible to obtain sufficient appropriate audit evidence simply from substantive procedures. This might be the case if the entity conducts its business using IT systems which do not produce documentation of transactions.

6.9 In carrying out tests of controls, auditors must use **inquiry**, but must not only use inquiry. Other procedures must also be used. In testing controls, **reperformance** by the auditor will often be a helpful procedure, as will **inspection**.

6.10 When considering timing in relation to tests of controls, the purpose of the test will be important. For example, if the company carries out a year end inventory count, controls over the inventory count can only be tested at the year end. Other controls will operate all year, and the auditor may need to test that controls have been effective all year.

6.11 Some controls may have been tested in prior audits and the auditor may choose to rely on that evidence of their effectiveness. If this is the case, the auditor must obtain evidence about any changes since the controls were last tested and must test the controls if they have changed. In any case, controls should be tested for effectiveness at least once in every three audits.

6.12 If the related risk has been designated a significant risk, the auditor should not rely on testing carried out in prior years, but should carry out testing in the current year.

Part B: Audit planning

Substantive procedures

6.13 **The auditor must always carry out substantive procedures on material items.** The ISA says 'irrespective of the assessed risk of material misstatement, the auditor should design and perform substantive procedures for each material class of transactions, account balance and disclosure'.

6.14 In addition, the auditor **must** carry out the following substantive procedures:

- Agreeing the financial statements to the underlying accounting records
- Examining material journal entries
- Examining other adjustments made in preparing the financial statements

6.15 As you know, substantive procedures fall into two categories: analytical procedures and other procedures. The auditor must determine when it is appropriate to use which type of substantive procedure.

6.16 **Analytical procedures** tend to be appropriate for large volumes of predictable transactions (for example, wages and salaries). **Other procedures** (**tests of detail**) may be appropriate to gain information about account balances (for example, stocks or trade debtors), particularly verifying the assertions of existence and valuation.

6.17 Tests of detail rather than analytical procedures are likely to be more appropriate with regard to matters which have been identified as **significant risks**, but the auditor must determine procedures that are specifically responsive to that risk, which may include analytical procedures. Significant risks are likely to be the most difficult to obtain sufficient appropriate evidence about.

Timing of substantive procedures and tests of controls

6.18 Auditors may carry out their audit work for one year in two or more sittings. When they do so, they call these sittings the **interim audit**(s) and the **final audit**.

> **KEY TERMS**
>
> The **final audit** is the main period of audit testing, when work if focused on the final financial statements.
>
> **Interim audits** are audits undertaken prior to the final audit, often during the period under review. The auditor is likely to carry out tests of controls at interim audits.

6.19 We have already highlighted the need for the auditors to obtain evidence that controls have operated effectively throughout the period. The ISA says 'when the auditor obtains evidence about the operating effectiveness of controls during an interim period, the auditor should determine what additional audit evidence should be obtained for the remaining period'.

6.20 The ISA makes a similar observation with regard to substantive procedures: 'when substantive procedures are performed at an interim date, the auditor should perform further substantive procedures or substantive procedures combined with tests of controls to cover the remaining period that provide a reasonable basis for extending the audit conclusions from the interim date to the period end'.

5: Risk assessment

6.21 In addition, with regard to substantive procedures, 'the use of audit evidence from the performance of substantive procedures in a prior audit is not sufficient to address a risk of material misstatement in the current period'. In other words, because the existence of non current assets was testing last year does not mean it does not have to be tested this year.

6.22 This is slightly different to testing the operation of controls, as the controls may be the same year on year, and operating in the same manner. Therefore, the auditor may judge that tests of controls carried out in a prior audit may be relevant to a current year audit, subject to the matters of judgement already discussed.

Key learning points

- Auditors should evaluate all audit evidence in terms of its **sufficiency** and **appropriateness**.
- Evidence can be in the form of **tests of controls** or **substantive procedures**.
- If carrying out tests of controls, auditors are looking for audit evidence on **design** and **operation** of controls.
- When carrying out substantive procedures, auditors are seeking to obtain audit evidence on all the **financial statement assertions**.
    - Existence
    - Occurrence
    - Valuation (and allocation)
    - Presentation and disclosure
    - Rights and obligations
    - Completeness and cut off
    - Measurement/accuracy
- **Materiality** should be calculated at the planning stages of all audits. The calculation or estimation of materiality should be based on experience and judgement. The materiality chosen should be reviewed during the audit.
- The auditor is required to obtain an **understanding** of the **entity** and its **environment** in order to be able to assess the risks of material misstatements.
- In doing so, the auditor should use a combination of:
    - **Inquiries** of management/others within the entity
    - **Analytical procedures**
    - **Observation** and **inspection**
- When the auditor has obtained an understanding of the entity, he must **assess the risks of material misstatement** in the financial statements, also identifying significant risks.
- Audit risk is the risk that the auditors give an inappropriate opinion on financial statements. It has two elements: the **risk that the financial statements contain a material misstatement** and the **risk that the auditors will fail to detect any material misstatements**.
- The risk that the financial statements contain a material misstatement has two elements, **inherent risk** and **control risk**. The risk that the auditors will fail to detect material misstatement is known as **detection risk**.
- **Significant risks** are complex or unusual transactions, those that may indicate fraud or other special risks.
- The auditors must then formulate an approach to the risks of material misstatement. He must formulate **overall responses** and **detailed further audit procedures**.
- The further audit procedures will be a combination of **tests of controls** and **substantive procedures** (a **systems approach**) or substantive tests only (a **direct verification approach**). Substantive procedures must be carried out on material items.

Part B: Audit planning

Quick quiz

1 What does ISA 500.2 say about the evidence that auditors should obtain?

2 When auditors are testing controls, about which two aspects are they seeking evidence?

3 List the financial statement assertions (single, two or three word descriptions will suffice).

4 What general comments can be made about audit evidence?

5 Of which type of audit procedure are the following examples?

   (a) Physical check of fixed assets
   (b) Watching the payment of wages
   (c) Receiving a letter from the client's bank concerning balances held at the bank by the client
   (d) Adding up the client's trial balance

6 Give examples of figures used as a basis for setting materiality.

7 What is audit risk?

8 What are the components of audit risk?

9 What procedures might an auditor use in gaining an understanding of the entity?

10 List three potential overall responses to assessed risks.

Answers to quick quiz

1 ISA 500.2 states that auditors should obtain sufficient appropriate audit evidence to be able to draw reasonable conclusions on which to base their opinion.

2 When testing controls, auditors are concentrating on their design and operation.

3 The financial statement assertions are:

   (a) Existence
   (b) Rights and obligations
   (c) Occurrence
   (d) Completeness and cut off
   (e) Valuation (and allocation)
   (f) Measurement/accuracy
   (g) Presentation and disclosure

4 General comments that can be made about audit evidence are as follows.

   (a) Audit evidence from external sources is more reliable than evidence from internal sources.

   (b) Evidence obtained form the client's records is more satisfactory if the accounting and internal control system is operating effectively.

   (c) Directly obtained audit evidence is more reliable than evidence obtained from the entity.

   (d) Written evidence is more reliable than oral evidence.

   (e) Original documents are more reliable than copies.

5 (a) Inspection
   (b) Observation
   (c) Confirmation
   (d) Computation

6 Common materiality is set using on or more of the following figures:

   (a) Profit before tax
   (b) Gross assets
   (c) Turnover

   Less frequently the following figures are used:

   (a) Gross profit
   (b) Profit before tax
   (c) Net assets

7 Audit risk is the risk that auditors may give an inappropriate opinion on the annual accounts.

5: Risk assessment

8   The three components of audit risk are inherent, control and detection risk.

9   Inquiry, analytical procedures, observation and inspection.

10 Any of:

- Emphasising the need for professional scepticism
- Assigning additional/more experienced staff
- Using experts
- Providing more supervision
- Incorporating more unpredictability

Answers to activities

Answer 5.1

(a) Control
(b) Substantive
(c) Substantive
(d) Substantive
(e) Control
(f) Control

Answer 5.2

Audit evidence should allow auditors to draw conclusions on the financial statement assertions.

(a) Existence
(b) Rights and obligations
(c) Occurrence and cut off
(d) Completeness
(e) Valuation (and allocation)
(f) Measurement/accuracy
(g) Presentation and disclosure

(a) The physical inspection of an asset by auditors is inherently strong audit evidence since it is evidence obtained directly by auditors rather than from the client.

The physical inspection of an asset gives auditors the strongest possible evidence concerning its existence.

It also may give auditors some evidence as to valuation if for example machines appear to be obsolete or buildings appear to be derelict. More likely however auditors will require specialist assistance to value very material assets.

Inspection also gives auditors some assurance that assets have been completely recorded. Auditors can check that all assets inspected have been recorded.

However ownership of assets cannot be verified solely by physical inspection. Auditors will need to inspect documents of title, vehicle registration documents and so forth depending on the assets being verified.

(b) Debtor confirmation of balances owed is inherently strong audit evidence since it is written confirmation by a third party.

The evidence is particularly relevant to the assertions of existence (the debtor exists) and rights and obligations (the debtor owes the client money).

Further evidence however is likely to be needed of valuation because although the debtor has acknowledged money is owed, that does not mean that the money will be paid.

(c) Oral representations from clients about what is owed at the year-end are inherently weak evidence since they are not in writing and do not come from an independent source. Auditors should seek written confirmation of the representations, and seek confirmation from other audit evidence, for example suppliers' statements, post year-end accounting records and invoices received after the year-end.

The representations do give some comfort on the completeness of creditors, and also the obligations of the client.

Part B: Audit planning

Answer 5.3

(a) Because the business is stable, auditors are likely to base overall materiality on a % of turnover or gross assets, or possibly an average of both. Profit before tax is unlikely to be used overall as its fluctuation does not appear to be significant. However a different materiality level may be set when considering the one-off expense, since it may be particularly significant to readers of the accounts.

(b) Auditors are likely here to pay some attention to the level of profit when setting materiality, because the outside members regard profit as significant. However the auditors are also likely to take into account gross and net assets. Low profits will be of less significance if the business has a strong asset base, but more significance if the business is in long-term financial difficulty.

Answer 5.4

The key risk arising from the above information is that trade debtors will not be carried at the appropriate **value** in the financial statements, as some may be irrecoverable. Where receipts are not matched against invoices in the ledger, the balance on the ledger may include old invoices that the customer has no intention of paying.

It is difficult to assess at this stage whether this is likely to be material. Trade debtors is likely to be a material balance in the financial statements, but the number of irrecoverable balances may not be material. Analytical procedures, for example, to see if the level of debtors has risen year on year, in a manner that is not explained by price rises or levels of production, might help to assess this.

A key factor that affects the likelihood of the material misstatement arising is the poor controls over the sales ledger. The fact that invoices are not matched against receipts increases the chance of old invoices not having been paid and not noticed by Tantpro Ltd. It appears reasonably likely that the trade debtors balance is overstated in this instance.

> **Now try Question 5 in the Exam Question Bank**

Chapter 6 Audit planning

Chapter topic list

1. Introduction
2. Aims of planning
3. Audit team and use of the work of others
4. Using computers
5. Audit plan
6. Sampling
7. Documentation

The following study sessions are covered in this Chapter:

Syllabus reference

3(c)	Identify the factors that external auditors should consider when evaluating the work of internal auditors	3
7(e)	Explain the role of audit programmes and summarise the advantages/ disadvantages of using standard programmes	4
7(f)	Outline planning issues with regard to audit planning meetings, the timing of audit work, staffing, training of the audit team, the use of suitable experts, and liaison with client staff including internal auditors	3
7(g)	Explain how auditors may plan to use computer assisted audit techniques	6
7(h)	Illustrate the use of an audit planning memorandum	4
10(a)	Discuss the reasons for maintaining audit working papers	4
10(b)	Explain the purpose of the current file and the permanent file	4
10(c)	Describe the contents of a current file and a permanent file	4
10(d)	Outline the quality control procedures that should exist over the review of audit working papers and in the reporting of important audit points to the audit engagement partner	4
10(e)	Illustrate how information technology can be used in the documentation of audit work	4
21(a)	Explain the relevance of sampling to the auditor	6
21(b)	Outline selection methods, including random selection, systematic selection and haphazard selection	6
21(c)	Outline the main factors affecting sample size	6
23(d)	Explain the rationale for designing audit programmes by reference to audit objectives	6

Part B: Audit planning

1 INTRODUCTION

1.1 In the previous chapter we introduced the idea of the auditor responding to assessed risks. In this chapter we look in more detail at the **responses to assessed risks**.

1.2 The **overall responses** to assessed risk will be incorporated to the **audit plan**, which will document the key findings of the risk assessment and the resultant important areas of the audit.

1.3 Overall responses include consideration of **audit staffing** and also the use of **work of others**, for example, experts or internal audit. We shall look at auditing guidance in these areas.

1.4 It might also involve consideration of the role of computers on the audit, and whether the team should use **computer assisted audit techniques** (CAATs) which we shall explain briefly.

1.5 Specific responses to assessed risks consist of developing **audit programs** to gather evidence in specific areas. We will introduce the concept of audit programs and related auditing guidance.

1.6 As we observed in Chapter 5, auditors often gather this evidence on a sample basis. We shall outline the concept of **sampling** and set out the related auditing standard.

1.7 Lastly in this chapter, we shall consider the issue of **documentation**. Auditors are required to document the audit plan and program and also evidence obtained.

2 AIMS OF PLANNING

2.1 An effective and efficient audit relies on proper planning procedures. The planning process is covered in general terms by ISA 300 *Planning*.

> **ISA 300.2**
>
> The auditor should plan the audit so that the engagement will be performed in an effective manner.

> **KEY TERMS**
>
> **Audit strategy** – sets the scope, timing and the direction of the audit, and guides the development of a more detailed audit plan.
>
> **Audit plan** – converts the audit strategy into a more detailed plan and includes the nature, timing and extent of audit procedures to be performed by engagement team members in order to obtain sufficient appropriate audit evidence to reduce audit risk to an acceptably low level.

2.2 The objectives of planning work involve ensuring that:
- **Appropriate attention is devoted** to the different areas of the audit.
- **Potential problems** are **identified.**
- **Work is completed effectively and efficiently.**
- The **proper tasks are assigned** to the members of the audit team.

6: Audit planning

2.3 Audit procedures should be discussed with the client's management, staff and/or audit committee in order to co-ordinate audit work, including that of internal audit. However, all audit procedures remain the responsibility of the external auditors.

2.4 A structured approach to planning will include the following stages:

- **Updating knowledge of the client** and **assessing risks** (as discussed in Chapter 5)
- **Preparing the detailed audit approach**
- Making **administrative decisions** such as staffing and budgets.

> **ISA 300.8**
>
> The auditor should establish the overall audit strategy for the audit.

2.5 The establishment of the audit strategy involves:

(a) Determining the characteristics of the engagement which define its scope.

- Financial reporting framework
- Industry – specific reporting requirements
- Location of components of the entity.

(b) Ascertaining the reporting objectives of the engagement to plan the timing of the audit and the nature of the communication required.

- Deadlines for interim and final reporting
- Key dates for expected communications with management and those charged with governance.

(c) Considering the important factors that will determine the focus of the engagement team's efforts.

- Materiality levels
- High risk areas
- Preliminary identification of material components and account balances
- Possible reliance on internal control
- Financial reporting/industry specific developments.

The strategy sets out:

- The resources to deploy for specific audit areas (eg experienced team managers for high risk areas, involvement of experts)
- The amount of resources to allocate to specific audit areas (eg number of team members assigned to observe the inventory count)
- When these resources are deployed (eg interim audit stage or key cut-off dates)
- How resources are to be managed, directed and supervised. (eg timing of team briefing/debriefing, partner/manager reviews, engagement quality control reviews).

3 AUDIT TEAM AND USE OF THE WORK OF OTHERS

Audit team

3.1 The audit engagement partner (sometimes called the reporting partner) must take responsibility for the quality of the audit to be carried out. He should assign staff with necessary competencies to the audit team.

Part B: Audit planning

3.2 Some audits are wholly carried out by a sole practitioner (an accountant who practises on his or her own) or a partner. More commonly however the engagement partner will take overall responsibility for the conduct of the audit and will sign the audit report. The engagement partner will however delegate aspects of the audit work such as the detailed testing to the staff of the firm. The usual hierarchy of staff on an audit assignment is:

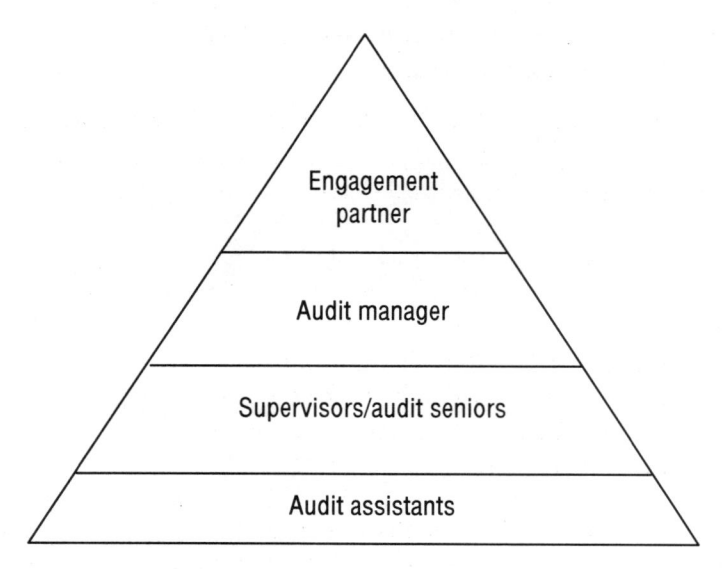

```
            /\
           /  \
          /Engagement\
         / partner  \
        /------------\
       /             \
      / Audit manager \
     /-----------------\
    /                   \
   / Supervisors/audit seniors \
  /---------------------------\
 /                             \
/      Audit assistants         \
---------------------------------
```

3.3 When planning the audit, the partner or manager must decide **how many staff** are to be allocated to the assignment, how **experienced** (what grade) and whether any of them will require any **special knowledge, skill or experience**. The partner or manager will review the level of staffing the previous year and consider whether that level of staffing was acceptable, he/she will also consider the results of the risk assessment in the current year.

3.4 The engagement partner is responsible for ensuring that:

- An appropriate level of professional scepticism is applied by audit staff in the conduct of the audit, and
- There is a proper communication both within the audit team and with the audited entity

3.5 Achieving these two objectives is likely to involve holding a **planning meeting** with the audit staff on the assignment to discuss the risks of material misstatement that could arise in the financial statements and making them aware of historical issues on the audit.

3.6 Ensuring communication between client staff and audit staff will be more difficult as the audit engagement partner is unlikely to visit the client site during the audit. However, given that he has a responsibility here, he must take appropriate steps. What these should be will depend on the individual circumstances of the audit. He should consider:

- Keeping in **regular contact** with both audit and client staff during the audit to assess the level of communication between them
- **Attending** the site during the audit to facilitate better communication if he feels that it is necessary
- Fostering lines of communication between client staff and audit staff during the period between audits, to ensure a good working relationship is built up between them

3.7 EXAMPLE

As we saw in Chapter 5 the team for the audit of Brown Ltd consists of the audit partner, Dougie Taylor, the audit senior, Jo Price and an audit assistant Jonathan Okacha.

Dougie Taylor will take overall responsibility for the audit and will sign the audit report.

Jo Price will be in charge on the site but will refer key issues back to Dougie Taylor. Jonathan will be responsible for routine aspects and his work will be supervised by Jo.

In this case no audit manager has been appointed. In small firms this can often be the case where the audit partner also assumes the role of the audit manager. In larger firms it is more likely that an audit manager would also be involved leaving the partner to deal with very high level issues only.

Dealing with client staff

3.8 An important skill that all staff chosen for the audit assignment should have is the ability to deal with the client staff with whom they come into contact. Discussions with staff operating the system should be conducted in a manner which **promotes professional relationships** between auditing and operational staff.

3.9 Relationships with the client will be enhanced if auditors aim to provide a high quality service that caters for the needs of the client. However more specific people skills will also be needed. Negotiation skills and interviewing skills are particularly important.

3.10 Auditors should also be trying to understand what managers and staff want from the audit and how hostility to the time they have to spend dealing with auditors can be overcome. This does not mean agreeing with management and staff on every issue, but it does enable the auditors to understand why difficulties have arisen and how those difficulties can be overcome.

Experts

> **KEY TERM**
>
> An **expert** is a person or firm possessing special skill, knowledge and experience in a particular field other than accounting and auditing.

3.11 Professional audit staff are highly trained and educated, but their experience and training is limited to accountancy and audit matters. In certain situations it will therefore be necessary to employ someone else with different expert knowledge. Auditors have **sole responsibility** for their opinion, but may use the work of an expert. An expert may be engaged by:

- A client to provide **specialist advice** on a particular matter which carries a risk of material misstatement in the financial statements
- The auditors in order to obtain **sufficient audit evidence** regarding certain financial statement assertions

Determining the need to use the work of an expert

3.12 The following list of examples is given by ISA 620 *Using the work of an expert* of the audit evidence which might be obtained from the opinion, valuation etc of an expert.

Part B: Audit planning

- **Valuations of certain types of assets**, eg land and buildings, plant and machinery
- **Determination of quantities or physical condition of assets**
- **Determination of amounts** using specialised methods, eg pensions accounting
- The **measurement of work completed** and **work in progress** on contracts
- **Legal opinions**

3.13 When considering whether to use the work of an expert, the auditors should review:

- The importance of matter being considered in the context of the accounts
- The **risk of misstatement** based on the nature and complexity of the matter
- The **quantity** and **quality** of other available **relevant audit evidence**

Competence and objectivity of the expert

3.14 The auditors should assess the professional competence of the expert. This will involve considering:

- The expert's **professional certification**, or licensing by, or membership of, an appropriate professional body
- The expert's **experience and reputation** in the field in which the auditors are seeking audit evidence

3.15 The risk that an expert's objectivity is impaired increases when the expert is:

- **Employed** by the entity
- **Related** in some other manner to the entity, for example, by being financially dependent upon, or having an investment in, the entity

3.16 If the auditors have **reservations** about the competence or objectivity of the expert they may need to carry out other procedures or obtain evidence from another expert.

The expert's scope of work

3.17 The auditors need to obtain evidence that the scope of the expert's work is adequate for the purposes of their audit. Written instructions usually cover the expert's terms of reference and such instructions may cover such matters as:

- The **objectives** and **scope** of the expert's work
- A **general outline** as to the specific matters the expert's report is to cover
- The **intended use** of the expert's work
- The **extent** of the **expert's access** to appropriate records and files
- Clarification of the **expert's relationship** with the entity, if any
- **Confidentiality** of the entity's information
- Information regarding the **assumptions and methods intended** to be used

3.18 Auditors should assess whether the substance of the expert's findings is properly reflected in the financial statements or supports the financial statement assertions. It will also require consideration of:

- The **source data used**
- The **assumptions and methods used**
- **When** the expert carried out the work
- The reasons for any **changes in assumptions and methods**

- The **results** of the expert's work in the light of the auditors' knowledge of the business and the results of other audit procedures

3.19 The auditors do *not* have the expertise to judge the assumptions and methods used; these are the responsibility of the expert. However, the auditors should seek to obtain an understanding of these assumptions etc, to consider their reasonableness based on other audit evidence, knowledge of the business and so on.

3.20 This may involve discussion with both the client and the expert. Additional procedures (including use of another expert) may be necessary.

Reference to an expert in the audit report

3.21 The auditor should not refer to the work of the expert in an unmodified audit report. Such a reference might be understood and interpreted as a qualification of the audit opinion or a division of responsibility, neither of which is appropriate.

3.22 If the auditors issue a modified audit report, then they may refer to the work of the expert. In such cases, auditors should obtain permission in advance from the expert. If such permission is not given, then the auditors may have to seek legal advice.

Activity 6.1

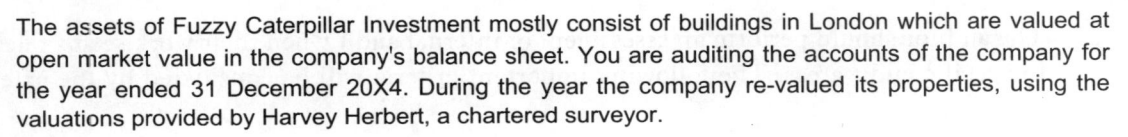

The assets of Fuzzy Caterpillar Investment mostly consist of buildings in London which are valued at open market value in the company's balance sheet. You are auditing the accounts of the company for the year ended 31 December 20X4. During the year the company re-valued its properties, using the valuations provided by Harvey Herbert, a chartered surveyor.

Required

(a) What work will you as auditor carry out on the valuation given by Harvey Herbert?
(b) How would your answer differ if Harvey Herbert was an employee of Fuzzy Caterpillar?

Exam alert

Expert opinions are generally obtained in 'difficult' audit areas, for example valuation of assets, and hence the topic is popular with auditing examiners.

Internal audit

3.23 Remember what we said earlier about internal audit. Large organisations may appoint full time staff whose function is to monitor and report on the running of the company's operations. Its objectives will be set by management.

3.24 ISA 610 *Considering the work of internal audit* examines the relationship between external and internal audit. It requires that external auditors consider what the internal audit department do, and whether it has an effect on the external audit. The ISA makes a most important point.

> 'While the external auditor has sole responsibility for the audit opinion expressed and for determining the nature, timing and extent of external audit procedures, certain parts of internal auditing work may be useful to the external auditor.'

Part B: Audit planning

3.25 The scope and objectives of internal audit vary widely. Normally however, internal audit operates in one or more of the following broad areas.

- Review of the accounting and internal control systems
- Examination of financial and operating information
- Review of economy, efficiency and effectiveness
- Review of compliance with laws and regulations
- Special investigations

Understanding and preliminary assessment of the role and scope of internal audit

> **ISA 610.9**
>
> The external auditor should obtain a sufficient understanding of internal audit activities to identify and asses the risks of material misstatement of the financial statements and to design and perform further audit procedures.

3.26 An effective IA function may reduce, modify or alter the timing of external audit procedures, but it can **never** eliminate them entirely. Where the IA function is deemed ineffective, it may still be useful to be aware of the IA conclusions. The effectiveness of IA will have a great impact on how the external auditors assess the whole control system and the assessment of audit risk.

3.27 The auditor should perform an assessment of internal audit when their work seems relevant in specific audit areas. The following important criteria will be considered by the external auditors.

ASSESSMENT OF INTERNAL AUDIT	
Organisational status	Consider **to whom** internal audit **reports** (should be board), whether internal audit has any **operating responsibilities** and constraints or restrictions on the function
Scope of function	Consider **extent** and **nature** of **assignments** performed and the action taken by management as a result of internal audit reports
Technical competence	Consider whether internal auditors have adequate **technical training** and proficiency
Due professional care	Consider whether internal audit is **properly planned**, **supervised**, **reviewed** and **documented**

3.28 When reporting, internal auditors should report to the whole board or the audit committee and should be free to discuss their concerns with external auditors. They should not report to management upon whose work or responsibilities they are likely to comment; this may mean for example that they should not report to the finance director.

Evaluating specific internal auditing work

> **ISA 610.16**
>
> When the external auditor intends to use specific work of internal auditing, the external auditor should evaluate and perform audit procedures on that work to confirm its adequacy for the external auditor's purpose.

3.29 The evaluation here will consider the scope of work and related audit programmes *and* whether the assessment of the IA function remains appropriate. This may include consideration of whether:

- The work is performed by persons having **adequate technical training** and **proficiency** as internal auditors.

- The work of assistants is **properly supervised, reviewed and documented**.

- **Sufficient appropriate audit evidence** is obtained to afford a reasonable basis for the conclusions reached.

- The **conclusions** reached are **appropriate** in the circumstances.

- Any **reports** prepared by internal audit are **consistent** with the results of the work performed.

- Any **exceptions** or unusual matters disclosed by internal auditing are **properly resolved**.

- **Amendments** to the external audit programme are **required** as a result of matters identified by internal audit work.

- There is a need to **test the work of internal audit** to confirm its adequacy.

3.30 The nature, timing and extent of the testing of the specific work of internal auditing will depend upon the external auditor's judgement of the risk and materiality of the area concerned, the preliminary assessment of internal auditing and the evaluation of specific work by internal auditing. Such tests may include examination of items already examined by internal auditing, examination of other similar items and observation of internal auditing procedures.

3.31 If the external auditors decide that the IA work is not adequate, they should extend their procedures in order to obtain appropriate evidence.

Exam alert

You should remember the distinction between:

(a) Assessing internal audit's effectiveness as part of the assessment of the accounting system (which external auditors should always do); and

(b) Assessing the work of internal audit if its work is to be used as audit evidence (which will only happen if the external auditor is seeking to rely on the work of internal audit).

Activity 6.2

(a) What are the major differences between internal and external audit?

(b) What should external auditors consider when deciding whether to rely on the work of internal auditors?

4 USING COMPUTERS

Computer assisted audit techniques (CAATs)

4.1 There is no mystery about using a computer to help with auditing. You probably use common computer assisted audit techniques all the time in your daily work without realising it.

(a) Most modern accounting systems allow data to be manipulated in various ways and extracted into an **ad hoc report**.

(b) Even if reporting capabilities are limited, the data can often be exported directly into a **spreadsheet** package (sometimes using simple Windows-type cut and paste facilities in very modern systems) and then analysed.

(c) Most systems have **searching** facilities that are much quicker to use than searching through print-outs by hand.

4.2 There are a variety of packages specially designed either to ease the auditing task itself, or to carry out audit interrogations of computerised data automatically. There are also a variety of ways of testing the processing that is carried out. Much of this work can now be done using PCs such as laptops that are independent of the organisation's systems.

4.3 Auditors customarily audit '**through the computer**'. This involves an **examination** of the **detailed processing routines** of the computer to determine whether the **controls** in the **system** are **adequate** to ensure complete and correct processing of all data. In these situations it will often be necessary to **employ computer assisted audit techniques**.

Audit software

4.4 Audit software performs the sort of checks on data that auditors might otherwise have to perform by hand. Examples of uses of audit software are:

- Interrogation software, which accesses the client's data files without the need to ask the client for information, or use the client's own programs
- Comparison programs which compare versions of a program
- Interactive software for interrogation of on-line systems
- Resident code software to review transactions as they are processed

4.5 The use of audit software is particularly appropriate during substantive testing of transactions and especially balances. Interrogation software in particular can help auditors prepare tests, by for example **selecting** a sample of balances or dividing populations according to set criteria such as amounts owed (this is called **stratification** and is discussed further later in this chapter).

4.6 Interrogation software can also help auditors scrutinise large volumes of data, and concentrate resources on the investigation of results. Examples of uses include the following.

Use of interrogation software	Comment
Analytical procedures	Programs can **identify trends in data**, and also **highlight exceptions** and **potential areas of concern**, for example expenses varying from previous years by more than a certain amount or percentage.
Identification of items that fulfil certain criteria	Programs can highlight items according to criteria set by the auditors, for example debtor balances owed for longer than a certain period of time.
Confirming completeness of processing	Programs can check to see whether all items in a sequence of invoices have been processed.
Checking calculations	Programs can check that the ageing of debtors has been carried out correctly.
Testing for unauthorised relationships	Programs can achieve this by comparison of different data, for example employee and supplier addresses.

Test data

4.7 An obvious way of seeing whether a system is **processing** data in the way that it should be is to input some test data and see what happens. The expected results can be calculated in advance and then compared with the results that actually arise. Test data has two aspects.

(a) Data representing **valid transactions**. Here the auditor is looking to check that the systems **produces** the **required documentation** such as sales invoices and **updates** the **accounting records.**

(b) Data that is **invalid** for any reason. Here the auditors are checking on **controls** that **prevent processing** of data that is clearly wrong, negative amounts or non-existent customers for example, or which breaches limits set down by the company (for example transactions which take credit customers over their credit limit). Auditors are interested in seeing not only that the system rejects the transaction, but also that **breaches** are **reported** (by means of exception reports).

4.8 The problem with test data is that any resulting corruption of the data files has to be corrected. This is difficult with modern real-time systems, which often have built in (and highly desirable) controls to ensure that data entered **cannot** easily be removed without leaving a mark. Consequently test data is used less and less as a CAAT.

Embedded audit facilities

4.9 The results of using test data would, in any case, be completely distorted if the programs used to process it were not the ones **normally** used for processing.

4.10 EXAMPLE

A fraudulent member of the IT department might substitute a version of the program that gave the correct results, purely for the duration of the test, and then replace it with a version that siphoned off the company's funds into his own bank account.

4.11 To allow a **continuous** review of the data recorded and the manner in which it is treated by the system, it may be possible to use CAATs referred to as 'embedded audit facilities'. An

Part B: Audit planning

embedded facility consists of audit modules that are incorporated into the computer element of the enterprise's accounting system.

EXAMPLES OF EMBEDDED AUDIT FACILITIES	
Integrated test facility (ITF)	Creates a **fictitious entity** within the company applications, where transactions are posted to it alongside regular transactions, and actual results of fictitious entity compared with what it should have produced
Systems control and review file (SCARF)	Allows auditors to have transactions above a **certain amount** from **specific ledger account** posted to a file for later auditor review

Simulation

4.12 Simulation (or 'parallel simulation)' entails the preparation of a separate program that simulates the processing of the organisation's real system. Real data can then be passed not only through the system proper but also through the simulated program.

4.13 EXAMPLE

The simulation program may be used to re-perform controls such as those used to identify any missing items from a sequence.

Knowledge-based systems

4.14 Decision support systems and expert systems can be used to assist with the auditors' own judgement and decisions.

5 AUDIT PLAN

> **ISA 300**
>
> The auditor should develop an audit plan for the audit in order to reduce audit risk to an acceptably low level.

5.1 The audit plan includes:

- A description of the nature, timing and extent of planned risk assessment procedures sufficient to assess the risks of material misstatement.

- A description of the nature, timing and extent of planned further audit procedures at the assertion level for each material class of transactions, account balance and disclosure. This will include tests of controls and substantive procedures.

- Any other audit procedures required.

5.2 The following is an example extract from an audit plan covering fixed assets.

Procedures	Sample	Ref	Completed by
Existence			
1 Inspect a sample of assets that are recorded in the fixed asset register.	All assets costing >$10,000 + 10 others chosen randomly	B6	
2 Examine invoices, department of transport roadworthiness certificates and other independent documentary records of assets' existence.	All assets costing >$10,000 + 10 others chosen randomly	B7	
3 Examine invoices for smaller furniture + equipment additions to see if any have been incorrectly capitalised.	20 additions costing <$1,000	B8	

Changes to the overall audit strategy and audit plan

> **ISA 300.16**
>
> The overall audit strategy and the audit plan should be updated and changed as necessary during the course of the audit.

5.3 An accurate record of changes to the audit strategy must be maintained in order to explain the general approach finally adopted for the audit.

5.4 **EXAMPLE**

The auditors find errors in the client's computer processing procedures or fixed assets are held by the client which are not recorded in the fixed asset register. Further testing may be required in these areas. The audit strategy may also alter if major administrative matters change, for example the deadline for audited accounts is brought forward.

6 SAMPLING   6/04

6.1 Audit sampling is the subject of ISA 530 *Audit sampling and other means of testing*.

> **ISA 530.2**
>
> When designing audit procedures, the auditor should determine appropriate means for selecting items for testing so as to gather sufficient, appropriate audit evidence to meet the objectives of the audit procedures.

6.2 This ISA is based on the premise that auditors do not normally examine all the information available to them; it would be impractical to do so and using audit sampling will produce valid conclusions.

Part B: Audit planning

> **KEY TERMS**
>
> **Audit sampling** involves the application of audit procedures to less than 100% of items within a class of transactions or account balance such that all sampling units have a chance of selection. This will enable the auditor to obtain and evaluate audit evidence about some characteristic of the items selected in order to form or assist in forming a conclusion concerning the population from which the sample is drawn. Audit sampling can use either a statistical or a non-statistical approach.
>
> **Statistical sampling** is any approach to sampling that involves random selection of a sample, and use of probability theory to evaluate sample results, including measurement of sampling risk.
>
> **Population** is the entire set of data from which a sample is selected and about which an auditor wishes to draw conclusions.
>
> **Sampling units** are the individual items constituting a population.
>
> **Stratification** is the process of dividing a population into sub-populations, each of which is a group of sampling units, which have similar characteristics (often monetary value).
>
> **Error** means either control deviations, when performing tests of controls, or misstatements, when performing tests of details.
>
> **Expected error** is the error that the auditor expects to be present in the population.
>
> **Tolerable error** is the maximum error in the population that the auditor would be willing to accept.
>
> **Anomalous error** means an error that arises from an isolated event that has not recurred other than on specifically identifiable occasions and is therefore not representative of errors in the population.
>
> **Sampling risk** arises from the possibility that the auditor's conclusion, based on a sample of a certain size, may be different from the conclusion that would be reached if the entire population were subjected to the same audit procedure.
>
> **Non-sampling risk** arises from factors that cause the auditor to reach an erroneous conclusion for any reason not related to the size of the sample. For example, most audit evidence is persuasive rather than conclusive, the auditor might use inappropriate procedures, or the auditor might misinterpret evidence and fail to recognise an error.

> **ISA 530.22**
>
> When designing audit procedures, the auditors should determine appropriate means of selecting items for testing.

6.3 The ISA points out that some testing procedures do *not* involve sampling, such as:

- **Testing 100%** of items in a population (this should be obvious)
- Testing all items with a **certain characteristic** as selection is not representative

6.4 Auditors are unlikely to test 100% of items when carrying out tests of controls, but 100% testing may be appropriate for certain substantive procedures. For example if the population is made up of a small number of high value items, inherent and control risks are high and other means do not provide sufficient appropriate audit evidence, 100% examination may be appropriate.

6.5 The auditor may alternatively select certain items from a population because of specific characteristics they possess. The results of items selected in this way cannot be projected onto the whole population but may be used in conjunction with other audit evidence concerning the rest of the population.

(a) **High value or key items.** The auditor may select high value items or items that are suspicious, unusual or prone to error.

(b) **All items over a certain amount.** Selecting items this way may mean a large proportion of the population can be verified by testing a few items.

(c) **Items to obtain information** about the client's business, the nature of transactions, or the client's accounting and control systems.

(d) **Items to test procedures,** to see whether particular procedures are being performed.

6.6 The ISA distinguishes between **statistically-based sampling**, which involves the use of techniques from which mathematically constructed conclusions about the population can be drawn, and **non-statistical methods**, from which auditors draw a judgmental opinion about the population. However the principles of the ISA apply to both methods.

Selection of the sample

> **ISA 530.42**
>
> The auditor should select items for the sample with the expectation that all sampling units in the population have a chance of selection.

6.7 The ISA then makes a very important point, that this requires that *all items* in the population to have an opportunity be selected.

6.8 There are a number of selection methods available.

(a) **Random selection** ensures that all items in the population have an equal chance of selection, eg by use of random number tables or computerised generator.

(b) **Systematic selection** involves selecting items using a constant interval between selections, the first interval having a random start. When using systematic selection auditors must ensure that the population is not structured in such a manner that the sampling interval corresponds with a particular pattern in the population.

(b) **Haphazard selection** may be an alternative to random selection provided auditors are satisfied that the sample is representative of the entire population. This method requires care to guard against making a selection which is biased, for example towards items which are easily located, as they may not be representative. It should not be used if auditors are carrying out statistical sampling.

(c) **Sequence or block selection.** Sequence sampling may be used to check whether certain items have particular characteristics. For example an auditor may use a sample of 50 consecutive cheques to check whether cheques are signed by authorised signatories rather than picking 50 single cheques throughout the year. Sequence sampling may however produce samples that are not representative of the population as a whole, particularly if errors only occurred during a certain part of the period, and hence the errors found cannot be projected onto the rest of the population.

Part B: Audit planning

> **ISA 530.44**
>
> The auditor should perform audit procedures appropriate to the particular audit objective on each item selected.

6.9 If the particular item is not **appropriate**, tests can be performed on alternative items. If however evidence about the item is not **available**, the auditor should normally treat it as an error.

Sample size

> **ISA 530.18/40**
>
> In obtaining evidence, the auditor should use professional judgement to assess the risk of material misstatement (which includes inherent and control risk) and design further audit procedures to ensure this risk is reduced to an acceptably low level.
>
> In determining the sample size, the auditor should consider whether sampling risk is reduced to an acceptably low level.

6.10 Examples of some factors affecting sample size are given in appendices to the ISA, summarised here.

Appendix 1: Examples of factors influencing sample size for tests of controls

Factor	Effect on sample size	Explanation
An increase in the extent to which the risk of material misstatement is reduced by the operating effectiveness of controls.	Increase	The more the auditor relies on the operating effectiveness of controls in the risk assessment the greater the extent of the tests of controls. Therefore the sample size is increased.
An increase in the tolerable error that the auditor is willing to accept.	Decrease	The higher the rate of deviation that the auditor is willing to accept the smaller the sample size needs to be.
An increase in the expected error that the auditor expects to find in the population.	Increase	The higher the rate of deviation expected, the larger the sample size needs to be so as to be in a position to make a reasonable estimate of the actual rate of deviation.
An increase in the auditor's required confidence level.	Increase	The greater the degree of confidence that the auditor requires that the results of the sample are in fact indicative of the actual incidence of error in the population, the larger the sample size needs to be.
An increase in the number of sampling units in the population.	Negligible effect	For small populations, however, sampling may not be the most efficient method of obtaining evidence.

6: Audit planning

Appendix 2: Examples of factors influencing sample size for tests of details

Factor	Effect on sample size	Explanation
An increase in the auditor's assessment of the risk of material misstatement.	Increase	In order to reduce audit risk to an acceptably low level, the auditor needs low detection risk. This results in increased sample sizes.
An increase in the use of other substantive procedures directed at the same assertion.	Decrease	The more the auditor is relying on other substantive procedures the less assurance the auditor will require from sampling.
An increase in the auditor's required confidence level.	Increase	The greater the degree of confidence that the auditor requires the larger the sample size needs to be.
An increase in the tolerable error.	Decrease	The lower the total error that the auditor is willing to accept, the larger the sample size need to be.
An increase in the expected error.	Increase	Factors relevant to the auditor's consideration of the expected error include the extent to which items are determined subjectively, the results of risk assessment procedures, the results of tests of controls and the results of other substantive procedures.
Stratification of the population when appropriate.	Decrease	Useful when there is a wide range in the monetary size of items in the population.
The number of sampling units in the population.	Negligible effect	For small populations though, sampling may not be the most efficient approach.

> **Exam alert**
>
> These factors will apply whether the auditors use statistical or non-statistical sampling methods.

Sampling risk

6.11 The auditors are faced with sampling risk in both tests of controls and substantive procedures, as follows.

(a) The risk the auditor will conclude, in the case of a test of controls, that controls are more effective than they actually are, or in the case of a test of details that a material error does not exist when in fact it does. This type of risk affects **audit effectiveness** and is more likely to lead to an inappropriate audit opinion.

(b) The risk the auditor will conclude, in the case of a test of controls, that controls are less effective then they actually are, or in the case of a test of details, that a material error exists when in fact it does not. This type of risk affects **audit efficiency** as it would usually lead to additional work to establish that initial conclusions were incorrect.

6.12 The **greater** their reliance on the results of the procedure in question, the **lower** the sampling risk auditors will be willing to accept and the **larger** the sample size will be.

Part B: Audit planning

6.13 The ISA also adds the following note:

> 'For both tests of controls and substantive tests of details, sampling risk can be reduced by increasing sample size while non-sampling risk can be reduced by proper engagement planning, supervision and review.'

6.14 EXAMPLE

At Brown Ltd, the auditors have an expectation that controls are operating effectively. This means that for the purposes of drawing their audit opinion, they will rely on a combination of tests of controls and substantive procedures. This will mean in general terms that their sample sizes for the substantive tests will be smaller than if they were not carrying out tests of controls as well.

In addition to considering the overall picture, the auditors will consider the inherent risk of each area and this too will have an additional impact on sample size. For example, stock at Brown Ltd is considered to be high risk. This means the auditors will be looking to have a substantial sample when testing stock. Fixed assets are lower risk, so the sample size will be comparably lower.

Tolerable error

6.15 Tolerable error is considered during the planning stage and, for substantive procedures, is related to the auditor's judgement about materiality. The smaller the tolerable error, the greater the sample size will need to be.

Expected error

6.16 Larger samples will be required when errors are expected than would be required if none were expected, in order to conclude that the *actual* error is *less* than the *tolerable* error. If the expected error rate is high then sampling may not be appropriate and auditors may have to examine 100% of a population.

Statistical and judgmental sampling

6.17 As mentioned above, auditors need to decide when sampling whether to use statistical or non-statistical methods. Statistical sampling means using statistical theory to measure the impact of sampling risk and evaluate the sample results. Non-statistical sampling relies on judgement to evaluate results.

6.18 Whether statistical or non-statistical methods are used, auditors will still have to take account of risk, tolerable and expected error, and population value for substantive tests when deciding on sample sizes.

6.19 **Statistical sampling** is likely to have the following **advantages**.

(a) At the conclusion of a test the auditors are able to state with a **definite level of confidence** that the whole population conforms to the sample result, within a stated precision limit.

(b) **Sample size** is **objectively determined**, having regard to the degree of risk the auditors are prepared to accept for each application.

(c) The process of fixing required precision and confidence levels compels the auditors to consider and clarify their audit objectives.

(d) The **results of tests** can be **expressed** in precise **mathematical terms**.

(e) **Bias is eliminated.**

6.20 Statistical sampling has a number of **disadvantages**.

(a) The **technique** may be **applied blindly** without prior consideration of the suitability of the statistical sampling for the audit task to be performed. This disadvantage may be overcome by establishing soundly-based procedures for use in the firm, incorporating standards on sampling in the firm's audit manual, instituting training programmes for audit staff and proper supervision.

(b) **Unsuspected patterns** or **bias** in **sample selection** may invalidate the conclusions. The probability of these factors arising must be carefully judged by the auditor before they decide to adopt statistical sampling.

(c) **Statistical sampling** frequently needs **back-up** by further tests within the population reviewed: large items, non-routine items, sensitive items like directors' transactions.

(d) At the conclusion of a statistical sampling-based test the auditors **may fail to appreciate** the **further action** necessary based on the results obtained. This potential disadvantage may be overcome by adequate training and supervision, and by requiring careful evaluation of all statistical sampling tests.

(e) **Statistical sampling** may be **applied carelessly**, without due confirmation that the sample selected is acceptably random.

(f) The **selection** exercise can be **time consuming**.

(g) The **degree of tolerance** of acceptable error must be predetermined.

6.21 The disadvantages listed above can all be overcome if the technique is applied sensibly and competently.

Evaluation of sample results

> **ISA 530.47/51/54**
>
> The auditor should consider the sample results, the nature and cause of any errors identified, and their possible effect on the particular audit objective and on other areas of the audit.
>
> For tests of details, the auditor should project monetary errors found in the sample to the population, and should consider the effect of the projected error on the particular audit objective and on other areas or the audit.
>
> The auditor should evaluate the sample results to determine whether the assessment of the relevant characteristic of the population is confirmed or needs to be revised.

Analysis of errors in the sample

6.22 To begin with, the auditors must consider whether the items in question are **true errors**, as they defined them before the test, eg a misposting between customer accounts will not affect the total accounts receivable.

6.23 When the expected audit evidence regarding a specific sample item cannot be found, the auditors may be able to obtain sufficient appropriate audit evidence by performing **alternative procedures**. In such cases, the item is not treated as an error.

6.24 The **qualitative** aspects of errors should also be considered, including the **nature and cause** of the error. Auditors should also consider any possible effects the error might have on

Part B: Audit planning

other parts of the audit including the general effect on the financial statements and on the auditors' assessment of the accounting and internal control systems.

6.25 Where common features are discovered in errors, the auditors may decide to identify all items in the population which possess the common feature (eg location), thereby producing a sub-population. Audit procedures could then be extended in this area.

6.26 On some occasions the auditor may decide that the errors are **anomalous errors**. To be considered anomalous, the auditors have to be certain that the errors are not representative of the population. Extra work will be required to prove that an error is anomalous.

6.27 **Section summary**

Key stages in the sampling process are as follows.

- Choosing method of **sample selection**
- Determining **sample size**
- Analysing the **results** and **projecting errors**

Activity 6.3

Describe three commonly-used methods of sample selection and the main problems involved in using each method.

7 DOCUMENTATION

7.1 All audit work must be documented: the working papers are the tangible evidence of the work done in support of the audit opinion. ISA 230 *Documentation* provides guidance.

KEY TERM

Working papers are the material prepared by and for, or obtained and retained by, the auditor in connection with the performance of the audit.

Working papers may be in the form of data stored on paper, film, electronic media or other media.

ISA 230.2

The auditor should document matters which are important in providing audit evidence to support the auditor's opinion and evidence that the audit was carried out in accordance with International Standards on Auditing.

7.2 The reasons why auditors use working papers to record their work, and why it is necessary for auditors to record all their work are as follows.

(a) The **reporting partner** needs **to be able to satisfy himself that work delegated** by him has been **properly performed**. The reporting partner can generally only do this by having available detailed working papers prepared by the audit staff who performed the work.

6: Audit planning

(b) **Working papers** will **provide**, for future reference, **details of audit problems** encountered, together with evidence of work performed and conclusions drawn in arriving at the audit opinion. This can be invaluable if, at some future date, the adequacy of the auditors' work is called into question in the event of **litigation** against them by either the client or some third party.

(c) Good working papers will not only **assist** in the **control** of the **current audit**, but will also be invaluable in the **planning** and **control** of **future audits**.

(d) The preparation of working papers **encourages** the auditors to adopt a **methodical approach** to their audit work, which in turn is likely to improve the quality of that work.

Form and content of working papers

> **ISA 230.5**
>
> The auditor should prepare working papers which are sufficiently complete and detailed to provide an overall understanding of the audit.

7.3 Auditors cannot record everything they consider. Therefore judgement must be used as to the extent of working papers, based on:

> 'What would be necessary to provide an experienced auditor, with no previous experience of the audit with an understanding of the work performed and the basis of the principle decisions taken, but not the detailed aspects of the audit.'

7.4 The form and content of working papers are affected by matters such as:

- The **nature** of the **engagement**
- The **form** of the **auditors' report**
- The **nature, size** and **complexity** of the entity's **business**
- The **nature** and **complexity** of the **entity's internal control**
- The **needs** for direction, supervision and review of the work of the audit team
- The **specific methodology** and technology the auditors use

7.5 Working papers should be designed and organised to meet auditor needs on each audit. Some firms use standardised working papers such as checklists or specimen letters. This may expedite the completion and review of working papers, and also mean that delegation is more straightforward, and quality control is easier. However standardised working papers must *not* mean that a standardised approach to the conduct and documentation of the audit is followed without regard to the need to exercise professional judgement.

7.6 While auditors may utilise schedules, analyses etc prepared by the entity, they require evidence that such information is properly prepared.

Examples of working papers

7.7 These include the following.

- Information obtained in understanding the entity and its environment including its internal control such as the following:

Part B: Audit planning

- Information concerning the legal and organisational structure of the client
- Information concerning the client's industry, economic and legal environment
- Extracts from the internal control manual

- Evidence of the planning process (including audit plans) and any changes thereto
- Evidence of the auditor's considerations of the work of internal audit
- Analyses of transactions and balances
- Analyses of significant ratios and trends
- The identified and assessed risks of material misstatement
- A record of the nature, timing, extent and results of auditing procedures
- Copies of communications with other auditors, experts and other third parties
- Copies of correspondence with the client about audit matters
- Conclusions reached by the auditors on significant aspects of the audit
- Letters of representation received
- Copies of the approved financial statements and auditors' reports

7.8 Working papers should be **headed with**:

- The **name** of the **client**
- The balance sheet **date**
- The **file reference** of the working paper
- The **name** of the **person** preparing the working paper
- The **date** the working paper was **prepared**
- The **subject** of the working paper
- The **name** of the person **reviewing** the working paper
- The **date** of the **review**

7.9 Working papers should also show:

- The **objective** of the work done
- The **sources of information**
- How any **sample** was **selected** and the sample size determined
- The **work done**
- A **key** to any **ticks** or **symbols**
- **Appropriate cross referencing**
- The **results obtained**
- **Analysis** of **errors** or other significant observations
- The **conclusions drawn**
- The **key points highlighted** including the need for further work

7.10 For recurring audits, working papers may be split between **permanent** and **current** audit files. **Permanent audit files** contain information of **continuing importance** to the audit. Current audit files contain information of relevance to the current year's audit.

7.11 Working papers should be clearly referenced. The referencing system used should be **logical, facilitate review** by enabling reviewers to be able to find their way about the audit file easily and help ensure that **audit work** is **completely carried out** and no important tasks are missed.

6: Audit planning

> **Exam alert**
>
> You should be able to discuss the uses and benefits of working papers.

> **Activity 6.4**
>
> The auditing standard ISA 230 *Documentation* contains the following statement on working papers.
>
> '... it may be useful for the auditor to consider what would be necessary to provide another auditor, who has no previous experience with the audit with an understanding of the work performed and the basis of the principle decisions taken ...'
>
> **Required**
>
> Describe four benefits that auditors will obtain from working papers that meet the above requirement in ISA 230.

Confidentiality, safe custody and ownership

> **ISA 230.13**
>
> The auditor should adopt appropriate procedures for maintaining the confidentiality and safe custody of the working papers and for retaining them for a period sufficient to meet the needs of the practice and in accordance with legal and professional requirements of record retention.

7.12 Working papers are the property of the auditors. They are not a substitute for, not part of, the entity's accounting records. Auditors must follow ethical guidance on the confidentiality of audit working papers. They may, at their discretion, release parts of or whole working papers to the client, as long as disclosure does not undermine 'the independence or validity of the audit process'. Information should not be made available to third parties without the permission of the client.

Review

7.13 Audit work performed by each assistant should be reviewed by personnel of appropriate experience to consider whether:

(a) The work has been **performed in accordance with the audit plan**.

(b) The work performed and the results obtained have been **adequately documented**.

(c) Any **significant matters** have been **resolved** or are reflected in audit conclusions.

(d) The **objectives** of the audit procedures have been **achieved.**

(e) The **conclusions** expressed are **consistent** with the results of the work performed and support the audit opinion.

7.14 When the audit work has been completed and reviewed, the audit engagement partner completes an overall review of the working papers to ensure that he is able to issue his opinion.

7.15 Throughout the audit, a system of review of all working papers will be used. In the case of a large audit, the work of assistants will be reviewed by the supervisor(s). When a review takes

Part B: Audit planning

place, the reviewer will often use a separate working paper to record queries **and** their answer.

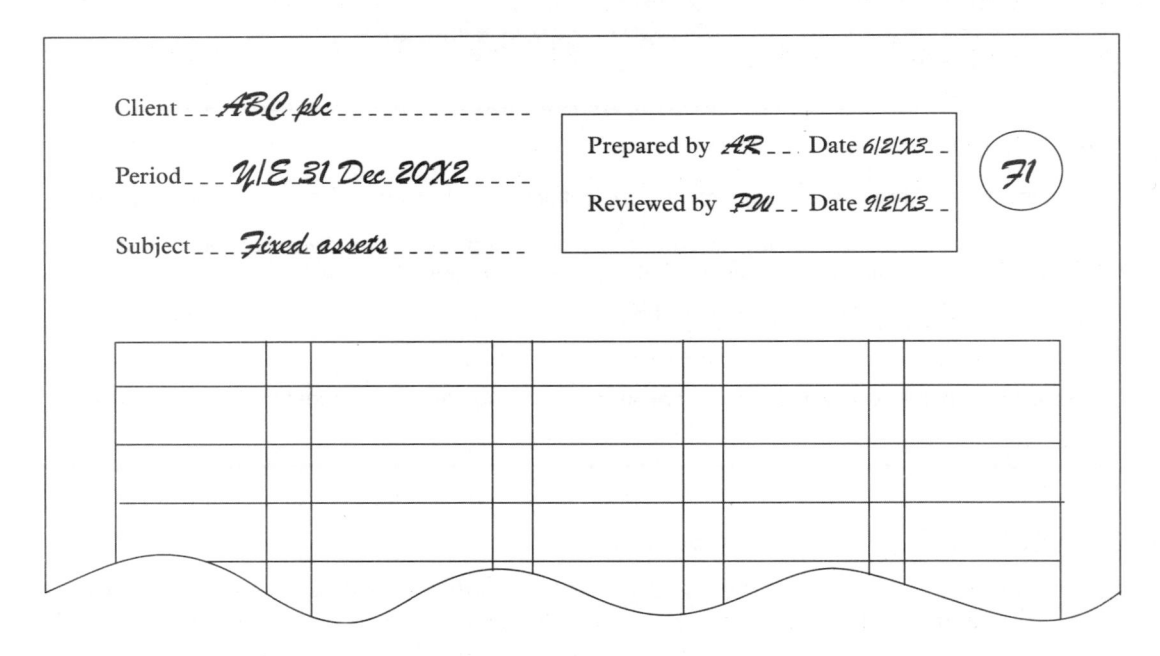

Client __ *ABC plc* _____		
Period __ *Y/E 31 Dec 20X2* ____	Prepared by *AR* __ Date *6/2/X3*	*F1*
Subject __ *Fixed assets* _____	Reviewed by *PW* __ Date *9/2/X3*	

Automated working papers

7.16 **Automated** working paper packages have been developed which can make the documenting of audit work much easier. These are automatically cross referenced and balanced by the computer. Whenever an adjustment is made, the computer will automatically update all the necessary schedules.

7.17 The **advantages** of automated working papers are as follows.

- The **risk** of **errors** is **reduced**.
- The **working papers** will be **neater** and **easier** to **review**.
- The **time saved** will be **substantial** as adjustments can be made easily to all working papers, including working papers summarising the key analytical information.
- **Standard forms** do **not** have to be **carried** to audit locations. Forms can be designed to be called up and completed on the computer screen.
- **Audit working** papers can be **transmitted** for review via a modem, or fax facilities (if both the sending and receiving computers have fax boards and fax software).

Documenting the planning process

7.18 In this chapter we have outlined two key audit documents, the audit strategy and the audit plan. The auditor is required by ISAs 315 and 330 to document the following (which may be contained within or referred to in the audit strategy):

- The discussion among the audit team concerning the susceptibility of the financial statements to material misstatements, including any significant decisions reached
- Key elements of the understanding gained of the entity including the elements of the entity and its control specified in the ISA as mandatory, the sources of the information gained and the risk assessment procedures carried out
- The identified and assessed risks of material misstatement

6: Audit planning

- Significant risks identified and related controls evaluated
- The overall responses to address the risks of material misstatement
- Nature, extent and timing of further audit procedures linked to the assessed risks at the assertion level
- If the auditors have relied on evidence about the effectiveness of controls from previous audits, conclusions about how this is appropriate

7.19 EXAMPLE: BROWN LTD AUDIT PLANNING MEETING

Once Jo Price has completed the audit strategy and it has been approved by Dougie Taylor, Dougie, Jo and Jonathan will have a planning meeting to ensure that all of them, and in particular, Jonathan in this case, are aware of all the relevant issues relating to the audit.

This will include:

- Jonathan being given the opportunity to gain an understanding of the business, particularly if he has not done any audit work on Brown Ltd before.
- Discussion of the susceptibility of Brown Ltd's financial statements to material misstatement. Particular emphasis will be given to the possibility of fraud. More specifically the risky areas of stock and debtors will be discussed and the overall concern about what impact the new competitor might have on the overall financial statements.
- The preliminary conclusions about the information system and internal control at Brown Ltd and its effect on the audit work.
- Discussion of the materiality level and any relevant non-value matters which might affect materiality.
- Discussion of the detailed audit plan and what aspects of work are to be carried out by each team member. As we have seen, Jo is likely to be allocated high risk areas such as stock and Jonathan is likely to be allocated low risk areas such as fixed assets.
- Any matters which need consideration prior to the final audit, such as attendance at the stock count at the year end and preparation of debtors' circularisation.
- Administrative details such as the date of the audit, the date audited financial statements are required by and the location of the audit.

Key learning points

- This chapter has covered some very important areas of the planning process.
- The auditors will formulate an **overall audit strategy** which will be translated into a **detailed audit plan** for audit staff to follow.
- In formulating the **audit strategy** the auditors will consider:
    - Knowledge of the entity's business (understanding the entity/ its environment)
    - Risk and materiality
    - Nature, timing and extent of procedures
    - Co-ordination, direction, supervision and review of the audit
- Any **changes** in the audit approach during the audit should be documented very carefully.
- Audits should be carried out by **staff** of **appropriate skills** and **experience**.

Part B: Audit planning

- All partners and staff involved on audits have a responsibility to maintain professional relationships with clients.

- Auditors may only rely on other **experts** once specific procedures have been carried out.

- External auditors may rely on the work of internal audit provided it has been assessed as a reliable internal control. General criteria include:
  - Organisational status
  - Scope of function
  - Technical competence
  - Due professional care

- External auditors should also evaluate specific internal work if they wish to use it to reduce the extent of external audit procedures.

- The main stages of audit sampling are:
  - Design of the sample
  - Selection of the sample
  - Evaluation of sample results

- **Sample sizes for tests of controls** are influenced by:
  - Sampling risk
  - Tolerable error rate
  - Expected error rate

- **Sample sizes for substantive procedures** are influenced by:
  - Inherent, control and detection risk
  - Tolerable error rate
  - Expected error rate
  - Population value
  - Stratification

- Sampling is not always possible or desirable and each set of circumstances must be judged for the appropriateness of testing procedures.

- **Samples** can be picked by a variety of means including:
  - Random selection
  - Systematic selection
  - Haphazard selection

- When **evaluating results**, auditors should:
  - Analyse any errors considering their amount and the reasons why they have occurred
  - Draw conclusions for the population as a whole

- **Working papers** must be properly completed since they provide a record of:
  - Audit planning and procedures
  - Supervision and review
  - Audit evidence

- You should be able to state what **information** is normally found in working papers.

- Auditors must ensure the **confidentiality** and **safe custody** of working papers.

6: Audit planning

Quick quiz

1   Which documents set out:

    (a)   The overall approach to the audit?
    (b)   The detailed work?

2   Can an audit partner delegate responsibility for the audit opinion to his staff?

3   What are the key tasks that should be performed when work is delegated to assistants?

4   May the auditor use the work of an expert employed by the organisation?

5   (a)   Why might auditors use the work of an expert?
    (b)   What should auditors consider when deciding whether to use the work of an expert?

6   What information does an audit plan usually contain?

7   What is the main danger of using standardised working papers?

8   Define:

    (a)   Error
    (b)   Tolerable error
    (c)   Sampling risk

9   Summarise the factors that affect sample sizes for substantive procedures.

10 What is the difference between random and haphazard selection?

Answers to quick quiz

1   (a)   The **audit strategy** sets out the overall approach to the audit.
    (b)   The **audit plan** sets out the detailed work.

2   No. A partner cannot delegate responsibility for the audit opinion. He can however delegate aspects of the detailed audit work.

3   The audit engagement partner has responsibility for the quality of the audit performed.

    He must ensure that the audit staff approach the job in the correct manner and have proper communication both between themselves and with the client.

    The engagement partner is also responsible for ensuring that the work of other members of the audit team is directed, supervised and reviewed.

4   Yes

5   (a)   Auditors might use the work of an expert to obtain sufficient audit evidence for certain items in the accounts.

    (b)   When deciding whether to use the work of an expert, auditors should consider:

        (i)   The importance of the audit area
        (ii)   The risks of misstatement
        (iii) The quantity and quality of other audit evidence

6   An audit plan usually contains:

    (a)   Audit tests
    (b)   Test objectives
    (c)   Timing of the tests
    (d)   Sample sizes
    (e)   Basis of sample selection

7   The main danger of using standardised working papers is that they can mean auditors mechanically follow a standard approach to the audit without using professional judgement.

8   (a)   An error is an unintentional mistake in the financial statements.

    (b)   Tolerable error is the maximum error in the population that auditors are willing to accept and still conclude the audit objectives have been achieved.

    (c)   Sampling risk is the risk that the auditors' conclusion, based on a sample, may be different from the conclusion that would be reached if the entire population was subject to the audit procedure.

Part B: Audit planning

9   Factors that affect the sample sizes of substantive procedures are:

(a) Inherent risk
(b) Control risk
(c) Detection risk
(d) Tolerable error rate
(e) Expected error rate
(f) Population value
(g) Number of items (in small population)

Stratification may also lead to smaller sample sizes.

10 Random selection involves selecting items using formal random methods such as random number tables, so that each item has an equal chance of being selected. Haphazard selection involves selecting items judgementally, but also aiming to select them without bias so that each item has an equal chance of being chosen.

Answers to activities

Answer 6.1

(a) When assessing Harvey Herbert's work, we as auditors should consider the following.

Competence and objectivity

If Harvey Herbert is practising as a chartered surveyor he should be professionally qualified.

We should also consider what experience Harvey Herbert has of valuing similar properties within the same geographical area as the properties owned by Fuzzy Caterpillar. If he does not have experience of the type of properties owned by the company or of the areas in which they are located, then the value of his evidence is likely to be reduced.

We should also consider Harvey Herbert's reputation, and the reputation of the firm for which he works. It is likely that more reliance can be placed on a valuation from a long-established firm with a good reputation than one from a little-known small firm.

Assessing the work

We should consider the following aspects of Harvey Herbert's work.

(i) The objectives and scope of his work. Harvey Herbert should have been aware of the purposes for which his work would be used.

(ii) The data that Harvey Herbert used.

(iii) The assumptions and methods employed by Harvey Herbert. In general a reasonable basis of valuation should be used. If the assumptions and methods differed significantly from those used for previous valuations of the same properties, we should satisfy ourselves that the change was for valid reasons.

(iv) When Harvey Herbert carried out the work. If the work was carried out during the year, we should confirm that there had been no events in the months between the valuation and the year-end that would undermine the basis of the valuation.

(v) The results of the valuation. Although we as auditors do not have the expertise to make a second valuation, we can nevertheless assess the valuation in the light of other evidence, which might include the following.

  (1) Previous valuations by Harvey Herbert can be compared against any subsequent profits or losses made on those properties, since those could indicate any tendency to over or under value the properties to a material extent.

  (2) The valuations may also be comparable with those used by other clients holding similar properties in the same locations.

We should also consider significant changes in the valuation of any of the properties since the last valuation, comparing those changes with the general behaviour of the commercial property market in the intervening period.

6: Audit planning

(b) If Harvey Herbert was employed by the company we need to consider carefully whether his lack of independence may diminish the value of his work. We may have to undertake additional audit procedures or consider obtaining a second opinion from another expert.

Answer 6.2

(a) The major differences between internal and external auditors are as follows.

Scope

Legislation prescribes that external auditors should report on the financial statements. In order to do so they have certain rights such as the rights to receive all the information and explanations they consider necessary for the purposes of their audit.

The scope of internal audit's work is determined by management. It varies from company to company but may include:

(i) Review of the accounting and internal control systems;
(ii) Examination of financial and operating information;
(iii) Review of economy, efficiency and effectiveness;
(iv) Review of compliance with laws and regulations;
(v) Special investigations, for example into fraud.

Objectives

The main objective of the work of external auditors is to report on the truth and fairness of the accounts. The objectives of internal audit will be determined by management. A major objective is likely to be to give assurance that the system of internal controls is working properly. Although external auditors will report weaknesses in control that they find, the external audit cannot be relied on to identify every weakness that may exist in internal control.

Reporting

The audit report of external auditors is to the shareholders.

Internal auditors report to management, ideally to top-level management. They should be able to contact the board or audit committee directly.

(b) The internal audit function is itself part of the system of internal control: it is an internal control over internal controls. As such, the external auditors should be able to test it and, if it is found to be reliable, they can rely on it.

To check the reliability of the work of the internal auditors, external auditors would consider the following matters.

(i) *The degree of independence of the internal auditors*

External auditors should assess the organisational status and reporting responsibilities of the internal auditors and consider any restrictions placed upon them. Although internal auditors are employees of the enterprise and cannot therefore be independent of it, they should be able to plan and carry out their work as they wish and have access to senior management. They should be free of any responsibility which may create a conflict of interest, and of a situation where those staff on whom they are reporting are responsible for their or their staff's appointment, promotion or pay.

(ii) *The scope and objectives of the internal audit function*

External auditors should examine the internal auditors' formal terms of reference and ascertain the scope and objectives of internal audit assignments.

(iii) *Quality of work*

External auditors should consider whether the work of internal audit is properly planned, controlled, recorded and reviewed. Examples of good practice include the existence of an adequate audit manual, plans and procedures for supervision of individual assignments, and satisfactory arrangements for ensuring adequate quality control, reporting and follow-up.

(iv) *Technical competence*

Internal audit should be performed by persons having adequate training and competence as auditors. Indications of technical competence may be membership of an appropriate professional body or attendance at regular training courses.

Part B: Audit planning

(v) *Reports*

External auditors should consider the quality of reports issued by internal audit and find out whether management considers and acts upon such reports.

If external auditors find that where the internal auditors' work is reliable, external auditors will be able to place reliance on that work when appropriate. This may mean that they will need to carry out less audit work.

However, it should be emphasised that external auditors cannot rely totally on the internal auditors' work in relation to any particular audit objective. Internal audit work provides only one form of evidence, and the internal auditors are not independent of company management. External auditors may be able to reduce the number of items which they test, but they will not be able to leave a particular type of test (for example, a debtors' circularisation) entirely to internal audit. External auditors remain responsible for the opinion which they form on the accounts.

Answer 6.3

The three commonly used methods are:

(a) *Random selection* involves using random number tables or other methods to select items. Random selection means that bias cannot affect the sample chosen; it means that all items in the population have an equal chance of being chosen. However if the auditors are more concerned about some items than others, they can modify their approach, either by selecting certain items automatically because they are above a certain value, and selecting the rest of the sample by random numbers, or by stratifying the sample.

(b) *Systematic selection* involves selecting items using a constant interval between selections, the first interval having a random start.

The main danger is that errors occur systematically in a pattern that means that none of the items in error will be sampled.

(c) *Haphazard selection* involves auditors choosing items subjectively without using formal random methods but avoiding bias.

The main danger is that bias (conscious or unconscious) affects the auditors' judgement, and that certain items are selected because for example they are easy to obtain.

Answer 6.4

Four benefits that auditors will obtain from preparing working papers that meet the requirement stated in the ISA are as follows.

(a) The reporting partner needs to be satisfied that the work delegated by him has been properly performed. He can only do this by having available detailed working papers prepared by the staff who performed the work.

(b) Working papers are a record for the future of work performed and conclusions drawn, also of problems encountered. This record would be very important in the event of litigation by the client or some other party.

(c) Good working papers will aid the planning and control of future audits.

(d) The preparation of working papers encourages auditors to adopt a methodical approach, which is likely to improve the quality of their work.

Now try Question 6 in the Exam Question Bank

Part C
Controls

Chapter 7   Internal control evaluation

Chapter topic list

1   Introduction
2   Features of information systems and internal control
3   Control problems in small computer systems
4   Assessment of information systems and internal control
5   Recording of information systems and internal control
6   Communications with management

The following study sessions are covered in this Chapter:

Syllabus reference

11(a)	Explain the following terms: (i) Internal control system (ii) Control environment (iii) Control procedures	5
11(b)	Describe the objectives of an internal control system	5
11(c)	Discuss the different types of internal control	5
11(d)	Describe and illustrate the inherent limitations of internal control systems	5
11(e)	Discuss the importance of internal control to auditors	5
15(a)	Distinguish between application controls and general controls in computer-based systems and identify the objectives of each control type	5
15(b)	Provide examples of specific general controls and application controls	5
15(c)	Outline the typical control problems encountered in small computer-based systems	5
16(a)	Describe the techniques used by auditors to record and evaluate manual and computer-based systems	5
16(b)	Provide examples of, and explain the format and contents of, internal control questionnaires (ICQs) and internal control evaluation questionnaires (ICEQs)	5
16(c)	Explain the purpose of tests of control	5
16(d)	Distinguish between tests of control and substantive procedures	5
18(b)	Explain the purpose of a management letter, indicating when it should be issued	5
18(c)	Provide information on an accounting system in a functional area and prepare points for inclusion in a management letter, in the following format: (i) Description of weakness (ii) Implication of weakness (iii) Recommendation(s) to address weakness	5

Part C: Controls

1 INTRODUCTION

1.1 Having discussed the process of risk assessment and response to assessed risks, we now turn to look at the control aspects of this more closely.

1.2 We shall first look at how auditors obtain understanding and consider the operation of **accounting** and **internal control systems**.

1.3 They consider the **adequacy** of the **accounting records** and whether the accounting systems are **capable** of **producing** a **reliable set of accounts**. This includes the context in which controls operate, the **control environment**. This involves examining the client's attitude to controls and how the business is organised, focusing particularly on the role of the directors and senior management.

1.4 The auditors then **assess** and (if considered necessary) **test** the client's controls. Auditors will only perform detailed tests of controls if they believe that the controls are strong, and hence they will be able to place some reliance on tests of controls and reduce the amount of substantive testing they need to carry out.

1.5 We shall look specifically at control problems that can arise in small computer systems.

1.6 We shall then go on to deal with how accounting systems and controls are **recorded**. Questionnaires are a common means of recording and assessing the strength of controls, and we shall consider Internal Control Questionnaires and Internal Control Evaluation Questionnaires.

1.7 Finally in this chapter we deal with how **control weaknesses** should be **reported** to **management** in a management letter.

1.8 We shall examine the detailed controls that businesses operate in Chapters 8 and 9. You should bear in mind the principles discussed in this chapter when considering the controls needed over specific accounting areas. Remember exam questions can cover the controls that ought to be operating, or how auditors should test the controls that are in place.

> **Exam alert**
>
> The examiner has stressed that the principles of control and the identification of control objectives are a key topic in this paper.

2 FEATURES OF INFORMATION SYSTEMS AND INTERNAL CONTROL

> **KEY TERM**
>
> **Internal control** is the process designed and effected by those charged with governance, management, and other personnel to provide reasonable assurance about the achievement of the entity's objectives with regard to reliability of financial reporting, effectiveness and efficiency of operations and compliance with applicable laws and regulations...designed and implemented to address identified business risks that threaten achievement of any of these objectives.

7: Internal control evaluation

2.1 ISA 315 *Understanding the entity and its environment and assessing the risks of material misstatements* deals with the whole area of controls.

> **ISA 315.41**
>
> The auditor should **obtain an understanding of internal control relevant to the audit**.

2.2 The ISA states that internal control has five elements:
- The control environment
- The entity's risk assessment process
- The information system (including related business processes/communication)
- Control activities
- Monitoring of controls

2.3 In obtaining an understanding of internal control, the auditor must gain an understanding of the **design** of the internal control (is it capable of effectively preventing or detecting and correcting material misstatements?) and the **implementation** of that control (has it been operated correctly in the year?).

Control environment

2.4 Control environment is the framework within which controls operate. The control environment is very much determined by the management of a business.

> **KEY TERM**
>
> **Control environment** includes the governance and management functions and the attitudes, awareness and actions of those charged with governance and management concerning the entity's internal control and its importance in the entity.

2.5 A strong control environment does not, by itself, ensure the effectiveness of the overall internal control system, but can be a positive factor when assessing the risks of material misstatement. A weak control environment can undermine the effectiveness of controls.

2.6 Aspects of the control environment (such as **management attitudes** towards control) will nevertheless be a significant factor in determining **how controls operate**. Controls are more likely to operate well in an environment where they are treated as being important. In addition consideration of the control environment will mean considering whether certain controls (internal auditors, budgets) actually exist.

> **ISA 315.67**
>
> The auditor should obtain an understanding of the control environment.

2.7 In evaluating the design of the entity's control environment, the auditor should consider the following elements:

Part C: Controls

CONTROL ENVIRONMENT	
Communication and enforcement of integrity and ethical values	Essential elements which influence the effectiveness of the design, administration and monitoring of controls
Commitment to competence	Management's consideration of the competence levels for particular jobs and how those levels translate into requisite skills and knowledge
Participation of those charged with governance	Independence from management, their experience and stature, the extent of their involvement and scrutiny of activities, the information which they receive, the degree to which difficult questions are raised and pursued with management and their interaction with internal and external auditors
Management's philosophy and operating style	Management's approach to taking and managing business risks, and management's attitudes and actions toward financial reporting, information processing and accounting functions and personnel
Organisational structure	The framework within which an entity's activities for achieving its objectives are planned, executed, controlled and reviewed
Assignment of authority and responsibility	How authority and responsibility for operating activities are assigned and how reporting relationships and authorization hierarchies are established
Human resource policies and practices	Recruitment, orientation, training, evaluating, counselling, promoting, compensating and remedial actions

2.8 The auditor should see whether control environment elements have been implemented by a combination of inquiries and other risk assessment procedures:

- Observation
- Inspection

Entity's risk assessment process

> **ISA 315.76**
>
> The auditor should obtain an understanding of the entity's process for identifying business risks relevant to financial reporting objectives and deciding about actions to address those risks, and the results thereof.

2.9 Factors to consider include how management:

- Identifies business risks relevant to financial reporting
- Estimates the significance of the risks
- Assesses the likelihood of their occurrence
- Decides upon actions to manage business risks

2.10 If the entity has a good risk management process, this should assist the auditor in determining the risks of material misstatement.

7: Internal control evaluation

Information system

2.11 The auditor is required to consider the information system relevant to financial reporting objectives, including the accounting system.

> **ISA 315.81**
>
> The auditor should obtain an understanding of the information system, including the related business processes, relevant to financial reporting, including the following areas:
>
> - The classes of transactions in the entity's operations that are significant to the financial statements (FS)
> - The procedures, within both IT and manual systems, by which those transactions are initiated, recorded, processed and reported in the FS
> - The related accounting records, whether electronic or manual, supporting information, and specific accounts in the FS, in respect of initiating, recording, processing and reporting transactions
> - How the information system captures events and conditions, other than classes of transactions, that are significant to the financial statements
> - The financial reporting process used to prepare the entity's financial statements, including significant accounting estimates and disclosures

2.12 So the auditor needs to understand the whole financial reporting system, including how items such as depreciation (not a transaction) are reported, how the use of journals is controlled, how incorrect processing of transactions is controlled (for example, by use of suspense accounts).

> **ISA 315.89**
>
> The auditor should understand how the entity communicates financial reporting roles and responsibilities and significant matters relating to financial reporting.

Control activities

> **KEY TERM**
>
> **Control activities** are those policies and procedures in addition to the control environment which are established to achieve the entity's specific objectives.

2.13 Control activities include those designed to **prevent** or to **detect** and **correct errors**. Examples include those relating to authorization, performance reviews, information processing, physical controls, segregation of duties.

Part C: Controls

Examples of specific control activities	
Approval and control of documents	Transactions should be approved by an appropriate person. For example, overtime should be approved by departmental managers.
Controls over computerised applications	The ISA requires the auditor to 'obtain an understanding of how the entity has responded to risks arising from IT'. We shall look at computer controls later in this chapter.
Checking the arithmetical accuracy of records	For example, checking to see if individual invoices have been added up correctly.
Maintaining and reviewing control accounts and trial balances	Control accounts bring together transactions in individual ledgers. Trial balances bring together unusual transactions for the organisation as a whole. Preparing these can highlight unusual transactions or accounts.
Reconciliations	Reconciliations involve comparison of a specific balance in the accounting records with what another source says the balance should be. Differences between the two figures should only be reconciling items. For example, a bank reconciliation.
Comparing the results of cash, security and inventory counts with accounting records	For example, a physical count of petty cash. The balance shown in the cash book should be the same amount as is in the tin.
Comparing internal data with external sources of information	For example, comparing records of goods despatched to customers with customers' acknowledgement if goods that have been received.
Limiting physical access to assets and records	Only authorised personnel should have access to certain assets (particularly valuable or portable ones). For example, ensuring that the stock store is only open when the store personnel are there and is otherwise locked. This can be a particular problem in computerised systems.

Segregation of duties

2.14 **Segregation** implies a **number of people** being involved in the accounting process. This makes it more difficult for fraudulent transactions to be processed (since a number of people would have to collude in the fraud), and it is also more difficult for accidental errors to be processed (since the more people are involved, the more checking there can be). Segregation should take place in various ways:

(a) **Segregation of function.** The key functions that should be segregated are the **carrying out** of a transaction, **recording** that transaction in the accounting records and **maintaining custody** of assets that arise from the transaction.

(b) The various **steps** in carrying out the transaction should also be segregated. We shall see how this works in practice when we look at the major control cycles in Chapters 8 and 9.

(c) The **carrying out** of various **accounting operations** should be segregated. For example the same staff should not record transactions and carry out the reconciliations at the period-end.

Monitoring of controls

> **ISA 315.96**
>
> The auditor should obtain an understanding of the major types of activities that the entity uses to monitor internal control over financial reporting, including those related to those control activities relevant to the audit, and how the entity initiates corrective actions to its controls.

2.15 In many organisations, as we discussed in Chapter 1, the role of monitoring controls fall to an internal audit department. As we discussed in Chapter 6, the auditors may make the use of the work of internal auditors in carrying out their own work.

Controls in a computer environment

2.16 Auditors must be able to cope with the special problems that arise when auditing in a computer environment and keep abreast of technical innovation.

> **KEY TERMS**
>
> **Application controls** are manual or automated procedures that typically operate at a business process level. Application controls can be preventative or detective in nature and are designed to ensure the integrity of the accounting records.
>
> Accordingly, application controls relate to procedures used to initiate, record, process and report transactions or other financial data.
>
> **General IT controls** are policies and procedures that relate to many applications and support the effective functioning of application controls by helping to ensure the continued proper operations of information systems. General IT controls commonly include controls over data centre and network operations; system software acquisition, change and maintenance; access security; and application system acquisition, development and maintenance.

> **Exam alert**
>
> Make sure you can distinguish clearly between application and general IT controls.

2.17 Application controls and general IT controls are inter-related. Strong general IT controls contribute to the assurance which may be obtained by an auditor in relation to application controls. On the other hand, unsatisfactory general IT controls may undermine strong application controls or exacerbate unsatisfactory application controls.

Part C: Controls

2.18 The following points will particularly influence the auditors' approach.

(a) Before auditors place reliance on application controls which involve computer programs, they need to obtain reasonable assurance that the programs have **operated properly**, by evaluating and testing the effect of relevant general IT controls or by other tests on specific parts of the programs.

(b) Sometimes a programmed accounting procedure may not be subject to effective application controls. In such circumstances, in order to put themselves in a position to limit the extent of substantive procedures, the auditors may choose to perform tests of controls by **testing** the **relevant general IT controls** either manually or by using CAATs, to gain assurance of the continued and proper operation of the programmed accounting procedure.

(c) In a computer environment there is the possibility of **systematic errors**. This may take place because of program faults or hardware malfunction in computer operations. However, many such potential recurrent errors should be prevented or detected by general controls over the development and implementation of applications, the integrity of the program and data files, and of computer operations.

(d) The extent to which the auditors can rely on general IT controls may be **limited** because many of these controls might not be evidenced, or because they could have been performed inconsistently.

Examples of application controls

2.19 To achieve the overall objectives of application controls identified above, the specific requirements are controls over:

- **Completeness, accuracy** and **authorisation** of **input**
- **Completeness** and **accuracy** of **processing**
- **Maintenance** of **master files** and **standing data files contained therein**

(Standing data is data that will be used over and over again, for example, staff grades or rates of pay. Master files use data and store an **accumulation** of **transactions**.)

APPLICATION CONTROLS	
Controls over **input**: completeness	Manual or programmed agreement of control totals
	Document counts
	One for one checking of processed output to source documents
	Programmed matching of input to a expected input control file
	Procedures over resubmission of rejected controls
Controls over **input**: accuracy	Programmes to check data fields (for example value, reference number, date) on input transactions for plausibility:
	Digit verification (eg reference numbers are as expected)
	Reasonableness test (eg VAT to total value)
	Existence checks (eg customer name)
	Character checks (no unexpected characters used in reference)
	Necessary information (no transaction passed with gaps)
	Permitted range (no transaction processed over a certain value)
	Manual scrutiny of output and reconciliation to source
	Agreement of control totals (manual/programmed)

7: Internal control evaluation

APPLICATION CONTROLS	
Controls over **input:**	Manual checks to ensure information input was
Controls over **processing**	Similar controls to input must be completed when input is completed, for example, batch reconciliations.
	Screen warnings can prevent people logging out before processing is complete
Controls over **master files and standing data**	One to one checking
	Cyclical reviews of all master files and standing data
	Record counts (number of documents processed) and hash totals (for example, the total of all the payroll numbers) used when master files are used to ensure no deletions
	Controls over the deletion of accounts that have no current balance

Examples of general controls

2.20 To achieve the overall objectives of general IT controls, controls may be needed in the following areas.

GENERAL IT CONTROLS	
Development of computer applications	Standards over **systems design, programming and documentation**
	Full **testing procedures** using test data
	Approval by **computer users** and **management**
	Segregation of duties so that those responsible for design are not responsible for testing
	Installation procedures so that data is not corrupted in transition
	Training of staff in new procedures and availability of adequate documentation
Prevention of unauthorised changes to programs	**Segregation of duties**
	Full records of program **changes**
	Password protection of programs so that access is limited to computer operations staff.
	Restricted access to **central computer**
	Maintenance of programs logs
	Virus checks on software
	Back-up copies of programs being taken and stored in other locations
	Control copies of programs being preserved and regularly **compared** with **actual programs**
	Stricter controls over certain programs (utility programs)
Testing and documentation of program changes	Complete **testing procedures**
	Documentation standards
	Approval of changes by computer users and management
	Training of staff using programs
Prevention of use of wrong programs or files	**Operation controls** over programs
	Libraries of programs
	Proper job scheduling
Prevention of unauthorised changes to data files	See section below on real-time systems

Part C: Controls

GENERAL IT CONTROLS	
Controls to ensure continuity of operation	**Storing extra copies** of programs and data files off site

Activity 7.1

You are responsible for the audit of purchases and creditors in Tigger Ltd. All data is processed through the computer, by full-time computer operators in the payables section. You are about to start the audit, and want to find out more about the controls operated over processing in the creditors section.

Required

List the main questions you would ask to ascertain whether computer controls over purchases and creditors were effective.

Activity 7.2

Six months ago fire destroyed most of the manual accounting records of Big Ted Ltd. Rather than set up the manual accounting system, the company has decided to computerise its accounting process. However the managing director is (perhaps not surprisingly) worried about what will happen if the company suffers another fire.

Required

Advise the managing director of the steps that can be taken to minimise the risk to the computerised system of fire.

Internal controls and their inherent limitations

2.21 Management of an entity will set up internal controls in the accounting system to assess the following.

- **Transactions** are executed in accordance with **proper authorisation**.

- All transactions and other events are **promptly recorded** at the **correct amount**, in the **appropriate accounts** and in the **proper accounting period.**

- **Access to assets** is permitted only in accordance with proper authorisation.

- **Recorded assets** are **compared** with the **existing assets** at reasonable intervals and appropriate action is taken with regard to any differences.

2.22 However, any internal control system can only provide the directors with **reasonable assurance** that their objectives are reached, because of **inherent limitations**, such as the following:

- The potential for **human error**.

    These include the fact that human judgement in decision-making can be faulty or simple errors and mistakes. For example if an entity's information system personnel do not completely understand how the company's order entry system operates they may incorrectly design changes to this system.

On the other hand, they may design the changes correctly but these may be misunderstood by the personnel responsible for translating them into program code. Errors may also occur in the use of information produced by IT. For example, automated controls may be designed to report transactions over a specified amount for management review, but individuals responsible for conducting the review may not understand the purpose of these reports, and fail to review them or investigate unusual items.

- The possibility of **controls being by-passed** or **over-ridden**

    Controls can be circumvented by the collusion of two or more people or management may inappropriately override controls. For example, management could enter into a side agreement with customers that alters the terms and conditions of sales contracts, which could result in improper revenue recognition.

    Also, edit checks in a software program that are designed to identify and report transactions that exceed specified credit limits may be overridden or disabled.

- The **costs of control** not **outweighing** their **benefits**

    This is a particular problem faced by smaller entities (see section 3). For example, smaller entities often have fewer employees which may limit the extent to which segregation of duties is practicable. It would not make commercial sense to employ additional staff purely for the purposes of achieving greater segregation of duties.

- Controls tending to be designed to **cope** with **routine** and not non-routine transactions.

    Non-routine transactions are by their very nature unusual. As a result it will be difficult to predict what these might be and therefore is less likely that a system will have been devised to deal with these effectively.

2.23 These factors show why auditors cannot obtain all their evidence from tests of the systems of internal control.

Activity 7.3

What objectives should internal control in a company aim to fulfil?

3 CONTROL PROBLEMS IN SMALL COMPUTER SYSTEMS

3.1 In this section we look at the control and audit problems peculiar to small computer systems concentrating on personal computers (PCs).

Summary of the control problems

3.2 The majority of the potential problems arise due to the departure from the formal structure of the traditional data processing department, where a controlled environment was provided over the acquisition, maintenance and distribution of computer information. In the world of the PC this controlled structure does not exist and the environment is more informal.

Lack of planning over the acquisition and use of PCs

3.3 When an organisation sets out to acquire a computer system, a series of steps should be undertaken before making the decision to purchase.

Part C: Controls

PLANNING PROCEDURES	COMMENT
Authorisation	A **feasibility study** should be carried out, examining the requirements, the costs and the benefits, to ensure that the expense is justified. Suppliers should be invited to tender, and responses from the suppliers should be evaluated and compared. All interested parties within the organisation should be identified and involved throughout the whole procedure.
Suitability	There is a risk that the client will not have the expertise to evaluate the relative merits of systems. Many first time users tend to purchase **standard software packages** which creates an even greater risk as regards suitability, for such systems may not fit precisely the company's trading methods.
Support facilities	The support facilities offered by the supplier and/or software house should be ascertained and a maintenance contract entered. The client should ensure that in the event of machine breakdown, **prompt service** and, if necessary, backup facilities are available and **adequate** systems **documentation** and operator manuals have been provided.
Standards	With PCs, where the time taken from ordering, through installation to operation, may be a matter of weeks only, there is great danger that standards are not set. Strict disciplines must be imposed to ensure that **recognised systems development controls** are **applied** and **sufficient administration procedures** are **implemented**.

Lack of documentary evidence

3.4 We have identified that many PCs operate in real time via VDUs, which allows users to have direct access to the computer thus enabling them to input data, update files and make one-off enquiries on data held on files.

3.5 Control can be enhanced by ensuring that **edit programs** are **in-built** at the **design stage** and by incorporating into the system a user-usage file which logs details of the user's identification, the application involved, the records accessed or updated and so on. Such a file can be reviewed periodically by a responsible official and the auditor. It may be prudent to implement manual controls to ensure that transactions can only be processed when supported by an appropriate initiating document.

Lack of security and confidentiality

Lack of segregation of duties

3.6 Poor segregation of duties all too easily occurs since frequently the same person prepares the data, **feeds** it into the computer, **supervises** the **processing** and **acts** as **end user**. This lack of division of duties leads to enhanced opportunities for fraud, the user having access to assets and the recording and disposal of assets. The auditors may well have to perform extensive substantive verification work to compensate for this serious lack of control.

Lack of control over users

3.7 Because PCs do not require a protected environment the **terminals** are **readily available** to any user. In order to safeguard the records, controls to prevent unauthorised users from using the computer are necessary (use of passwords and so on).

Lack of control over alterations to programs

3.8 We have emphasised that a lack of expertise, particularly in the case of first time users, may lead to imprudent purchase in terms of capacity and compatibility. Conversely, there are dangers arising because of the relative ease with which expertise may be acquired once a machine is installed and operational. PCs employ high level languages and a working knowledge can be grasped within a short time. In the wrong hands there is a danger that **programs** might be **altered** without **detection** or that programs are written at the time data is being processed without adequate testing.

3.9 Stringent supervisory arrangements are required to prevent unauthorised personnel from having access to the programs together with **programmed controls preventing unauthorised running**. A degree of security will be guaranteed to the extent that the programs are permanently etched onto silicon chips and are hence an integral part of the hardware ('ROMs'). Such programs can only be altered by specialist electronics engineers.

Activity 7.4
(a) What are the major problems involved in the use of a PC based system by a small company?
(b) What controls can a small company implement over such a system?

4 ASSESSMENT OF INFORMATION SYSTEMS AND INTERNAL CONTROL

4.1 Auditors:

- **Assess the adequacy** of the accounting system as a basis for preparing the accounts
- **Identify** the types of **potential misstatements** that could occur in the accounts
- **Consider factors** that affect the **risk of misstatements**
- **Design appropriate audit procedures**

Accounting system and control environment

4.2 The factors affecting the **nature, timing and extent** of the **procedures** performed in order to understand the systems include:

- **Materiality** considerations
- The **size and complexity** of the entity
- Their **assessment** of **inherent risk**
- The **complexity** of the entity's computer systems
- The **type of internal controls** involved
- The **nature of the entity's documentation** of specific internal controls

4.3 The auditors will normally update previous knowledge of the systems in the following ways.

- **Enquiries** of appropriate supervisory and other personnel
- **Inspection** of relevant documents and records produced by the systems
- **Observation** of the entity's activities and operations

4.4 In obtaining their understanding, the auditors should consider **knowledge** about the **presence** or **absence** of **control activities** obtained from the understanding of the control environment and accounting system.

4.5 For example in obtaining an understanding of the accounting system pertaining to cash, the auditors will become aware of whether bank accounts are reconciled. Development of the overall audit strategy does not usually require an understanding of every control activity.

Part C: Controls

4.6 As we have already discussed, auditors decide whether to carry out tests of controls. ISA 315 requires auditors to carry out of tests of controls in areas where they believe controls are operating effectively.

> **ISA 330.23**
>
> When the auditor's assessment of risks of material misstatement includes an expectation that controls are operating effectively, the auditor should perform tests of controls to obtain sufficient appropriate evidence that the controls were operating effectively at relevant times during the period under audit.

Tests of controls

> **KEY TERM**
>
> **Tests of controls** are performed to obtain audit evidence about the effectiveness of the:
>
> (a) Design of the accounting and internal control systems, ie whether they are suitably designed to prevent or detect and correct material misstatements; and
>
> (b) Operation of the internal controls throughout the period.

Tests of controls

Inspection of documents supporting controls or events to gain audit evidence that internal controls have operated properly, eg verifying that a transaction has been authorised

Inquiries about internal controls which leave no audit trail, eg determining who actually performs each function not merely who is supposed to perform it

Reperformance of control procedures, eg reconciliation of bank accounts, to ensure they were correctly performed by the entity

Examination of evidence of management views, eg minutes of management meetings

Testing of internal controls operating on **computerised systems** or over the overall information technology function, eg access controls

Observation of controls. Auditors will consider the manner in which the control is being operated

4.7 Auditors should consider:

- **How** controls were applied
- The **consistency** with which they were applied during the period
- **By whom** they were applied

4.8 Deviations in the operation of controls (caused by change of staff etc) may increase control risk and tests of controls may need to be modified to confirm effective operation during and after any change.

4.9 The use of CAATs (Computer Assisted Techniques) may be appropriate (see Chapter 6).

4.10 In a continuing engagement, the auditor will be aware of the accounting system and internal control through work carried out previously but will need to update the knowledge gained and consider the need to obtain further audit evidence of any changes in control.

4.11 The auditor would obtain audit evidence as to the nature, timing and extent of any changes in the entity's accounting systems and internal control since such procedures were performed and assess their impact on the auditor's intended reliance. The longer the time elapsed since the performance of such procedures the less assurance that may result.

4.12 Further evidence must be obtained to augment the results of tests carried out at an interim audit, ie before the period end. Radical changes in controls, including a periodic breakdown in controls, should be considered as separate periods by the auditors.

4.13 If deviations from controls mean that the level of control risk has to be revised, the nature, timing and extent of the auditors planned substantive procedures should be modified.

4.14 Significant weaknesses on internal controls should be communicated in writing to management. This is dealt with later in this chapter.

Activity 7.5

Explain the importance of the following controls.
(a) Segregation of duties
(b) Bank reconciliation
(c) Comparing the results of stock counts with accounting records.

5 RECORDING OF INFORMATION SYSTEMS AND INTERNAL CONTROL

5.1 As mentioned above, there are several techniques for recording the assessment of control risk, ie the system. One or more may be used, depending on the complexity of the system.

- Narrative notes
- Questionnaires (eg ICQ)
- Checklists
- Flowcharts

5.2 Whatever method of recording the system is used, the record will usually be retained on the permanent file and updated each year.

Narrative notes

5.3 Narrative notes have the advantage of being simple to record. However they are awkward to change if written manually. Editing in future years will be easier if they are computerised. The purpose of the notes is to **describe** and **explain** the **system**, at the same time making any comments or criticisms which will help to demonstrate an intelligent understanding of the system.

Flowcharts

5.4 There are two methods of flowcharting in regular use:

- Document flowcharts
- Information flowcharts

Part C: Controls

Document flowcharts

5.5 Document flowcharts are more commonly used because they are relatively easy to prepare.

- All documents are followed through from 'cradle to grave'.
- *All* operations and controls are shown.

Advantages and disadvantages of flowcharts

5.6 **Advantages**

(a) After a little experience they can be **prepared quickly**.

(b) As the information is presented in a standard form, they are fairly **easy to follow** and to review.

(c) They generally ensure that the system is **recorded in its entirety**, as all document flows have to be traced from beginning to end. Any 'loose ends' will be apparent from a cursory examination.

(d) They **eliminate** the need for **extensive narrative** and can be of considerable help in highlighting the salient points of control and any weaknesses in the system.

5.7 **Disadvantages**

(a) They are **only really suitable for describing standard systems**. Procedures for dealing with unusual transactions will normally have to be recorded using narrative notes.

(b) They are useful for recording the flow of documents, but once the **records** or the assets to which they relate have **become static** they **can no longer be used for describing the controls** (for example over non-current assets).

(c) Major **amendment is difficult** without redrawing.

(d) **Time** can be **wasted** by **charting areas** that are of no **audit significance** (a criticism of *document* not information flowcharts).

Questionnaires

5.8 We can look at two types of questionnaire here, each with a different purpose.

(a) **Internal Control Questionnaires (ICQs)** are used to ask whether controls exist which meet specific control objectives.

(b) **Internal Control Evaluation Questionnaires (ICEQs)** are used to determine whether there are controls which prevent or detect specified errors or omissions.

Internal Control Questionnaires (ICQs)

5.9 The major question which internal control questionnaires are designed to answer is 'How good is the system of controls?'

5.10 Where strengths are identified, the auditors will perform work in the relevant areas. If, however, weaknesses are discovered they should then ask:

(a) **What errors or irregularities** could be made possible by these weaknesses?

(b) Could such errors or irregularities be **material** to the accounts?

(c) What **substantive procedures** will enable such errors or irregularities to be discovered and quantified?

5.11 Although there are many different forms of ICQ in practice, they all conform to the following basic principles:

(a) They **comprise a list of questions** designed to determine whether desirable controls are present.

(b) They are formulated so that there is one to **cover each of the major transaction cycles.**

5.12 Since it is the primary purpose of an ICQ to evaluate the system rather than describe it, one of the most effective ways of designing the questionnaire is to phrase the questions so that all the answers can be given as 'YES' or 'NO' and a 'NO' answer indicates a weakness in the system. An example would be:

Are purchase invoices checked to goods received notes before being passed for payment?	YES/NO/Comments

A 'NO' answer to that question clearly indicates a weakness in the company's payment procedures.

5.13 The ICQ questions below dealing with goods inward provide additional illustrations of the ICQ approach.

Goods inward

(a) Are supplies examined on arrival as to quantity and quality?

(b) Is such an examination evidenced in some way?

(c) Is the receipt of supplies recorded, perhaps by means of goods inwards notes?

(d) Are receipt records prepared by a person independent of those responsible for:

  (i) Ordering functions?
  (ii) The processing and recording of invoices?

(e) Are goods inwards records controlled to ensure that invoices are obtained for all goods received and to enable the liability for unbilled goods to be determined (by pre-numbering the records and accounting for all serial numbers)?

(f) (i) Are goods inward records regularly reviewed for items for which no invoices have been received?

  (ii) Are any such items investigated?

(g) Are these records reviewed by a person independent of those responsible for the receipt and control of goods?

Internal Control Evaluation Questionnaires (ICEQs)

5.14 In recent years many auditing firms have developed and implemented an evaluation technique more concerned with assessing whether specific errors (or frauds) are possible rather than establishing whether certain desirable controls are present. This is achieved by reducing the control criteria for each transaction stream down to a handful of key questions (or control questions). The characteristic of these questions is that they concentrate on the significant errors or omissions that could occur at each phase of the appropriate cycle if controls are weak.

5.15 The nature of the key questions may best be understood by reference to the examples on the following pages.

Part C: Controls

Internal control evaluation questionnaire: control questions

The sales (revenue) cycle

Is there reasonable assurance that:

(a) Sales are properly authorised?
(b) Sales are made to reliable payers?
(c) All goods despatched are invoiced?
(d) All invoices are properly prepared?
(e) All invoices are recorded?
(f) Invoices are properly supported?
(g) All credits to customers' accounts are valid?
(h) Cash and cheques received are properly recorded and deposited?
(i) Slow payers will be chased and that bad and doubtful debts will be provided against?
(j) All transactions are properly accounted for?
(k) Cash sales are properly dealt with?
(l) Sundry sales are controlled?
(m) At the period end the system will neither overstate nor understate debtors?

The purchases (expenditure) cycle

Is there reasonable assurance that:

(a) Goods or services could not be received without a liability being recorded?

(b) Receipt of goods or services is required in order to establish a liability?

(c) A liability will be recorded:

    (i) Only for authorised items
    (ii) At the proper amount?

(d) All payments are properly authorised?

(e) All credits due from suppliers are received?

(f) All transactions are properly accounted for?

(g) At the period end liabilities are neither overstated nor understated by the system?

(h) The balance at the bank is properly recorded at all times?

(i) Unauthorised cash payments could not be made and that the balance of petty cash is correctly stated at all times?

Wages and salaries

Is there reasonable assurance that:

(a) Employees are only paid for work done?
(b) Employees are paid the correct amount (gross and net)?
(c) The right employees actually receive the right amount?
(d) Accounting for payroll costs and deductions is accurate?

Stocks

Is there reasonable assurance that:

(a) Stock is safeguarded from physical loss (eg fire, theft, deterioration)?
(b) Stock records are accurate and up to date?
(c) The recorded stock exists?
(d) The recorded stock is owned by the company?
(e) The cut off is reliable?
(f) The costing system is reliable?
(g) The stock sheets are accurately compiled?
(h) The stock valuation is fair?

Fixed assets

Is there reasonable assurance that:

(a) Recorded assets actually exist and belong to the company?
(b) Capital expenditure is authorised and reported?
(c) Disposals of fixed assets are authorised and reported?
(d) Depreciation is realistic?
(e) Fixed assets are correctly accounted for?
(f) Income derived from fixed assets is accounted for?

Investments

Is there reasonable assurance that:

(a) Recorded investments belong to the company and are safeguarded from loss?
(b) All income, rights or bonus issues are properly received and accounted for?
(c) Investment transactions are made only in accordance with company policy and are appropriately authorised and documented?
(d) The carrying values of investments are reasonably stated?

Management information and general controls

Is the nominal ledger satisfactorily controlled?

Are journal entries adequately controlled?

Does the organisation structure provide a clear definition of the extent and limitation of authority?

Are the systems operated by competent employees, who are adequately supported?

If there is an internal audit function, is it adequate?

Are financial planning procedures adequate?

Are periodic internal reporting procedures adequate?

5.16 Each key control question is supported by detailed control points to be considered. For example, the detailed control points to be considered in relation to key control question (b) for the expenditure cycle (Is there reasonable assurance that receipt of goods or services is required to establish a liability?) are as follows.

(1) Is segregation of duties satisfactory?

(2) Are controls over relevant master files satisfactory?

(3) Is there a record that all goods received have been checked for:

- Weight or number?
- Quality and damage?

(4) Are all goods received taken on charge in the detailed inventory ledgers:

- By means of the goods received note?
- Or by means of purchase invoices?
- Are there, in a computerised system, sensible control totals (hash totals, money values and so on) to reconcile the inventory system input with the creditors system?

(5) Are all invoices initialled to show that:

- Receipt of goods has been checked against the goods received records?
- Receipt of services has been verified by the person using it?
- Quality of goods has been checked against the inspection?

Part C: Controls

> (6) In a computerised invoice approval system are there print-outs (examined by a responsible person) of:
>
> - Cases where order, GRN and invoice are present but they are not equal ('equal' within predetermined tolerances of minor discrepancies)?
> - Cases where invoices have been input but there is no corresponding GRN?
>
> (7) Is there adequate control over direct purchases?
>
> (8) Are receiving documents effectively cancelled (for example cross-referenced) to prevent their supporting two invoices?

5.17 Alternatively, ICEQ questions can be phrased so that the weakness which should be prevented by a key control is highlighted, such as the following.

Question	Answer	Comments or explanation of 'yes' answer
Can goods be sent to unauthorised suppliers?		

5.18 In these cases a 'yes' answer would require an explanation, rather than a 'no' answer.

Advantages and disadvantages of ICQs and ICEQs

5.19 ICQs have various advantages.

- If drafted thoroughly, they can ensure **all controls** are **considered.**
- They are **quick** to **prepare.**
- They are **easy** to **use** and **control.**

5.20 However they also have some disadvantages.

- The client may be able to **overstate controls.**
- They may contain a large number of **irrelevant controls.**
- They may not include **unusual controls**, which are nevertheless effective in particular circumstances.
- They can give the impression that all controls are of **equal** weight. In many systems one NO answer (for example lack of segregation of duties) will cancel out a string of YES answers.

5.21 ICEQs have the following advantages.

- Because they are drafted in terms of **objectives** rather than specific controls, they are easier to apply to a variety of systems than **ICQs.**
- Answering ICEQs should enable auditors to **identify the key controls** which they are most likely to test during control testing.
- ICEQs can **highlight areas of weakness** where extensive substantive testing will be required.

5.22 The principal disadvantage is that they can be **drafted vaguely**, hence **misunderstood** and important controls not identified.

6 COMMUNICATIONS WITH MANAGEMENT

6.1 Several ISAs refer to the auditors' relationship with management. Some aspects of this relationship are determined by legal and professional **requirements**, some by the auditors' own internal procedures and practices.

6.2 Communications between auditors and management are important throughout the audit, but may be particularly crucial in the closing stages.

Communications with management during the audit

6.3 During the audit, the auditors will wish to discuss with **management** various matters including the following.

- An **understanding of the business**
- The **audit strategy**
- The **effect of new legislation** or professional standards on the audit
- **Information necessary** for audit risk assessments
- **Explanations, evidence and representations** from management or from a lower level in the organisation
- Any **observations and suggestions** arising from the audit on such matters as operational or administrative efficiencies, business strategies
- **Unaudited information management** is intending to publish with the audited accounts which the auditors consider is inconsistent or appears to be misleading
- **Details of inefficiencies** or delays in the agreed timetable for preparation of the accounts or of workings schedules which delayed the completion of the audit
- Any **significant differences** between the accounts and any **management accounts** or budgets
- Any **results of the auditors' analytical procedures** of which management may not be aware and may be of benefit to them.

6.4 Important points for the auditors to bear in mind are as follows.

(a) Such discussions are normally conducted during **audit visits** to the client, but may take place at other times.

(b) When discussions are held for the purpose of obtaining audit evidence, the auditors need to **identify** the **most appropriate person** from whom to obtain audit evidence.

(c) All **important discussions** with management should be **documented** in the auditors' working papers. Such documentation would include **explanations** and **representations** regarding material transactions.

Communications with management at the end of the audit

6.5 At the end of the audit the auditors will need to discuss with **management** matters such as the following.

- Any **practical difficulties** encountered in performing the audit
- Any **disagreements** with management relating to the financial statements
- **Significant audit adjustments,** whether or not reflected in the financial statements

- **Significant concerns** or problems relating to accounting policies and the disclosure of items in the financial statements that might lead to a modification of the audit report
- Any **irregularities** or suspected non-compliance with laws and regulations which came to the attention of the auditors
- **Significant risks** or exposures faced by the entity such as matters that have the potential to jeopardise the ability of the entity to continue as a going concern
- **Recommendations** (eg regarding internal control matters: see below) that the auditors wish to make as a result of the audit

6.6 The auditors should bear the following points in mind.

- The auditors should communicate such matters to the **appropriate level** of management.
- The **communication** may be **oral or written**. If the communication is oral, the auditors document communication in the working papers.
- A **specific meeting** will usually **take place** at the **end of the audit** with the board of directors, audit committee or other senior **management**.

Communications on internal control

6.7 Recommendations regarding internal control are a by-product of the financial statement audit, not a primary objective, but nonetheless are frequently of great value to a client. The auditors should make management aware, on a timely basis, of material weaknesses in the design or operation of the accounting and internal control systems which have come to the auditors' attention.

6.8 When auditors prepare a written communication on internal control matters, the following points are suggested by the statement.

(a) It should not **include language** that **conflicts** with the **opinion** expressed in the audit report.

(b) It should state that the **accounting and internal control** system were **considered only** to the **extent necessary** to **determine** the **auditing procedures** to report on the financial statements and not to determine the adequacy of internal control for management purposes or to provide assurances on the accounting and internal control systems.

(c) It will state that it **discusses only weaknesses** in internal control which have **come to the auditors' attention** as a result of the **audit** and that other weaknesses in internal control may exist.

(d) It should also include a statement that the **communication is provided for use only** by **management** (or another specific named party).

6.9 After the above items and the auditors' suggestions for corrective action are communicated to management, the auditors will usually ascertain the actions taken, including the reasons for those suggestions rejected. The auditors may encourage management to respond to the auditors' comments in which case any response can be included in the report.

6.10 The significance of findings relating to the accounting and internal control systems may change with the passage of time. Suggestions from previous years' audits which have not been adopted, if any, should normally be repeated or referred to.

6.11 Communication with management by the auditors regarding internal control, or any other matter, does not remove the need for the auditors to consider any effect on the financial statement or the audit nor is it an adequate substitute for an emphasis of matter or qualification.

Specimen letter on internal control

6.12 This is an example of a letter on internal controls which demonstrates how the principles described in the previous paragraphs might be put into practice.

AB & Co
Certified Accountants
29 High Street

The Board of Directors,
Manufacturing Limited,
15 South Street

1 April 20X8

Members of the board,

Financial statements for the year ended 31 May 20X8

In accordance with our normal practice we set out in this letter certain matters which arose as a result of our review of the accounting systems and procedures operated by your company during our recent interim audit.

We would point out that the matters dealt with in this letter came to our notice during the conduct of our normal audit procedures which are designed primarily for the purpose of expressing our opinion on the financial statements of your company. In consequence our work did not encompass a detailed review of all aspects of the system and cannot be relied on necessarily to disclose defalcations or other irregularities or to include all possible improvements in internal control.

1 *Purchases: ordering procedures*

   Present system
   During the course of our work we discovered that it was the practice of the stores to order certain goods from X Co orally without preparing either a purchase requisition or purchase order.

   Implication
   There is therefore the possibility of liabilities being set up for unauthorised items and at a non-competitive price.

   Recommendation
   We recommend that the buying department should be responsible for such orders and, if they are placed orally, an official order should be raised as confirmation.

2 *Purchase ledger reconciliation*

   Present system
   Although your procedures require that the purchase ledger is reconciled against the control account on the nominal ledger at the end of every month, this was not done in December or January.

   Implication
   The balance on the purchase ledger was short by some £2,120 of the nominal ledger control account at 31 January 20X8 for which no explanation could be offered. This implies a serious breakdown in the purchase invoice and/or cash payment batching and posting procedures.

   Recommendation
   It is important in future that this reconciliation is performed regularly by a responsible official independent of the day to day purchase ledger, cashier and nominal ledger functions.

Part C: Controls

3 *Sales ledger: credit control*

Present system
As at 28 February 20X8 trade debtors accounted for approximately 12 weeks' sales, although your standard credit terms are cash within 30 days of statement, equivalent to an average of about 40 days (6 weeks) of sales.

Implication
This has resulted in increased overdraft usage and difficulty in settling some key suppliers accounts on time.

Recommendation
We recommend that a more structured system of debt collection be considered using standard letters and that statements should be sent out a week earlier if possible.

4 *Preparation of payroll and maintenance of personnel records*

Present system
Under your present system, just two members of staff are entirely and equally responsible for the maintenance of personnel records and preparation of the payroll. Furthermore, the only independent check of any nature on the payroll is that the chief accountant confirms that the amount of the wages cheque presented to him for signature agrees with the total of the net wages column in the payroll. This latter check does not involve any consideration of the reasonableness of the amount of the total net wages cheque or the monies being shown as due to individual employees.

Implications
It is a serious weakness of your present system, that so much responsibility is vested in the hands of just two people. This situation is made worse by the fact that there is no clearly defined division of duties as between the two of them. In our opinion, it would be far too easy for fraud to take place in this area (eg by inserting the names of 'dummy workmen' into the personnel records and hence on to the payroll) and/or for clerical errors to go undetected.

Recommendations

(i) Some person other than the two wages clerks be made responsible for maintaining the personnel records and for periodically (but on a surprise basis) checking them against the details on the payroll.

(ii) The two wages clerks be allocated specific duties in relation to the preparation of the payroll, with each clerk independently reviewing the work of the other.

(iii) When the payroll is presented in support of the cheque for signature to the chief accountant, that he should be responsible for assessing the reasonableness of the overall charge for wages that week.

Our comments have been discussed with your finance director and the chief accountant and these matters will be considered by us again during future audits. We look forward to receiving your comments on the points made. Should you require any further information or explanations do not hesitate to contact us.

This letter has been produced for the sole use of your company. It must not be disclosed to a third party, or quoted or referred to, without our written consent. No responsibility is assumed by us to any other person.

We should like to take this opportunity of thanking your staff for their co-operation and assistance during the course of our audit.

Yours faithfully

ABC & Co

Activity 7.6

(a) What are the main purposes of preparing a letter on internal control?

(b) What are the major advantages in each point made in the letter on internal control being made in the format

'Present system'

'Implication'

'Recommendations'?

Discuss what should be included under each heading.

Exam alert

The pilot paper asked about the reasons for a letter on internal control and for one to be drafted.

Part C: Controls

> **Key learning points**
>
> - The auditors must understand the information system and control environment in order to determine the audit approach. They must also assess whether accounting records fulfil legal requirements.
>
> - Specific control activities include the following.
>
>   - Approval and control of documents
>   - Controls over computerised applications and the information technology environment
>   - Checking the arithmetical accuracy of the records
>   - Maintaining and reviewing control accounts and trial balances
>   - Reconciliations
>   - Comparing the results of cash, security and stock counts with accounting records
>   - Comparing internal data with external sources of information
>   - Limiting direct physical access to assets and records
>
> - **Application controls** should ensure:
>
>   - Completeness, accuracy and authorisation of input
>   - Completeness and accuracy of processing
>   - Proper maintenance of master files and standing data
>
> - **General IT controls** are required to:
>
>   - Ensure proper application development
>   - Prevent or detect unauthorised changes to programs
>   - Ensure that all program changes are adequately tested and documented
>   - Prevent or detect errors during use of programs
>   - Prevent unauthorised amendments to data files
>   - Ensure that systems software is properly installed and maintained
>   - Ensure that proper documentation is kept
>   - Ensure continuity of operations
>
> - Many small computer systems use **personal computers (PCs)**. The major problems with use of PCs are lack of:
>
>   - Planning over acquisition and use
>   - Documentary evidence
>   - Security and confidentiality
>
> - There are always **inherent limitations** to internal controls, including cost-benefit requirements and the possibility of controls being by-passed and over-ridden.
>
> - Auditors should assume **control risk** is high, unless it is assessed, and the assessment confirmed by **tests of controls.**
>
> - Tests of controls must cover the whole accounting period.
>
> - Auditors can use a number of methods to **record** accounting and control systems.
>
>   - Narrative notes
>   - Flowcharts
>   - ICQs (which ask if various controls exist)
>   - ICEQs (which ask if controls fulfil key objectives)
>
> - Auditors should report material control weakness to management, usually in a letter on internal control.

Quick quiz

1. What are the main features of a business's control environment according to ISA 315?
2. What are the main limitations of a system of internal controls?
3. What application controls can help ensure the completeness of input?
4. What are the major objectives of controls over processing?
5. What are the key controls over the testing and documentation of program changes?
6. What support facilities should a supplier offer the user of a small computer system?
7. Give five examples of tests of controls by auditors.
8. What is the main disadvantage of recording systems by means of manual narrative notes?
9. What is the main difference between ICQs and ICEQs?

Answers to quick quiz

1. The main features of a business's control environment per ISA 315 are the overall attitude, and actions of those charged with governance and management towards internal controls and their importance to the entity.

2. The main limitations of a system of internal controls are:

    (a) Costs of implementing controls may outweigh benefits.
    (b) Most internal controls are directed towards routine rather than non-routine transactions.
    (c) Mistakes may occur when controls are being operated.
    (d) Controls may be bypassed by people acting in collusion.
    (e) Controls may be over-ridden.
    (f) Changes in conditions or decreased compliance may mean control procedures become inadequate over time.

3. Completeness of input can be ensured by:

    (a) Manual or programmed agreement of control totals
    (b) One for one checking of processed output to source documents
    (c) Manual or programmed sequence checking
    (d) Programmed matching of input to a control file, containing details of expected inputs
    (e) Procedures for re-submission of rejected inputs

4. The major objectives of controls over processing are to ensure that:

    (a) All input data is processed.
    (b) The correct master files and standing data files are used.
    (c) The processing of each transaction is accurate.
    (d) The updating of data/new data is accurate and authorised.
    (e) Output reports are complete and accurate.

5. The key controls over testing and documentation of program changes are:

    (a) Testing procedures
    (b) Documentation controls and standards
    (c) Approval of changes by users and computer management
    (d) Internal audit involvement and segregation of duties
    (e) Training and supervision of staff

6. The support facilities that should be obtained include:

    (a) There should be prompt service and back-up facilities in the event of a breakdown.
    (b) Bugs should be sorted easily.
    (c) Minor modifications to programs should be carried out easily.
    (d) Adequate documentation should be provided including program documentation, operator instructions and user manuals.
    (e) Operators should be given adequate instruction.

Part C: Controls

7   Examples of control tests include:

(a) Enquiries about and observation of internal controls
(b) Inspection of documents
(c) Examination of evidence of management views
(d) Re-performance of control procedures
(e) Testing controls on specific computerised applications or overall information technology controls

8   The main disadvantage of manual narrative notes is that they can be difficult to change.

9   ICQs concentrate on whether specific controls exist, whereas ICEQs concentrate on whether the control system has specific strengths or can prevent specific weaknesses.

Answers to activities

Answer 7.1

The questions to be asked in order to review the computer controls in existence over purchases and creditors must cover controls over input, processing, access, files and output. The following questions could be asked of the accountant responsible for the creditors section.

(a) What systematic action is taken to ensure the completeness, accuracy and authorisation of input of purchase invoices, credit notes, journal entries, cash and so on? For example, batch totalling, sequence checking, programmed matching of input to control files containing details of expected input, and authorisation limits and reasonableness checks.

(b) By what methods is it established that all input is fully and accurately processed? Examples are batch reconciliation after records update, summary totals, programmed validity checks.

(c) What controls are in place to prevent or detect unauthorised amendments to programs and data files (for example, restrictions of access to programs and to users of the on-line terminals)?

(d) What controls exist over the work done by computer operators (for example, division of duties, job scheduling, computer logs, cross-checks to input control, authorisation of file issue)?

(e) What procedures are in operation to ensure the continuing correctness of master files and the standing data they contain? For example, record counts or hash totals for the files, produced and checked each time they are used, regular checks of all contents, run-to-run control totals.

(f) Are there procedures for the review and despatch of output by the computer operators? Examples are: comparison of output with prelist totals of input, checking all queries have been properly dealt with, distribution list for all output and close control over exception reports, audit totals and so on.

(g) Is the reasonableness of output tested? For example, is output tested against file totals after update, and compared with manually prepared totals and balances on individual debtor accounts?

(h) Is there an adequate management (audit) trail of generated data and regular listing of ledger balances and creditors analysis?

(i) Is there an accounting manual in existence, detailing all procedures and clerical processes relating to the purchases and creditors system, and is it up to date?

Answer 7.2

The following procedures should be undertaken to prevent fire from damaging the system.

(a) The computer room should be constructed of fire-proof materials.

(b) The computer room should have an adequate alarm system which not only warns of fire but also of high-risk conditions, for example the room becoming too hot, so that emergency procedures can be operated.

(c) The computer room should be fitted with fire extinguishers and sprinklers to minimise the effect of fire.

(d) Emergency procedures should be tested regularly.

If fire does damage computer equipment the following precautions can minimise the damage.

(a) Regular back-up copies should be taken of files processed, and these should be held in fire-proof accommodation away from the computer room.

(b) A second computer in a different location within the company can be used as a back-up system if the main computer is damaged by fire.

(c) The company may enter maintenance and repair agreements to ensure back-up facilities are provided externally, and damage to the main computers can be quickly repaired.

Answer 7.3

It is the responsibility of those charged with governance and management to implement an appropriate system of financial and non-financial controls. Good management is itself an internal control, but other procedures must be in place as directors and senior managers cannot supervise everything, particularly in large companies. Hence overseeing an effective internal control system is how senior management discharge their responsibilities.

The general objectives of internal controls is to ensure that the company achieves its objectives regarding reliability of financial reporting, effectiveness and efficiency of operations and compliance with applicable laws and regulations.

In practical terms this involves the following:

Accuracy and completeness of accounting records

Directors are required by the Companies Act to maintain proper accounting records. As we have stated, this objective also relates to safeguarding of assets.

Timely preparation of financial information

Directors have a statutory responsibility to prepare accounts which show a true and fair view within time limits set by statute. Internal financial information such as management accounts and budgets also helps directors monitor what is going on, and if any areas of the business are causing concern.

Adherence to internal policies

In order for management to be able to implement their decisions, there have to be policies in place to ensure management directives are followed.

Safeguarding of assets

Safeguarding of assets is a vital objective of internal control, since directors have the responsibility of stewardship over a company's assets. Safeguarding means not only physical protection of assets but also their proper recording.

Prevention and detection of fraud and error

This objective is related to the safeguarding of assets. If the company's internal control systems cannot prevent or detect fraud or error, there would be serious legal consequences if frauds are allowed to continue, or if the company publishes inaccurate information.

Answer 7.4

(a) The problems involved in a PC based small company accounting system include the following.

   (i) Small companies often have to buy in packages from outside suppliers and these may not be suitable for all their needs.

   (ii) Small companies are unlikely to have a separate specialist computer department. Hence clerical staff may lack training and hence lack an understanding of how the system works. If therefore errors are made or malfunctions occur, there may be no-one who can identify or correct them, and this may mean data is lost or corrupted.

   (iii) Small companies may have few accounting staff so there may be a lack of segregation of duties. It may be that the accountant is the only person in the company who is fully conversant with the system. If one person does have specialised programming knowledge not shared by the others, he may be able to put through unauthorised program changes undetected.

   (iv) Small systems are often real-time systems which means that data can be input and all the associated processing can be carried out at once. Therefore errors may be difficult to correct.

Part C: Controls

- (v) Users can become dependent on the system to produce basic accounting information such as debtors listing. Therefore there may no longer be staff available who can carry out manual processing efficiently, and manual processing might be a necessary back-up if there are problems with the system.
- (vi) Many important files will be held on floppy disks. These can be misappropriated or damaged easily.
- (vii) There may be no security arrangements over the custody of computers, and hence they may be at risk of being stolen or sabotaged.
- (viii) The small company environment may be hostile to controls. This may not only mean that controls necessary to safeguard the system and ensure the completeness and accuracy of processing are not implemented, but also controls required by statute, for example controls over confidential personal information required by the data protection legislation, are not put into practice.

(b) Possible controls over small company computer systems include the following.

- (i) Accounting controls such as batching and reconciliations can be used over input.
- (ii) Programmed procedures within the computer can ensure correctness of processing. Examples include check digits, sequence checks and hash totals.
- (iii) The computer can produce reports on changes to master files for example sales prices.
- (iv) The computer should also be able to produce exception reports of transactions requiring authorisation or investigation, in accordance with parameters set down by the organisation.
- (v) Output should be checked for reasonableness.
- (vi) Standing data should be checked on a regular basis.
- (vii) File menus can be used to help users run programs in the correct sequence and for example prevent processing for a new period before the previous period was closed down.
- (viii) Password systems can be used to aid security. These should be confidential and subject to frequent change. The more sensitive the application, the more passwords should be required, operated in hierarchical systems.
- (ix) Physical security arrangements may also be used, for example physical controls by senior staff over confidential files and vital programs.
- (x) The software house used by the company should supply adequate systems documentation, training and prompt service if the systems break down.
- (xi) Proper back-up procedures should be in place. These include copying of hard disk files onto floppy disks, and storing the files offsite in secure accommodation.
- (xii) The information on the system should be regularly checked and out of date or inaccurate information deleted.
- (xiii) Hardware should be maintained on a regular basis.
- (xiv) Small companies should have contingency plans if the system does break down. These include additional computers and ability to process data manually.

Answer 7.5

(a) Segregation of duties is important because the more people that are involved in all the stages of processing a transaction, the more likely it is that fraud or error by a single person will be identified. In addition the more people that are involved, the less the changes of fraudulent collusion between them.

(b) A bank reconciliation is important because it reconciles the business's records of cash held at bank with the bank's records of cash held at bank. Written confirmation from the bank is strong evidence since it arises from an independent source and is in writing. Generally the only differences on the reconciliation should be timing differences on unpresented cheques or uncleared bankings. For large unpresented cheques and for all uncleared bankings the timing differences involved should be small.

(c) Stock is an important figure in the accounts often materially affecting both the income statement and balance sheet. In addition the stock of many businesses is highly portable, and it is thus subject to a high risk of theft.

A main comparison of stock as recorded in the accounting records with actual stock held, may identify differences which have to be investigated. The differences may be due to theft of stock but may also be due to failure to record stock movements properly. This may also mean that purchases or sales have been recorded incorrectly.

Answer 7.6

(a) The principal purposes of a letter on internal control are as follows.

   (i) To enable the auditors to highlight weaknesses in the accounting records, systems and controls which they have identified during the course of their audit, and which may lead to material errors

   (ii) To provide management with constructive advice on various aspects of the business which the auditors may have identified during the course of the audit

   (iii) To highlight matters that may have an effect on future audits

   (iv) To comply with specific requirements as laid down by, for example, government departments

(b) In order for management letters to be effective, they must clearly describe the weaknesses, consequences and auditor suggestions. The three stage format described enables auditors to do that.

   'Present system'. This section should confirm in writing auditor understanding of the system, and describe the weaknesses in precise terms.

   'Implications'. Although weaknesses are stated under 'present system' their consequences may not necessarily be understood by management. A separate section on implications means that auditors can emphasise what the weaknesses mean and highlight effects on the accounts and on the safeguarding of assets.

   'Recommendations'. Putting these in a separate section emphasises their importance. Clients may well view management letters negatively if recommendations are not clear. The recommendations should be practical and cost-effective and be as specific as possible, stating for instance that named members of staff should be responsible for reviews.

Now try Question 7 in the Exam Question Bank

Chapter 8 Tests of controls: income cycles

Chapter topic list

1 Introduction
2 The sales system
3 The purchases system
4 The wages system

The following study sessions are covered in this Chapter:

Syllabus reference

12(a) Describe and illustrate control procedures to meet specified objectives for each of the following function areas: 5

    (i) Purchases and trade creditors
    (ii) Sales and trade debtors
    (iii) Wages and salaries

18(a) Explain the audit approach to testing accounting system controls over the following functional areas: 5

    (i) Purchases and trade creditors
    (ii) Sales and trade debtors
    (iii) Wages and salaries

1 INTRODUCTION

1.1 In the last chapter we talked about controls. We have stated that on all audits auditors must ascertain the accounting system and internal control. If auditors decide to rely on controls, they must test them. The next two chapters describe the controls that may operate and the tests auditors may carry out.

1.2 It is best to examine controls in terms of the various components of the accounting system. Most commonly these will be: sales, purchases, wages, cash and other systems such as stock, fixed assets and investments.

1.3 For each of the components we shall examine the controls from the client and the auditors' viewpoint. The key **objectives** that clients ought to be trying to fulfil are summarised and we shall look at **common controls** that should generally achieve those objectives. We shall look at how auditors will test them.

1.4 For **sales**, businesses want to give credit only to **customers** who will pay their debts. In addition there are various stages of the selling process - **ordering, dispatch and charging**, all of which should be **documented** and **matched** so that customers receive what they ordered and are appropriately billed. In order to keep track of who owes what and to be able to identify slow-paying customers, a **sales ledger** should be maintained.

1.5 Similarly **purchases** must be controlled. Businesses should ensure that only **properly authorised purchases** which are necessary for the business are made. Again all stages of the purchase process, ordering, receiving goods and being charged for them should be **documented** and **matched** so that the business gets what it ordered and only pays for what it ordered and received. Businesses also need to keep track of what they owe to each supplier by maintaining a **purchase ledger**.

1.6 For **wages and salaries** businesses are trying to ensure that they only pay for **hours worked** and that they pay the **right staff** the **right amount**. Controls should also be in place to ensure **PAYE** and **VAT liabilities** are calculated correctly otherwise penalties may be imposed by the tax authorities.

> **Exam alert**
>
> In the exam you may well be given a practical situation and asked about the controls that should be in operation and the audit work that should be carried out. You should consider the **objectives** that the controls should be trying to achieve, and remember that audit tests should be designed to check whether the controls have fulfilled those objectives. Focusing on the objectives will help you avoid suggesting controls or audit tests which are unnecessary, whilst omitting controls or audit tests which should prevent or highlight weaknesses.

Part C: Controls

2 THE SALES SYSTEM 6/04

Control objectives

2.1 The most important aims of internal control relating to debtors and sales are:

Feature	Aims
Ordering and granting of credit	• **Goods** and **services** are **only supplied** to **customers** with **good credit ratings** • **Customers** are encouraged to **pay promptly** • **Orders** are **recorded correctly** • **Orders** are **fulfilled**
Despatch and invoicing	• All **despatches** of goods are **recorded** • All **goods and services** sold are **correctly invoiced** • All **invoices** raised **relate to goods and services** that have been **supplied** by the business • **Credit notes** are only given for **valid reasons**
Recording, accounting and credit control	• All sales that have been **invoiced** are **recorded** in the general and sales ledgers • All **credit notes** that have been **issued** are **recorded** in the general and sales ledgers • All **entries** in the sales ledger are **made** to the **correct** sales ledger **accounts** • **Cut-off** is applied correctly to the sales ledger • Potentially **doubtful debts** are **identified**

Activity 8.1

What can go wrong at the following stages of the sales cycle?

(a) Ordering by customers
(b) Despatch of goods
(c) Accounting

Controls

2.2 The following controls relate to the **ordering** and **credit control** process; note the importance of controls over credit terms, ensuring that goods are only sent to customers who are likely to pay promptly.

- **Segregation** of duties; credit control, invoicing and stock despatch
- **Authorisation** of **credit terms** to customers
  - References/credit checks obtained
  - Authorisation by senior staff
  - Regular review
- **Authorisation** for changes in **other customer data**
  - Change of address supported by letterhead
  - Requests for deletion supported by evidence balances cleared/customer in liquidation

- **Orders** only **accepted** from **customers** who have no credit problems
- **Sequential numbering** of blank **order documents**
- **Matching** of **customer orders** with production orders and despatch notes

2.3 The following checks relate to **despatches** and **invoice preparation**.
- **Authorisation** of **despatch** of **goods**
  - Despatch only on sales order
  - Despatch only to authorised customers
  - Special authorisation of despatches of goods free of charge or on special terms
- **Examination** of **goods outwards** as to quantity, quality and condition
- **Recording** of **goods outwards**
- **Agreement** of **goods outwards records** to **customer orders**, **despatch notes** and **invoices**
- **Prenumbering** of despatch notes and delivery notes and regular checks on sequence
- **Condition** of **returns checked**
- Recording of goods returned on **goods returned notes**
- **Signature** of **delivery notes** by customers
- Preparation of invoices and credit notes
  - **Authorisation** of **selling prices**/use of **price lists**
  - **Authorisation** of **credit notes**
  - **Checks** on **prices, quantities, extensions** and totals on invoices and credit notes
  - **Sequential numbering of** blank invoices and credit notes, and regular tests on sequence
- **Stock records updated**
- **Matching** of **sales invoices** with despatch and delivering notes and sales orders
- Regular **review** for **orders** which have not yet been delivered

2.4 The following controls relate to **accounting** and **recording**.
- **Segregation of duties:** recording sales, maintaining customer accounts and preparing statements
- **Recording** of **sales invoices** sequence and **control** over **spoilt invoices**
- **Matching** of **cash receipts** with **invoices**
- **Retention** of **customer remittance advices**
- **Separate recording** of **sales returns, price adjustments** etc
- **Cut-off procedures** to ensure goods despatched and not invoiced (or vice versa) are properly dealt with the correct period
- Regular **preparation** of **debtor statements**
- **Checking** of **debtors' statements**
- **Safeguarding** of **debtor statements** so that they cannot be altered before despatch
- **Review** and **follow-up** of **overdue accounts**
- **Authorisation** of **writing off** of **bad debts**
- **Reconciliation** of **sales ledger control account**
- **Analytical review** of **sales ledger** and **profit margins**

Part C: Controls

Tests of controls

2.5 Auditors should carry out the following tests on **ordering** and granting of **credit control** procedures.

- **Check** that **references** are being **obtained** for **all new customers**
- **Check** that all **new accounts** on the sales ledger have been **authorised** by senior staff
- **Check** that **orders** are only **accepted** from customers who are **within** their **credit terms** and **credit limits**
- **Check** that **customer orders** are being **matched** with **production orders** and **despatch notes**

2.6 The following tests should be carried out over **despatches** and **invoices**

- Verify trade sales with **sales invoices checking**:
    - Quantities
    - Prices charged with official price lists
    - Trade discounts have been properly dealt with
    - Calculations and additions
    - Entries in sales day book are correctly analysed
    - VAT, where chargeable, has been properly dealt with
    - Postings to sales ledger
- Verify details of trade sales with entries in stock records
- Verify non-routine sales (scrap, fixed assets etc) with:
    - Appropriate supporting evidence
    - Approval by authorised officials
    - Entries in plant register etc
- Verify **credit notes** with:
    - **Correspondence** or other supporting evidence
    - **Approval** by authorised officials
    - **Entries** in **stock records**
    - **Entries** in **goods returned records**
    - **Calculations** and **additions**
    - **Entries** in **day book**, checking these are correctly analysed
    - **Postings** to **sales ledger**
- Test numerical sequence of despatch notes and enquire into missing numbers
- Test numerical sequence of invoices and credit notes, enquire into missing numbers and inspect copies of those cancelled
- Test numerical sequence of order forms and enquire into missing numbers
- Check that despatches of goods free of charge or on special terms have been authorised by management

8: Tests of controls: income cycles

2.7 The following tests should be carried out over **recording** and **accounting** for sales, and **credit control.**

Sales day book

- **Check entries** with **invoices** and **credit notes** respectively
- **Check additions** and **cross casts**
- **Check postings** to **sales ledger control account**
- Check postings to sales ledge

Sales ledger

- **Check** entries in a **sample of accounts** to sales day book
- **Check additions** and **balances** carried down
- **Note** and **enquire** into contra entries
- Check that **control accounts** have been **regularly reconciled** to total of sales ledger balances

Credit control

- **Scrutinise accounts** to see if credit limits have been observed
- **Check** that debtor statements are **prepared and sent out regularly**
- **Check** that **overdue accounts have been followed up**
- **Check that all bad debts written off have been authorised by management**

Exam alert

This area is very popular in auditing exams, particularly credit control procedures.

Activity 8.2

You are the audit manager on Auckland Ltd, which manufactures computer equipment. Unfortunately the audit senior had to go off on another audit before she could draft the management letter for the final audit for the year ended 31 December 20X7. She has however left the following notes on the system.

Despatch of computer equipment

Customers have to complete a written order before any equipment is despatched. When an order is received Miss Lea in the sales section sends out a pre-numbered despatch note, which is in three parts to Miss Lang in the stock room. The goods are delivered by one of the company's delivery team who takes with him a copy of the despatch note. One copy of the despatch note is sent to Mrs Rawle in the financial accounts section and Miss Lang keeps a third copy.

If the goods are not in stock, Miss Lang sends one copy of the despatch note to the customer together with a note of when the stock is likely to arrive. She places the second copy in an awaiting goods file and destroys the third copy. When the goods arrive in stock Miss Lang notifies Miss Lea, sending her the second copy of the previous despatch note. Miss Lea places this copy in a cancelled despatches file and makes out a new despatch note, which is then processed in the usual way.

Billing

When the second copy of the despatch note of a completed order arrives in the financial accounts section, Mrs Rawle prepares a two-copy invoice. The section supervisor, Mrs McGillivray, checks the details of the invoice. One copy is sent to the customer and one copy is filed in the financial accounts section. Mrs Rawle posts the invoice details to the sales ledger. Each week the total of sales invoices for the week is posted by Miss Bamsey to the sales ledger control account.

Part C: Controls

Receipts

Customers' cheques are received in the company's post room and cheques received each day are added up. The cheques and add-list are sent to Mrs Rawle who posts the payments into the sales ledger control account. The cheques are banked by Mrs McGillivray on her way home. Miss Bamsey enters the total monies received in the cash book and sales ledger control account.

Reconciliation

Every month Miss Gallant, who is the head of the financial accounts section reconciles the sales ledger and sales ledger control account.

Required

Prepare a management letter highlighting weaknesses in the company's sales system and make recommendations about improvements that can remedy those weaknesses.

Activity 8.3

What tests of controls can give auditors assurance that the company's system of control ensures that sales are completely recorded?

3 THE PURCHASES SYSTEM 6/04

3.1 We will follow much the same procedure for the purchases system.

Control objectives

3.2 The most important aims of internal control relating to creditors and purchases are:

Feature	Aims
Ordering	• All **orders for,** and expenditure on, **goods and services** are properly **authorised**, and are for **goods and services** that are actually **received** and are **for the company**
	• **Orders** are only **made** to **authorised suppliers**
	• **Orders** are **made** at **competitive prices**
Receipt and invoices	• **Goods and services** received are **used** for the **organisation's purposes** and not private purposes
	• **Goods and services** are **only accepted** if they have been **ordered**, and the **order** has been authorised
	• All **goods and services received** are accurately **recorded**
	• **Liabilities** are **recognised** for all **goods and services** that have been **received**
	• All **credits** to which business is due are **claimed**
	• **Receipt** of goods and services is **necessary** to **establish** a **liability**
Accounting	• All **expenditure** is **authorised** and is for goods that are **actually received**
	• All **expenditure** that is made is **recorded** correctly in the general and purchase ledger
	• All **credit notes** that are received are **recorded** in the general and purchase ledger
	• All **entries** in the **purchase ledger** are **made** to the **correct purchase ledger accounts**
	• **Cut-off** is **applied correctly** to the purchase ledger

8: Tests of controls: income cycles

> **Activity 8.4**
> What can go wrong at the following stages of the purchase cycle?
> (a) Ordering
> (b) Receipt of goods
> (c) Accounting

Controls

3.3 The following controls should be in place over **ordering**.

- **Central policy** for choice of suppliers
- Evidence required of **requirements** for purchase before purchase authorised (re-order quantities and re-order levels)
- **Order forms** prepared only when a purchase requisition has been received
- **Authorisation** of order forms
- **Prenumbered order forms**
- **Safeguarding** of blank order forms
- **Review** of orders not received
- **Monitoring** of **supplier terms** and taking advantage of favourable conditions (bulk order, discount)

3.4 The client should carry out the following checks on **goods received** and **invoices** from **suppliers**

- **Examination** of goods inwards
  - Quality
  - Quantity
  - Condition
- **Recording arrival** and **acceptance** of goods (prenumbered goods received notes)
- **Comparison** of **goods received notes** with **purchase orders**
- **Referencing** of supplier invoices; numerical sequence and supplier reference
- **Checking** of **suppliers' invoices**
  - Prices, quantities, accuracy of calculation
  - Comparison with order and goods received note
- **Recording return of goods** (prenumbered good returned notes)
- Procedures for **obtaining credit notes** from suppliers

3.5 The following controls should be in place over **accounting procedures**.

- **Segregation** of **duties:** accounting and checking functions
- Prompt **recording** of **purchases** and **purchase returns** in day books and ledgers
- **Regular maintenance** of **purchase ledger**
- **Comparison** of **supplier statements** with **purchase ledger balances**
- **Authorisation** of **payments**
  - Authority limits

Part C: Controls

- Confirmation that goods have been received, accord with purchase order, and are properly priced and invoiced
- **Review** of **allocation** of expenditure
- **Reconciliation** of **purchase ledger** control account to total of purchase ledger balances
- **Cut-off** accrual of unmatched goods received notes at year-end

Tests of controls

3.6 A most important test of controls is for auditors to check that all **purchases** have been **authorised**. The officials who approve the invoices should be operating within laid-down authority limits.

3.7 Auditors should carry out the following tests on **receipts of goods** and **invoices**.

> - Check invoices for goods, raw materials are:
>   - Supported by goods received notes and inspection notes
>   - Entered in stock records
>   - Priced correctly by checking to quotations, price lists to see the price is in order
>   - Properly referenced with a number and supplier code
>   - Correctly coded by type of expenditure
> - **Trace entry** in **record of goods returned** etc and see credit note duly received from the supplier, for invoices not passed due to defects or discrepancy
> - For invoices of all types:
>   - Check calculations and additions
>   - Check entries in purchase day book and verify that they are correctly analysed
>   - Check posting to purchase ledger
> - For credit notes:
>   - **Verify** the **correctness** of credit received with correspondence
>   - **Check entries** in **stock records**
>   - **Check entries** in **record of returns**
>   - **Check entries** in **purchase day book** and verify that they are correctly analysed
>   - **Check postings** to **purchase ledger**
> - Check for **returns** that **credit notes** are duly **received** from the suppliers.
> - Test **numerical sequence** and enquire into missing numbers of:
>   - Purchase requisitions
>   - Purchase orders
>   - Goods received notes
>   - Goods returned notes
>   - Suppliers' invoices
> - **Obtain explanations** for **items** which have been **outstanding** for a long time:
>   - Unmatched purchase requisitions
>   - Purchase orders
>   - Goods received notes (if invoices not received)
>   - Unprocessed invoices

8: Tests of controls: income cycles

3.8 The following tests should be carried out on the recording of purchases.

> - Verify that invoices and credit notes recorded in the purchase day book are:
>   - **Initialled** for prices, calculations and extensions
>   - **Cross-referenced** to purchase orders, goods received notes etc
>   - **Authorised** for payment
> - Check additions
> - Check postings to nominal ledger accounts and control account
> - Check postings of entries to purchase ledger
>
> *Purchase ledger*
>
> - For a sample of accounts recorded in the purchase ledger:
>   - **Test check entries** back into books of prime entry
>   - **Test check additions** and **balances** forward
>   - **Note** and **enquire** into all contra entries
> - Confirm **control account balancing** has been regularly carried out during the year
> - **Examine control account** for unusual entries

3.9 EXAMPLE

Jo has established that Brown Ltd operate a number of controls in the purchases system.

These include the following:

- All goods received are recorded on pre-numbered multi-part goods received notes (GRNs).
- Goods inwards are checked regarding quantity against the supplier's delivery note. They are also checked for quality. These checks are evidenced on the GRN.
- The purchase ledger clerk compares the details on the purchase invoice with the order and GRN. Any discrepancies are followed up.

If Jo wishes to rely on these controls she must perform suitable tests of controls on them and evaluate the results. These would include:

- Testing the numerical sequence of GRNs and enquiring into any missing numbers.
- For a sample of purchase invoices check that these are supported by a GRN.
- Review a sample of GRNs for evidence of quantity and quality check. This would normally be evidenced by a signature.
- Observe procedures on delivery day.
- Review a sample of purchase invoices for evidence of matching to invoice and GRN. Again this would normally be evidenced by a signature.

If Jo identified any breakdowns in the application of controls she would then need to decide whether this was an isolated or systematic error. In some instances it may be necessary to extend the sample in order to draw a conclusion.

3.10 The following question should help you to apply 'standard' tests to a question.

Part C: Controls

Activity 8.5

Derek Limited operates a computerised purchase system. Invoices and credit notes are posted to the bought ledger by the bought ledger department. The computer subsequently raises a cheque when the invoice has to be paid.

Required

List the controls that should be in operation:

(a) Over the addition, amendment and deletion of suppliers, ensuring that the standing data only includes suppliers from the company's list of authorised suppliers

(b) Over purchase invoices and credit notes, to ensure only authorised purchase invoices and credit notes are posted to the purchase ledger

---

4 THE WAGES SYSTEM 12/04

Control objectives

4.1 The most important aims of internal control relating to wages and salaries are:

Feature	Aims
Setting of wages and salaries	• **Employees** are **only paid** for **work** that they have **done** • **Gross pay** has been **calculated correctly** and **authorised**
Recording of wages and salaries	• **Gross** and **net pay** and **deductions** are **accurately recorded** on the payroll • **Wages** and **salaries paid** are **recorded correctly** in the **bank** and **cash records** • Wages and salaries are **correctly recorded** in the **general ledger**
Payment of wages and salaries	• The **correct employees** are **paid**
Deductions	• Statutory and non-statutory **deductions** have been **calculated correctly** and are **authorised** • The **correct amounts** are **paid** to the **taxation authorities**

Controls

4.2 While in practice separate arrangements are generally made for dealing with wages and salaries, the considerations involved are broadly similar and for convenience the two aspects are here treated together.

General arrangements

4.3 Responsibility for the preparation of pay sheets should be delegated to a suitable person, and adequate staff appointed to assist him. The extent to which the staff responsible for preparing wages and salaries may perform other duties should be clearly defined. In this connection full advantage should be taken where possible of the division of duties, and checks available where automatic wage-accounting systems are in use.

4.4 Setting of wages and salaries

- **Staffing** and **segregation of duties**
- **Maintenance of personnel records** and regular checking of wages and salaries to details in personnel records
- **Authorisation**
  - Engagement and discharge of employees
  - Changes in pay rates
  - Overtime
  - Non-statutory deductions (for example pension contributions)
  - Advances of pay
- **Recording** of **changes** in **personnel** and **pay rates**
- **Recording** of hours worked by **timesheets, clocking in and out** arrangements
- **Review of hours worked**
- **Recording** of **advances** of **pay**
- **Holiday pay** arrangements
- **Answering queries**
- **Review** of **wages against budget**

4.5 Recording of wages and salaries

- **Bases** for **compilation** of payroll
- **Preparation, checking** and **approval** of payroll
- Dealing with **non-routine matters**

4.6 Payment of cash wages

- **Segregation of duties**
  - Cash sheet preparation
  - Filling of pay packets
  - Distribution of wages
- **Authorisation** of **wage cheque**
- **Custody** of cash
  - Encashment of cheque
  - Security of pay packets
  - Security of transit arrangements
  - Security and prompt banking of unclaimed wages
- **Verification of identity**
- **Recording** of distribution

4.7 Payment of salaries

- **Preparation** and **signing** of cheques and bank transfer lists
- **Comparison** of **cheques** and **bank transfer list** with payroll
- **Maintenance** and **reconciliation** of wages and salaries bank account

Part C: Controls

4.8 Deductions from pay

- **Maintenance** of **separate employees' records**, with which pay lists may be compared as necessary
- **Reconciliation** of **total pay** and **deductions** between one pay day and the next
- **Surprise cash counts**
- **Comparison** of actual pay totals with **budget estimates** or standard costs and the investigation of variances
- **Agreement** of **gross earnings** and **total tax deducted** with PAYE returns to the Inland Revenue

4.9 Appropriate arrangements should be made for dealing with statutory and other authorised deductions from pay, such as national insurance, PAYE, pension fund contributions, and savings held in trust. A primary consideration is the establishment of adequate controls over the **records** and **authorising** deductions.

Tests of controls

Setting of wages and salaries

4.10 Auditors should check that the **wages** and **salary summary** is approved for payment. They should confirm that procedures are operating for **authorising changes** in **rates of pay**, overtime, and holiday pay.

4.11 A particular concern will be joiners and leavers. Auditors will need to obtain evidence that staff only start being paid when they join the company, and are removed from the payroll when they leave the company. They should check that the **engagement** of **new employees** and **discharges** have been **confirmed in writing**.

4.12 Auditors will also wish to check calculations of wages and salaries. This test should be designed to check that the client is carrying out **checks** on **calculations** and also to provide substantive assurance that **wages** and **salaries** are being **calculated correctly**.

4.13 For wages, this will involve checking **calculation** of **gross pay** with:

- Authorised rates of pay
- Production records. See that production bonuses have been authorised and properly calculated
- Clock cards, time sheets or other evidence of hours worked. Verify that overtime has been authorised

4.14 For salaries, auditors should **verify that gross salaries and bonuses are in accordance with personnel records, letters of engagement** etc and that increases in pay have been properly authorised.

Payment of wages and salaries

4.15 If wages are paid in cash, auditors should carry out the following procedures.

> - **Arrange to attend** the **pay-out** of wages to confirm that the official procedures are being followed
> - Before the wages are paid, **compare payroll** with **wage packets** to ensure all employees have a wage packet
> - **Check** that **no employee receives more than one wage packet**
> - **Check entries** in the **unclaimed wages book** with the entries on the payroll
> - **Check that unclaimed wages** are **banked regularly**
> - **Check** that unclaimed wages book shows **reasons** why wages are unclaimed
> - **Check pattern** of **unclaimed wages** in unclaimed wages book; variations may indicate failure to record
>
> Holiday pay
>
> - **Verify** a sample of **payments** with the **underlying records** and **check** the **calculation** of the amounts paid

4.16 For salaries, auditors should check that comparisons are being made between payment records and they should themselves **examine paid cheques** or a **certified copy** of the **bank list** for employees paid by cheque of banks transfer.

Recording of wages and salaries

4.17 A key control auditors will be concerned with will be the reconciliation of wages and salaries.

4.18 For wages, there should have been reconciliations with:

> - The **previous week's payroll**
> - **Clock cards/time sheets/job cards**
> - **Costing analyses, production budgets**

4.19 The total of **salaries** should be **reconciled** with the **previous week/month** or the **standard payroll.**

4.20 In addition auditors should confirm that important calculations have been checked by the clients and re-perform those calculations.

4.21 These include checking for wages, for a number of weeks:

> - **Additions** of **payroll sheets**
> - **Totals** of **wages sheets** selected to summary
> - **Additions** and **cross-casts** of summary
> - **Postings** of **summary** to **general ledger** (including control accounts)
> - **Check casts** of **net cash column** to cash book

Part C: Controls

4.22 For salaries, they include checking for a number of weeks/months:

- **Additions** of **payroll sheets**
- **Totals** of **salaries sheets** to **summary**
- **Additions** and **cross-casts** of **summary**
- **Postings** of **summary** to **general ledger** (including control accounts)
- **Total** of **net pay column** to cash book

Deductions

4.23 Auditors should **check** the **calculations** of **PAYE, National Insurance** and **non-statutory deductions.** For PAYE and NI they should carry out the following tests.

- **Scrutinise** the **control accounts** maintained to see **appropriate deductions** have been **made**
- **Check** to see that the **employer's contribution** for national insurance has been **correctly calculated**
- **Check** that the **payments** to the **Inland Revenue** and other bodies are **correct**

They should **check other deductions to appropriate records. For voluntary deductions, they should see** the **authority completed** by the relevant employees.

Activity 8.6

The following questions have been selected from an internal control questionnaire for wages and salaries.

Internal control questionnaire - wages and salaries

		Yes	No
1	Does an appropriate official authorise rates of pay?		
2	Are written notices required for employing and terminating employment?		
3	Are formal records such as time cards used for time keeping?		
4	Does anyone verify rates of pay, overtime hours and computations of gross pay before the wage payments are made?		
5	Does the accounting system ensure the proper recording of payroll costs in the financial records?		

Required

(a) Describe the internal control objective being fulfilled if the controls set out in the above questions are in effect.

(b) Describe the audit procedures which would test the effectiveness of each control and help determine any potential material error.

(c) Identify the potential consequences for the company if the above controls were not in place.

You may answer in columnar form under the headings:

ICQ question	Internal control objective	Audit procedures	Consequences

8: Tests of controls: income cycles

Key learning points

- The sales and purchases systems will be the most important components of most company accounting systems.
- The tests of controls of the **sales system** will be based around:
  - **Selling** (authorisation)
  - **Goods outwards** (custody)
  - **Accounting** (recording)
- Similarly, the **purchases systems** tests will be based around:
  - **Buying** (authorisation)
  - **Goods inwards** (custody)
  - **Accounting** (recording)
- Important **tests of controls** by auditors include:
  - Checking documentation for correct details, calculations and authorisation
  - Comparing documents
  - Checking completeness of documentation sequences
- Note that all weaknesses discovered in these tests will be included in a **report to management**.
- Obviously, most manufacturing companies will have a large payroll. **Wages and salaries** are usually dealt with in very different ways, but they are often grouped together for audit testing purposes.
- Key controls over **wages** cover:
  - **Documentation** and **authorisation** of staff changes
  - **Calculation** of wages and salaries
  - **Payment** of wages and salaries
  - **Authorisation** of **deductions**

Quick quiz

1. What are the key elements in authorisation of credit terms to customers?
2. What should auditors check when reviewing sales invoices?
3. How can a company ensure that quantities of goods ordered do not exceed those that are required?
4. What are the important checks that should be made on invoices received from suppliers?
5. What procedures should auditors carry out on credit notes received?
6. What are the most important authorisation controls over amounts to be paid to employees?
7. How should auditors confirm that wages have been paid at the correct rate to individual employees?

Answers to quick quiz

1. References and credit checks should be obtained before customers are given credit. Credit limits should be authorised by senior staff and should be regularly reviewed.

2. When checking sales invoices, auditors should check:
   (a) Quantities
   (b) Prices charged with price lists
   (c) Correct calculation of discounts
   (d) Calculations and additions
   (e) Invoices have been correctly entered and analysed in the sales day book
   (f) VAT has been properly dealt with
   (g) Invoices have been posted to the sales ledger

3. A company can ensure goods ordered do not exceed requirements by setting re-order quantities and re-order limits.

4. Invoices from suppliers should be checked for correctness of prices and quantities and accuracy of calculation. They should be compared with purchase orders and goods received notes.

Part C: Controls

5   Auditors should:

  (a) Verify the correctness of credit notes with previous correspondence.
  (b) Confirm by reviewing stock records and records of returns that goods have been returned.
  (c) Check credit notes have been correctly accounted for by checking entries in the purchase day book and purchase ledger.

6   The most important authorisation controls over wages and salaries are controls over:

  (a) Engagement and discharge of employees
  (b) Changes in pay rates
  (c) Overtime
  (d) Non-statutory deductions
  (e) Advances of pay

7   Auditors should confirm that wages have been paid at the correct rate by checking calculation of gross pay to:

  (a) Authorised rates of pay
  (b) Production records
  (c) Clock cards, time sheets or other evidence of hours worked

Answers to activities

Answer 8.1

(a) (i)   Orders may never be recorded.
    (ii) The goods may never be sent.
    (iii) Goods may be sold to a customer who is unable to pay.
(b) (i)   Goods may never be despatched.
    (ii) Damaged or incorrect goods may be despatched.
    (iii) The customer may never receive the goods.
(c) (i)   Goods may never be invoiced.
    (ii) Invoicing errors may occur.
    (iii) Accounts may remain overdue.
    (iv) Accounts may not be correctly updated.

Answer 8.2

XYZ & Co
Chartered Accountants
10 Kinson Street
Northbourne
N10 10MM

Board of Directors
Auckland Ltd
11 Moordown Road
Winton
N11 10 WW

25 February 20X8

Dear Sirs

Points arising from the audit for the year ended 31 December 20X7

In accordance with our normal practice, we set out in this letter certain matters which arose as a result of our review of the accounting system and procedures operated by your company during our recent audit visit.

We would point out that the matters dealt with in this letter came to our notice during the conduct of our normal audit procedures which are designed primarily for the purpose of expressing our opinion of the financial statements of your company. In consequence, our work cannot be relied on necessarily to disclose defalcations or other irregularities or to be regarded as a comprehensive statement of all weaknesses that exist or of all improvements that might be made.

This report has been prepared for the sole use of your company. Its contents should not be disclosed to a third party without our written consent. No responsibility is assumed by us to any other person.

8: Tests of controls: income cycles

Sales, debtors and cash collection system

Sales

(a) Present system

There is no check when orders are received as to whether:

(i) They are from an established credit customer.
(ii) The customer is within their credit limit.

(b) Implication

Goods can be supplied to a bad credit risk.

(c) Recommendations

(i) Credit ratings/references should be obtained for all customers and a credit limit set.

(ii) Miss Lea should ensure individual orders do not place customers above their credit limit and evidence the order as such.

Despatch

(a) Present system

No evidence is obtained from customers that they have accepted delivery of their goods.

(b) Implication

Bad debts may occur if customers claim that they have not received goods.

Recommendation

Customers should sign a copy of the despatch note which should then be returned to Auckland as proof of delivery.

Invoicing

(a) Present system

Sequentially pre-numbered invoices are not used and there is no checking between orders, despatch notes and invoices.

(b) Implications

(i) Customer goodwill may be lost as it is not possible to check that all orders have been fulfilled correctly.

(ii) Sales and debtors may be understated because there is no guarantee that invoices are eventually raised in respect of goods despatched.

(c) Recommendations

(i) Sequentially pre-numbered invoices should be used. Despatch notes should be matched and filed with order forms. A sequence check should be periodically performed to chase up unfulfilled orders.

(ii) Invoices should be matched and filed with order forms and despatch notes in sequence order. A periodic sequence check would reveal uninvoiced sales.

(iii) A sequence check on sales invoice posting should also be carried out monthly.

Cash receipts

(a) Present system

Mrs Rawle is responsible for recording of both invoices and cheques received in the sales ledger.

(b) Implication

It is possible for Mrs Rawle to suppress the recording of sales invoices and then misappropriate the cheques on receipt from customers without any need for collusion with another member of staff.

(c) Recommendation

There must be segregation of duties between recording of invoices and recording payments received. The cheques received should be sent directly to Mrs McGillivray alongside a copy of the add list supplied to Mrs Rawle. The add list should be extended to contain the customer details needed by Mrs Rawle.

Part C: Controls

Our comments have been discussed with your finance director and the chief accountant and these matters will be considered by us again during future audits. We look forward to receiving your comments on the points made. Should you require any further information or explanations please do not hesitate to contact us.

We should like to take this opportunity to thank your staff for their co-operation and assistance during the course of our audit.

Yours faithfully.

XYZ & Co.

Answer 8.3

Tests of controls over completeness of recording of sales include:

(a) Sequence tests on sales orders, despatch notes, invoices and credit notes to ensure that there are no missing numbers or two documents with the same number

(b) Comparisons of despatch notes with order and invoices, checking documents are cross-referenced to each other

(c) Checking posting of sales day book to sales ledger control account and sales ledger

(d) Checking control account reconciliations have been carried out and have been reviewed by senior staff

(e) Reviewing controls over computerised input including:

    (i) Control totals
    (ii) Checking of output to source documents
    (iii) Procedure over resubmission of rejected inputs

Answer 8.4

(a)   (i) All purchases may not be recorded.
     (ii) Goods and services may be purchased which are not required.
     (iii) The company may fail to buy at the best prices.

(b)   (i) Goods may be accepted which have not been ordered.
     (ii) Goods may be damaged or the quantity may be wrong.

(c)   (i) Invoices may be received for goods that have not been ordered.
     (ii) Invoices may be incorrect.
     (iii) Accounts may not be correctly updated.

Answer 8.5

(a) Controls over the standing data file containing suppliers' details will include the following. These should prevent fraud by the creation of a fictitious supplier.

    (i) All amendments/additions/deletions to the data should be authorised by a responsible official. A standard form should be used for such changes.

    (ii) The amendment forms should be input in batches (with different types of change in different batches), sequentially numbered and recorded in a batch control book so that any gaps in the batch numbers can be investigated. The output produced by the computer should be checked to the input.

    (iii) A listing of all such adjustments should automatically be produced by the computer and reviewed by a responsible official, who should also check authorisation.

    (iv) A listing of suppliers' accounts on which there has been no movement for a specified period (6 months, 12 months) should be produced to allow decisions to be made about possible deletions, thus ensuring that the standing data is current. The buying department manager might also recommend account closures on a periodic basis.

    (v) Users should be controlled by use of passwords. This can also be used as a method of controlling those who can amend data.

    (vi) Periodic listings of standing data should be produced in order to verify details (for example addresses) with suppliers' documents (invoices/ statements).

(b) The input of authorised purchase invoices and credit notes should be controlled in the following ways.

(i) Authorisation should be evidenced by the signature of the responsible official (say the Chief Accountant). In addition, the invoice or credit note should show initials to demonstrate that the details have been agreed: to a signed GRN; to a purchase order; to a price list; for additions and extensions.

(ii) There should be adequate segregation of responsibilities between the posting function, stock custody and receipt, payment of suppliers and changes to standing data.

(iii) Input should be restricted by use of passwords linked to the relevant site number.

(iv) A batch control book should be maintained, recording batches in number sequence. Invoices should be input in batches using pre-numbered batch control sheets. The manually produced invoice total on the batch control sheet should be agreed to the computer generated total. Credit notes and invoices should be input in separate batches to avoid one being posted as the other.

(v) A program should check calculation of VAT at standard rate and total (net + VAT = gross) of invoice. Non-standard VAT rates should be highlighted.

(vi) The input of the supplier code should bring up the supplier name for checking by the operator against the invoice.

(vii) Invoices for suppliers which do not have an account should be prevented from being input. Any sundry suppliers account should be very tightly controlled and all entries reviewed in full each month.

(viii) An exception report showing unusual expense allocation (by size or account) should be produced and reviewed by a responsible official. Expenses should be compared to budget and previous years.

(ix) There should be monthly reconciliations of purchase ledger balances to suppliers' statements by someone outside the purchasing (accounting) function.

Answer 8.6

	ICQ question	Internal control objective	Audit procedures	Consequences
1	Does an appropriate official authorise rates of pay?	Employees are paid amounts authorised	Test rates of pay from payroll to schedule of authorised pay rates (personnel files, board minutes etc)	Incorrect rates of pay could lead to over/under statement of profit
2	Are written notices required for employing and terminating employment?	All employees paid through payroll exist	Check a sample of employees from payroll files for authorisation of employment or termination Check details for cheque or credit transfer salary payments to personnel files	Payroll may include fictitious employees
3	Are formal records such as time cards used for time keeping?	Employees are only paid for work done	Review time records to ensure they are properly completed and controlled Observe procedures for time recording Check time records where absences are recorded to payroll to ensure they have been accounted for Review the wages account and investigate any large or unusual amounts	Overstatement of payroll costs. Employees over/under paid
4	Does anyone verify rates of pay, overtime hours and computation of gross pay before wage payments are made?	Employees are paid the correct amount	Examine payroll for evidence of verification Recompute gross pay (including overtime) Check wage rates to authorised schedule	Misstatement of payroll costs
5	Does the accounting system ensure the proper recording of payroll costs in the financial records?	Payroll costs are properly recorded	Check posting of payroll costs to the nominal ledger	Misstatement of payroll costs

Now try Question 8 in the Exam Question Bank

Chapter 9   Tests of controls: asset cycles

Chapter topic list

1 Introduction
2 The cash system
3 The stock system
4 Fixed assets
5 Management information

The following study sessions are covered in this Chapter:

Syllabus reference

12(a) Describe and illustrate control procedures to meet specified objectives for each
of the following functional areas: 5

   (iv) Tangible fixed assets
   (v) Stock
   (vi) Bank receipts and payments
   (vii) Cash receipts and payments

18(a) Explain the audit approach to testing accounting system controls over the
following functional areas: 5

   (iv) Tangible fixed assets
   (v) Stock
   (vi) Bank receipts and payments
   (vii) Cash receipts and payments

1 INTRODUCTION

1.1 This chapter deals with other areas of the accounts for which significant controls are likely to exist.

1.2 Controls over **cash** and **bank balances** cannot be seen in complete isolation from controls over the sales, purchases and wages cycle. In this chapter we concentrate on controls over and testing of the safe **custody** and **recording** of cash.

1.3 You should note in particular the emphasis on prompt recording of receipts and payments, and prompt banking of cash and cheques received. Bear in mind also when you work through the section on bank and cash that controlling cheque receipts and payments is significantly easier than controlling cash receipts and payments.

1.4 For **stock**, there should obviously be **proper security arrangements** and **prompt recording**. You should note however the other aspects of control of stock, particularly reviews of the condition of stock, and stockholding policies designed to ensure that the business is not holding too much or too little stock. These controls interest auditors since they may impact upon how stock is valued. We shall discuss valuation of stock further in Chapter 11.

1.5 With **fixed assets**, controls over the **recording** and **condition** of fixed assets are important, also the **custody** of portable fixed assets such as computer equipment. Given that much fixed asset expenditure is for significant amounts, auditors will also be interested in **controls** over the **acquisition** and **disposal** of fixed assets, particularly **authorisation** controls.

2 THE CASH SYSTEM

Control objectives

2.1 The most important aims of internal control relating to cash receipts and payments are:

- All **monies received** are **recorded**
- All **monies received** are **banked**
- **Cash** and **cheques** are **safeguarded** against loss or theft
- All **payments** are **authorised, made** to the **correct recipients** and **recorded**
- **Payments** are **not made twice** for the same liability

2.2 Segregation of duties is particularly important here. The person responsible for receiving and recording cash when it arrives in the post should not be the same as the person responsible for banking it. Ideally the cash book should be written up by a further staff member, and a fourth staff member should reconcile the various records of amounts received.

2.3 Records of cash are obviously also at the heart of a company's accounting records; therefore if these accounting records are to fulfil Companies Act requirements, cash must be recorded **promptly**.

2.4 The following detailed matters should be considered.

Control considerations

Cash at bank and in hand - receipts

2.5 **Segregation of duties** between the various functions listed below is particularly important.

Part C: Controls

2.6 Recording of receipts by post

- **Safeguards** to **prevent interception of mail** between receipt and opening
- Appointment of **responsible person** to supervise mail
- **Protection** of **cash and cheques** (restrictive crossing)
- **Amounts received listed** when post opened
- **Post stamped** with date of receipt

2.7 Recording of cash sales and collections

- **Restrictions** on **receipt of cash** (by cashiers only, or by salesmen etc)
- **Evidencing** of receipt of cash
  - Serially numbered receipt forms
  - Cash registers incorporating sealed till rolls
- **Clearance** of cash offices and registers
- **Agreement** of **cash collections** with **till rolls**
- **Agreement** of **cash collections** with **bankings** and cash and sales records
- **Investigation** of cash shortages and surpluses

2.8 General controls over recording

- **Prompt maintenance** of records (cash books, ledger accounts)
- **Limitation** of **duties** of receiving cashiers
- **Holiday arrangements**
- **Giving** and **recording** of **receipts**
  - Retained copies
  - Serially numbered receipts books
  - Custody of receipt books
  - Comparisons with cash book records and bank paying in slips

2.9 Banking

- **Daily bankings**
- **Make-up** and **comparison** of **paying-in** slips against initial receipt records and cash book
- **Banking** of receipts **intact**/control of disbursements

2.10 Safeguarding of cash and bank accounts

- **Restrictions** on **opening new bank accounts**
- **Limitations** on **cash floats** held
- **Restrictions** on **payments** out of **cash received**
- **Restrictions** on **access** to cash registers and offices
- **Independent checks** on cash floats
- **Surprise cash counts**
- **Custody** of **cash outside office hours**
- **Custody** over **supply** and issue of cheques
- **Preparation** of **cheques** restricted (person responsible should be separate from purchase ledger)
- **Safeguards** over **mechanically signed cheques**/cheques carrying printed signatures

- **Restrictions** on issue of **blank** or **bearer** cheques
- **Safeguarding** of **IOUs**, cash in transit
- **Insurance arrangements**
- **Bank reconciliations**
    - Issue of bank statements
    - Frequency of reconciliations by independent person
    - Reconciliation procedures
    - Treatment of longstanding unpresented cheques
    - Stop payment notice on unpresented cheques
    - Sequence of cheque numbers is confirmed as complete
    - Comparison of reconciliation with cash books

Cash at bank and in hand - payments

2.11 The arrangements for controlling payments will depend to a great extent on the nature of business transacted, the volume of payments involved and the size of the company.

2.12 The cashier should generally not be concerned with keeping or writing-up books of account other than those recording disbursements nor should he have access to, or be responsible for the custody of, securities, title deeds or negotiable instruments belonging to the company.

2.13 The person responsible for preparing cheques or traders' credit lists should not himself be a cheque signatory. Cheque signatories in turn should not be responsible for recording payments.

2.14 Cheque payments

- **Cheque requisitions**
    - Appropriate supporting documentation
    - Approval by appropriate staff
    - Presentation to cheque signatories
    - Cancellation (crossing/recording cheque number)
- **Authority** to sign cheques
    - Signatories should not also approve cheque requisitions
    - Limitations on authority to specific amounts
    - Number of signatories (all cheques/larger cheques require more than one signature)
    - Prohibitions over signing of blank cheques
- **Prompt despatch** of signed **cheques**
- **Obtaining** of paid **cheques** from **banks**
- Payments **recorded promptly** in **cash book** and **ledger**

2.15 Cash payments

- **Authorisation** of **expenditure**
- **Cancellation** of **vouchers** to ensure cannot be paid
- **Limits** on **disbursements**
- **Rules** on **cash advances** to employees, IOUs and cheque cashing

Part C: Controls

Tests of controls

2.16 Auditors will carry out the following procedures to ensure receipts are being recorded. Note that as well as testing controls over receipts, auditors are obtaining evidence to support the assertion that sales and receipts are **completely recorded**.

2.17 Receipts received by post

> - Observe procedures for post opening are being followed.
> - **Observe** that **cheques** received by post are immediately **crossed** in the company's favour of the company.
> - For items entered in the rough cash book (or other record of cash, cheques etc received by post), **trace entries** to:
>   - **Cash book**
>   - **Paying-in book**
>   - **Counterfoil** or carbon copy receipts
> - **Verify amounts entered** as **received** with remittance advices or other supporting evidence.

2.18 Cash sales, branch takings

> - For a sample of cash sales summaries/branch summaries from different locations:
>   - **Verify with till rolls** or copy cash sale notes
>   - **Check to paying-in slip** date-stamped and initialled by the bank
>   - **Verify that takings** are banked intact daily
>   - **Vouch expenditure** out of takings

2.19 Collections

> - For a sample of items from the original collection records:
>   - **Trace amounts** to **cash book** via collectors' cash sheets or other collection record
>   - **Check entries** on **cash sheets** or collection records with collectors' receipt books
>   - **Verify** that **goods delivered** to travellers/salesmen have been regularly **reconciled** with sales and stocks in hand
>   - **Check numerical sequence** of collection records

2.20 Receipts cash book

> - For cash receipts for several days throughout the period:
>   - **Check to entries in rough cash book**, receipts, branch returns or other records
>   - **Check to paying-in slips** obtained direct from the bank, observing that there is no delay in banking monies received. Check additions of paying-in slips
>   - **Check additions of cash book**
>   - **Check postings to the sales ledger**
>   - **Check postings to the general ledger**, including control accounts
> - **Scrutinise the cash book** and **investigate items** of a **special** or **unusual nature**.

9: Tests of controls: asset cycles

2.21 Auditors will be concerned with whether payments have been authorised and are to the correct payee. The following procedures may be performed on the payments cash book.

- For a sample of payments:
    - **Compare** with paid cheques to ensure payee agrees
    - **Check** that **cheques** are **signed** by the **persons authorised** to do so within their authority limits
    - **Check** to **suppliers' invoices** for goods and services. Verify that supporting documents are signed as having been **checked** and **passed for payment** and have been stamped 'paid'
    - **Check supplier details and amounts to suppliers' statements**
    - **Check** to **other documentary evidence,** as appropriate (agreements, authorised expense vouchers, wages/salaries records, petty cash books etc)

2.22 When checking the **recording** of payments, auditors will carry out the following procedures on the payments cash book.

- For a sample of weeks:
    - **Check the sequence of cheque numbers** and enquire into missing numbers
    - **Trace transfers** to other bank accounts, petty cash books or other records, as appropriate
    - **Check additions,** including extensions, and balances forward at the beginning and end of the months covering the periods chosen
    - **Check postings** to the **purchase ledger**
    - **Check postings** to the **general ledger,** including the control accounts
    - **Scrutinise the cash book** for the rest of the year and **examine items of a special** or **unusual nature**

2.23 When checking that bank and cash are **secured,** auditors should consider the security arrangements over blank cheques and cash. Bank reconciliations are also a very important control and auditors should carry out the following tests on these.

- For a period which includes a reconciliation date, **re-perform reconciliation**
- **Verify** that **reconciliations have been prepared and reviewed** at **regular intervals** throughout the year
- **Scrutinise reconciliations** for **unusual items**

Auditors should also perform the substantive procedures on bank reconciliations detailed in Chapter 13.

Part C: Controls

2.24 The following procedures should be carried out on petty cash.

> - For a sample of payments:
>   - **Check** to supporting vouchers
>   - **Check** whether they are properly **approved**
>   - **See** that **vouchers** have been **marked and initialled** by the cashier to prevent their re-use
> - For a sample of weeks:
>   - **Trace amounts** received to **cash books**
>   - **Check additions** and **balances carried** forward
>   - **Check postings** to the **nominal ledger**

> **Exam alert**
>
> In the exam you may be asked to devise audit procedures for the particular purpose of testing security.

3 THE STOCK SYSTEM   *Pilot paper*

3.1 The stock system can be very important in an audit because of the high value of stock or the complexity of its audit. It is closely connected with the sales and purchases systems covered in Chapter 8.

Control objectives

3.2 The most important aims of internal control relating to stock are:

Feature	Aims
Recording	• All **stock movements** are **authorised** and **recorded** • **Stock records** only **include items** that **belong** to the client • **Stock records include stock** that **exists** and is **held** by the client • **Stock quantities** have been **recorded correctly** • **Cut-off procedures** are **properly applied** to stock
Protection of stock	• **Stock** is **safeguarded** against loss, pilferage or damage
Valuation of stock	• The **costing system values stock correctly** • **Allowance** is **made** for **slow-moving, obsolete** or **damaged stock**
Stock-holding	• **Levels** of **stocks held** are **reasonable**

Controls

3.3 Significant controls are as follows.

Recording of stock

- **Segregation** of duties; custody and recording of stocks
- **Reception, checking** and **recording** of goods inwards

- **Stock issues supported** by **appropriate documentation**
- **Maintenance** of **stock records**
    - Stock ledgers
    - Bin cards
    - Transfer records

Protection of stock

- **Precautions** against **theft, misuse** and **deterioration**
    - Restriction of access to stores
    - Controls on stores environment (right temperature, precautions against damp etc)
- **Security** over **stock** held by third parties, and third party stock held by entity
- **Stocktaking** (see also Chapter 11)
    - Regular stocktaking
    - Fair coverage so that all stock is counted at least once a year
    - Counts by independent persons
    - Recording
    - Cut-off for goods in transit and time differences
    - Reconciliation of stock count to book records and control accounts

Valuation of stock

- **Computation** of **stock valuation**
    - Accords with SSAP 9
    - Checking of calculations
- **Review** of **condition** of stock
    - Treatment of slow-moving, damaged and obsolete stock
    - Authorisation of write-offs
- **Accounting** for **scrap** and **waste**

Stockholding

- **Control** of **stock levels**
    - Maximum stock limits
    - Minimum stock limits
    - Re-order quantities and levels
- Arrangements for dealing with **returnable containers**

Tests of controls

3.4 Most of the testing relating to stock has been covered in the purchase and sales testing outlined in Chapter 8.

3.5 Auditors will primarily be concerned at this stage with ensuring that the business keeps track of stock. To confirm this, checks must be made on how stock movements are recorded and how stock is secured.

Part C: Controls

> - **Select** a sample of **stock movements records** and **agree** to **goods received** and goods **despatched notes**
> - **Confirm** that **movements** have been **authorised** as appropriate
> - **Select** a sample of **goods received** and **goods despatched** notes and agree to **stock movement records**
> - **Check sequence** of stock records
> - **Test** check **stock counts** carried out from time to time (eg monthly) during the period and confirm:
>   - **All discrepancies** between **book** and **actual** figures have been fully investigated
>   - **All discrepancies** have been **signed off** by a senior manager
>   - **Obsolete, damaged or slow-moving goods** have been **marked accordingly** and written down to net realisable value
> - **Observe security arrangements** for stocks
> - **Consider environment** in which stocks are held

3.6 Auditors will carry out extensive tests on the **valuation** of stock at the substantive testing stage (see Chapter 11).

Activity 9.1

Jonathan is the sole shareholder of Furry Lion Stores Ltd, a company which owns five stores in the west of England. The stores mainly stock food and groceries, and four of the stores have an off-licence as well.

Each store is run by a full-time manager and three or four part-time assistants. Jonathan spends on average ½ a day a week at each store, and spends the rest of his time at home, dealing with his other business interests.

All sales are for cash and are recorded on till rolls which the manager retains. Shop manager wages are paid monthly by cheque by Jonathan. Wages of shop assistants are paid in cash out of the takings.

Most purchases are made from local wholesalers and are paid for in cash out of the takings. Large purchases (over £250) must be made by cheques signed by the shop manager and countersigned by Jonathan.

Shop managers bank surplus cash once a week, apart from a float in the till.

All accounting records including the cash book, wages and VAT records are maintained by the manager. Jonathan reviews the weekly bank statements when he visits the shops. He also has a look at stocks to see if stock levels appear to be about right. All invoices are also kept in a drawer by a manager and marked with a cash book reference, and where appropriate a cheque number when paid.

Required

Discuss the weaknesses in the control systems of Furry Lion Ltd, and how the weaknesses can be remedied.

4 FIXED ASSETS   Pilot paper

4.1 These systems tend to be of lesser importance, although this depends on the nature of the business.

Control objectives

4.2 The most important aims of internal control relating to fixed assets are to ensure:

> - Fixed assets are **properly accounted** for and **recorded**
> - **Security arrangements** over fixed assets are sufficient
> - Fixed assets are **maintained properly**
> - Fixed asset **acquisitions are authorised**
> - Fixed asset **disposals are authorised** and proceeds of disposals are accounted for
> - **Depreciation rates are reasonable**
> - All **income is collected** from income-yielding fixed assets

Controls

4.3 Key controls are as follows.

- **Segregation** of **duties**; authorisation, custody and recording
- **Maintenance** of **accounting records** (including distinction between capital and revenue expenditure)

Security and maintenance

- **Maintenance** of plant and property **registers**
  - Agreement with general ledger
  - Inspection of assets recorded
- **Inspection** of fixed assets to ensure **properly maintained** and **used**

Acquisition and disposal

- **Authorisation** of capital expenditure
- **Authorisation** of **sales**, scrapping or transfer of fixed assets

Depreciation

- **Authorisation** of **depreciation rates**
- **Calculation** and **checking** of depreciation rates
  - Arithmetical check
  - Assessment of asset lives

Income from fixed assets

- **Identification** of income **producing assets**
  - Monitoring of income
  - Receipt of cash
- Adequate **insurance cover**

4.4 **Maintenance** of a **fixed asset register** is a key control. The register should contain details of all the company's **tangible fixed assets**. It is an important control over the **completeness of recording** and **safe custody** of those assets. To preserve **segregation of duties,** it should be maintained by someone who does not use, and is not responsible for the custody of, fixed assets.

4.5 The fixed asset register acts as a point of **comparison** against which the fixed assets that physically exist can be compared, and also the fixed asset accounts in the general ledger. It is of most use for assets that can easily be stolen.

Part C: Controls

4.6 Information that should be included within the register for individual assets includes the following.

- **Cost**
- **Additions** or **alterations** to the assets
- **Total depreciation** charged over the asset's life
- The **serial number** or other means of identification
- **Description** of the asset
- The **location** of the asset
- The **manufacturer** and **supplier**
- **Insurance** details
- **Maintenance** record

Tests of controls

4.7 A key concern of auditors will be proper controls over **movements** (acquisitions and disposals) during the year.

- For a sample of fixed asset purchases during the year in the general ledger:
  - **Check authorisation** (and board approval if necessary)
  - **Vouch purchase price** to invoice and cash book
  - Check asset has been **recorded** in the **fixed asset register**
  - Check **correct depreciation** rates applied
- For a sample of fixed asset disposals during the year:
  - **Check disposal authorised** by senior official
  - **Check invoice** issued for any proceeds
  - **Agree recording** of proceeds in the cash books
  - Check **asset** has been **removed** from fixed asset register
  - Check **calculations of profit** or loss on disposal

4.8 Auditors should also carry out some testing on **security, maintenance** and **recording** of fixed assets.

- For a sample of fixed assets from the fixed asset register:
  - **Check physical existence** of asset
  - **Ensure asset** in good condition
  - Consider whether asset **value** should be **written down**
- Check whether fixed asset register has been **reconciled to general ledger**.
- For a sample of fixed assets of all varieties:
  - **Agree existence** to fixed asset register
  - **Consider whether write down required**

Activity 9.2

Describe the main controls that a business should implement in order to ensure safe custody of:

(a) Stock
(b) Tangible fixed assets

5 MANAGEMENT INFORMATION

5.1 The **management information system** is an important aspect of the control environment, since timely and accurate information helps management supervise operations. There should be controls in place to ensure **budgets** are **regularly set,** and reports and information are provided **on time** to the specified degree of **accuracy** and **detail.**

5.2 As well as the **control** aspects, auditors will be concerned with the management information system's ability to provide useful data for analytical procedures.

5.3 Auditors will also be particularly concerned of course with the accounting records, with the procedures that ensure **transactions** are **completely posted**, and journal adjustments are authorised and backed up by **appropriate documentation**.

Management information procedures

5.4 Auditors will review the contents of **internal management accounting reports**, and check in particular that budgets are being **set** and that actual results are being **compared** with **budgeted figures.**

5.5 As well as procedures based on individual components of the accounting system, the auditor will also perform some general tests, including the following.

- **Test postings** from **books of prime entry** to the general ledger
- **Check** that the **general ledger** is regularly **balanced**
- **Test vouch** a sample of **journal entries** to **original documentation**

Key learning points

- Controls over cash receipts and payments should prevent fraud or theft.
- Key controls over **receipts** include:
  - Proper **post-opening** arrangements
  - **Prompt recording**
  - **Prompt banking**
  - **Reconciliation** of records of cash received and banked
- Key controls over **payments** include:
  - **Restriction of access** to cash and cheques
  - Procedures for **preparation and authorisation** of payments
- A further important control is **regular independent bank reconciliations.**
- **Stock controls** are designed to ensure safe custody. These include:
  - **Restriction of access** to stock
  - **Documentation** and **authorisation** of movements
- Other important controls over stock include regular **independent stock-taking** and **review of stock condition.**
- Important controls over **tangible fixed assets** include **physical custody** and authorisation of **purchases** and **disposals.**
- Tangible fixed assets should be recorded in a **fixed asset register**.
- Controls over investments should include maintenance of an **investment register** and **investment control account** and **custody** of documents of title.

Part C: Controls

Quick quiz

1. How frequently should cashiers bank money received?
2. What are the key controls over a system of cheque requisitions?
3. What are the most important controls over the signing of cheques?
4. What work should auditors carry out on bank reconciliations prepared by the client?
5. If the client has a system of regular stocktakes, what are the most important features this system should have?
6. What controls should businesses exercise over stock levels?
7. What tests would auditors normally carry out on controls over fixed asset purchases?

Answers to quick quiz

1. Cash receipts should ideally be banked every day.

2. The key controls over a system of cheque requisitions are as follows.

    (a) Requisitions should be supported by appropriate documentation.

    (b) Requisitions should be approved by appropriate staff, who should not be the same as the staff authorised to sign cheques.

    (c) Requisitions should be presented to the cheque signatories.

    (d) Once a cheque has been drawn, requisitions should be cancelled and marked with the cheque number.

3. The most important controls over the signing of cheques are as follows.

    (a) Signatories should not also approve cheque requisitions.
    (b) All cheques/cheques for larger amounts should be signed by more than one person.
    (c) Signatories should be restricted to signing cheques for a prescribed maximum amount.
    (d) Documentation supporting cheques should be cancelled once the cheque has been signed.
    (e) The signing of blank cheques should be prohibited.

4. Auditors should check whether:

    (a) Reconciliations have been prepared at regular intervals throughout the year.

    (b) Reconciliations have been prepared by staff other than those responsible for writing up the cash book.

    (c) Reconciliations have been reviewed by a second person.

    Auditors should also carry out more in-depth testing on the year-end reconciliation and perhaps others as well.

5. (a) The stocktakes should be carried out regularly.
    (b) All stock should be counted at least once a year.
    (c) Counts should be carried out by staff independent of the stock/stores function.
    (d) The results of the stocktakes should be properly recorded, and take account of goods in transit.
    (e) The results of the stocktakes should be reconciled to book stock records.

6. Clients should set maximum and minimum stock levels, also stock levels at which stock should be ordered and the normal re-order quantities.

7. Auditors should normally check that:

    (a) Fixed asset purchases have been authorised.
    (b) The purchase price can be confirmed to supporting documentation.
    (c) The asset has been recorded in the cash book and fixed asset register.
    (d) An appropriate depreciation rate has been chosen and has been applied correctly to the asset.

Answers to activities

Answer 9.1

Weaknesses in the system, and their remedies are as follows.

Stock

The shops do not appear to have any stock movement records. This would appear to breach the Companies Act s 221 requirement for the company to maintain proper accounting records. Jonathan has also only a very approximate indication of stock levels. Hence it will be difficult to detect whether stock levels are too high, or too low with a risk of running out of stock. Theft of stock would also be difficult to detect. The company should therefore introduce stock movement records, detailing values and volumes.

In addition regular stock counts should be made either by Jonathan or by staff from another shop. Discrepancies between the stock records and the actual stock counted should be investigated.

Cash controls

Too much cash appears to be held on site. In addition the fact that most payments appear to be for cash may mean inadequate documentation is kept. The level of cash on site can be decreased by daily rather than weekly bankings. In addition the need for cash on site can be decreased by paying wages by cheque, and by paying all but the smallest payments by cheque.

The cash book should obviously still be maintained but cheque stubs should also show details of amounts paid. The cash book should be supported by invoices and other supporting documentation, and should be cross-referenced to the general ledger (see below).

Cash reconciliations

There is no indication of the till-rolls that are kept being reconciled to cash takings.

There should be a daily reconciliation of cash takings and till rolls; this should be reviewed if not performed by the shop manager.

Bank reconciliations

There is no mention of bank reconciliations taking place.

Bank reconciliations should be carried out at least monthly by the shop manager, and reviewed by the owner.

Purchases

There is no formal system for recording purchases. Invoices do not appear to be filed in any particular way. It would be difficult to see whether accounting records were complete, and hence it would be difficult to prepare a set of accounts from the accounting records available.

In addition the way records are maintained means that accounts would have to be prepared on a cash basis, and not on an accruals basis, as required by the Companies Act.

A purchase day book should be introduced. Invoices should be recorded in the purchase day book, and filed in a logical order, either by date received or by supplier.

General ledger

There is no general ledger, and again this means that annual accounts cannot easily be prepared (and also management accounts).

A general ledger should be maintained with entries made from the cash book, wages records and purchase day book. This will enable accounts to be prepared on an accruals basis.

Supervision

Jonathan does not take a very active part in the business, only signing cheques over £250, and visiting the shops only half a day each week. This may mean that assets can easily go missing, and Jonathan cannot readily see whether the business is performing as he would wish.

Jonathan should review wage/VAT/cash book reconciliations. Management accounts should also be prepared by shop managers for Jonathan.

Tutorial note. This question deals with controls that are possible given the circumstances of the business. Greater segregation of duties does not appear to be possible as the shops are small, and Jonathan cannot spend more time at the shops (although he can use his time more productively by reviewing reconciliations).

Part C: Controls

Answer 9.2

(a) The most important controls over the safe custody of stock are as follows.

   (i) **Physical**

   Access to the stock-rooms should be restricted to authorised staff. Outside working hours, the stock area should be locked.

   (ii) **Segregation of duties**

   Stock movements should be recorded by different staff from those responsible for ensuring the safe custody of stocks.

   (iii) **Stock records**

   Appropriate documentation should be maintained including stores ledger accounts giving details of movements, quantities held and pricing of stock lines, bin cards giving details of movements and quantities held, and materials requisitions and return notes.

   (iv) **Controls over movements**

   (1) Stock being delivered should be logged in by goods received notes and goods inwards records, which should be reconciled with supplier delivery notes and purchase orders.

   (2) All internal movements of stock should be authorised.

   (3) Stock should only be despatched if a sales order has been received, and should only be despatched to authorised customers. Stock despatches should be recorded on despatch notes and in goods outwards records, and these should subsequently be reconciled to sales order and invoices.

   (v) **Stocktakes**

   Regular stock-takes should be carried out by someone who is independent of the stores department. All stock should be counted at least once a year. Stock counted should be compared with stock records, and differences investigated.

(b) The most important controls over the custody of tangible fixed assets are as follows.

   (i) **Physical**

   As with stock, fixed assets, particularly portable ones should be locked away when not in use or outside business hours. Companies may also mark fixed assets with identification codes.

   (ii) **Segregation of duties**

   There should be segregation of duties between the people responsible for authorising fixed assets purchases and disposals, those responsible for custody and those responsible for recording fixed assets.

   (iii) **Fixed asset register**

   Fixed assets held should be recorded in a fixed asset register, maintained separately from the company's general ledger and cash systems.

   (iv) **Purchases and disposals**

   All fixed asset purchases, disposals and scrappings should be authorised by staff of appropriate seniority. Major purchases and disposals should be authorised by the board.

   (v) **Reconciliations**

   The fixed asset register should be reconciled to the general ledger on a regular basis by someone other than the staff member who maintains the fixed asset register. There should also be comparisons made by independent staff to check if fixed assets recorded in the fixed asset register are actually held, and to check that assets held are recorded in the fixed asset register.

Now try Question 9 in the Exam Question Bank

Part D
Substantive procedures

Chapter 10 Analytical procedures and estimates

Chapter topic list

1   Introduction
2   Analytical procedures
3   Accounting estimates

The following study session is covered in this Chapter:

Syllabus reference

22(c)   Describe and give examples of procedures used by auditors to obtain audit evidence, including the use of analytical procedures   6

Part D: Substantive procedures

1 INTRODUCTION

1.1 Having looked at tests of controls in detail, we now move on to **substantive procedures**. In Chapters 11-14 we shall consider substantive testing in each of the major audit areas. In this chapter however we consider two general auditing issues that affect substantive procedures generally, analytical procedures (also referred to as analytical review) review and the audit of estimates.

1.2 **Analytical procedures** impact upon the whole audit process. We mentioned briefly in Chapter 6 that auditors are required to carry out analytical procedures when **planning** an audit as part of the risk assessment process; this chapter goes into more detail. We then go on to discuss how substantive analytical procedures can provide **audit evidence**. Lastly analytical procedures are required at the final stage of the audit, as a key part of the **overall review** of the final accounts. The purpose of analytical procedures at this stage is to answer the question 'Do the figures make sense?'

1.3 In the second part of this chapter we examine **accounting estimates**. We have mentioned in previous chapters that judgement has to be used in accounting for several figures in the accounts. Often these judgements depend on uncertain future events - what percentage of outstanding receivables will fail to pay their debts, or for how much will inventory which has been in the warehouse eventually sell.

1.4 Since there may be a range of plausible answers to questions such as these, estimates can cause problems for auditors. We shall see that there are a number of possible ways in which estimates can be tested, and auditors will often wish to use a combination of procedures to obtain the required assurance.

2 ANALYTICAL PROCEDURES   Pilot paper

> **KEY TERM**
>
> **Analytical procedures** consist of evaluations of financial information made by a study of plausible relationships among both financial and non-financial data. Analytical procedures also encompass the investigation of identified fluctuations and relationships that are inconsistent with other relevant information or deviate significantly from predicted amounts.

> **ISA 520.2**
>
> The auditor should apply analytical procedures as risk assessment procedures to obtain an understanding of the entity and its environment and in the overall review at the end of the audit.

2.1 In addition to the uses of analytical procedures above, they may also be used as substantive procedures, to obtain audit evidence directly.

10: Analytical procedures and estimates

Nature and purpose of analytical procedures

2.2 ISA 520 *Analytical procedures* states that analytical procedures include:

(a) The consideration of comparisons with:

(i) **Similar information** for prior periods

(ii) **Anticipated results** of the entity, from budgets or forecasts

(iii) **Predictions** prepared by the auditors

(iv) **Industry information,** such as a comparison of the client's ratio of sales to trade debtors with industry averages, or with the ratios relating to other entities of comparable size in the same industry.

(b) Those between elements of financial information that are expected to conform to a predicted pattern based on the entity's experience, such as the relationship of gross profit to sales.

(c) Those between financial information and relevant non-financial information, such as the relationship of payroll costs to number of employees.

2.3 A variety of methods can be used to perform the procedures discussed above, ranging from **simple comparisons** to **complex analysis** using statistics, on a company level, branch level or individual account level. The choice of procedures is a matter for the auditors' professional judgement.

Analytical procedures as risk assessment procedures

> **ISA 520.8**
>
> Auditors should apply analytical procedures as risk assessment procedures to obtain an understanding of the entity and its environment.

2.4 Possible sources of information about the client include:

- Interim financial information
- Budgets
- Management accounts
- Non-financial information
- Bank and cash records
- VAT returns
- Board minutes
- Discussions or correspondence with the client at the year-end

Auditors may also use specific industry information or general knowledge of current industry conditions to assess the client's performance.

2.5 As well as helping to determine the nature, timing and extent of other audit procedures, such analytical procedures may also indicate aspects of the business of which the auditors were previously unaware. Auditors are looking to see if developments in the client's business have had the expected effects. They will be particularly interested in changes in audit areas where problems have occurred in the past.

Part D: Substantive procedures

Analytical procedures as substantive procedures

2.6 ISA 520 *Analytical procedures* states that auditors must decide whether using available analytical procedures as substantive procedures will be effective and efficient in **reducing the assessed risk of material** misstatement at the assertion level to an acceptably low level. Auditors may efficiently use analytical data produced by the entity itself, provided they are satisfied that it has been properly prepared.

2.7 The ISA lists a number of factors which the auditors should consider when using analytical procedures as substantive procedures.

Factors to consider	Explanation
The **suitability** of using substantive analytical procedures given the assertions.	Substantive analytical procedures are generally more applicable to large volumes of transactions that tend to be predictable over time.
The **reliability** of the data, whether internal or external, from which the expectation of recorded amounts or ratios is developed.	Source: information is more reliable when it is obtained from independent sources outside the entity.
	Comparability: broad industry data may need to be supplemented to be comparable to that of an entity that produces and sells specialised products.
	Nature and relevance: whether budgets have been established as results to be expected rather than as goals to be achieved.
	Controls over preparation: eg review and maintenance of budgets. (The auditor may consider testing these).
Prior year knowledge and understanding	Eg knowledge gained during previous audits.
Whether the information is produced **internally**	If information is produced internally its reliability is enhanced if it is produced independently of the accounting system or there are adequate controls over its preparation.
Whether the expectation is **sufficiently precise** to identify a material misstatement at the desired level of assurance.	Accuracy with which results can be predicted: the auditor would expect greater consistency in comparing gross profit margins than in comparing research or advertising.
	Degree to which information can be disaggregated: substantive analytical procedures may be more effective when applied to financial information on individual sections of an operation.
	Availability of information: financial (budgets or forecasts) Non-financial (eg the number of units produced or sold).
	The frequency with which a relationship is observed, eg monthly/annually.

10: Analytical procedures and estimates

Factors to consider	Explanation
The amount of any **difference** of recorded amounts from expected values that is acceptable.	The auditor considers the amount of difference from expectation that can be accepted without further investigation. This is affected by risk and materiality assessments.
	The auditor also needs to consider: the assessment of the risk of material misstatement – where controls are weak the auditor may place more reliance on tests of details.

2.8 Auditors will need to consider testing the controls, if any, over the **preparation** of **information** used in applying analytical procedures. When such controls are effective, the auditors will have greater confidence in the reliability of the information, and therefore in the results of analytical procedures.

2.9 The **controls** over **non-financial information** can often be tested in conjunction with tests of **accounting-related controls**. For example, in establishing controls over the processing of sales invoices, a business may include controls over unit sales recording. In these circumstances the auditors could test the controls over the recording of unit sales in conjunction with tests of the controls over the processing of sales invoices.

2.10 Reliance on the results of analytical procedures depends on the auditors' assessment of the **risk** that the procedures may identify relationships (between data) as expected, whereas a material misstatement exists (ie the relationships, in fact, do not exist).

Analytical procedures as part of the overall review

> **ISA 520.13**
>
> The auditor should apply analytical procedures at or near the end of the audit when forming an overall conclusion as to whether the financial statements as a whole are consistent with the auditor's understanding of the entity.

2.11 The conclusions from these analytical procedures should corroborate the conclusions formed from other audit procedures on parts of the financial statements. However, these analytical procedures may highlight areas which require further investigation and audit.

Investigating significant fluctuations or unexpected relationships

> **ISA 520.17**
>
> When analytical procedures identify significant fluctuations or relationships that are inconsistent with other relevant information or that deviate from predicted patterns, the auditor should investigate and obtain adequate explanations and appropriate corroborative audit evidence.

2.12 Investigations will start with **enquires** to management and then corroboration of management's responses:

(a) By **comparing** them with the auditors' understanding of the entity's business and with other audit evidence obtained during the course of the audit

Part D: Substantive procedures

(b) If the analytical procedures are being carried out as substantive procedures, by **undertaking additional audit procedures** where appropriate to confirm the explanations received

2.13 If explanations cannot be given by management, or if they are insufficient, the auditors must determine which further audit procedures to undertake to explain the fluctuation or relationship.

Practical techniques

2.14 When carrying out analytical procedures, auditors should remember that every industry is different and each company within an industry differs in certain respects.

Important accounting ratios	
	Gross profit margin = $\dfrac{\text{Gross profit}}{\text{Turnover}} \times 100\%$
	This should be calculated in total and by product, area and month/quarter if possible.
	Debtors turnover period = $\dfrac{\text{Debtors}}{\text{Sales}} \times 365$
	Stock turnover ratio = $\dfrac{\text{Cost of sales}}{\text{Stock}}$
	Current ratio = $\dfrac{\text{Current assets}}{\text{Current liabilities}}$
	Quick or acid test ratio = $\dfrac{\text{Current assets (excluding stock)}}{\text{Current liabilities}}$
	Gearing ratio = $\dfrac{\text{Loans}}{\text{Share capital and reserves}} \times 100\%$
	Return on capital employed = $\dfrac{\text{Profit before tax}}{\text{Total assets - current liabilities}}$
Significant items	Creditors and purchases
	Stocks and cost of sales
	Fixed assets and depreciation, repairs and maintenance expense
	Intangible assets and amortisation
	Loans and interest expense
	Investments and investment income
	Debtors and bad debt expense
	Debtors and sales

2.15 Ratios mean very little when used in isolation. They should be **calculated** for **previous periods** and for **comparable companies**. The permanent file should contain a section with summarised accounts and the chosen ratios for prior years.

2.16 In addition to looking at the more usual ratios the auditors should consider examining **other ratios** that may be **relevant** to the particular **clients' business**, such as revenue per passenger mile for an airline operator client, or fees per partner for a professional office.

10: Analytical procedures and estimates

2.17 One further important technique is to examine **important related accounts** in conjunction with each other. It is often the case that revenue and expense accounts are related to balance sheet accounts and comparisons should be made to ensure that the relationships are reasonable.

2.18 Other areas that might be investigated as part of the analytical procedures include the following.

> - Examine changes in products, customers and levels of returns
> - **Assess** the effect of **price and mix changes** on the cost of sales
> - **Consider** the effect of **inflation, industrial disputes, changes in production methods** and **changes in activity** on the charge for wages
> - **Obtain explanations** for all **major variances** analysed using a standard costing system. Particular attention should be paid to those relating to the over or under absorption of overheads since these may, inter alia, affect inventory valuations
> - **Compare trends in production and sales** and assess the effect on any provisions for obsolete inventories
> - **Ensure** that **changes in the percentage labour or overhead content** of production costs are also reflected in the inventory valuation
> - **Review other profit and loss expenditure,** comparing:
>   - Rent with annual rent per rental agreement
>   - Rates with previous year and known rates increases
>   - Interest payable on loans with outstanding balance and interest rate per loan agreement
>   - Hire or leasing charges with annual rate per agreements
>   - Vehicle running expenses to vehicles
>   - Other items related to activity level with general price increase and change in relevant level of activity (for example telephone expenditure will increase disproportionately if export or import business increases)
>   - Other items not related to activity level with general price increases (or specific increases if known)
> - **Review** income statement for **items** which may have been **omitted** (eg scrap sales, training levy, special contributions to pension fund, provisions for dilapidation etc)
> - **Ensure expected variations** arising from the following have occurred:
>   - Industry or local trends
>   - Known disturbances of the trading pattern (for example strikes, depot closures, failure of suppliers)

2.19 Certain of the comparisons and ratios measuring liquidity and longer-term capital structure will assist in evaluating whether the company is a **going concern**, in addition to contributing to the overall view of the accounts. We shall see in Chapter 15, however, that there are factors other than declining ratios that may indicate going concern problems.

Part D: Substantive procedures

2.20 The working papers must contain the completed results of analytical procedures. They should include:

- The **outline programme** of the work
- The **summary of significant figures** and relationships for the period
- A **summary** of **comparisons made** with budgets and with previous years
- Details of all **significant fluctuations** or **unexpected relationships** considered
- Details of the **results of investigations** into such fluctuations/relationships
- The **audit conclusions** reached
- **Information considered necessary** for assisting in the planning of subsequent audits

2.21 EXAMPLE

Brown Limited

EXTRACT DRAFT FIGURES
FOR YEAR ENDED 30 SEPTEMBER 2004

	£
Turnover	6,408,279
Gross profit	2,412,797
Profit before tax	527,112
Fixed assets	308,947
Stock	1,247,487
Debtors	1,491,498
Trade creditors	998,123
Other current liabilities (incl. bank)	107,501

Jo Price can use this information during her planning process. She has calculated the following ratios.

Ratio	Calculation	Result
Gross profit margin	$\dfrac{2{,}412{,}797}{6{,}408{,}279} \times 100 =$	37.65%
Debtors' turnover period	$\dfrac{1{,}247{,}487}{6{,}408{,}279} \times 365 =$	71 days
Stock turnover ratio	$\dfrac{6{,}408{,}279 - 2{,}412{,}797}{1{,}247{,}487} =$	3.2 times
Current ratio	$\dfrac{1{,}247{,}487 + 1{,}491{,}498}{998{,}123 + 107{,}501} =$	2.47
Acid test ratio	$\dfrac{1{,}491{,}498}{998{,}123 + 107{,}501} =$	1.35
Return on capital employed	$\dfrac{527{,}112}{(308{,}947 + 1{,}247{,}487 + 1{,}491{,}498) - (998{,}123 + 107{,}501)} =$	26.6

However, this information is only of limited use to her in isolation. She should refer to previous audit files to compare these ratios to last years'.

For instance, if she discovered that last year, turnover was £7,794,301, she should discuss this drop in turnover of £1,386,022 with the client. It could indicate several things.

- That the company has had a bad year in 2004, with potential impact on going concern
- that the company had an amazing year in 2003, and 2004 is more representative of what the company expected
- A major customer has been lost
- There have been errors in recording sales

Jo should carry out further analysis to assess any explanations given to her by the client. For instance, if gross profit percentage and debtor days are similar to last year, that might indicate that there was not an error in sales recording.

As sales appear to require further work, Jo could plan to carry out a more detailed substantive analytical review on the sales figure, by obtaining detailed analysis of sales by month and by product to see if this reveals any more answers abut why the sales figure has dropped in 2004.

> **Exam alert**
>
> When analysing figures, make sure that the points which you make are consistent with each other.
>
> The examiner has stated that analytical procedures are an important means of gathering audit evidence. On a practical note, remember to take calculator to the exam in case of a question like this.

Activity 10.1

(a) What are the purposes of analytical procedures?
(b) At what stages of the audit should and can analytical procedures be carried out?

Activity 10.2

The following information has been provided to you in advance of the finalisation of the audit for the year to 30 June 20X7 of Moony plc, a large sports goods and sportswear manufacturer.

PROFIT AND LOSS ACCOUNTS

	20X7	20X6
	£'000	£'000
Turnover	62,200	51,000
Cost of sales	46,000	35,800
	16,200	15,200
Distribution costs*	6,650	6,500
Administration expenses*	4,400	4,350
	11,050	10,850
Trading profit	5,150	4,350
Interest paid	1,800	850
Profit before taxation	3,350	3,500
*Note. Depreciation included as part of these figures	4,950	4,400

Part D: Substantive procedures

BALANCE SHEETS

	20X7 £'000	20X6 £'000
Fixed assets	50,350	50,100
Current assets		
Stock	10,800	8,650
Debtors	9,150	5,200
	19,950	13,850
Current liabilities		
Trade creditors	5,750	5,400
Other creditors	1,200	1,000
Bank overdraft	3,600	2,050
	10,550	8,450
Net current assets	9,400	5,400
Total assets less current liabilities	59,750	55,500
Long-term loan (repayable 20X9)	15,600	12,800
	44,150	42,700
Share capital	5,000	5,000
Reserves	39,150	37,700
	44,150	42,700

Required

(a) Identify five matters which you consider require special attention when auditing the accounts of Moony plc.

(b) For each of these state why you consider them to be of importance.

---

3 ACCOUNTING ESTIMATES

3.1 ISA 540 *Audit of accounting estimates* provides guidance on the audit of accounting estimates contained in financial statements.

> **ISA 540.2**
> Auditors should obtain sufficient appropriate audit evidence regarding accounting estimates

> **KEY TERM**
> An **accounting estimate** is an approximation of the amount of an item in the absence of a precise means of measurement.

3.2 ISA 540 gives these examples.

- Allowances to reduce inventories and receivables to their estimated realisable value
- Provisions to allocate the cost of long-term assets over their estimated useful lives
- Accrued revenue
- Provision for a loss from a lawsuit
- Losses on construction contracts in progress
- Provision to meet warranty claims

3.3 **Directors and management** are responsible for making accounting estimates included in the financial statements. These estimates are often made in conditions of uncertainty regarding the outcome of events and involve the use of judgement. The risk of a material misstatement therefore increases when accounting estimates are involved. **Audit evidence** supporting accounting estimates is **generally less than conclusive** and so auditors need to exercise greater judgement than in other areas of an audit.

The nature of accounting estimates

3.4 Accounting estimates may be produced as part of the routine operations of the information system, or may be a non-routine procedure at the period end. Where, as is frequently the case, a **formula** based on past experience is used to calculate the estimate, it should be reviewed regularly by management (eg actual vs estimate in prior periods).

3.5 If there is no objective data to assess the item, or if it is surrounded by uncertainty, the auditors should consider the implications for their report.

Audit procedures responsive to the risk of material misstatement

> **ISA 540.8**
>
> Auditors should design and perform further audit procedures to obtain sufficient appropriate evidence as to whether the entity's accounting estimates are reasonable in the circumstances and, when required, appropriately disclosed.

3.6 Auditors should gain an understanding of the procedures and methods used by management to make accounting estimates. This will aid the auditors in identifying and assessing the risks of material misstatement and in designing the nature, timing and extent of further audit procedures.

> **ISA 540.10**
>
> The auditor should adopt one or a combination of the following approaches in the audit of an accounting estimate:
> (a) review and test the process used by management or the directors to develop the estimate;
> (b) use an independent estimate for comparison with that prepared by management or the directors; or
> (c) review of subsequent events which provide audit evidence of the reasonableness of the estimate made.

Review and testing the process

3.7 The auditors will carry out the following steps.

- **Consider whether data** is **accurate, complete and reliable**
- **Seek appropriate evidence from outside client** (eg industry sales projections to confirm internal estimates of future sales orders)
- **Check** whether **data is appropriately analysed** and **projected** (eg age analysis of accounts receivable)
- **Evaluate** whether **base used** for assumptions is **appropriate**

Part D: Substantive procedures

- **Evaluate** whether **assumptions** are **reasonable** in light of **prior period results**
- **Consider** whether **formulae** used remain **appropriate**
- Consider whether **assumptions** are **consistent**
    - With those used for other accounting estimates
    - With management's plans
- **Consider** whether **expert opinion** is required if estimates are complex
- **Test calculations** involved in the estimate considering:
    - Complexity of calculation
    - Procedures and methods used by the client
    - Materiality of estimate
- **Compare previous estimates** with actual results, aiming to obtain evidence about:
    - General reliability of the client's estimating procedures
    - Whether adjustments to estimating formulae will be required
    - Whether differences between previous estimates and actual figures ought to be disclosed
- Consider management's approval procedures, confirming it is performed by the **appropriate level of management** and **evidenced**

Use of an independent estimate

3.8 The auditors may seek evidence from sources outside the entity. Such an estimate (made or obtained by the auditors) may be compared with the accounting estimate. The auditors should evaluate the data, consider the assumptions and test the calculation procedures used to develop the independent estimate. Prior period independent assessments and actual results could also be compared.

Review of subsequent events

3.9 The auditors should review transactions or events after the period end which may reduce or even remove the need to test accounting estimates (as described above).

Evaluation of results of audit procedures

> **ISA 540.24**
>
> The auditor should make a final assessment of the reasonableness of the entity's accounting estimates based on the auditor's understanding of the entity and its environment and whether the estimates are consistent with other audit evidence obtained during the audit.

3.10 Auditors must assess the differences between the amount of an estimate supported by evidence and the estimate calculated by management. If the auditors believe that the difference is unreasonable then an adjustment should be made. If the directors or management refuse to revise the estimate, then the difference is considered a misstatement and will be treated as such.

3.11 EXAMPLE

Jo has identified a provision of £40,000 in the accounts. She has been informed that this is a provision for damages likely to result from litigation pending against Brown Ltd by a customer for breach of contract.

In her audit of this balance Jo would need to consider the following:

- Whether the amount is material. This will determine the extent of the audit procedures. Based on a profit before tax figure of £527,112 the provision is approximately 7.5% of this. It is therefore likely to be material.

- Whether the treatment complies with FRS 12. Recognition will depend upon the assessment of the outcome. If it is likely that Brown Ltd will lose the case the provision should be recognised. Jo will need to asses the assumptions on which this decision has been based. This may involve reviewing legal advice provided and by considering the outcome of any similar situations encountered in the past.

- The amount of the provision. Here Jo may need to consider advice provided by the company's legal team and will need to review correspondence between them and Brown Ltd.

- The possibility of mitigating factors. Brown Ltd may have recourse to others depending on the nature of the issue.

- The possibility that this problem has affected other contracts which also require provisions.

Jo would also look for the following audit evidence.

- The contract with the customer to determine the nature of the breach and the consequences.

- Documentation produced by the legal advisers and any correspondence with the customer to assess the likely outcome.

- Discussion with management to assess the basis of the assumptions. These discussions should be documented and key points should be corroborated where possible.

- Previous years' working papers on similar matters to establish management's ability to asses this type of situation.

- A review of events after the balance sheet date to establish whether the claim has been settled subsequently.

- A review of other major customer contracts to establish whether there is the possibility of other similar breaches.

- Discussions (documented) with management regarding the possible existence of other breaches.

- Management representations confirming that all contingencies have been disclosed.

Part D: Substantive procedures

Key learning points

- **Analytical procedures** cover comparisons of financial data with other financial or non-financial data of the same or previous periods, also comparisons of financial data with expected data.
- Analytical procedures aim to **identify inconsistencies** or **significant fluctuations**.
- Analytical procedures **must** be undertaken as part of the **risk assessment** stage of audits.
- Analytical procedures can be used as substantive procedures, depending on the **available information** and the plausibility and predictability of the relationships.
- Analytical procedures **must** be undertaken at the **final stage** of an audit on the final accounts.
- **Significant fluctuations** and **unexpected variations** should be investigated by enquiries of management, comparisons with other evidence and further audit procedures as required.
- Accounts may contain **accounting estimates** in a number of areas.
- Auditors can test accounting estimates by:
    - **Reviewing** and **testing** the management process
    - **Using an independent estimate**
    - **Reviewing subsequent events**

Quick quiz

1. Give four examples of information that can be compared with this year's financial information.
2. Give four examples of sources of information for analytical procedures at the risk assessment stage.
3. What factors determine the reliance that auditors can place on analytical procedures?
4. What are:
    - (a) The current ratio
    - (b) The acid test ratio
    - (c) The return on capital employed
5. (a) What is an accounting estimate?
   (b) Give three examples of an accounting estimate.
6. When auditors are testing the process that management use to arrive at estimates what procedures should they undertake?

Answers to quick quiz

1. Examples include:
    - (a) Comparable information for prior periods
    - (b) Anticipated results
    - (c) Predictive estimates
    - (d) Industry information

2. Examples include:
    - (a) Interim financial information
    - (b) Budgets
    - (c) Management accounts
    - (d) Non-financial information
    - (e) Bank and cash records
    - (f) VAT returns
    - (g) Board minutes
    - (h) Discussions or correspondence with the client at the year end

3. The reliance auditors can place on substantive analytical procedures is determined by:
    - (a) The materiality of the item involved
    - (b) Other audit procedures directed towards the same assertions
    - (c) The accuracy with which results can be predicted
    - (d) The frequency with which a relationship is observed
    - (e) Assessment of inherent and control risk

4 (a) Current ratio = $\dfrac{\text{Current assets}}{\text{Current liabilities}}$

    (b) Acid test ratio = $\dfrac{\text{Current assets (excluding stock)}}{\text{Current liabilities}}$

    (c) Return on capital employed = $\dfrac{\text{Profit before tax}}{\text{Total assets less current liabilities}}$

5 (a) An accounting estimate is an approximation of the amount of an item in the absence of a precise means of measurement.

    (b) Examples of accounting estimates include:

        (i)   Allowances against stock and debtors
        (ii)   Depreciation allowances
        (iii) Accrued revenue
        (iv) Allowance for loss from a lawsuit
        (v)   Profits or losses on construction contracts in progress
        (vi) Allowance to meet warranty claims

6 When testing the management process, auditors should:

- Consider whether data is accurate, complete and reliable
- Seek appropriate evidence from outside client (eg industry sales projections to confirm internal estimates of future sales orders)
- Check whether data is appropriately analysed and projected (eg age analysis of accounts receivable)
- Evaluate whether base used for assumptions is appropriate
- Evaluate whether assumptions are reasonable in light of prior period results
- Consider whether formulae used remain appropriate
- Consider whether assumptions are consistent
    - With those used for other accounting estimates
    - With management's plans
- Consider whether expert opinion is required if estimates are complex
- Test calculations involved in the estimate considering:
    - Complexity of calculation
    - Procedures and methods used by the client
    - Materiality of estimate
- Compare previous estimates with actual results, aiming to obtain evidence about:
    - General reliability of the client's estimating procedures
    - Whether adjustments to estimating formulae will be required
    - Whether differences between previous estimates and actual figures ought to be disclosed
- Consider management's approval procedures, confirming it is performed by the appropriate level of management and evidenced

Answers to activities

Answer 10.1

(a) Analytical procedures are used to identify relationships between financial data or between financial and non-financial data. Their purpose is to identify consistencies and patterns, or significant fluctuations and unexpected relationships. They assist in increasing auditors' understanding of a business and can be used to aid audit efficiency by highlighting risk areas and providing an alternative means of audit assurance to extensive tests of details.

Part D: Substantive procedures

(b) Analytical procedures are used:

(i) At the planning stage as part of the risk assessment of an audit, to ascertain which areas of the accounts require particular attention

(ii) As a substantive procedure, to provide evidence for the various financial statement assertions

(iii) As part of the final review of the accounts, to see if the accounts are consistent with the auditors' knowledge of the business

Answer 10.2

(a) The matters which require special attention include (any five of) the following.

    (i) The increase in turnover by 22%
    (ii) The fall in gross profit percentage from 29.8% to 26.0%
    (iii) The 18% increase in trading profit
    (iv) The reason why profit before taxation has fallen despite increased turnover
    (v) Fixed asset additions/revaluation amounting to a minimum £5.2 million
    (vi) The 25% increase in stock
    (vii) The increase in debtor days from 37 days to 54 days
    (viii) The 76% increase in bank overdraft
    (ix) The £2.8 million increase in long-term loan

(b) Each of the matters is important for the following reasons.

    (i) Turnover might be overstated as the result of including post year end sales. The same error could have understated stocks. Analysing sales on a monthly basis might reveal inconsistencies, for example unusually high sales in June 20X7 and unusually low sales in July 20X7.

    (ii) The gross profit percentage may have fallen due to changed trading conditions such as increased supplier prices, or a change in the company's pricing policy to boost turnover. There may however have been errors which have misstated purchases or stock.

    (iii) The increase in trading profits suggests that distribution costs or administrative expenses may be incorrect. Distribution costs have only increased by 3% while turnover has increased by 22%. Normally, distribution costs would be expected to increase in line with turnover.

    (iv) Profit before taxation is affected by the further figure of interest paid. Interest paid could be over- or under-stated. Understatement could result from failing to accrue for all interest payable up to the year end.

    (v) All additions should be checked to ensure that cost has been correctly recorded, and that the additions have been authorised. If revaluations of fixed assets have taken place, it is important to check that the revaluations are reasonable.

    (vi) A misstatement in the stock valuation has a direct effect on profit. The large increase in stock could indicate overvaluation of stocks held. Increased stock levels alternatively suggest that there may be significant quantities of stock which cannot be sold (for example obsolete stock).

    (vii) The rise in debtor days could indicate possible bad debts for which provision should be made. However, it will be more useful if debtor days were calculated using monthly sales figures: it may be that much of the increased turnover for 20X6/7 occurred in the final months of the year, in which case the debtors' collection position may not be as bad as our figures suggest.

    (viii) The bank overdraft may have increased because of cash flow problems brought about by excessive purchases of stock or failure to collect money from debtors.

    (ix) The reasons for the increase in the loan should be ascertained. It may be due to increased investment in fixed assets, but it may be of concern if it has resulted from cash flow problems mentioned in (viii).

Now try Question 10 in the Exam Question Bank

Chapter 11 Stocks and work in progress

Chapter topic list

1. Introduction
2. Accounting for stock
3. The stocktake
4. Stock cut-off
5. Valuation of stock

The following study sessions are covered in this Chapter:

Syllabus reference

26(a)	Explain why the audit of stock is often an area of high audit risk	6
26(b)	Describe the procedures that should be undertaken before, during and after attending a stocktake	6
26(c)	Discuss the extent to which an auditor can rely on a system of continuous stocktaking	6
26(d)	Design an audit programme to meet specific audit objectives for the audit of stock	6
23(b)	For each area in the financial statements of an incorporated company, provide examples of the representations made by directors	6

Part D: Substantive procedures

1 INTRODUCTION

1.1 **Stock causes more problems for auditors than any other audit area.** As you will know from your accounting studies, closing stock appears on both the profit and loss account and balance sheet and often has a material effect on both.

1.2 However stock does **not** form part of the double entry; hence it is not possible to find errors in stock as a result of finding errors in other areas. Stock errors can arise for a number of reasons.

1.3 Verifying the **existence** and **completeness** of stock can cause problems. Stock often is very portable and hence easy to steal. Companies face problems controlling stock because stock is often held in a number of different locations or is held by third parties.

1.4 Another very difficult aspect of stock is **stock valuation** for the following reasons:

   (a) If a company sells a large number of different products, then stock will be made up of a large number of diverse items with different unit values.

   (b) Different stock valuation methods are allowed under by the Companies Act and by SSAP 9 *Stocks and long term contracts* although they must be applied consistently.

   (c) Stock does get damaged; other stock may be difficult to sell because fashions change or technology has moved on. The Companies Act requires stock to be written down to its ultimate selling price if that price is below the cost of the stock. However identifying stock the value of which has fallen is a subjective process and can prove difficult.

   (d) Valuing work in progress can also be difficult. Its valuation depends on the state of completion it has reached; this may be quite difficult to gauge.

   (e) For both stock and work in progress, valuation will include overheads, production overheads and other overheads attributable to bringing the product or service to its present location or condition. Which overheads constitute overheads attributable is again a subjective decision.

1.5 How should auditors view stock? They must understand how stock is **accounted for** and thus we summarise the relevant provisions of the Companies Act and SSAP 9.

1.6 The central audit procedure in auditing stock is **attending the stocktake.** Most companies count their stock at the year-end and auditors should aim to attend the stocktake. The reason for this is that the stocktake can provide evidence for a significant number of assertions, including completeness, existence, ownership and valuation (by observing the condition of stock).

1.7 Much audit time after the stocktake will be taken up checking the **valuation** of stock. This has several aspects. Partly it involves checking costs to invoices, and it also involves review of the absorption of overheads. Auditors may also have gained at the stocktake a view of what stock was old or in poor condition, and will follow this up by reviewing post year end sales. General analytical procedures on stock are also important.

Exam alert

Perhaps the most important thing to remember about stock is that there is nearly always a question about it in auditing exams. You **must** know the procedures involved before, during and after the stocktake, and should not neglect what tests are required to check valuation. You must also read the question carefully to make sure you know precisely what it is asking for. A question on valuation of stock may ask about valuation of overheads **or** it may ask about obsolete or slow-moving stock.

2 ACCOUNTING FOR STOCK

2.1 The rules surrounding the audit of stocks and the related reporting requirements come from three sources:

- Companies Act 1985 (disclosure, basis of valuation)
- SSAP 9 *Stocks and long-term contracts* (departure, disclosure and valuation)
- Part of ISA 501 *Audit evidence – additional considerations for specific items* which relates to attendance at the stock count

Companies Act 1985

2.2 CA 1985 lays out the format of the balance sheet and under stock in current assets the following headings must be used.

1. Raw materials and consumables
2. Work in progress
3. Finished goods and goods for resale
4. Payments on account

2.3 In terms of valuation, CA 1985 states that all current assets should be stated at the lower of their **purchase price** or production cost and their **net realisable value**.

- 'Purchase price' can be interpreted as 'fair value'.
- 'Production cost' is determined according to the provision of SSAP 9.

2.4 CA 1985 allows certain methods of identifying cost, because it recognises that it is impossible to identify cost for each item individually. The methods allowed are:

- First in first out (FIFO)
- Last in first out (LIFO)
- Weighted average cost
- Other similar methods

SSAP 9 does *not* allow last in first out (LIFO) as a method of valuation except in rare circumstances.

SSAP 9 *Stocks and long-term contracts*

> **KEY TERMS**
>
> **Net realisable value** is the estimated or actual selling price, (net of trade discounts but before settlement discounts) less all further costs to completion and all cost to be incurred in marketing, selling and distributing the good or service.
>
> **Cost** is that expenditure which has been incurred in the normal course of business in bringing the product or service to its present location and condition. This includes the purchase price plus production costs appropriate to the location and condition of the stock.

2.5 Production costs (**costs of conversion**) include:

- Costs specifically attributable to units of production
- Production overheads

Part D: Substantive procedures

- Other overheads attributable to bringing the product or service to its present location and condition

---

Activity 11.1

Why is the audit of stock and work-in-progress one of the most difficult areas of the audit?

---

3 THE STOCKTAKE

Pilot paper

Exam alert

You **must** have a thorough knowledge of audit procedures before, during and after the stocktake.

Responsibilities in relation to stock	
Management	Ensure stock figure in accounts: • Represents stock that **exists** • Includes all stock **owned** Ensure accounting records include **stocktaking statements**
Auditors	**Obtain sufficient audit evidence** about stock figure from • Stock records • Stock control systems • Results of stocktaking • Test counts by auditors **Attend stocktaking if** stock is material and evidence of existence is provided by management stocktake

Methods of stocktaking

3.1 A business may take stock by one or a combination of the following methods.

(a) **Stocktaking** at the **year-end.**

From the viewpoint of the auditor, this is often the best method.

(b) **Stocktaking before** or **after** the **year-end.**

This will provide audit evidence of varying reliability depending on:

- The **length of time** between the stocktake and the year-end; the greater the time period, the less the value of audit evidence
- The business's system of **internal controls**
- The **quality of records** of stock movements in the period between the stocktake and the year-end

(c) **Continuous stocktaking** where management has a programme of stock-counting throughout the year.

3.2 If continuous stocktaking is used, auditors will check that:

(a) **All stock lines** are **counted at least once a year.**

(b) **Adequate stock records** are maintained and kept up-to-date. Auditors may compare sales and purchase transactions with stock movements, and carry out other tests on the stock records, for example checking casts and classification of stock.

(c) **Satisfactory procedures** for **stocktaking** and **test-counting exist.** Auditors should confirm the stocktaking arrangements and instructions are as rigorous as those for a year-end stocktake by reviewing instructions and observing counts. Auditors will be particularly concerned with **cut-off,** that there are no stock movements whilst the count is taking place, and stock records are updated up until the time of the stocktakes.

(d) **Management investigates** and **corrects** all **material differences.** Reasons for differences should be recorded and any necessary **corrective action taken,** including improvements in recording and custody procedures. All corrections to stock records should be **authorised** by a manager who has not been involved in stocktaking and checking; these procedures are necessary to guard against the possibility that stock records may be adjusted to conceal shortages. **Unusual stock movements** during the year should also be **investigated.**

3.3 Auditors should:

> (a) **Attend one** of the stock counts (to observe and confirm that instructions are being adhered to)
>
> (b) **Follow up** the **stock counts attended** to compare quantities counted by the auditors with stock records, obtaining and verifying explanations for any differences, and checking that the client has reconciled count records with book stock records
>
> (c) **Review** the **year's stock counts** to confirm the extent of counting, the treatment of discrepancies and the overall accuracy of records (If matters are not satisfactory, auditors will only be able to gain sufficient assurance by a full count at the year-end.)
>
> (d) Assuming a full count is not necessary at the year-end, **compare** the **listing of stock with** the **detailed stock records,** and carry out other procedures (**cut-off, analytical review**) to gain further comfort

Work-in-progress

3.4 Evidence of the existence of work-in-progress should be obtained by:

(a) **Attending** a **stocktake**

(b) **Reviewing management controls** over completeness and accuracy of accounting records and inspection of work-in-progress. (These procedures will be required if the nature of work-in-progress means that a stocktake is impractical.)

3.5 The auditors need to do this to gain assurance that the stock-checking system as a whole is effective in maintaining accurate stock records from which the amount of stocks in the financial statements can be derived.

The main stocktaking procedures

3.6 The following paragraphs set out the principal procedures which may be carried out by an auditors when attending a stocktake, but are not intended to provide a comprehensive list of the audit procedures which the auditors may find it necessary to perform during their attendance.

Part D: Substantive procedures

PLANNING STOCKTAKE	
Gain understanding	**Review** previous year's **arrangements**
	Perform **analytical procedures**
	Discuss with **management stock-taking arrangements** and **significant changes**
Assess key factors	The **nature** and **volume** of the **stocks**
	Risks relating to stock (see below)
	The **identification** of **high value items**
	Method of accounting for stocks
	Location of stock and how it affects stock control and recording
	Internal control and **accounting systems** to identify potential areas of difficulty
	Possible **internal audit** involvement
Plan procedures	**Ensure** a **representative selection** of **locations, stocks** and **procedures** are covered
	Ensure sufficient attention is given to **high value items**
	Arrange to obtain from **third parties confirmation** of stocks they hold
	Consider the need for **expert help**

3.7 Risk factors include:

- reliability of accounting and stock recording systems

- timing of physical counts relative to the year-end date and the reliability of records used in any 'roll-forward' of balances

- location of stock including that held by third parties

- physical controls over the stock and its susceptibility to theft or deterioration

- objectivity, experience and reliability of the counters and of those monitoring their work

- the degree of fluctuation in stock levels

- nature of stock, for example whether specialist knowledge is needed to identify the quantity, quality and/or identity of stock items

- whether a significant degree of estimation is involved in assessing quantity

- potential for fraud (eg movement of stocks between entity sites with stock counts at different dates, deliberate alteration of stock count records after the event, false stock count records being added to those prepared during the count)

Review of stock-taking instructions

REVIEW OF STOCK-TAKING INSTRUCTIONS	
Organisation of count	**Supervision** by senior staff including senior staff not normally involved with stock
	Tidying and **marking** stock to help counting
	Restriction and **control** of the production process and stock movements during the count
	Identification of damaged, obsolete, slow-moving, third party and **returnable** stock

11: Stocks and work in progress

REVIEW OF STOCK-TAKING INSTRUCTIONS	
Counting	**Systematic counting** to ensure all stock is counted
	Teams of **two counters,** with one counting and the other checking or two **independent counts**
Recording	**Serial numbering, control** and **return** of all stock sheets
	Stock sheets being **completed** in **ink** and **signed**
	Information to be recorded on the **count records** (location and identity, count units, quantity counted, conditions of items, stage reached in production process)
	Recording of **quantity, conditions** and **stage of production** of **work-in-progress**
	Recording of last numbers of **goods inwards** and **outwards** records and of internal transfer records
	Reconciliation with **stock records** and **investigation** and correction of any **differences**

If the instructions are inadequate the auditor should ask management to improve them.

During the stocktaking

3.8 Key tasks during the stocktake are as follows.

- **Check** the **client's staff** are following instructions (if not, the auditor should immediately draw this to the attention of management)

- **Make test counts** to ensure procedures and internal controls are working properly

- **Ensure** that the **procedures** for **identifying damaged, obsolete** and **slow-moving** stock operate properly; the auditors should **obtain information** about the stocks' **condition, age, usage** and in the case of work in progress, its **stage of completion**

- **Confirm** that **stock held** on behalf of **third parties** is separately identified and accounted for

- **Ensure** that **proper account** is taken of **stock movements** during the stock-take, and noting the last numbers of stock documentation for cut-off purposes (see below)

- **Consider** whether any **amendment** is necessary to subsequent **audit procedures**.

3.9 When carrying out test counts the auditors should select items from the count records and from the physical stocks and check one to the other, to confirm the accuracy of the count records. The auditors should concentrate on high value stock. If the results of the test counts are not satisfactory, the auditors may request stock be recounted.

3.10 The auditors should conclude by trying to gain an **overall impression** of the levels and values of stocks held so that they may, in due course, judge whether the figure for stocks appearing in the financial statements is reasonable.

3.11 Working papers should include:

- Details of their **observations** and **tests**
- The manner in which **points** that are **relevant** and **material** to the stocks being counted or measured have been dealt with by the client
- Instances where the **client's procedures** have **not been satisfactorily carried out**

Part D: Substantive procedures

- **Items for subsequent testing**, such as photocopies of (or extracts from) rough stocksheets
- **Details** of the **sequence** of **stocksheets**
- The **auditors' conclusions**

After the stocktaking

3.12 After the stocktaking, the matters recorded in the auditors' working papers at the time of the count or measurement should be followed up.

3.13 Key tests include the following.

- **Trace items** that were **test counted** during the stocktake to final stocksheets
- **Check all count** records have been **included** in final stocksheets
- **Check final stocksheets** are **supported by** count records
- **Ensure** that **continuous stock records** have been **adjusted** to the amounts physically counted or measured, and that differences have been investigated
- **Confirm cut-off** by using details of the last serial number of goods inwards and outwards notes; and of movements during the stocktake (see below)
- **Check replies** from **third parties** about stock held by or for them
- **Confirm** the client's final **valuation** of stock has been calculated correctly
- **Follow up queries** and **notifying problems** to management
- **Consider** whether attendance at the stock take has provided **sufficient** reliable audit evidence for determining the existence of stocks

3.14 EXAMPLE

Jonathan will be attending the stocktake at Brown Limited. The stores manager at Brown Limited has sent him the stocktaking instructions and he has assessed them and believes that the stocktake should be capable of producing a reliable figure for stock.

Jonathan has also reviewed the prior year working papers relating to the stocktake. He has ascertained the following key facts:

- Stock at Brown Limited consists of a high number of medium value items.
- No individual stock line is likely to have a material value.
- Stock is straightforward to count and there will be no need to use the assistance of an expert.

Because stock is a highly material and risky balance, and the population consists of a high number of medium value items, the sample sizes which will be used in the audit of stock will be high. Jonathan therefore needs to pick large samples of items to test count. He will also need to ensure that client staff are following the stock take procedures and ensure that procedures over slow moving (damaged stock and stock movements during the count) are being observed properly. He should make a note of the key cut-off details (last goods in and out) and any items of damaged stock.

On the audit plan, Jonathan has been allocated the task of following up this stocktake work at the final audit and ensuring that the items he has sampled have been included in the final stocksheets. He must therefore ensure that he notes down sufficient detail about the items he is counting, and may find it useful to photocopy the count sheets with the items he has selected on, if this is possible.

Activity 11.2

How can stocktaking instructions ensure that stock is counted completely and accurately?

Activity 11.3

What planning procedures should auditors undertake when planning attendance at a stocktake?

4 STOCK CUT-OFF

4.1 Auditors should consider whether management has instituted adequate cut-off procedures: procedures intended to ensure that movements into, within and out of stocks are properly identified and reflected in the accounting records.

4.2 Cut-off is most critical to the accurate recording of transactions in a manufacturing enterprise at particular points in the accounting cycle as follows:

- **Point of purchase** and **receipt** of **goods and services**
- **Requisitioning** of **raw materials** for production
- **Transfer** of **completed work-in-progress** to **finished goods stocks**
- **Sale** and **despatch of finished goods**

4.3 **Purchase invoices** should be recorded as liabilities only if the goods were received *prior* to the stock count. A schedule of 'goods received not invoiced' should be prepared, and items on the list should be accrued for in the accounts.

4.4 **Sales cut-off** is generally more straightforward to achieve correctly than purchases cut-off. Invoices for goods despatched after the stock count should not appear in the profit and loss accounts for the period.

4.5 Prior to the stock-take management should make arrangements for cut-off to be properly applied.

(a) **Appropriate systems of recording** of receipts and despatches of goods should be in place, and also a system for documenting materials requisitions. Goods received notes (GRNs) and goods despatched notes (GDNs) should be sequentially pre-numbered.

(b) **Final GRN and GDN** and **materials requisition numbers should be noted**. These numbers can then be used to check subsequently that purchases and sales have been recorded in the current period.

(c) **Arrangements** should be made to ensure that the **cut-off arrangement** for stock held by **third parties** are satisfactory.

4.6 There should ideally be no movement of stocks during the stock count. Preferably, receipts and despatches should be suspended for the full period of the count. It may not be practicable to suspend all deliveries, in which case any deliveries which are received during the count should be segregated from other stocks and carefully documented.

Part D: Substantive procedures

Audit procedures on cut-off

4.7 At the stocktake the auditors should carry out the following procedures.

> - Record **all movement notes** relating to the period, including:
>   - All interdepartmental requisition numbers
>   - The last goods received notes(s) and despatch note(s) prior to the count
>   - The first goods received notes(s) and despatch note(s) after the count
> - **Observe** whether correct cut-off procedures are being followed in the despatch and receiving areas
> - **Discuss procedures** with company staff performing the count to ensure they are understood
> - **Ensure** that **no goods finished** on the day of the count are **transferred** to the warehouse

4.8 During the final audit, the auditors will use the cut-off information from the stocktake to perform the following tests.

> - **Match up** the last **goods received notes** with **purchase invoices** and ensure the **liability** has been **recorded** in the **correct period**. Only goods received before the year end should be recorded as purchases.
> - **Match up** the last **goods despatched notes** to **sales invoices** and ensure the **income** has been **recorded** in the **correct period**. Only stocks despatched before the year-end should be recorded as sales.
> - **Match up** the **requisition notes** to the **work in progress** details for the receiving department to ensure correctly recorded.

4.9 **EXAMPLE**

At the final audit of Brown Limited, because stock is high risk, the audit of stock has been allocated to Jo Price. However, she has asked Jonathan to follow up the cut off details he obtained at the stocktake. He is uncertain of exactly what to do because he has never audited stock cut off before. Jo Price has left him the following note to follow:

'Take the goods received notes you obtained at the stocktake and match them up with the relevant purchase invoices. Only goods received before the stocktake should be included in purchases, so you should trace those purchase invoices to the purchase day book and ledger and ensure that they were recorded before the year end.

Similarly, with sales, match the last goods despatched notes to the relevant sales invoices and through to the ledger. These should be recorded as sales in the year.

The goods received and despatch notes after the ones you obtained at the stocktake should be recorded after the year end in the next years' ledger. You should check a sample of five of each to be sure this is the case.'

5 VALUATION OF STOCK

Assessment of cost and net realisable value *Pilot paper*

> **Exam alert**
>
> You must know the audit work needed to confirm valuation of stock when overheads have been absorbed, and to confirm stock is stated at the lower of cost and net realisable value.
>
> Knowledge of the requirements of SSAP 9 is essential when considering absorption of overheads, hence we have gone into detail about these provisions. You should refer back to your Drafting Financial Statements notes if you are still unsure about this area.

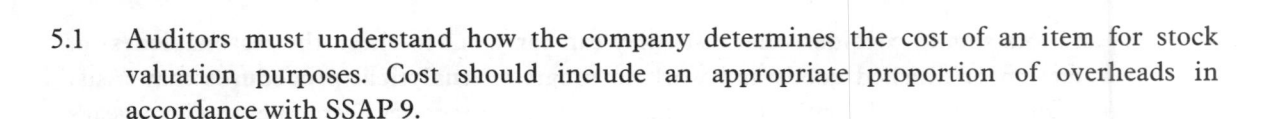

5.1 Auditors must understand how the company determines the cost of an item for stock valuation purposes. Cost should include an appropriate proportion of overheads in accordance with SSAP 9.

5.2 There are several ways of determining cost. Auditors must ensure that the company is **applying** the method **consistently** and that each year the method used **gives** a **fair approximation** to cost. They may need to support this by additional procedures such as:

- **Reviewing price** changes near the year-end
- **Ageing the stock** held
- **Checking gross profit** margins to reliable management accounts

Valuation of raw materials and brought in components

5.3 The auditors should check that the correct prices have been used to value raw materials and brought in components valued at actual costs by **referring** to **suppliers' invoices**.

5.4 If standard costs are used, auditors should **check** the **basis** of the **standards**, compare **standard costs** with **actual costs** and **confirm** that **variances** are being **treated appropriately**.

5.5 EXAMPLE

Jo Price is carrying out the audit of valuation of stock at Brown Limited. Her sample sizes are high so it is a time consuming task!

She is currently tracing a large sample of raw material values to the original supplier invoices. This has involved her asking the stores manager to tell her who the relevant suppliers of each part sampled are, and then searching for those invoices to verify the unit cost for each of them.

Next she will be looking at samples for work-in-progress and finished goods. She will test both the cost of these goods and the net realisable value, and then compare the two values to ensure that the goods are valued at the lower of these two costs.

Valuation of work in progress and finished goods (other than long-term contract work in progress)

5.6 As we saw above, SSAP 9 defines 'cost' as comprising the cost of purchase plus the cost of conversion (production costs). The costs of conversion comprises:

Part D: Substantive procedures

- Costs **specifically attributable** to units of production
- **Production overheads**
- Other **overheads attributable** to bringing the product or service to its present **location and condition**

Audit procedures

5.7 The audit procedures will depend on the methods used by the client to value work in progress and finished goods, and on the adequacy of the system of internal control.

Reasonableness tests

5.8 The auditors should consider what tests they can carry out to check the reasonableness of the valuation of finished goods and work in progress. **Analytical procedures** may assist comparisons being made with stock items and stock categories from the previous year's stock summaries. A **reasonableness check** will also provide the auditors with **assurance** regarding **completeness**.

Costs attributable to production

5.9 The auditors should carry out the following tests.

- For materials:
    - Check the valuation of raw materials to invoices and price lists
    - Confirm appropriate basis of valuation (eg FIFO) is being used
    - Confirm correct quantities are being used when calculating raw material value in work in progress and finished goods
- For labour costs:
    - Check labour costs to wage records
    - Check labour hours to time summaries and production reports
    - Review standard labour costs in the light of actual costs and production

Overhead allocation

5.10 The auditors should ensure that the client includes a proportion of overheads **appropriate** to **bringing** the **stock** to its **present location** and **condition**. The basis of overhead allocation should be **consistent** with **prior years**, and **calculated** on the **normal level** of **production activity**.

5.11 Thus, overheads arising from **reduced levels** of **activity, idle time** or **inefficient production** should be written off to the profit and loss account, rather than being included in stock.

5.12 In an appendix to SSAP 9 there is general guidance on the allocation of overheads which the auditors should follow. SSAP 9 comments that auditors should note that overheads are **classified by function** when being allocated (for example whether they are a function of production, marketing, selling or administration).

(a) All **abnormal conversion** costs (such as idle capacity) must be **excluded**.

11: Stocks and work in progress

(b) Where **firm sales contracts** have been entered into for the provision of goods or services to customer's specification, **design, marketing and selling costs** incurred before manufacture may be **included**.

(c) Overheads are **classified** by **function** when being allocated.

(d) The costs of **general management**, as distinct from functional management, are not directly related to current production and are, therefore, **excluded**.

(e) The allocation of costs of **central service departments** should depend on the function or functions that the department is serving. **Only** those costs that can reasonably be allocated to the **production function** should be **included**.

(f) In determining what constitutes 'normal' activity, a number of factors need to be considered:

- The **volume** of **production** which the production facilities are **designed to achieve**
- The **budgeted level** of **activity** for the year under review and for the ensuing year
- The **level** of **activity achieved** both in the **year** under review and in previous years

Although temporary changes in the load of activity may be ignored, persistent variation should lead to revision of the previous norm.

Activity 11.4
How should auditors determine whether a company is operating at a normal level of activity?

5.13 Difficulty may be experienced if the client operates a system of total overhead absorption. It will be necessary for those overheads that are of a general, non-productive nature to be identified and excluded from the stock valuation.

5.14 EXAMPLE

Jo will commence her work on work-in-progress and finished goods the same way as she did her raw materials test – checking original costs to supplier invoices. The client should be able to give her breakdowns showing each element of cost within work-in-progress and finished goods so that she is able to test each element.

Once she has completed her tests on the original costs of materials, she will test the other costs attributed to the stock; labour and overheads. Labour costs are attributed to the stock in terms of staff wage grade and hours worked on each stage of the production process. She will compare the hours worked to previous years to see if it reasonable, and ensure (for work-in-progress) that the number of hours attributed is reasonable given the degree of completion of the stock. She will agree wage rates to the payroll.

The basis of overhead allocation should be consistent with prior years, so she will again compare this year's calculation to last year's to ensure that it appears reasonable. She will then verify figures within the calculation (for example, electricity) to invoices. Lastly she will ensure the allocation to each individual item of stock has been done properly.

Part D: Substantive procedures

Cost vs Net Realisable Value

5.15 Auditors should **compare cost and net realisable value** for each item of stock of all types - raw materials, work in progress and finished goods. Where this is impracticable, the comparison may be done by stock group or category.

5.16 Net realisable value is likely to be less than cost when there has been:

- An **increase in costs** or a fall in selling price
- **Physical deterioration** of stocks
- **Obsolescence** of products
- A **decision** as part of a company's **marketing strategy** to manufacture and sell products at a loss
- **Errors in production** or **purchasing**

5.17 The following audit tests are important.

> - **Review and test the client's system** for **identifying slow-moving, obsolete** or **damaged stock**
> - **Follow up** any such **items** that were **identified** at the **stocktaking**, ensuring that the client has made adequate provision to write down the items to net realisable value
> - **Examine stock records** to identify slow-moving items. It may be possible to incorporate into a computer audit program certain tests and checks such as listing items whose value or quantity has not moved over the previous year
> - **Examine the prices** at which finished goods have been sold after the year-end and ascertain whether any finished goods items need to be reduced below cost
> - **Review quantities of goods sold after the year end** to determine that year end stock has, or will be, realised
> - If significant quantities of finished goods stock remain unsold for an unusual time after the year-end, **consider** the **need** to make **appropriate provision**

5.18 For work in progress, the **ultimate selling price** should be **compared** with the **carrying value** at the year end plus **costs to be incurred** after the year end to bring work in progress to a finished state.

5.19 EXAMPLE

The last test Jo will carry out on valuation of stock is an NRV test. For each of the items of work-in-progress and finished goods she has selected, she will ascertain the selling price after the year end. The best way to do this is to find examples of sales of the stocks and look at the sales price in the invoice. If the stock item has not been sold, she may look at the sales catalogue to ascertain the price, but this may be an indication that the stock is slow-moving or obsolete and should be written down. She should check the order book to see if there are any orders in progress for that stock item.

She will also carry out a series of general tests – looking at the level of sales after the year end to ensure stocks are being sold generally, looking at any specific items notes as damaged or obsolete at the stocktake and comparing sales prices to previous years' to ensure they are not dropping unduly.

Activity 11.5

(a) What types of stock might be valued at less than cost?

(b) What audit work would you carry out to find stock that should be carried at net realisable value, and to confirm the value at which that stock should be carried?

Activity 11.6

What general analytical procedures can be applied to test whether the valuation of stock is reasonable?

Activity 11.7

What are the major tasks auditors should carry out:

(a) During a stocktake
(b) After a stocktake

Activity 11.8

What procedures should auditors undertake to ensure stock cut-off has operated correctly?

Key learning points

- The audit of stocks and work in progress is difficult and time consuming, because of problems of control over stock (affecting **existence and cut-off**) and **problems over valuation**.

- The **valuation** and **disclosure** rules for stock are laid down in SSAP 9 and CA 1985.

- ISA 501 *Audit evidence – additional considerations for specific items* provides guidance to auditors.

- Stocktake procedures are vital as they provide evidence which cannot be obtained elsewhere or at any other time about the quantities and conditions of stocks and work in progress.

    - Before the stocktake auditors should ensure audit **coverage** of **stock-taking** is **appropriate**, and that the client's **stock-taking instructions** have been reviewed.

    - During the stocktake the auditors should **check the stock count** is being carried out according to instructions, carry out **test counts**, and watch for **third party, slow moving stock, cut-off problems.**

    - After the stocktake the auditors should check that **final stock sheets** have been **properly compiled** from stock count records and that **book stock records** have been **appropriately adjusted**.

- Auditors should check **cut-off** by noting the **serial numbers** of items received and despatched just before and after the year-end, and subsequently checking that they have been included in the correct period.

- Auditing the valuation of stock includes:

    - Checking the **allocation of overheads** is appropriate
    - Confirming stock is carried at the lower of **cost** and **net realisable value**

Part D: Substantive procedures

Quick quiz

1. Under what headings does the Companies Act 1985 require stock to be classified?
2. What methods of identifying cost of stock does the Companies Act allow to be used? Which method is not allowed by SSAP 9?
3. How does SSAP 9 define net realisable value?
4. What factors determine the reliability of an annual stocktake which takes place other than at the year-end?
5. What should auditors include in their working papers concerning the work that they have carried out at a stock-take?
6. At what points of the accounting cycle is cut-off of most importance?
7. How should auditors check that a company's method of valuing stock (FIFO, LIFO etc) is reasonable?
8. What tests should auditors carry out to check the valuation of raw materials and brought in components which are valued at actual cost?
9. What guidance does SSAP 9 give on the type of overheads that should be included and excluded from the costs of stock?
10. How should auditors test whether work-in-progress is being carried at the lower of cost and net realisable value?

Answers to quick quiz

1. Companies Act 1985 prescribes the following headings.

   (a) Raw materials and consumables
   (b) Work in progress
   (c) Finished goods and goods for resale
   (d) Payments on account

2. Companies Act 1985 allows the following methods of stock valuation to be used.

   (a) First in first out (FIFO)
   (b) Last in first out (LIFO) (not allowed by SSAP 9)
   (c) Weighted average cost
   (d) Other similar methods

3. SSAP 9 defines net realisable value as the estimated or actual selling price, net of trade discounts but before settlement discounts less all further costs to completion and all costs to be incurred in marketing, selling or distributing the good or service.

4. The factors which determine the reliability of a stocktake other than at the year-end are:

   (a) The length of time between the stocktake and the year-end
   (b) The internal control system
   (c) The quality of stock movement records

5. Auditors' working papers should include:

   (a) Details of their observations and tests
   (b) How the client has dealt with material points
   (c) Instances where client procedures have not been carried out satisfactorily
   (d) Items for subsequent testing
   (e) Details of the sequence of stocksheets
   (f) The auditors' conclusions

6. Stock cut-off is particularly important at the following points of the cycle.

   (a) The point of purchase and receipt of goods and services
   (b) The requisitioning of raw materials for production
   (c) The transfer of completed work-in-progress to finished goods stocks
   (d) The sale and despatch of finished goods

7   Auditors should check whether the client is using the same method consistently. They should also:

    (a) Review price movements around the year-end
    (b) Consider the ageing of the stock
    (c) Check gross profit margins to reliable management accounts

8   Auditors should check that raw materials and brought in components are valued at actual cost by referring to suppliers' invoices.

9   The guidance SSAP 9 gives regarding overheads is as follows.

    (a) All abnormal conversion costs should be excluded.

    (b) Design, marketing and selling costs incurred before manufacture may be included where sales contracts for goods or services according to the customer's specification have been entered.

    (c) The costs of general management should be excluded.

    (d) The allocation of costs of central service departments should depend on the functions of that department. Only costs that can reasonably be allocated to production should be included.

10 For work-in-progress, auditors should compare the ultimate selling price with the carrying value at the year-end plus costs to be incurred after the year-end to bring work-in-progress to a finished state.

Answers to activities

Answer 11.1

Stock can pose auditors particular problems for the following reasons.

(a) Closing stock does not normally form part of the double entry bookkeeping system; thus a misstatement cannot be detected by finding corresponding errors in other audit areas.

(b) Stock existence must generally be verified by attendance at stock-take and follow-up procedures.

(c) Control over stocktaking can be difficult to achieve if it is taking place in a number of locations.

(d) Cut-off may be difficult to test because it may be necessary to move stock during the stock-take.

(e) Valuation of stock can be difficult for a number of reasons.

   (i)   Stock is often made up of a large number of different items.
   (ii) The Companies Act and SSAP 9 allow a variety of methods to be used to value stock.
   (iii) The allocation of overheads which is required by Companies Act and SSAP 9 is a subjective process.
   (iv) Assessment of the valuation of work-in-progress depends on assessment of its state of completion, which is generally subjective.
   (v)   Assessment of the valuation of slow-moving, obsolete and damaged stock is also subjective.

Answer 11.2

If instructions are to ensure stock is counted completely and accurately, they must be clear, and include the following features.

(a) Someone, preferably someone not normally responsible for stock, should supervise the count and deal with queries.

(b) Stock should be tidied and laid out in an orderly manner.

(c) All stock should be clearly identified.

(d) Goods received on the day of the stocktake should be physically segregated until the count has been completed.

(e) Goods due to be despatched to customers or issued internally on the day should be separately identified so that they are not included in stock.

(f) Records should be kept of goods received or issued during the day.

Part D: Substantive procedures

(g) Prenumbered stock sheets should be issued to counters.

(h) Counters should be given responsibility for a specific area.

(i) All stock should be marked after being counted so that it is evident it has been counted.

(j) Each area should be subject to a recount.

(k) One of the counts should be by someone who is not normally responsible for stock.

(l) All stock sheets should be accounted for at the end of the audit.

Answer 11.3

In planning attendance at a stocktake the auditors should carry out the following tests.

(a) Review previous year's audit working papers and discuss any developments in the year with management.

(b) Assess risk of material misstatement.

(c) Obtain and review a copy of the company's stocktaking instructions.

(d) Arrange attendance at stockcount planning meetings, with the consent of management.

(e) Gain an understanding of the nature of the stock and of any special stocktaking problems this is likely to present, for example liquid in tanks, scrap in piles.

(f) Consider whether expert involvement is likely to be required as a result of any circumstances noted in (d) above.

(g) Obtain a full list of all locations at which stock is held, including an estimate of the amount and value of stock held at different locations.

(h) Using the results of the above steps, plan for audit attendance by appropriately experienced audit staff at all locations where material stocks are held, subject to other factors (for example rotational auditing, reliance on internal controls).

(i) Consider the impact of internal controls upon the nature and timing of the stocktaking attendance.

(j) Ascertain whether stocks are held by third parties and if so make arrangements to obtain written confirmation of them or, if necessary, to attend the stocktake of them.

Answer 11.4

The normal level of activity is likely to be determined in the following way.

(a) Compare the level of production with previous years.

(b) Compare production/sales with budget.

(c) Investigate overtime levels of production staff, compared to previous years.

(d) Enquire of management about any changes in production during the year, and investigate:

    (i) Board/management minutes
    (ii) New machinery/production space

Answer 11.5

(a) (i) Stock which may be worth less than cost will include:

    (1) Slow moving stock
    (2) Obsolete or superseded stock
    (3) Seconds stock and items that have been damaged
    (4) Stock which is being, or is soon likely to be, sold at reduced prices
    (5) Discontinued stock lines

(b) (i) To identify stock which may be worth less than cost the following work will be carried out.

    (1) Examine the computerised stock control system and list items showing an unacceptably low turnover rate. An unacceptable rate of turnover may be different for different items, but stock representing more than six months' sales is likely to qualify.

11: Stocks and work in progress

      (2)   Check the stock printout for items already described as seconds or recorded as damaged.

      (3)   Discuss with management the current position regarding slow moving stock and their plans and expectations in respect of products that may be discontinued. The standard system must be carefully considered and estimates obtained of the likely selling price of existing stock. The most likely outcome regarding the use and value of discontinued components must be decided.

      (4)   At the stocktake, look for stock which is dusty, inaccessible and in general not moving and mark on the stock sheets.

      (5)   Find out whether any lines are unreliable and therefore frequently returned for repairs as these may be unpopular.

      (6)   Check with the trade press or other sources to see whether any of the equipment is out of date.

(ii) Determining the net realisable value of stock is a difficult task and involves management in judging how much stock can be sold and at what price, together with deciding whether to sell off raw materials and components separately or to assemble them into finished products. Each separate type of stock item should be considered separately in deciding on the level of prudent provision.

To determine the net realisable value of the stock the following procedures should be carried out.

      (1)   Find the actual selling prices from the latest sales invoice. For items still selling, invoices will be very recent, but for slow moving and obsolete items the invoiced prices will be out of date and allowance will have to be made for this (probably a reduction in estimating the most likely sale price of the stock concerned).

      (2)   Estimate the value of marketing, selling and distribution expenses using past figures for the types of finished goods concerned as a base. I would update and check for reasonableness against the most recent accounting records.

      (3)   Discuss with management what selling prices are likely to be where there is little past evidence. Costs to completion will be questioned where these are difficult to estimate and where there are any unusual assembly, selling or distribution problems.

      (4)   Discuss any large differences between auditor estimation of net realisable value and management estimation, and consider the basis for the company's estimates.

      (5)   Value any damaged stock at zero since it is unlikely to fetch any money.

      (6)   Conclude line by line what stock ought to be carried at cost, and what at net realisable value.

Answer 11.6

The figures calculated should be broken down as far as possible, by product or by location. Significant variations from last year's figures, or from what may be expected (average figures for other products or other locations for example) should be investigated, particularly variations in the key stock ratios mentioned in (a)). Comparisons that can be made include the following.

(a) Comparisons of stock ratios with previous years. These include gross profit margins and stock turnover.

(b) Comparisons of values of stock held compared with previous years.

(c) Comparisons of quantities of stock held compared with previous years.

(d) Comparisons of stock provisions, both in absolute terms and as a percentage of stock held. Auditors should consider whether provisions made in previous years were excessive or insufficient.

(e) Comparisons of costings with previous years. Auditors should consider unit stock prices, also percentage of material, labour and overhead in production costs.

(f) If standard costing is used, auditors should ascertain the reasons for changes in standards and also significant variances.

(g) Comparisons of selling prices to those charged elsewhere. If selling prices charged elsewhere are lower, this may mean the stock being audited will be difficult to sell. On the other hand if prices charged by competitors are higher, it is possible that the stock being audited will be sold for less than cost.

(h) Selling prices should be checked as long after the year-end as possible, to make sure that prices were not kept artificially high over the year-end and then reduced at a later date. Auditors should also consider stock turnover after the year-end.

Part D: Substantive procedures

(i) Auditors should consider levels and costs of stock held in the light of what they know about what is happening in the industry. In particular auditors might have to consider the effect of new technology and new fashions, and hence the possible risk of stock obsolescence.

Answer 11.7

(a) During a stocktake the auditors should carry out the following procedures.

   (i) Check that the client's staff are following instructions. If auditors see a breach of instructions for example client staff counting stock together when one should be counting and one checking, they should draw this to the attention of whoever is supervising the stock count.

   (ii) Make test counts. Auditors should compare count records with actual stock and vice versa, concentrating on high value stock. If the results of these are not satisfactory, auditors may have to request the stock to be recounted.

   (iii) Ensure that the procedures for identifying damaged, obsolete and slow-moving stock are operating. Auditors should record details of stock likely to be valued at lower than cost including condition, age and usage.

   (iv) Ensure that stock held on behalf of third parties is separately identified and accounted for.

   (v) Ensure that proper account is taken of stock movements during the stock-take, and noting the last numbers of stock documentation for cut-off purposes.

   (vi) Conclude whether the stock-take provides sufficient evidence of the existence of stocks.

   (vii) Consider whether any amendment is necessary to subsequent audit procedures.

   (viii) Gain an overall impression of the valuation of stock.

(b) After a stocktake, auditors should carry out the following tests.

   (i) Trace items that were test counted during the stock count to the final stock sheets.

   (ii) Check all count records have been included in the final stock sheets.

   (iii) Check final stock sheets are supported by count records.

   (iv) Ensure that book stock records have been adjusted to reflect actual stock counted, and differences have been investigated.

   (v) Confirm cut-off by checking correct treatment of last goods inwards and outwards before the stock-take, and first goods inwards and outwards after the stock-take. Auditors should also check that stock movements during the stock-take have been treated correctly.

   (vi) Check confirmations by third parties of stock held by them.

   (vii) Discuss queries and problems with management.

   (viii) Conclude whether the final valuation of stock has been calculated correctly.

Answer 11.8

(a) Auditors should ensure management instructions cover cut-off arrangements properly. Instructions should specify the following.

   (i) Receipts, despatches and material requisitions should be recorded by pre-numbered documentation.

   (ii) Final numbers of goods received, despatched and requisitions should be noted.

   (iii) Cut-off arrangements with third parties should be satisfactory.

(b) At the stocktake auditors should carry out the following procedures.

   (i) Record details themselves of the last goods received and goods despatched notes, together with any requisitions for movements during the stock-take.

   (ii) Observe whether correct cut-off procedures are being followed in the despatch and receiving areas. Stock coming in or going out during the stock-take should be separately segregated.

   (iii) Ensure no goods finished on the day of the stocktake are transferred into stock.

11: Stocks and work in progress

After the stocktake, auditors should carry out the following procedures.

(i) Match up the last goods received notes and the first notes for the following year with purchase invoices and ensure that the liability has been recorded in the correct period.

(ii) Match up the last goods despatched notes and the first notes for the following year to sales invoices and ensure that the income has been recorded in the correct period.

(iii) Match up the internal requisitions for movements during the period with work in progress details for the receiving department to ensure that movements have been correctly recorded.

Now try Question 11 in the Exam Question Bank

Chapter 12 Fixed assets

Chapter topic list

1 Introduction
2 Tangible fixed assets
3 Investments

The following study sessions are covered in this Chapter:

Syllabus reference

23(b) For each area in the financial statements of an incorporated company, provide examples of the representations made by directors 6

24(a) Design audit programmes to meet specific audit objectives with regard to the following balance sheet items: 6

    (i) Tangible fixed assets
    (ii) Investments

1 INTRODUCTION

1.1 In this chapter we discuss the audit of fixed assets, which may include intangible and tangible fixed assets and also investments.

1.2 We shall concentrate first on **tangible fixed assets** such as land and buildings, plant and machinery and motor vehicles. These will be the major items that many companies own, and hence the figure for tangible fixed assets is likely to be very material in the accounts. That said, the major tangible fixed assets tend to be few in number, so that not many items have to be tested in order to gain assurance about a large proportion of the amount shown.

1.3 Assertions of particular significance for tangible fixed assets are **rights and obligations** (that is, ownership), **existence and valuation**. Different tests will be needed on ownership and existence. Although ownership may be verified by inspecting appropriate documentation (for example, land deeds or vehicle registration documents) those documents do not guarantee that the asset still exists. Physical inspection of the asset may be required to prove existence.

1.4 Valuation is the other important assertion. The auditors will concentrate on **testing** any **valuations** made **during the year**, and also whether other values appear reasonable given asset usage and condition. A very important aspect of testing valuation is **reviewing depreciation rates**. Auditors should check that the rates used appear reasonable and are consistently applied from year to year.

1.5 We shall also consider **investments**. Gaining sufficient assurance concerning the client's **ownership** of investments can be a particular problem in this area.

1.6 Two topics which we covered in earlier chapters may well be important in the audit of fixed assets, using the work of an expert (which we covered in Chapter 6) and the usefulness of third party confirmations (which we covered in Chapter 5). You should refer back to your notes in these subjects.

> **Exam alert**
>
> Most exam questions on fixed assets cover the audit of tangible fixed assets, although auditing examiners do on occasions ask about the other types of fixed asset. Sometimes questions are confined to the audit work required, but questions can also refer to whether the accounting treatment proposed by the client is reasonable.

2 TANGIBLE FIXED ASSETS   Pilot paper

Internal control considerations

2.1 As we have seen, a key element of good internal control is a **fixed asset register**, which should help identify assets. In any event auditors should record movements in fixed assets in their working papers.

2.2 Auditors should also ensure that the company has good controls over substantial asset expenditure and disposals.

Part D: Substantive procedures

Activity 12.1

What do you think the auditors can do if a company does not maintain a fixed asset register?

Summary of audit procedures

> **Exam alert**
>
> In the exam you may be asked generally how to audit certain aspects of tangible fixed assets (such as valuation) or you may be given a specific example and asked what audit work you would carry out (for example, X Limited has revalued its properties by £40,000 this year using a valuation by a director).

2.3 Completeness (and cut off)

- **Obtain** or **prepare** a **summary** of tangible fixed assets showing:
    - Gross book value
    - Accumulated depreciation
    - Net book value

    and reconcile with the **opening position**

- Compare fixed assets in the general ledger with the fixed assets register and obtain explanations for differences
- Check whether assets which physically exist are recorded in fixed asset register
- If a fixed asset register is not kept, obtain a schedule showing the original costs and present depreciated value of major fixed assets
- Reconcile the schedule of fixed assets with the general ledger

2.4 Existence

- **Confirm** that the **company physically inspects** all items in the fixed asset register each year
- **Inspect assets,** concentrating on high value items and additions in year. Confirm items inspected are:
    - Exist
    - Are in use
    - Are in good condition
    - Have correct serial numbers
- **Review records** of **income yielding assets** to see whether **all income** has been received
- **Reconcile** opening and closing **vehicles** by numbers as well as amounts

2.5 Valuation (and allocation)

- **Verify valuation** to valuation certificate
- **Consider reasonableness** of **valuation**, reviewing:
  - Experience of valuer
  - Scope of work
  - Methods and assumption used
- Check revaluation surplus has been correctly calculated
- Consider whether permanent diminution in value of assets has occurred

2.6 Rights and obligations (ownership)

- **Verify title** to land and buildings by inspection of:
  - Title deeds
  - Land registry certificates
  - leases
- Obtain a certificate from solicitors/bankers:
  - **Stating purpose** for which the deeds are being held (custody only)
  - **Stating deeds** are **free** from **mortgage** or **lien**
- **Inspect registration documents** for vehicles held, checking that they are in client's name
- **Confirm** all vehicles held are used for the **client's business**
- **Examine documents** of **title** for other assets (including purchase invoices, architects' certificates, contracts, hire purchase or lease agreements)

2.7 Additions (to confirm rights and obligations, valuation and completeness)

- **Verify additions** by inspection of architects' certificates, solicitors' completion statements, suppliers' invoices etc.
- **Check capitalisation** of **expenditure** is correct by considering for fixed assets additions and items in relevant expense categories (repairs, motor expenses, sundry expenses) whether:
  - Capital/revenue distinction is correctly drawn
  - Capitalisation is in line with consistently applied company policy
- Check **purchases** have been **properly allocated** to correct fixed asset accounts
- Check **purchases** have been **authorised** by directors/senior management
- **Ensure** that appropriate **claims** have been made for **grants**, and grants received and receivable have been received
- **Check additions** have been **recorded** in fixed asset register and general ledger

Part D: Substantive procedures

2.8 Self-constructed assets

- **Verify material** and **labour** costs and **overheads** to invoices and wage records
- **Ensure expenditure** has been **analysed correctly** and **properly charged** to capital
- **Check no profit element** has been included in costs
- Check **finance costs** have been **capitalised** on a consistent basis

2.9 Disposals (to confirm rights and obligations, valuation and completeness)

- **Verify disposals** with supporting documentation, checking transfer of title, sales price and dates of completion and payment
- **Check calculation** of profit or loss is **accurate** and **in accordance with accounting standards**
- Check that **disposals** have been **authorised**
- **Consider** whether **proceeds** are **reasonable**
- If the property was **used as security**, ensure **release from security** has been correctly made

2.10 Depreciation (to confirm valuation)

- Review depreciation rates applied in relation to:
    - Asset lives
    - Residual values
    - Replacement policy
    - Past experience of gains and losses on disposal
    - Consistency with prior years and accounting policy
    - Possible obsolescence
- Check **depreciation** has been **charged on all** assets with a limited useful life
- For **revalued assets**, ensure that the charge for **depreciation** is **based** on the **revalued amount**
- **Check calculation** of depreciation rates
- **Compare ratios** of depreciation to fixed assets (by category) with:
    - Previous years
    - Depreciation policy rates
- Ensure no further depreciation provided on fully depreciated assets
- Check that depreciation policies and rates are disclosed in the accounts

2.11 Charges and commitments

- **Review for evidence** of charges in statutory books and by company search
- **Review leases** of leasehold properties to ensure that company has fulfilled covenants therein
- **Examine invoices received after year-end, orders and minutes** for evidence of capital commitments

2.12 **Insurance**

> - **Review insurance policies** in force for all categories of tangible fixed assets and consider the adequacy of their insured values and check expiry dates

Exam alert

A question on depreciation may involve considering whether the rates used in specific circumstances are reasonable.

2.13 **EXAMPLE**

Because the audit of fixed assets at Brown Limited is low risk, it has been allocated to Jonathan. The client has provided him with the following information.

	Motor vehicles	Plant/ machinery	Fittings	Total
Cost at 1 October 2003	157,444	302,973	119,372	579,789
Additions	–	47,219	1,099	48,318
Disposals	–	–	–	–
Cost at 30 September 2004	157,444	350,192	120,471	628,107
Accumulated depreciation at 1 October 2003	38,809	169,581	30,224	238,614
Charge for the year	20,214	30,214	30,118	80,546
Accumulated depreciation at 30 September 2004	59,023	199,795	60,342	319,160
Net realisable value 1 October 2003	118,635	133,392	89,148	341,175
Net realisable value 30 September 2004	98,421	150,397	60,129	308,947

Additions	£	**Depreciation rates**	%
Cutting machine	25,620	Motor vehicles	15
XZO machine	21,599	Plant/machinery	10
Computer	1,099	Fittings	25

Jonathan should carry out the following tests:

- Agree the opening position to last year's file and accounts
- Select a sample of assets (including the three additions) to physically inspect
- Select a sample of physical assets and trace to fixed asset register
- Agree closing position to general ledger and accounts
- Agree value of sample (including additions) to purchase invoices
- Check additions were properly authorised (purchase order)
- Check a sample of motor vehicles to registration documents for ownership
- Confirm depreciation rates to last year's file
- Check depreciation in total if possible, if not, obtain breakdown
- Review minutes/ask directors if there are capital commitments

Activity 12.2

The following material items have been included in the fixed asset note of the year-end accounts of Growler Ltd. Explain the audit tests you would carry out on them.

(a) Plant and machinery additions of £80,000
(b) A depreciation charge of £15,000 for motor vehicles

Part D: Substantive procedures

Activity 12.3

You are the audit manager in charge of the audit of Freddo Ltd. The audit senior has contacted you with a number of problems he has encountered when considering the audit of fixed assets.

(a) The client has stated that the motor vehicles the senior wished to inspect cannot be inspected, as they are all being driven by salesmen who are not due to return to office until after the accounts are signed.

(b) The client has capitalised furniture in its new office block, although it has not previously capitalised furniture. The furniture has an expected life of three years.

(c) A large crane, previously written off by the client has been brought back into use at a valuation of £10,000 because of problems with its replacements. The £10,000 has been included as a re-valuation in this year's accounts.

Required

Outline the audit work that should be carried out in the light of the problems found.

3 INVESTMENTS

3.1 This section applies to companies where dealing in investments is secondary to the main objectives of the company.

- Investments in companies, whether listed or unlisted, fixed interest or equity
- Income arising from investments

(*Note.* The following comments apply equally to investments treated as fixed or current.)

Internal control considerations

3.2 The key controls are:

(a) **Authorisation** over investment dealing; authorisation from high level management should be required.

(b) **Segregation of duties:**
- The recording and custody roles should be kept separate.
- As investments may be misappropriated by being pledged as collateral, those responsible for custody should not have access to cash.

Existence and rights and obligations

3.3 Stockbrokers should not normally be entrusted with the safe custody of share certificates on a continuing basis since they have ready access to the Stock Exchange. Auditors should not therefore rely on a certificate from a broker stating that he holds the company's securities.

3.4 If securities are being transferred over the year-end the auditors should obtain a broker's certificate. The transaction should be further verified by examining contract notes, and in the case of purchases, examination of the title documents after the year-end.

3.5 Rights and obligations

- **Examine certificates** of **title** to investments listed in investment records and confirm that they are:
    - *Bona fide* complete title documents
    - In the client's name
    - Free from any charge or lien
- **Examine confirmation** from **third party investment custodians** (such as banks) and check:
    - Investments are in client's name
    - Investments are free from charge or lien
- **Inspect certificates** of **title** which are held by third parties who are not bona fide custodians
- **Inspect blank transfers** and **letters of trust** to confirm client owns shares in name of nominee
- **Review minutes** and **other statutory books** for evidence of charging and pledging

3.6 Additions

- **Verify purchases** to agreements, contract notes and correspondence
- **Confirm purchases** were **authorised**
- **Check** with Stubbs, Extel or appropriate financial statements that all **reported capital changes** (bonus or rights issues) have been correctly **accounted for** during the period

3.7 Disposals of investments

- **Verify disposals** with contract notes or sales agreements correspondence
- **Check** whether investment **disposals** have been **authorised**
- **Confirm** that **profit** or **loss** on sale of investments has been **correctly calculated** taking account of:
    - Bonus issue of shares
    - Consistent basis of identifying cost of investment sold
    - Rights issues
    - Accrued interest
    - Taxation

Valuation

3.8 The auditors should establish that the company's policy on valuing investments has been correctly applied and is consistent with previous years, for example cost or market value.

Part D: Substantive procedures

3.9 Substantive procedures

> - **Confirm** the **value** of **listed investments** by reference to the Stock Exchange Daily Lists or the quotations published in the *Financial Times* or *Times*; the middle market value should be used
> - Review accounts of unlisted investments and:
>   - Check the **basis on** which the **shares** are **valued** (expert help may be required)
>   - **Ensure** that the **valuation** of the investment is **reasonable**
> - **Check** that **no substantial fall** in the value of the investments has taken place since the balance sheet date
> - **Consider** whether there are any **restrictions** on **remittance** of **income** and ensure these are properly disclosed
> - **Check** whether **current asset investments** are included at the **lower of cost** or **net realisable value**

Investment income

3.10 The basis of recognising investment income may vary from company to company particularly for dividends, for example:

- Credit taken only when received (cash basis)
- Credit taken when declared
- Credit taken after ratification of the dividend by shareholders in general meeting.

A consistent basis must be applied from year to year.

3.11 Substantive procedures

> - **Check** that all **income** due has been **received**, by reference to Stubbs or Extel cards for listed investments, and financial statements for unlisted investments
> - **Review investment income** account for **irregular** or unusual **entries**, or those not apparently pertaining to investments held (particular attention should be paid to investments bought and sold during the year
> - **Ensure** that the **basis** of **recognising** income is **consistent** with previous years
> - **Compare investment income** with **prior years** and **explain** any **significant fluctuations**
> - **Consider whether** there are likely to be any **restrictions** on **realisation** of the investment or remittance of any income due (especially for investments abroad) and ensure these are properly disclosed in the financial statements

3.12 If the client is a charity or pension scheme, auditors would check that tax deducted at source has been reclaimed from the Inland Revenue.

Other procedures

3.13 Other tests that are likely to be carried out include the following.

> - **Obtain** or prepare a **statement** to be placed on the current file **reconciling the book value** of listed and unlisted investments at the last balance sheet date and the current balance sheet date (tests completeness)
> - **Ensure** that the **investments** are **properly disclosed and categorised** in the financial statements into listed and unlisted

Activity 12.4

You are auditing the accounts of the Crossroads Motel trust. The trust owns significant investments, the income from which is used to support retired stars of television soap operas. The investments include large investments in the shares of listed companies.

Tasks

(a) Explain how you would confirm the trust's ownership of the listed company shares.
(b) Explain how you would check that all income due during the year has been received.
(c) Explain what work you would carry out on the disposals of investments.

Key learning points

- The disclosure and valuation requirements for all fixed assets under CA 1985 are relevant here.
- Key areas when testing **tangible fixed assets** are:
    - **Confirmation** of ownership
    - **Inspection** of fixed assets to confirm **existence**
    - **Valuation** by third parties
    - **Adequacy** of **depreciation** rates
- **Investments** (if quoted) should be **valued** at **mid-market price** at the balance sheet date.
- Auditors may need to **inspect share certificates** to confirm ownership.

Quick quiz

1. What documentation should auditors inspect when reviewing deeds to registered land?
2. How should auditors check whether a company has capitalised expenditure correctly?
3. What are the major audit procedures that should be carried out on the disposal of fixed assets?
4. What audit work should be carried out in order to check whether a company has capital commitments and charges on fixed assets?
5. How would an auditor test whether the valuation of listed investments is reasonable?

Part D: Substantive procedures

Answers to quick quiz

1. When inspecting title to registered land, auditors should inspect the land registry certificate which is conclusive evidence of title. Other documents should only normally be inspected in cases of doubt.

2. When checking capitalisation of expenditure, auditors should check fixed asset additions and expense categories which may contain capital items such as repairs or motor expenses. They should check whether the capital/revenue distinction has been correctly drawn, and whether the capitalisation is consistent with company policy.

3. Auditors should carry out the following work on disposals:

    (a) Verify disposals with supporting documentation.
    (b) Check the calculation of profit or loss on disposal.
    (c) Check disposals have been authorised.
    (d) Consider whether proceeds received appear reasonable.

4. Auditors should review statutory books and carry out company searches for evidence of charges. They should review invoices raised after the year-end, orders and board minutes for evidence of capital commitments.

5. The valuation of listed investments should be confirmed by referring to the Stock Exchange Daily Lists, or the quotations published in the *Financial Times* or *Times*.

Answers to activities

Answer 12.1

If a company does not maintain a fixed asset register, the auditors should ask the client for a schedule listing the major items of fixed assets. This schedule should show the original cost and estimated depreciated value; it should also indicate additions and disposals during the year. (Alternatively auditors may have a schedule from previous years on file, and would need information about movements in fixed assets to update it.)

The schedule should be reconciled to the draft accounts.

Auditors should verify additions to supporting documentation and should inspect assets acquired.

Auditors may have problems obtaining evidence on the completeness of disposals. If they have a schedule from previous years, they can inspect the assets recorded on it to see if they still exist and can confirm ownership to appropriate supporting documentation. If however the auditors do not have information about what was held at the start of the year they will have to scrutinise the cash book for any large unexplained receipts, and also inspect board minutes for reference to disposals.

Auditors should also use their knowledge of the business to consider whether fixed asset additions should have resulted in corresponding disposals (for example new motor vehicles replacing old). Alternatively changes in the business such as discontinuation of certain products may be expected to result in disposals.

Ultimately auditors may be forced to conclude that they have insufficient evidence on fixed assets.

Answer 12.2

(a) We should carry out the following work on plant and machinery additions.

   (i) Check that the purchase has been authorised by examining board minutes or other evidence of authorisation.

   (ii) Confirm the purchase price paid to suppliers' invoice and cash book.

   (iii) Inspect the new plant and machinery to confirm its existence.

   (iv) Check whether any security has been granted over the plant and machinery; if it has, we should ensure that it has been properly recorded and disclosed in the accounts.

(b) We should carry out the following work on the depreciation charge.

   (i) Check whether the depreciation charge is consistent with charges for previous years, and consistent with the company's accounting policies relating to depreciation.

   (ii) Check the calculation of the depreciation charge for individual vehicles/in total.

12: Fixed assets

(iii) Review the profits or losses on disposals of motor vehicles during the year to ensure that the charge is not excessive.

(iv) Check that depreciation rates appear reasonable in the light of vehicle usage and replacement policy.

(v) Check that all vehicles are being depreciated.

(vi) Check that no further depreciation is being charged on fully depreciated vehicles.

(vii) Check that the client's depreciation policy and depreciation charge are disclosed in the accounts.

Answer 12.3

(a) Alternative means of obtaining evidence of the existence of vehicles include the following.

   (i) Insurance policies

   (ii) Evidence of repair and maintenance expenditure

   (iii) MOT certificate

   (iv) Correspondence with the salesmen, including acknowledgement by the salesmen that they have the cars

(b) We should consider whether:

   (i) The change in accounting policy is reasonable; the new office block may have meant the company has purchased furniture that is significantly more expensive than previously.

   (ii) The furniture purchased is expensive enough to warrant capitalisation.

   (iii) The expected life of the furniture is reasonable (has the board decided that all furniture will be replaced after three years?).

   Audit work on the furniture should include:

   (i) Confirm costs to purchase invoices.

   (ii) Inspect the furniture to confirm its existence and condition, and to check if the expected life appears reasonable.

(c) Audit work should include:

   (i) Inspect the crane to confirm its condition and the fact that it is still being used.

   (ii) Check the invoices which detail the expenditure on the crane.

   (iii) If the client has used internal labour in bringing the crane back into use, check labour costs to wage records.

   (iv) Check the insurance policy on the crane for evidence of valuation.

Answer 12.4

(a) Ownership could be verified by the following procedures.

   (i) Select a sample of fixed investments stock held at the year end and inspect the relevant certificates. These should be in the scheme's name.

   (ii) For listed companies, again select a sample of investments held at the year end and agree to the share certificate in the scheme's name.

   (iii) Compare the list of investments held with the list of income received and investigate any discrepancies between the two.

   (iv) Check dividend and interest vouchers for scheme's name and number of shares held.

(b) Income is received from two sources - fixed interest investments and shares in listed companies.

   However, there is also the question of tax deducted at source on this income which will be recoverable by the scheme from the Inland Revenue. Because not all the tax will have been recovered by the year-end it will be necessary to reconcile the amount received in the year and the opening and closing debtor.

   (i) For fixed interest stocks, verify the overall income in the accounts by analytical review. In overall terms as the income is fixed the expected income can be calculated. It will be necessary to take into account tax reclaimed from the Inland Revenue and opening and closing debtors for tax.

Part D: Substantive procedures

- (ii) For fixed interest stocks, test individual receipts to the cash books to ensure that the expected interest was received, and check the calculations.
- (iii) For shares in listed companies select a sample of investments and obtain from Extel or a similar reference details of dividend payments made during the year.
- (iv) Trace receipt of these dividends to the cash book via dividend vouchers.
- (v) For shares in listed companies, reconcile total income in accounts to total income in cash book.
- (vi) Carry out comparison of dividends received as compared with previous year and check changes to Extel.
- (vii) For shares disposed of in year, check to Extel or broker's note that all dividends to which the scheme was entitled have been received in the year.
- (viii) For shares bought in year, check to Extel or broker's note that dividends to which the scheme was entitled have been received.
- (ix) Review the reclaims of tax made by the scheme to the Inland Revenue to ensure that all reclaims had been made.

(c) The following procedures should be carried out on investments disposed of during the year.

- (i) Verify disposals to contract notes, sales agreements or other relevant information.
- (ii) Check whether the disposal of shares had been authorised.
- (iii) Confirm that the profit or loss on the sale of investments has been correctly calculated, taking account of:
    - (1) Basis of identifying costs of investment
    - (2) Bonus issues of shares
    - (3) Rights issues
    - (4) Accrued interest
    - (5) Taxation

Now try Question 12 in the Exam Question Bank

Chapter 13 Debtors and cash

Chapter topic list

1. Introduction
2. Debtors and prepayments
3. Bank and cash

The following study sessions are covered in this Chapter:

Syllabus reference

23(b) For each area in the financial statements of an incorporated company, provide examples of the representations made by directors — 6

24(a) Design audit programmes to meet specific audit objectives with regard to the following balance sheet items: — 6
- (iii) Trade debtors
- (iv) Prepayments
- (v) Bank and cash

Part D: Substantive procedures

1 INTRODUCTION

1.1 In this chapter we deal with the remaining major current assets, debtors and bank and cash.

1.2 With debtors, auditors are primarily concerned to prove that:

- Debtors represent **amounts** due to the company (the assertions of existence and rights and obligations).

- **Adequate allowance** has been made for bad debts, discounts and returns (valuation).

- **Cut-off of goods** despatched and invoiced is satisfactory (measurement, rights and obligations).

1.3 The primary procedure for obtaining evidence of the correctness of the **rights and obligations** of debtor balances is the **debtors' circularisation**, asking debtors for confirmation of balances owed. Satisfactory responses to the circularisation are strong audit evidence, as they are **written evidence** from **third parties**.

1.4 You need to know the specific procedures auditors follow when carrying out a circularisation. Inevitably also auditors will not obtain exact confirmation from all of the debtors circularised, and you should be aware of what auditors do in those circumstances.

1.5 Although debtors may agree that they owe the amount stated in the client's books, that does not mean that they will pay that amount. Therefore auditors will also need to carry out tests to confirm the **valuation of** debtors and the **adequacy** of **bad debt provisions**.

1.6 Finally **cut-off** will need to be tested. Most often this will be done along with testing of stock and purchases cut-off.

1.7 The other major current asset is **cash at bank** and in hand. Cash at bank will be confirmed by obtaining confirmation in the form of a **bank letter** from the clients' bank(s) of balances held at the year-end. Auditors will then check that the balances shown in the bank letter can be reconciled to the balances shown in the client's records by carrying out a bank reconciliation or checking the reconciliation that the client has prepared.

1.8 **Cash in hand** can be confirmed by a **cash count**. Cash counts are not carried out on many audits since cash balances held as floats are small. However you need to know the procedures involved, because cash counts may be necessary when the amount of cash passing through a business is large (retail operations, for example), or a cash count is performed to test controls over cash as well as to substantiate the balances held.

2 DEBTORS AND PREPAYMENTS   Pilot paper, 6/04

Debtors' listing and aged debtor analysis

2.1 Much of the auditors' detailed work will be based on a selection of debtors' balances chosen from a listing of sales ledger balances, prepared by the client or auditors. Ideally the list should be aged, showing the period or periods of time money has been owed. The following substantive procedures are necessary to check the **completeness** and **accuracy** of the listing.

> - **Check** the **balances** from the **individual sales ledger accounts** to the **list of balances** and vice versa
> - **Check** the **total** of the **list** to the **sales ledger control account**
> - **Cast** (ie add up) the **list of balances** and the **sales ledger control account**
> - **Confirm** whether **list of balances reconciles** with the **sales ledger control account**

The debtors' circularisation

2.2 *Objectives of circularisation*

ISA 501 *External confirmations* covers confirmation of debtors. This begins by stating that, when it is reasonable to expect customers to respond, the auditors should ordinarily plan to obtain direct confirmation of debtors to individuals entries in the account balance.

2.3 The verification of trade debtors by contacting them directly to confirm balances (direct circularisation) is therefore the normal means of checking whether debtors exist and owe *bona fide* amounts due to the company (rights and obligations, existence).

2.4 Circularisation should produce a written statement from each debtor contacted that the amount owed at the date of the circularisation is correct. This is, *prima facie*, reliable audit evidence, being from an independent source and in 'documentary' form.

Timing

2.5 Ideally the circularisation should take place immediately after the year-end and hence cover the year-end balances to be included in the balance sheet. However, time constraints may make it impossible to achieve this ideal. In these circumstances it may be acceptable to carry out the circularisation **prior to the year-end** provided that circulation is no more than three months before the year end and internal controls are strong.

Client's mandate

2.6 Confirmation is essentially an act of the **client**, who alone can authorise third parties to divulge information to the auditors. Should the client refuse to co-operate the auditors will need to consider the potential impact on the audit opinion, as they may not be able to satisfy themselves by means of other audit procedures as to the validity and accuracy of the balances.

Positive v negative circularisation

2.7 When circularisation is undertaken the method of requesting information from the debtor may be either 'positive' or 'negative'.

- Under the **positive** method the debtor is requested to confirm the accuracy of the balance shown or state in what respect he is in disagreement.
- Under the **negative** method the debtor is requested to reply **only** if the amount stated is disputed.

2.8 In either case, the customer is requested to reply **direct** to the auditors. Both methods may be used in conjunction.

Part D: Substantive procedures

2.9 The positive method is generally preferable as it is designed to encourage definite replies from those circularised. The negative method may be used if the client has good internal control, with a large number of small accounts. In some circumstances, say where there is a small number of large accounts and a large number of small accounts, a combination of both methods may be appropriate.

2.10 The following is a specimen 'positive' confirmation letter.

MANUFACTURING CO LIMITED
15 South Street
London

Date

Messrs   (debtor)

In accordance with the request of our auditors, Messrs Arthur Daley & Co, we ask that you kindly confirm to them directly your indebtedness to us at (insert date) which, according to our records, amounted to £.......... as shown by the enclosed statement.

If the above amount is in agreement with your records, please sign in the space provided below and return this letter direct to our auditors in the enclosed stamped addressed envelope.

If the amount is not in agreement with your records, please notify our auditors directly of the amount shown by your records, and if possible detail on the reverse of this letter full particulars of the difference.

Yours faithfully,

For Manufacturing Co Limited

Reference No: ....

....

(Tear off slip)

The amount shown above is/is not * in agreement with our records as at

Account No   ....   Signature   ....

Date   ....   Title or position ....

* The position according to our records is shown overleaf.

Note:

- The letter is on the client's paper, signed by the client.
- A copy of the statement is attached.
- The reply is sent directly to the auditor in a pre-paid envelope.

2.11 The statements will normally be prepared by the client's staff, from which point the auditors, as a safeguard against the possibility of fraudulent manipulation, must maintain **strict control** over the **checking** and **despatch** of the statements. Precautions must also be taken to ensure that undelivered items are returned, not to the client, but to the auditors' own office for follow-up by them.

Sample selection

2.12 Auditors will normally only circularise a sample of debtors. If this sample is to yield a meaningful result it must be based upon a complete list of all debtor accounts. In addition, when constructing the sample, the following classes of account should receive special attention:

- **Old unpaid accounts**
- **Accounts written off** during the period under review
- **Accounts** with **credit balances**
- **Accounts settled** by **round sum payments**

Similarly, the following should not be overlooked:

- **Accounts** with **nil balances**
- **Accounts** which have been **paid** by the date of the examination

2.13 Auditors may apply stratification techniques to ensure that a sufficient proportion of debtors are confirmed.

Follow-up procedures

2.14 Auditors will have to carry out further work in relation to those debtors who:

- **Disagree** with the **balance stated** (positive and negative circularisation)
- **Do not respond** (positive circularisation only)

2.15 In the case of disagreements, the debtor response should have identified specific amounts which are disputed.

2.16 Disagreements can arise for the following reasons.

(a) There is a **dispute** between the client and the customer. The reasons for the dispute would have to be identified, and provision made if appropriate against the debt.

(b) **Cut-off problems exist,** because the client records the following year's sales in the current year or because goods returned by the customer in the current year are not recorded in the current year. Cut-off testing may have to be extended (see below).

(c) The customer may have sent the **monies before** the year-end, but the monies were **not recorded** by the client as receipts until **after** the year-end. Detailed cut-off work may be required on receipts.

(d) Monies received may have been posted to the **wrong account** or a cash-in-transit account. Auditors should check if there is evidence of other mis-posting. If the monies have been posted to a cash-in-transit account, auditors should ensure this account has been cleared promptly.

(e) Customers who are also suppliers may **net off balances** owed and owing. Auditors should check that this is allowed.

(f) **Teeming and lading** (**stealing** monies and **incorrectly posting** other receipts so that no particular debtor is seriously in debt) is a fraud that can arise in this area. If auditors suspect teeming and lading has occurred, detailed testing will be required on cash receipts, particularly on prompt posting of cash receipts.

2.17 When the positive request method is used the auditors must follow up by all practicable means those debtors who **fail to respond**. Second requests should be sent out in the event of no reply being received within two or three weeks, and if necessary, this may be followed by phoning the debtor.

Part D: Substantive procedures

2.18 After two, or even three, attempts to obtain confirmation, a list of the outstanding items will normally be passed to a responsible company official, preferably independent of the sales accounting department, who will arrange for them to be investigated.

2.19 If it proves impossible to get confirmations from individual debtors, alternative procedures include the following.

- Check receipt of cash after date
- Verify valid purchase orders if any
- Examine the account to see if the balance outstanding represents specific invoices and confirm their validity
- Obtain explanations for invoices remaining unpaid after subsequent ones have been paid
- Check if the balance on the account is growing, and if so, why
- Test company's control over the issue of credit notes and the write-off of bad debts

Additional procedures where circularisation is carried out before year-end

2.20 The auditors will need to carry out the following procedures where their circularisation is carried out before the year-end.

- **Review** and **reconcile entries** on the **sales ledger control account** for the intervening period
- **Verify sales entries** from the control account by checking sales day book entries, copy sales invoices and despatch notes
- **Check** that **appropriate credit entries** have been made for goods returned notes and other evidence of returns/allowances to the sales ledger control account
- **Select a sample** from the **cash received records** and **ensure** that **receipts** have been **credited** to the control account
- **Review** the **list of balances** at the **circularisation** date and year end and **investigate** any **unexpected movements** or lack of them (it may be prudent to send further confirmation requests at the year end to material debtors where review results are unsatisfactory)
- **Carry out analytical review** procedures, comparing debtors' ratios at the confirmation date and year-end
- **Carry out** year end **cut-off tests**, in addition to any performed at the date of the confirmation (see below)

Evaluation and conclusions

2.21 All circularisations, regardless of timing, must be properly recorded and evaluated. All **balance disagreements** and **non-replies** must be **followed up** and their effect on total debtors evaluated.

2.22 **Differences** arising that merely represent **invoices** or **cash in transit** (normal timing differences) generally do not require adjustment, but disputed amounts, and errors by the client, may indicate that further substantive work is necessary to determine whether material adjustments may be required.

Activity 13.1

(a) How reliable a source of audit evidence is a debtors' circularisation?

(b) Describe the audit procedures that should be followed when planning and performing a circularisation to be carried out at the client's year end. (You are not required to consider follow-up procedures.)

(c) Describe the audit work you would carry out on the following replies to a debtors' circularisation.

    (i) Balance agreed by debtor
    (ii) Balance not agreed by debtor
    (iii) Debtor is unable to confirm the balance because of the form of records kept by the debtor
    (iv) Debtor does not reply to the circularisation

2.23 EXAMPLE

At the year end, Jonathan arranged for client staff to send out debtors' circularisation requests to a sample (chosen by him) of Brown Limited's debtors. Now, at the final audit, he is processing the replies.

From a sample of 15 debtors, he has obtained 13 replies. Of these 13, 10 agreed the balance that was on Brown Limited's sales ledger, so Jonathan has confirmed these balances.

He is now turning his attention to the other five balances. He has asked the client if they would follow up the two that have not yet replied, and the sales ledger clerk is telephoning then now.

He must now perform a reconciliation between the balances the three other customers have stated they are and the sales ledger figure. The details from the customers are given below:

Ashleys Limited

Balance per sales ledger: £24,219
Balance per customer: £16,704

Difference per customer: remittance of £7,515 dated 28 September

Melanie Limited

Balance per sales ledger: £32,591
Balance per customer: £30,204

Difference per customer: credit requested re invoice no S5201497 (£2,387).

Wilkes plc

Balance per sales ledger: £938
Balance per customer: £692

Difference per customer: unexplained (£246)

Jonathan must investigate each of these reconciling items. He should review sales ledger receipts around the year end to verify the difference on Ashleys' account (if the remittance was not received until October the sales ledger balance is correct) and to see if the £246 on Wilkes' account is a similar receipt. If it is not, he must scrutinise the ledger account for Wilkes to see if he can discover the difference and also discuss it with the sales ledger clerk.

Part D: Substantive procedures

He might wish to review credit notes to see if it a credit that has been omitted from the ledger in error.

In terms of the Melanie balance, Jonathan should discuss the requested credit with the sales director to determine if it justified and likely to be issued. Even if the director says the credit will not be issued, it might be wise to include this amount on a schedule of bad debts as it appears that the customer is not prepared to pay the debt.

If replies from the other two customers with replies outstanding are not forthcoming Jonathan will have to carry out alternative procedures on these balances, for example cash after date tests.

Bad debts

2.24 A significant test here will be reviewing the cash received after date. This will provide evidence of collectability of debts (and hence **valuation**). It also provides some evidence of correctness of title (**rights and obligations**), although ideally it should be carried out as well as a debtors' circularisation (which is the main test on rights and obligations).

2.25 The following procedures will be important to check for bad debts and thus **confirm** valuation.

- **Confirm necessity/adequacy** of allowance against **write-off** of debts by review of correspondence, solicitors' debt collection, agencies' letters, liquidation statements
- **Examine customer files** on **overdue debts**, and **assess** whether **provision** is required in the circumstances
- **Consider** whether **amounts owed** may be **not recovered** where there have been:
    - Round sum payments on account
    - Invoices unpaid after subsequent invoices paid
- **Review customer files/correspondence** from solicitors for evidence of potential bad debts
- **Confirm allowance** for bad debts
    - How well previous year's provision predicted actual debts
    - Calculation correct
    - Formula used reasonable and consistent with previous years
- **Examine credit notes** issued after the year-end for **provisions** that should be made against current period balances
- **Check accuracy** of **aged debtor analysis** by comparing analysis with dates on invoices and **matching cash receipts** against outstanding invoices
- **Investigate unusual features** on aged debtors analysis, such as:
    - Unapplied credits
    - Unallocated cash
- **Investigate unusual items** in the sales ledger, such as:
    - Journal entries transferring balances from one account to another
    - Journal entries that clear post year-end debtor balances
    - Balances not made up of specific invoices
    - Sales ledger accounts with significant adjustments or credit notes

2.26 Auditors should also consider the collectability of material debtor balances other than those contained in the sales ledger. Auditors should request certificates of loan balances from employees and others, and inspect the authority if necessary.

Sales   Pilot paper, 6/04

2.27 Debtors will often be tested in conjunction with sales. Auditors are seeking to obtain evidence that sales are **completely** and **accurately recorded**. This will involve carrying out certain procedures to test for **completeness** of sales and also testing **cut-off**.

Completeness and occurrence of sales

2.28 **Analytical procedures** are likely to be important when testing completeness. Auditors should consider the following.

- The **level of sales** over the year, compared on a month-by-month basis with the previous year
- The effect on sales value of **changes in quantities** sold
- The effect on sales value of changes in **products** or **prices**
- The level of **goods returned, sales allowances** and **discounts**
- The **efficiency of labour** as expressed in sales or pre-tax profit per employee

2.29 In addition auditors must record reasons for changes in the **gross profit margin** ($\frac{\text{Gross profit}}{\text{Turnover}} \times 100\%$). Analysis of the gross profit margin should be as detailed as possible, ideally broken down by **product area** and **month or quarter**.

2.30 As well as analytical procedures, auditors may feel that they need to test completeness of recording of individual sales in the accounting records. To do this, auditors should start with the documents that first record sales (**goods despatched notes** or **till rolls** for example). They should trace details of sales recorded in these through intermediate documents such as the sales **day book invoices** and **summaries through** to the **sales ledger**.

2.31 Auditors must **ensure** that the **population of documents** from which the sample is originally taken is itself complete, by checking for example the completeness of the sequence of goods despatched notes. Auditors should also **review reconciliations** of the sales ledger control account and other relevant reconciliations, and **investigate unusual items**.

> **Exam alert**
>
> You must remember the direction of this test. Since we are checking the completeness of recording of sales in the sales ledger, we cannot take a sample from the ledger since the sample cannot include what has not been recorded.

2.32 If on the other hand, the auditors suspect that sales may have been **invalidly** recorded (may **not** have **occurred**), then the sample will be taken from the sales ledger and confirmed to supporting documentation (orders, despatch notes etc).

Part D: Substantive procedures

Measurement of sales

2.33 The following tests should be performed.

> - Check the **pricing calculations** and **additions** on invoices
> - Check whether **discounts** have been **properly calculated**
> - Check whether **VAT** has been **added appropriately**
> - Check casting of the **sales ledger accounts** and **sales ledger control account**
> - Trace **debits** in the **sales account** to credit notes
> - Check casting of **sales ledger accounts** and **sales ledger control account**
> - **Review reconciliations** of sales ledger control account and other relevant reconciliations (for example till rolls) and investigate unusual items

Sales cut-off

2.34 During the stocktake the auditors will have obtained details of the last serial numbers of goods outward notes issued before the commencement of the stocktaking.

2.35 The following substantive procedures are designed to test that goods taken into stock are not also treated as sales in the year under review and, conversely, goods despatched are treated as sales in the year under review and not also treated as stock.

> - Check **goods despatched** and **returns inwards** notes around year-end to ensure:
>   - **Invoices** and **credit notes** are **dated** in the **correct period**
>   - **Invoices** and **credit notes** are **posted** to the **sales ledger** and **general ledger** in the correct period
> - **Reconcile entries** in the **sales ledger control account** around the **year-end** to daily batch invoice totals ensuring batches are posted in correct year
> - **Review sales ledger control account** around year-end for **unusual items**
> - **Review material after-date invoices, credit notes** and **adjustments** and ensure that they are properly treated as following year sales

Goods on sale or return

2.36 Care should be exercised to ensure that goods on sale or return are properly treated in the accounts. Except where the client has been notified of the sale of the goods they should be reflected in the accounts as **stock** at cost and not as debtors, otherwise profits may be incorrectly anticipated.

Inter-company indebtedness

2.37 Where significant trading occurs between group companies the auditors should have ascertained as a result of their tests of controls whether trading has been at arm's length. As regards the balances at the year end, the following substantive procedures are suggested.

> - **Confirm balances** owing from group and associated companies (current and loan accounts) with the other companies' records (directly, or by contacting other group members' auditors)

> - **Ensure** that **cut-off procedures** have operated properly regarding inter company transfers
> - **Assess realisability** of amounts owing
> - **Ascertain** the **nature** of the entries comprised in the balances at the year-end
> - **Ensure** that any **management charges** contained therein have been **calculated** on a **reasonable** and **consistent basis** and have been acknowledged by the debtor companies

Prepayments

2.38 The extent of audit testing will depend on the materiality of the amounts.

> - **Verify prepayments** by reference to the cash book, expense invoices, correspondence and so on
> - **Check calculations** of prepayments
> - **Review** the **detailed profit and loss account** to ensure that all likely prepayments have been provided for
> - **Review** the **prepayments** for **reasonableness** by comparing with prior years and using analytical procedures where applicable

Activity 13.2

Based on past events Itchy and Scratchy Ltd has decided that an allowance equal to 5% of debtors is required.

Required

State the audit work you would perform on this allowance.

3 BANK AND CASH

Bank balances

3.1 The audit of bank balances will need to cover completeness, existence, rights and obligations and valuation. All of these elements can be audited directly through the device of obtaining third party confirmations from the client's banks and reconciling these with the accounting records, having regard to cut-off.

3.2 As preparation, the auditors should update details of bank accounts held, ensuring the client holds accounts with bona fide banks.

The bank letter

3.3 The bank confirmation letter is an important third party confirmation.

3.4 The procedure is simple but important.

(a) The banks will require **explicit written authority** from their client to disclose the information requested.

Part D: Substantive procedures

(b) The **auditors' request** must **refer** to the **client's letter** of authority and the date thereof. Alternatively it may be countersigned by the client or it may be accompanied by a specific letter of authority.

(c) In the case of joint accounts, **letters of authority** signed by all **parties** will be necessary.

(d) Such **letters** of **authority** may either **give permission** to the bank to disclose information for a specific request or grant permission for an indeterminate length of time.

(e) The request should **reach** the **branch manager** at least **two weeks in advance** of the client's **year-end** and should state both that year-end date and the previous year-end date.

(f) The **auditors** should themselves **check** that the **bank response covers all the information** in the standard and other responses.

3.5 Bank confirmation request letter – illustration

[XXXXXX Bank plc
25 XXX Street
Warrington
Cheshire
WA1 1XQ]

Dear Sirs,

In accordance with the agreed practice for provision of information to auditors, please forward information on our mutual client(s) as detailed below on behalf of the bank, its branches and subsidiaries. This request and your response will not create any contractual or other duty with us.

COMPANIES OR OTHER BUSINESS ENTITIES
(attach a separate listing if necessary)

[Parent Company Ltd
Subsidiary 1 Ltd
Subsidiary 2 Ltd]

AUDIT CONFIRMATION DATE (30 APRIL 2000)

Information required	Tick
Standard	
Trade finance	
Derivative and commodity trading	
Custodian arrangements	
Other information (see attached)	

The authority to disclose information signed by your customer is attached / already held by you (delete as appropriate). Please advise us if this authority is insufficient for you to provide full disclosure of the information requested.

The contract name is [John Caller]   Telephone [01 234 5678]

Yours faithfully,
[XXX Accountants]

Standard request for information

3.6 The following information should always be disclosed by banks upon receipt of a request for information for audit purposes. Responses should be given in the order below and if no information is available then this must be stated as 'None' in the response.

1 **Account and balance details**

Give full titles of all bank accounts including loans, (whether in sterling or another currency) together with their account numbers and balances. For accounts closed during the 12 months up to the audit confirmation date give the account details and date of closure.

Note. Also give details where your customer's name is joined with that of other parties and where the account is in a trade name.

State if any account or balances are subject to any restriction(s) whatsoever. Indicate the nature and extent of the restriction, eg garnishee order.

2 **Facilities**

Give the following details of all loans, overdrafts and associated guarantees and indemnities:

- Term
- Repayment frequency and/or review date
- Details of period of availability of agreed finance, ie finance remaining undrawn
- Detail the facility limit

3 **Securities**

With reference to the facilities detailed in (2) above give the following details:

- Any security formally charged (date, ownership and type of charge). State whether the security supports facilities granted by the bank to the customer or to another party.

  Note. Give details if a security is limited in amount or to a specific borrowing or if to your knowledge there is a prior, equal or subordinate charge.

- Where there are any arrangements for set-off of balances or compensating balances eg back to back loans, give particulars (ie, date, type of document and accounts covered) of any acknowledgement of set-off, whether given by specific letter of set-off or incorporated in some other document.

> 4 **Additional Banking Relationships**
>
> State if you are aware of the customer(s) having any additional relationships with branches or subsidiaries of the Bank not covered by the response. Supply a list of branches etc.

Cut-off

3.7 Care must be taken to ensure that there is no **window dressing**, by checking cut-off carefully. Window dressing in this context is usually manifested as an attempt to overstate the liquidity of the company by:

(a) Keeping the cash book open to take credit in the year for **remittances actually received** after the year end, thus enhancing the balance at bank and reducing debtors

(b) **Recording cheques** as **paid** in the period under review which are not actually despatched until after the year end, thus decreasing the balance at bank and reducing creditors

A combination of (a) and (b) can contrive to present an artificially healthy looking current ratio.

3.8 With the possibility of (a) above in mind, where lodgements have not been cleared by the bank until the new period the auditors should **examine** the **paying-in slip** to ensure that the amounts were actually paid into the bank on or before the balance sheet date.

3.9 As regards (b) above, where there appears to be a particularly **large number** of **outstanding cheques** at the year-end, the auditors should check whether these were **cleared** within a **reasonable time** in the new period. If not, this may indicate that despatch occurred after the year-end.

Summary of bank balance procedures

3.10 The following suggested substantive balance sheet tests summarise the principal audit procedures discussed above relevant to bank balances. The procedures apply to all bank accounts.

> - **Obtain standard bank confirmations** from each bank with which the client conducted business during the audit period
>
> - **Check arithmetic** of bank reconciliation
>
> - **Trace cheques shown as outstanding** from the bank reconciliation to the cash book prior to the year-end and to the **after date bank statements** and **obtain explanations** for any large or unusual **items not cleared** at the time of the audit
>
> - **Compare cash book(s)** and **bank statements** in detail, and **check items outstanding** at the reconciliation date to bank reconciliations concerned
>
> - **Obtain explanations** for **all items** in the **cash book** for which there are **no corresponding entries in** the **bank statement** and vice versa
>
> - **Verify contra items** appearing in the cash books or bank statements

- **Verify** by checking pay-in slips that **uncleared bankings** are **paid in** prior to the year end
- **Examine all lodgements** in respect of which payment has been refused by the bank. Ensure that they are cleared on re-presentation or that other appropriate steps have been taken to effect recovery of the due amount
- **Verify** balances per **cash book** according to the **bank reconciliation** with **cash book, bank statements and general ledger**
- **Verify** the **bank balances** with reply to **standard bank letter** and with the **bank statements**
- **Scrutinise** the cash book and bank statements before and after the balance sheet date for **exceptional entries** or **transfers** which have a material effect on the balance shown to be in hand
- **Identify** whether any **accounts** are **secured** on the **assets** of the company
- **Consider** whether there is a **legal right** of **set-off** of overdrafts against positive bank balances
- **Determine** whether the **bank accounts** are **subject** to any **restrictions**
- **Obtain explanations** for **all items** in the **cash book** for which there are **no corresponding entries in** the **bank statement** and vice versa

Note. Auditors should ensure that all cheques are despatched immediately after signature and entry in the cash book. Examine the interval between dates of certain of the larger cheques in the cash book and payment by the bank since this may indicate that cheques were despatched after the year-end (window dressing).

3.11 EXAMPLE

Jonathan is auditing the bank balance at Brown Limited. He has obtained a copy of the reconciliation from the client and has checked that it adds up properly. He has also confirmed that the balance on the reconciliation for the bank balance agrees to the bank letter the auditors have received from the bank and the cash book balance agrees to the cash book.

He now has to obtain the post balance sheet date bank statements from the client so that he can trace the reconciling items and ensures that they all cleared the bank in reasonable time. Cheques are likely to take longer to clear than receipts as the clearance time will depend on the cheque reaching the supplier in the first place and then the supplier's system for banking it.

Jonathan should also scrutinise the cash book and the bank statements for unusual items.

Cash balances

3.12 Cash balances/floats are often individually immaterial but they may require some audit emphasis because of the opportunities for fraud that could exist where internal control is weak and because in total they may be material. However, in enterprises such as hotels, the amount of cash in hand at the balance sheet date could be considerable; the same goes for retail organisations.

Part D: Substantive procedures

3.13 Where the auditors determine that cash balances are potentially material they may conduct a cash count, ideally at the balance sheet date. Rather like attendance at stocktaking, the conduct of the count falls into three phases: planning, the count itself and follow up procedures.

Planning

3.14 Planning is an essential element, for it is an important principle that all cash balances are counted at the same time as far as possible. Cash in this context may include unbanked cheques received, IOUs and credit card slips, in addition to notes and coins.

3.15 As part of their planning procedures the auditors will hence need to determine the **locations** where cash is held and which of these locations warrant a count.

3.16 Planning decisions will need to be recorded on the current audit file including:

- The **precise time** of the count(s) and location(s)
- The **names** of the **audit staff** conducting the counts
- The **names** of the **client staff** intending to be present at each location

Where a location is not visited it may be expedient to obtain a letter from the client confirming the balance.

Cash count

3.17 The following matters apply to the count itself.

- All cash/petty **cash books** should be **written up** to date in ink (or other permanent form) at the time of the count.
- All **balances** must be **counted** at the **same time**.
- All **negotiable securities** must be **available** and **counted** at the time the cash balances are counted.
- At **no time** should the **auditors** be left **alone** with the cash and negotiable securities.
- **All cash** and securities **counted** must be **recorded** on working papers subsequently filed on the current audit file. Reconciliations should be prepared where applicable (for example imprest petty cash float).

Follow-up procedures

3.18 Follow up procedures should ensure that:

- **Certificates** of **cash-in-hand** are **obtained** as appropriate.
- **Unbanked cheques/cash receipts** have subsequently been **paid in** and agree to the bank reconciliation.
- **IOUs** and cheques cashed for employees have been **reimbursed**.
- **IOUs or cashed cheques outstanding** for **unreasonable periods** of time have been provided for.
- The **balances** as **counted** are **reflected** in the **accounts** (subject to any agreed amendments because of shortages and so on).

13: Debtors and cash

Activity 13.3
(a) List the contents of a standard bank letter for audit purposes.
(b) What tests should auditors normally carry out on the bank reconciliation?

Exam alert
Remember that the bank letter contains the balance held by the client at the bank **per the bank's records**. This must be reconciled to the balance held with the bank **per the client's records**.

Key learning points

- **Circularisation** of debtors is a major procedure. Generally circularisation will be **positive** (debtors confirm client's figures are correct).
- Auditors must follow up:
  - Debtor disagreements
  - Failure by debtors to respond
- Testing of the **bad debt allowance** and sales **cut-off** is also important.
- Bank balances are usually confirmed directly with the **bank** by a bank letter. Balances confirmed by the bank must be reconciled to the balances shown in the client cash book.
- **Cash balances** should be **checked** if irregularities are suspected.

Quick quiz

1 In what circumstances might it be acceptable to carry out a debtors' circularisation prior to the year end?
2 (a) What is the difference between a positive and negative debtors' circularisation?
   (b) In what circumstances might a negative circularisation be undertaken?
3 What types of account require special attention when selecting a sample for a debtors' circularisation?
4 What audit work should be carried out on prepayments?
5 What must auditors get in order to obtain a response to a bank letter from a client's bank?
6 How far in advance of the year-end should a bank letter normally be sent?
7 Give two examples of 'window-dressing' of year-end bank balances?
8 What are the main procedures that auditors should perform when carrying out a cash count?

Answers to quick quiz

1 A debtors' circularisation can be carried out prior to the year-end provided:

   (a) The circularisation takes place not more than two or three months before the year-end.

   (b) The internal control system is strong enough to ensure that the circularisation plus work on the intervening period gives auditors sufficient assurance.

2 (a) A positive circularisation is when the debtor is requested to reply whether or not he disagrees with the balance stated. A negative circularisation is where the debtor is requested to reply only when he disagrees with the balance stated.

   (b) A negative circularisation can be used when the client has a good internal control system and debtors consist of a large number of small balances. It can also be used to confirm smaller balances in a ledger with positive circularisation being used for larger balances.

Part D: Substantive procedures

3   The following accounts require special attention in a debtors' circularisation.

   (a)   Old unpaid accounts
   (b)   Accounts written off during the period under review
   (c)   Accounts with credit balances
   (d)   Accounts settled by round-sum payments

4   Prepayments should be tested using the following tests.

   (a)   Verify amounts provided to supporting evidence such as cash book, expense invoices and correspondence.

   (b)   Check calculations.

   (c)   Review the profit and loss account to see whether all likely prepayments have been provided.

   (d)   Review for reasonableness by comparing with previous years and using appropriate analytical procedures.

5   Clients must give explicit written authority for the bank to disclose balances held.

6   Bank letters should normally be sent so as to reach the bank at least two weeks in advance.

7   Two examples of window-dressing are:

   (a)   Including cash received after the year-end as cash receipts during the year
   (b)   Recording cheques as paid during the year, but not sending the cheques out until after the year-end

8   When counting cash, auditors should:

   (a)   Ensure all records are written up to date in ink.

   (b)   Count all balances of cash and negotiable securities at the same time.

   (c)   Count cash in the presence of the individuals responsible (auditors should not be left alone with the cash).

   (d)   Record all amounts counted and confirm balances to accounting records.

Answers to activities

Answer 13.1

(a)   The debtors' circularisation can often provide strong evidence of the existence and valuation of a balance shown as outstanding from a customer. This is because the circularisation provides confirmation from an independent third party and in documentary form, and is therefore the most reliable type of audit evidence available.

Because of the quality of evidence it produces, a debtors' circularisation is normally considered a standard procedure and only omitted under special circumstances. It can be strengthened by asking customers who disagree with the balance to state the make-up of their purchase ledger balance.

However on occasions the assurance provided by the circularisation will be limited for the following reasons.

   (i)   The circularisation is generally carried out on a sample, and hence there is sampling risk that the circularisation will show an incorrect result.

   (ii)   Some debtors confirm balances automatically without checking the circularisation letter to their own records.

   (iii) Some debtors report that they cannot confirm the balance from their accounting records. However this sort of reply does at least provide evidence that the balance exists.

   (iv)   Some debtors will disagree with the balance, and the client's balance is correct. Usually this is due to cash or purchases in transit, or customer failure to update its purchase ledger.

   (v)   A debtors' circularisation may confirm debtors agree that the money is owed, but it does not confirm that they will pay the money. Hence further tests will be required on recoverability.

The above observations apply to a positive circularisation. On occasions a negative circularisation (asking the debtor to reply only if he disagrees with the balance) will be used. However this procedure is weaker than a positive circularisation because of the risk that debtors will not reply even though their records show different balances to the client's.

(b) The debtors' circularisation should normally take place immediately after the year-end covering balances outstanding at the year-end. When planning the debtors' circularisation, auditors should obtain a list of debtor balances, reconciled to the total in the sales ledger control account. The auditors should review the list for any obvious omissions or misstatements (customers where large balances were expected).

The auditors should then select a sample from the list, concentrating on the following accounts:

(i) Overdue accounts
(ii) Accounts written off in the period under review
(iii) Accounts with credit balances
(iv) Accounts settled by round-sum payments

The sample should also include:

(i) Accounts with nil balances
(ii) Accounts that had been paid since the year-end

The auditors should ensure a letter is prepared for each debtor sampled. The letter should be on the client's headed notepaper and should be signed by the client. It should authorise the debtor to contact the auditors about the amount owed. A pre-paid envelope addressed to the auditors should be provided for this purpose. The letter would normally state that if the debtor agrees with the amount, they should sign the letter to indicate agreement. If they do not agree with the amount, they shoal notify the auditors directly of the amount they believe is owed, and if possible give full details of the difference.

The letter should be accompanied by a debtors' statement which should be prepared by the client at the year-end.

Auditors should check the letters and statements to the debtors' listing prior to despatch, and should supervise despatch themselves.

(c) The audit work required on the various replies to a debtors' circularisation would be as follows.

(i) *Balances agreed by debtor*

Where the balance has been agreed by the debtor all that is required would be to ensure that the debt does appear to be collectable. This would be achieved by reviewing cash received after date or considering the adequacy of any provision made for a long outstanding debt.

(ii) *Balances not agreed by debtor*

All balance disagreements must be followed up and their effect on total debtors evaluated. Differences arising that merely represent invoices or cash in transit (which are normal timing differences) generally do not require adjustment, but disputed amounts, and errors by the client, may indicate that further substantive work is necessary to determine whether material adjustments are required.

(iii) *Debtor is unable to confirm the balance because of the form of records he or she maintains*

Certain companies, often computerised, operate systems which make it impossible for them to confirm the balance on their account. Typically in these circumstances their purchase ledger is merely a list of unpaid invoices. However, given sufficient information the debtor will be able to confirm that any given invoice is outstanding. Hence the auditors can circularise such enterprises successfully, but they will need to break down the total on the account into its constituent outstanding invoices.

(iv) *Debtor does not reply to circularisation*

When the positive request method is used the auditors must follow up by all practicable means those debtors who fail to respond. Second requests should be sent out in the event of no reply being received within two or three weeks and if necessary this may be followed by telephoning the customer with the client's permission.

If no reply has been received a list of the outstanding items will normally be passed to a responsible company official, preferably independent of the sales department, who will arrange for them to be investigated.

Other auditing tests that can establish that there existed a valid debt from a genuine customer at the date of the verification are as follows.

(1) Check receipt of cash after date.
(2) Verify valid purchase orders, if any.
(3) Examine the account to see if the balance represents specific outstanding invoices.
(4) Obtain explanations for invoices remaining unpaid after subsequent ones have been paid.
(5) See if the balance on the account is growing, and if so, why.
(6) Test the company's control over the issue of credit notes and the write-off of bad debts.

Part D: Substantive procedures

Answer 13.2

I would carry out the following tests on Itchy and Scratchy Ltd's bad debt provision.

(a) Check that the basis used is consistent with previous years.

(b) Consider whether the basis was reasonable, reviewing recent years to see the allowance made had been adequate but not excessive.

(c) Review the sales ledger for this year, checking the ageing of debtors, and considering whether the pattern of debtors had changed in terms of amounts owed and collection period.

(d) Review the sales ledger for all large debts against which specific allowance might be required.

(e) Check the calculation of the allowance.

(f) Confirm that the debtors' balances used agreed with the adjusted control account provision.

(g) Confirm that the provision had been posted to the accounting records.

Answer 13.3

(a) The main elements of a standard bank letter are as follows.

   (i) Titles, account numbers and balances on all bank accounts including loans

   (ii) Details of accounts where the customer's name is joined with that of other parties or where the amount is in a trade name

   (iii) Account details and date of closure for accounts closed during the twelve months up to the audit confirmation date

   (iv) Details of loans, overdrafts and associated guarantees and indemnities:

   (1) Term
   (2) Repayment frequency and/or review date
   (3) Detail of period of availability of agreed finance ie finance remaining undrawn
   (4) The facility limit

   (v) In relation to the facilities:

   (1) Details of any supporting security formally charged
   (2) Details if a security is limited in amount or to a specific borrowing, or if there is another charge

   (vi) Set-off arrangements

   (vii) Additional relationships with other branches or subsidiaries of the bank

(b) The following tests should be carried out on the bank reconciliation.

   (i) Check the arithmetic of the bank reconciliation.

   (ii) Trace cheques shown as unpresented on the bank reconciliation to the cash book before the year-end and the bank statement after the year-end.

   (iii) Check uncleared bankings per the bank reconciliation to paying-in-slips to confirm that they have been paid in prior to the year-end, and check they appear on bank statements soon after the year-end.

   (iv) Investigate other reconciling items.

   (v) Verify balance per cash book on reconciliation with cash book and general ledger.

   (vi) Verify balance per bank on reconciliation with bank statements and bank letter.

   (vii) Scrutinise cash book and bank statements before and after the year-end for unusual items which may materially affect the bank balance.

> **Now try Question 13 in the Exam Question Bank**

Chapter 14 Liabilities

Chapter topic list

1. Introduction
2. Current liabilities
3. Long-term liabilities
4. Provisions and contingencies

The following study sessions are covered in this Chapter:

Syllabus reference

23(b) For each area in the financial statements of an incorporated company, provide examples of the representations made by directors   6

24(a) Design audit programmes to meet specific audit objectives with regard to the following balance sheet items: 6

   (vi) Trade creditors
   (vii) Accruals
   (viii) Provisions

Part D: Substantive procedures

1 INTRODUCTION

1.1 In this chapter we deal with the testing of creditors, share capital and reserves. **Creditors** is often one of the most sensitive areas of a company's accounts. It significantly affects the company's liquidity, and may be closely related to bank borrowing covenants or debenture agreements. There may thus be significant incentives for a company to carry creditors at less than their true value.

1.2 Testing of creditors therefore is designed primarily to obtain evidence that the balances owed to creditors are **completely** and **accurately recorded**. Testing for completeness of creditors can be particularly difficult. We shall see how auditors can gain some assurance on completeness from a variety of sources, and also have to use their knowledge of the business.

1.3 Testing of **purchases** and **expenses** is primarily concerned with testing that the amounts shown are for valid expenditure.

1.4 We shall consider in a separate section of this chapter **long-term liabilities** such as loans and debentures. These may be major long-term sources of finance for a company. Auditors will thus be concerned with how **onerous the terms** are that the company has to fulfil, and whether the company has kept up with the repayments it is required to make.

2 CURRENT LIABILITIES

2.1 The purchases cycle tests of controls will have provided the auditors with some assurance as to the completeness of liabilities.

2.2 Auditors should however be particularly aware, when conducting their balance sheet work, of the possibility of understatement of liabilities.

2.3 As regards **trade creditors**, auditors should particularly consider the following.

- Is there a **satisfactory cut-off** between goods received and invoices received, so that purchases and trade creditors are recognised in the correct year?
- Do trade creditors **represent** all the **bona fide amounts** due by the company?

2.4 Before we ascertain how the auditors design and conduct their tests with these objectives in mind, we need to establish the importance, as with trade debtors, of the list of balances.

Trade creditors listing and accruals listing

2.5 The list of balances will be one of the principal sources from which the auditors will select their samples for testing. The listing should be extracted from the purchase ledger by the client. The auditors will carry out the following substantive tests to verify that the extraction has been properly performed and is **complete**.

> - Check from the purchase ledger accounts to the list of balances and *vice versa*
> - Reconcile the total of the list with the purchase ledger control account
> - Cast the list of balances and the purchase ledger control account

The client should also prepare a detailed schedule of trade and sundry accrued expenses.

Completeness and accuracy of trade creditors

2.6 The most important test when considering **trade creditors** is comparison of suppliers' statements with purchase ledger balances. This provides evidence of **existence, rights and obligations** and **completeness.**

2.7 When selecting a sample of creditors to test, auditors must be careful not just to select creditors with large year-end balances. Remember, it is errors of **understatement** that auditors are primarily interested in when reviewing creditors, and errors of understatement could occur equally in creditors with low or nil balances as with high balances.

2.8 When **comparing supplier statements** with **year-end purchase ledger balances**, auditors should include within their sample creditors with nil or negative purchase ledger balances. Auditors should be particularly wary of low balances with major suppliers.

2.9 You may be wondering as we normally carry out a debtors' circularisation whether we would also circularise creditors. The answer is generally no. The principal reason for this lies in the nature of the purchases cycle: third party evidence in the form of suppliers' invoices and even more significantly, **suppliers' statements**, is available as part of the standard documentation of the cycle.

2.10 In the following circumstances the auditors may, however, determine that a circularisation is necessary.

- Where **suppliers' statements** are, for whatever reason, **unavailable** or **incomplete**
- Where **weaknesses in internal control** or the nature of the client's business make possible a material misstatement of liabilities that would not otherwise be picked up
- Where it is thought that the **client** is **deliberately** trying to **understate creditors**
- Where the **accounts** appear to be **irregular** or if the nature or size of balances or transactions is abnormal

In these cases confirmation requests should be sent out and processed in a similar way to debtors' confirmation requests. 'Positive' requests will be required.

2.11 EXAMPLE

Jo is responsible for the audit of trade creditors. Analytical evidence suggests that trade creditors is low risk.

The client does not usually keep supplier statements after they have been reconciled with the purchase ledger. However, the purchase ledger clerk always keeps the statements as at 30 September for the auditors.

There is a statement available for every supplier that Jo has sampled, so she now has to work through and ensure that the purchase ledger balance agrees to what the supplier says. There may be small timing differences, for example when Brown Limited has made a payment near the year end that has not yet been received by the supplier at the date of the statement. Given that Brown Limited does a payment run of liabilities due, if this is true for one supplier it is likely to be true for more than one. If differences do arise due to payments having been made, Jo should cross refer to the bank reconciliation as these payments should be reconciling items and she can judge by when they cleared the bank whether they are likely to have genuinely been sent out before the year end, thus reducing creditors and bank.

Part D: Substantive procedures

Purchases and other expenses

2.12 When testing purchases, auditors are testing whether they have **occurred**, are **measured correctly** and have been made for **valid reasons**, (that goods and services purchased have provided benefits to the company). They are also checking for **accuracy of recording** of purchases so again cut-off procedures will be important.

Occurrence and accuracy of purchases

2.13 As with sales, **analytical procedures** will be important. Auditors should consider:

- The **level of purchases** over the year, compared on a month-by-month basis with the previous year
- The effect on value of purchases of **changes in quantities purchased**
- The effect on value of purchases of changes in **products** purchased (for example a change in ingredients), or **prices of products**
- How the **ratio of trade creditors to purchases** compares with previous years
- How the **ratio of trade creditors to stock** compares with previous years
- How **major expenses** other than purchases compare with previous years

2.14 In addition auditors may carry out the following additional substantive procedures on individual purchases or expenses.

- **Check purchases and other expenses recorded** in the **general or purchase ledger** or **cash book** to supporting documentation (books of prime entry, invoices, delivery notes, purchase orders) considering:
    - Whether **purchases** and **expenses** are **valid** (invoices addressed to the client, for goods and services ordered by the client, for the purposes of the business)
    - Whether **purchases** and **expenses** have been allocated to the correct **purchase** or **general ledger** account
    - Whether amounts have been **calculated correctly**
- Consider **reasonableness of deductions** from purchases or expenses by reference to subsequent events
- Consider whether **valid debits** are **recorded** in **purchase ledger** by **checking credit notes**

2.15 If auditors are concerned about the completeness of recording of purchases, the following procedures may be necessary.

- **Check** a **sample** of **purchase orders/goods received notes** to **purchase invoices**
- **Review the file** of **unprocessed invoices** and **obtaining explanations**
- **Check** the **total** of the **purchase day book** to the **general ledger**
- Analytically **review** the **gross profit percentage** and obtaining explanations for fluctuations

Purchases cut-off

2.16 The procedures applied by the auditors will be designed to ascertain whether:

- **Goods received** for which **no invoice** has been **received** are **accrued**.
- **Goods received** which have been **invoiced** but **not yet posted** are **accrued**.
- **Goods returned prior** to the **year-end** are **excluded** from **stock** and **trade creditors**.

2.17 At the year-end stocktaking the auditors will have made a note of the last serial numbers of goods received notes. Suggested substantive procedures are as follows.

- **Check from goods received notes** with serial numbers before the year-end to ensure that invoices are either:
    - Posted to purchase ledger prior to the year-end, or
    - Included on the schedule of accruals.
- **Review the schedule of accruals** to ensure that goods received after the year-end are not accrued
- **Check from goods returned notes prior to year-end** to ensure that **credit notes** have been **posted** to the purchase ledger prior to the year-end or accrued
- **Review large invoices** and **credit notes** included after the year-end to ensure that they refer to the following year
- **Reconcile daily batch invoice totals** around the year-end to purchase ledger control ensuring batches are posted in the correct year
- **Review** the **control account** around the year-end for **any unusual items**

Purchase of goods subject to reservation of title clauses

2.18 We have already mentioned briefly the existence of transactions where the seller may retain legal ownership of goods passed to a 'purchaser' in the context of the audit of debtors. The main burden is, however, on the auditors of the **purchaser not the seller**. We now look at the audit implications of such 'reservation of title clauses' in more detail.

2.19 The cases of *Borden (UK) Limited v Scottish Timber Products*, *Re Bond Worth* and *Romalpa* suggest that a reservation of title clause will only be upheld if it states that the seller has a charge over the goods, and the goods, any products made from them and any sale proceeds are kept separately and are readily identifiable.

2.20 Generally, the auditors' approach should be as follows.

- **Ascertain** how the **client identifies suppliers selling** on terms which **reserve title** by enquiry of those responsible for purchasing and the board
- **Review** and test the **procedures** for **quantifying** or **estimating** the **liabilities**
- **Consider** whether **disclosure** is **sufficient** by itself if the directors have decided quantification is impractical
- **Consider** the adequacy of the **disclosures** in the accounts
- **Review the terms of sale** of **major suppliers** to confirm that liabilities not provided for do not exist or are immaterial

Part D: Substantive procedures

Verification of accruals

2.21 Accruals is an area that lends itself to analytical procedures and reconciliation techniques.

2.22 A variety of sources may indicate possible accruals. These include **last year's accruals**, **expense items** where an accrual would be expected, and **invoices received** and **cash paid** after the year-end. Auditors should also use their **knowledge of** the **business** to consider whether there are accruals which they would expect to be there, but which may not be invoiced or paid until long after the year-end.

2.23 The following substantive procedures are suggested.

> - Check that accruals are fairly calculated and verify by reference to subsequent payments and supporting documentation
>
>   *Note.* For PAYE and VAT the following approach should be adopted.
>   - **PAYE**. Normally this should represent one month's deductions. **Check amount paid** to **Inland Revenue** by inspecting receipted annual declaration of tax paid over, or returned cheque.
>   - **VAT. Check reasonableness** to **next VAT return. Verify last amount paid in** year per cash book to VAT return.
> - **Review the profit and loss account** and **prior years' figures** and consider liabilities inherent in the trade to **ensure** that all **likely accruals have been provided**
> - **Scrutinise payments** and invoices received made **after year-end** to ascertain whether they should be accrued
> - **Consider basis** for **round sum accruals** and ensure it is reasonable and consistent with prior years
> - **Ascertain** why any **payments on account** are being **made** and **ensure** that the **full liability is provided**

Inter-company indebtedness

2.24 The same procedures apply as discussed in the section on inter-company indebtedness in the last chapter.

Wages and salaries

2.25 Although auditors may test other expenses solely by analytical review, they may carry out more detailed testing on wages and salaries, partly because of the consequences of failure to deduct PAYE and NIC correctly.

2.26 Analytical procedures will nonetheless be used to give some assurance on wages and salaries. Auditors should consider:

> - **Wages and salaries levels** month-by-month with **previous years**
> - **Effect on wages and salaries of salary changes** during the year
> - **Average wage** per month **over the year**
> - **Sales/profits per employee**

2.27 In addition auditors may carry out the following substantive procedures.

14: Liabilities

2.28 **Occurrence**

- **Check individual remuneration** per payroll to **personnel records, records of hours** worked or **salary agreements**
- **Confirm existence of employees** on payroll by meeting them, attending wages payout etc.
- **Check benefits** (pensions) on payroll to **supporting documentation**

2.29 **Accuracy**

- **Check accuracy of calculation** of **benefits**
- **Check whether calculation of statutory deductions** (PAYE, NIC) is **correct**
- **Check validity of other deductions** (pension contributions, share save etc) by agreement to supporting documentation (personnel files, conditions of pension scheme) and **check accuracy of calculation** of other deductions

2.30 **Completeness**

- **Check** a sample of employees from **personnel records** and ensure **included** in **payroll records**
- **Check details** of **joiners** and ensure **recorded** in **correct month**
- **Check casts of payroll records**
- **Confirm payment of net pay** per payroll records to **cheque or bank transfer** summary
- **Agree net pay** per cash book to **payroll**
- **Scrutinise payroll** and **investigate** unusual items

Exam alert
Wages and salaries is an important profit and loss account topic.

Activity 14.1

You are carrying out the audit of creditors and accruals of Rodney Rabbit Limited, which manufactures baskets and cages to be sold in pet shops.

The company operates a central warehouse to which all raw materials are delivered. Stores reception checks all deliveries for quantity and quality to the delivery note, and the stores receptionist completes a goods received note, keeping one copy and sending one copy to the bought ledger department.

The bought ledger department receives invoices, and when details have been checked as correct, invoices are posted to the bought ledger. Accounts with suppliers are settled monthly.

Required

Describe the audit work you will carry out:

(a) To confirm purchase cut-off is correct

(b) To confirm balances on the purchase ledger

Part D: Substantive procedures

(c) To confirm accruals (you can assume the only accruals are VAT, PAYE and time-apportioned expenses)

3 LONG-TERM LIABILITIES

3.1 We are concerned here with long-term liabilities comprising debentures, loan stock and other loans repayable at a date more than one year after the year-end.

3.2 Auditors will primarily try and determine:

- **Completeness:** whether all long-term liabilities have been disclosed
- **Accuracy:** whether interest payable has been calculated correctly and included in the correct accounting period
- **Disclosure:** whether long-term loans and interest have been correctly disclosed in the financial statements

Substantive procedures applicable to all audits

3.3 The following suggested substantive procedures are relevant.

- **Obtain/prepare schedule of loans** outstanding at the balance sheet date showing, for each loan: name of lender, date of loan, maturity date, interest date, interest rate, balance at the end of the period and security.
- **Compare opening balances** to previous year's working papers
- **Test the clerical accuracy** of the analysis
- **Compare balances** to the **general ledger**
- **Check name** of **lender** etc, to **register** of **debenture holders** or equivalent (if kept)
- **Trace additions** and **repayments** to **entries** in the **cash book**
- **Confirm repayments** are in accordance with **loan agreement**
- **Examine cancelled cheques** and **memoranda of satisfaction** for **loans repaid**
- **Verify** that **borrowing limits** imposed either by Articles or by other agreements are **not exceeded**
- **Examine signed Board minutes** relating to **new borrowings/repayments**
- **Obtain direct confirmation** from **lenders** of the amounts outstanding, accrued interest and what security they hold
- **Verify interest charged** for the period and the adequacy of accrued interest
- **Confirm assets charged** have been **entered** in the **register of charges** and **notified** to the **Registrar**
- **Review restrictive covenants** and provisions relating to default:
  - Review any **correspondence relating** to the **loan**
  - **Review confirmation** replies for non-compliance
  - If a **default appears to exist, determine** its **effect**, and **schedule findings**
- **Review minutes, cash book** to **check** if all **loans have been recorded**

4 PROVISIONS AND CONTINGENCIES

FRS 12 *Provisions, contingent liabilities and contingent assets*

4.1 The objective of FRS 12 is to ensure that contingent liabilities and assets and provisions are properly accounted for and disclosed.

> **KEY TERMS**
>
> A **provision** is a liability that is of uncertain timing or amount, to be settled by the transfer of economic benefits.
>
> A **contingent liability** is either (a) a possible obligation arising from past events whose existence will be confirmed only by the occurrence of one or more uncertain future events not wholly within the entity's control; or (b) a present obligation that arises from past events but is not recognised because it is not probable that a transfer of economic benefits will be required to settle the obligation or because the amount of the obligation cannot be measured with sufficient reliability.
>
> A **contingent asset** is a possible asset arising from past events whose existence will be confirmed only by the occurrence of one or more uncertain future events not wholly within the entity's control.

4.2 The key distinction therefore is between provisions which are accrued in the accounts, and contingent assets and liabilities, which are not accrued but which may be disclosed.

Recognition

4.3 A provision should be recognised when an entity has a **present obligation** as a result of a past event, it is **probable** that a **transfer** of **economic benefits** will be **required** to settle the obligation, and a **reasonable estimate** can be made of the amount of the obligation. Unless these conditions are met, no provision should be recognised.

Measurement

4.4 The amount recognised as a provision should be the **best estimate** of the expenditure required to settle the present obligation at the balance sheet date.

Reimbursements

4.5 Where some or all of the expenditure required to settle a provision is expected to be reimbursed by another party, the reimbursement should be recognised only when it is **virtually certain** that the reimbursement will be received if the entity settles the obligation. The reimbursement should be treated as a separate asset.

Changes in provisions

4.6 Provisions should be reviewed at each balance sheet date and adjusted to reflect the current best estimate.

CONTINGENT LIABILITIES		
Where, as a result of past events, there may be a transfer of future economic benefits in settlement of (a) a present obligation or (b) a possible obligation whose existence will be confirmed by the occurrence of one or more uncertain future events not wholly within the entity's control, and		
there is a present obligation that probably requires a transfer of economic benefits in settlement,	there is a possible obligation or a present obligation that may, but probably will not, require a transfer of economic benefits in settlement,	there is a possible obligation or a present obligation where the likelihood of a transfer of economic benefits in settlement is remote,
a provision is recognised and disclosures are required for the provision.	no provision is recognised but disclosures are required for the contingent liability.	no provision is recognised and no disclosure is required.

4.7 A contingent liability also arises in the extremely rare case **where there is a liability** that cannot be recognised because it cannot be **measured reliably**. Disclosures are required for the contingent liability.

CONTINGENT ASSETS		
Where, as a result of past events, there is a possible asset whose existence will be confirmed by the occurrence of one or more uncertain future events not wholly within the entity's control, and		
the inflow of economic benefits is virtually certain,	the inflow of economic benefits is probable but not virtually certain,	the inflow is not probable,
the asset is not contingent.	no asset is recognised but disclosures are required.	no asset is recognised and no disclosure is required.

4.8 Examples of the principal types of contingencies disclosed by companies are:

- Guarantees
    - for other group companies
    - of staff pension schemes
    - of completion of contracts
- Discounted bills of exchange
- Uncalled liabilities on shares or loan stock
- Lawsuits or claims pending
- Options to purchase assets

Obtaining audit evidence of contingencies

4.9 Part of ISA 501 *Audit evidence – additional considerations for specific items* covers contingencies relating to litigation and legal claims, which will represent the major part of audit work on contingencies. Litigation and claims involving the entity may have a material effect on the financial statements, and so will require adjustment to/disclosure in those financial statements.

14: Liabilities

> **ISA 501.32**
>
> The auditor should carry out audit procedures in order to become aware of any litigation and claims involving the entity which may result in a material misstatement of the financial statements.

4.10 Such procedures would include the following.

- Make appropriate inquiries of management including obtaining representations
- Review minutes of those charged with governance and correspondence with the entity's legal counsel.
- Examine legal expense account.
- Use any information obtained regarding the entity's business including information obtained from discussions with any in-house legal department.

> **ISA 501.33**
>
> When the auditor assesses a risk of material misstatement regarding litigation or claims that have been identified or when the auditor believes they may exist, the auditor should seek direct communication with the entity's legal counsel.

4.11 This will help to obtain sufficient appropriate audit evidence as to whether potential material litigation and claims are known and management estimates of the financial implications, including costs, are reliable.

4.12 Other audit procedures that should be carried out on provisions and contingent assets and liabilities are as follows.

- **Obtain details** of all **provisions** which have been included in the **accounts** and all **contingencies** that have been disclosed
- **Obtain** a **detailed analysis** of all **provisions** showing opening balances, movements and closing balances
- **Determine** for each material provision **whether** the **company** has a **present obligation** as a result of past events by:
  - **Review** of **correspondence** relating to the item
  - **Discussion** with the **directors**. Have they created a valid expectation in other parties that they will discharge the obligation?
- **Determine** for each material provision **whether** it is **probable** that a **transfer of economic benefits** will be required to settle the obligation by the following tests:
  - **Check** whether any **payments** have been **made** in the post balance sheet period in respect of the item
  - **Review of correspondence** with solicitors, banks, customers, insurance company and suppliers both pre and post year-end
  - **Send** a **letter** to the **solicitor** to obtain their views (where relevant)
  - **Discuss** the **position** of similar **past provisions** with the directors. Were these provisions eventually settled?
  - Consider the likelihood of reimbursement

Part D: Substantive procedures

- **Recalculate** all **provisions** made
- **Compare** the **amount provided** with any post year end payments and with any amount paid in the past for similar items
- In the event that it is not possible to estimate the amount of the **provision**, check that this **contingent liability** is **disclosed** in the accounts
- **Consider** the **nature** of the **client's business**. Would you expect to see any other provisions eg warranties?
- **Ensure disclosures** of **provisions** and contingencies **are sufficient** and **comply** with **FRS 12**

Exam alert

You should appreciate that the problems of accounting for provisions and contingencies makes their audit difficult.

Key learning points

- The largest figure in **current liabilities** will normally be **trade creditors** generally checked by comparison of **suppliers' statements** with **purchase ledger accounts.**
- A **creditors' circularisation** might be appropriate, although they are relatively rare in practice compared to the frequency of debtors' circularisations.
- **Accruals** can be significant in total. Expense accruals will tend to repeat from one year to the next. Auditors should review **after-date invoices and payments**, and consider whether anything else that would have been expected has not been accrued.
- **Long-term liabilities** are usually **authorised** by the board and should be well documented.
- Auditors should ensure that **provisions** are accounted for correctly and that **contingent liabilities** are correctly disclosed.

Quick quiz

1. How would you check whether a list of purchase ledger balances had been correctly extracted?
2. In what circumstances may a creditors' circularisation be necessary?
3. What tests should auditors normally carry out on:
   (a) The PAYE liability
   (b) The VAT liability?
4. What information should be contained on a schedule of long-term loans?

Answers to quick quiz

1. The following procedures should be carried out to check the proper extraction of a list of purchase ledger balances:

   (a) Check from the purchase ledger accounts to the list of balances and vice-versa.
   (b) Reconcile the total of the list of balances with the purchase ledger control account.
   (c) Cast the list of balances and the purchase ledger control account.

14: Liabilities

2   A creditors' circularisation may be necessary where:

   (a)   Suppliers' statements are unavailable or incomplete.
   (b)   There are serious weaknesses in internal control.
   (c)   There is a high risk that the client is trying to understate creditors.
   (d)   The accounts appear to be irregular or the nature or size of balances is unusual.

3   (a)   Auditors should check whether PAYE represents one month's deduction. They should check the amount paid to the Inland Revenue by inspecting the annual declaration of tax paid over or the returned cheque.

   (b)   Auditors should check whether the amount of VAT paid appears reasonable to the next VAT return, and the last amount paid in the year per the cash book should be verified to the VAT return.

4   The following information should be included on a schedule of long-term loans.

   (a)   Name of lender
   (b)   Date of loan
   (c)   Maturity date
   (d)   Interest date
   (e)   Interest rate
   (f)   Balance at period-end
   (g)   Security

Answer to activity

Answer 14.1

(a)   The audit work I would carry out to verify that purchases cut-off has been correctly carried out at the year end is as follows.

   (i)   From my notes taken at the stocktake I will have the number of the last GRN that was issued before the year end.

   (ii)   I will then select a sample of GRNs issued in the period immediately before and immediately after the year end. The period to be covered would be at least two weeks either side of the year end.

   (iii) I will concentrate my sample on high value items, and more on those GRNs from before the year end as these represent the greatest risk of cut-off error.

   (iv)   I will check that the GRNs have a correct number, according to the last GRN issued in the year and whether the goods were received before or after the year end.

   (v)   For GRNs issued before the year end I will ensure that the stock has been included in the year end stock total. In addition, I will ensure that the creditor is either included in trade creditors or purchase accruals.

   (vi)   For GRNs issued after the year end, I will need to ensure that the stock is only included in the stock records after the year end balance has been extracted. In addition, I will need to check to the purchase ledger to ensure that the relevant invoice has been posted to the supplier account after the year end.

(b)   The audit work I will carry out to check balances on the purchase ledger is as follows.

   I will select a sample of creditors and compare suppliers' statements with purchase ledger balances. The extent of the sample will depend on the results of my tests of controls and my assessment of the effectiveness of controls within the purchases system (ie if internal control is strong I will check fewer items).

   I will select the sample on a random basis. Selection of only large balances or those with many transactions will not yield an appropriate sample as I am looking for understatement of liabilities. Nil and negative balances will also need to be included in the sample.

   If no statement was available for the supplier, I would ask for confirmation of the balance from the creditor.

   If the balance agrees exactly, no further work needs to be carried out.

   Where differences arise these need to be categorised as either in-transit items or other (including disputed) items.

Part D: Substantive procedures

In-transit items will be either goods or cash.

If the difference relates to goods in transit, I would ascertain whether the goods were received before the year end by reference to the GRN and that they are included in year end stock and purchase accruals. If the goods were received after the year end, the difference with the suppliers' accounts is correct. If not, a cut-off error has occurred and should be investigated.

Similarly, cash in transit would arise where the payment to the supplier was made by cheque before the year end but was not received by him until after the year end. The date the cheque was raised and its subsequent clearing through the bank account after the year end should be verified by checking the cash book and the post year end bank statements.

However, if the cheque clears after the year end date, it may indicate that the cheque, though raised before the year end was not sent to the supplier until after the year end, and the relevant amount should be added back to year end creditors and to the end of year bank balance.

Differences which do not arise from in-transit items need to be investigated and appropriate adjustments made where necessary.

These differences may have arisen due to disputed invoices, where for example the client is demanding credit against an invoice which the supplier is not willing to agree to. The client may decide not to post the invoice to the supplier account as he does not consider it to be a liability of the company. However, differences may also arise because invoices have been held back in order to reduce the level of year-end creditors.

If significant unexplained differences are discovered it may be necessary to extend my testing. There may also be a problem if sufficient suppliers' statements are not available. Alternative procedures, eg a circularisation may then need to be required.

(c) The audit work I will carry out to ensure that accruals are correctly stated is as follows.

(i) I will assess internal control instituted by management to identify and quantify accruals and creditors. Where controls are strong, I will perform fewer substantive procedures, taking the materiality of the amounts into consideration.

(ii) From the client's sundry creditors and accruals listing I will check that accruals are calculated correctly and verify them by reference to subsequent payments. I will check that all time apportionments have been made correctly (eg for electricity).

(iii) *PAYE and VAT balance*

(1) I will check the amount paid to the Inland Revenue for PAYE and NI. The balance at the year end would normally represent one month's deductions and can be verified to the payroll records. The payment should be traced from the cash book to the PAYE payment book (if used) and subsequent bank statements.

(2) For the VAT balance I will review for reasonableness to the next VAT return. I would also ensure that the payment for the previous return was for the correct amount and had cleared through the bank.

(iv) I will review the profit and loss account and prior year figures (for any accruals which have not appeared this year or which did not appear last year) and consider liabilities inherent in the trade (eg weekly wages) to ensure that all likely accruals have been provided.

(v) I will scrutinise payments made after the year end to ascertain whether any payments made should be accrued. This will include consideration of any payments relating to the current year which are made a long time after the year-end.

(vi) I will consider and document the basis for round sum accruals and ensure it is consistent with prior years.

(vii) I will ascertain why any payments on account are being made and ensure that the full liability is provided.

(viii) Accrued interest and basic charges on loans or overdrafts can be agreed to the bank letter received for audit purposes.

Now try Question 10 in the Exam Question Bank

Part E
Audit completion

Chapter 15 Forming an audit judgement

Chapter topic list

1 Introduction
2 Overall review of financial statements
3 Opening balances
4 Comparatives
5 Subsequent events
6 Going concern
7 Management representations
8 Completion

The following study sessions are covered in this Chapter:

Syllabus reference

28(a) Explain the purpose and nature of carrying out an overall review of the financial statements prior to expressing an audit opinion and outline the purpose and nature of: 7

    (i) The application of analytical procedures
    (ii) A review of opening balances and comparatives
    (iii) A review of events after the balance sheet date
    (iv) An evaluation of going concern

28(b) Explain the purpose of a letter of representation 7

28(c) Describe the contents of a letter of representation and provide examples of typical representations made in such a letter 7

Part E: Audit completion

1 INTRODUCTION

1.1 This chapter deals with **review** and **completion procedures** on an audit. Review procedures have two aspects. Firstly auditors need to **review** the **final accounts**, considering whether the accounts comply with **statutory requirements**, the figures **make sense** (final analytical review) and the **accounts** give a **true and fair view**. Auditors have a specific responsibility to consider **opening balances** and **comparatives**, and information published along with the accounts.

1.2 The second part of the review deals with **events** that have taken place **since the balance sheet date**.

1.3 Auditors need to consider whether the accounts should be prepared on a **going concern** basis. This is a very important task since **going concern** is one of the fundamental accounting concepts, and misjudgements in this area can lead to considerable bad publicity.

1.4 It can be very difficult to explain why a company whose accounts did not contain any mention of going concern problems, and who received an unqualified audit report, shortly afterwards went into liquidation.

1.5 Completion procedures auditors undertake include obtaining **representations** from management in areas where those representations are significant audit evidence. Auditors may also send a final internal control report to management, and there are various other procedures involved in signing the accounts and tidying the audit file which are best dealt with by means of a completion checklist.

1.6 Many of the topics covered in this chapter are popular in auditing exams.

2 OVERALL REVIEW OF FINANCIAL STATEMENTS

2.1 Once the bulk of the substantive procedures have been carried out, the auditors will have a draft set of financial statements which should be supported by appropriate and sufficient audit evidence. As the beginning of the end of the audit process, it is usual for the auditors to undertake an **overall review** of the financial statements.

2.2 This review of the financial statements, in conjunction with the conclusions drawn from the other audit evidence obtained, gives the auditors a reasonable basis for their opinion on the financial statements. It should be carried out by a senior member of the audit team, with appropriate skills and experience.

Compliance with accounting regulations

2.3 The auditors should consider whether:

(a) The information presented in the financial statements is in accordance with statutory requirements.

(b) The accounting policies employed are in accordance with accounting standards, properly disclosed, consistently applied and appropriate to the entity.

2.4 When examining the **accounting policies,** auditors should consider:

(a) Policies **commonly adopted in particular industries**

(b) Policies for which there is **substantial authoritative support**

(c) Whether any **departures from applicable accounting standards** are necessary for the financial statements to give a true and fair view

(d) Whether the **financial statements reflect the substance** of the underlying transactions and not merely their form

2.5 When compliance with statutory requirements and accounting standards is considered, the auditors may find it useful to use a **checklist**.

Analytical procedures

2.6 In Chapter 10 we discussed how analytical procedures are used as part of the overall review procedures at the end of an audit.

2.7 Remember the areas that the analytical procedures at the final stage must cover.

- Important accounting ratios
- Related items
- Changes in products; customers
- Price and mix changes
- Wages changes
- Variances
- Trends in production and sales
- Changes in material and labour content of production
- Other income statement expenditure
- Variations caused by industry or economy factors

2.8 As at other stages, significant fluctuations and unexpected relationships must be investigated and documented. At this stage, the auditor is concerned whether the financial statements are internally consistent, so predictable relationships in particular will be important.

Review for consistency and reasonableness

2.9 The auditors should consider whether the financial statements are consistent with their knowledge of the entity's business and with the results of other audit procedures, and the manner of disclosure is fair.

2.10 The principal considerations are as follows.

(a) Whether the financial statements adequately reflect the **information** and **explanations** previously obtained and conclusions previously reached during the course of the audit

(b) Whether it reveals any **new factors** which may affect the presentation of, or disclosure in, the financial statements

(c) Whether analytical procedures applied when completing the audit, such as comparing the information in the financial statements with other pertinent data, **produce results** which assist in arriving at the overall conclusion as to whether the financial statements as a whole are consistent with their knowledge of the entity's business

(d) Whether the **presentation** adopted in the financial statements may have been unduly influenced by the **directors' desire** to present matters in a favourable or unfavourable light

Part E: Audit completion

(e) The potential impact on the financial statements of the **aggregate of uncorrected misstatements** (including those arising from bias in making accounting estimates) identified during the course of the audit and the preceding period's audit, if any

3 OPENING BALANCES

> **KEY TERM**
>
> **Opening balances** are those account balances which exist at the beginning of the period. Opening balances are based upon the closing balances of the prior period and reflect the effects of:
>
> (a) Transactions of prior periods
> (b) Accounting policies applied to the prior period

3.1 ISA 510 *Initial Engagements - Opening Balances* provides guidance on opening balances.

- When the financial statements of an entity are audited for the first time
- When the financial statements for the prior period were audited by another auditor

> **ISA 510.2**
>
> For initial audit engagements, the auditor should obtain sufficient appropriate audit evidence that:
> (a) the opening balances do not contain misstatements that materially affect the current period's financial statements;
> (b) the prior period's closing balances have been correctly brought forward to the current period or, when appropriate, have been restated; and
> (c) appropriate accounting policies are consistently applied or changes in accounting policies have been properly accounted for and adequately presented and disclosed.

> **ISA 510.2-1**
>
> The auditor should also obtain sufficient appropriate audit evidence for the matters set out in Paragraph 2 for continuing audit engagements.

Audit procedures

3.2 Appropriate and sufficient audit evidence is required on the opening balances and this depends on matters such as the following.

(a) The **accounting policies** followed by the entity

(b) Whether the **prior period's financial statements were audited** and, if so, whether the auditors' report was modified

(c) The **nature of the accounts** and the risk of their misstatement in the current period's financial statements

(d) The **materiality** of the opening balances relative to the current period's financial statements

15: Forming an audit judgement

3.3 The auditor must consider whether **opening balances reflect the application of appropriate accounting policies** and that those policies are **consistently applied** in the current period's financial statements. When there are any changes in the accounting policies or application thereof, the auditor should consider whether they are appropriate and properly accounted for and adequately disclosed.

3.4 When the prior period's financial statements were audited by another auditor, the current auditor may be able to obtain sufficient appropriate audit evidence regarding opening balances by **reviewing** the predecessor auditor's **working papers**. In these circumstances, the current auditor would also consider the professional competence and independence of the predecessor auditor.

3.5 If the prior period's audit report was **modified**, the auditor would pay particular attention in the current period to the matter which resulted in the modification.

3.6 Before communicating with the predecessor auditor, the current auditor must consider the relevant ethical matters.

3.7 When the prior period's financial statements were not audited or when the auditor is not able to be satisfied by using the procedures described above, the auditor must perform other procedures such as those discussed below.

3.8 For **current assets and liabilities** some audit evidence can usually be obtained as part of the current period's audit procedures. For example, the **collection** (payment) of opening **debtors** (creditors) during the current period will provide some audit evidence of their existence, rights and obligations, completeness and valuation at the beginning of the period.

3.9 In the case of **stock**, however, it is more difficult for the auditor to be satisfied as to stock on hand at the beginning of the period. Therefore, additional procedures will usually be necessary such as:

   (a) **Observing a current physical stock count** and reconciling it back to the opening stock quantities

   (b) **Testing the valuation** of the opening stock items

   (c) **Testing gross profit** and cut-off

   A combination of these procedures may provide sufficient appropriate audit evidence.

3.10 For **fixed assets and liabilities**, the audit will ordinarily examine the records underlying the opening balances. In certain cases, the auditor may be able to obtain confirmation of opening balances with third parties, eg for long-term debt and investments. In other cases, the auditor may need to carry out additional audit procedures.

Continuing auditors

3.11 If a continuing auditor has issued an unqualified report on the preceding period's financial statements and the audit of the current period has not revealed any matters which cast doubt on those financial statements the auditor should ensure that:

- opening balances have been appropriately brought forward
- accounting policies have been consistently applied

Part E: Audit completion

3.12 If a qualified report was issued on the preceding period's financial statements the auditor, in addition to carrying out the above procedures should consider whether the matter which gave rise to the qualification has been resolved and properly dealt with in the current period's financial statements.

Audit conclusion and reporting

> **ISA 510.11**
>
> If, after performing audit procedures including those set out above, the auditor is unable to obtain sufficient appropriate evidence concerning opening balances, the auditor's report should include:
> (a) a qualified opinion;
> (b) a disclaimer of opinion; or
> (c) an opinion which is qualified or disclaimed regarding the results of operations and unqualified regarding financial position.

3.13 If the opening balances contain misstatements which could materially affect the current period's financial statements, the auditor should inform those charged with governance and seek their authorisation to inform the predecessor auditor, if any.

> **ISA 510.12**
>
> If the effect of the misstatement is not properly accounted for and adequately presented and disclosed, the auditor should express a qualified opinion or an adverse opinion, as appropriate.

3.14 The report will also be modified if **accounting policies** are **not consistently applied**.

> **ISA 510.13**
>
> If the current period's accounting policies have not been consistently applied in relation to the opening balances and if the change has not been properly accounted for and adequately presented and disclosed, the auditor should express a qualified opinion or an adverse opinion as appropriate.

3.15 If the prior period auditor's report was modified, the auditor should **consider the effect on the current period's financial statements**. For example, if there was a scope limitation, such as one due to the inability to determine opening stock in the prior period, the auditor may not need to qualify or disclaim the current period's audit opinion. The ISA finishes:

> **ISA 510.14**
>
> However, if a modification regarding the prior period's financial statements remains relevant and material to the current period's financial statements, the auditor should modify the current auditor's report accordingly.

4 COMPARATIVES

4.1 ISA 710 *Comparatives* establishes standards and provides guidance on the auditors' responsibilities regarding comparatives.

> **ISA 710.2**
>
> The auditor should determine whether the comparatives comply in all material respects with the financial reporting framework applicable to the financial statements being audited.

> **ISA 710.2-1**
>
> The auditor should obtain sufficient appropriate audit evidence that amounts derived from the preceding period's financial statements are free from material misstatements and are appropriately incorporated in the financial statements for the current period.

4.2 Comparatives are presented differently under different countries' financial reporting frameworks. Generally comparatives can be defined as **corresponding amounts** and **other disclosures** for the preceding financial reporting period(s), presented for comparative purposes. Because of these variations in countries' approach to comparatives, the ISA refers to the following frameworks and methods of presentation.

> **KEY TERMS**
>
> **Corresponding figures** are amounts and other disclosures for the preceding period included as part of the current period financial statements, which are intended to be read in relation to the amounts and other disclosures relating to the current period (referred to as 'current period figures'). These corresponding figures are not presented as complete financial statements capable of standing alone, but are an integral part of the current period financial statements intended to be read only in relationship to the current period figures.
>
> **Comparative financial statements** are amounts and other disclosures of the preceding period included for comparison with the financial statements of the current period, but do not form part of the current period financial statements.

4.3 Comparatives are presented in compliance with the relevant financial reporting framework. The essential audit reporting differences are that:

- For **corresponding figures,** the auditors' report only refers to the financial statements of the current period.

- For **comparative financial statements,** the auditors' report refers to each period that financial statements are presented.

ISA 710 provides guidance on the auditors' responsibilities for comparatives and for reporting on them under the two frameworks in separate sections.

In the UK the **corresponding figures method** of presentation is usually required.

Part E: Audit completion

Corresponding figures

The auditors' responsibilities

> **ISA 710.6**
>
> The auditor should obtain sufficient appropriate audit evidence that the corresponding figures meet the requirements of the applicable financial reporting framework.

4.4 Audit procedures performed on the corresponding figures are usually limited to checking that the corresponding figures have been correctly reported and are appropriately classified. Auditors must assess whether:

(a) **Accounting policies** used for the corresponding figures are **consistent** with those of the current period and appropriate adjustments and disclosures have been made where this is not the case.

(b) **Corresponding amounts agree** with the **amounts** and other disclosures presented in the preceding period and are free from errors in the context of the financial statements of the current period.

(c) Where corresponding amounts have been adjusted as required by relevant legislation and accounting standards, appropriate disclosures have been made.

4.5 When the financial statements of the prior period:

- Have been audited by other auditors
- Were not audited

the incoming auditors assess whether the corresponding figures meet the conditions specified above and also follow the guidance in ISA 510 *Initial engagements - opening balances*.

4.6 If the auditors become aware of a possible material misstatement in the corresponding figures when performing the current period audit, then they must perform any necessary additional procedures.

Reporting

> **ISA 710.10**
>
> When the comparatives are presented as corresponding figures, the auditor should issue an audit report in which the comparatives are not specifically identified because the auditor's opinion is on the current period financial statements as a whole, including the corresponding figures.

4.7 The auditor's report will only make any specific reference to corresponding figures in the circumstances described below. We will look at specific examples of the wording of auditors' reports in such circumstances below.

4.8 Firstly, there is the problem of what happens when the auditor's report for the previous period was modified.

> **ISA 710.12**
>
> When the auditor's report on the prior period, as previously issued, included a qualified opinion, disclaimer of opinion, or adverse opinion and the matter which gave rise to the modification is:
>
> (a) unresolved, and results in a modification of the auditor's report regarding the current period figures, the auditor's report should also be modified regarding the corresponding figures; or
>
> (b) unresolved, but does not result in a modification of the auditor's report regarding the current period figures, the auditor's report should be modified regarding the corresponding figures

4.9 If a modified report was issued, but the matter which gave rise to it is resolved and properly dealt with in the financial statements, the current report will not usually refer to the previous modification. If the matter is material to the **current period**, however, the auditors may include an **emphasis of matter paragraph** to deal with it. In some circumstances the auditor may consider it appropriate to qualify the audit opinion on the current period's financial statements. For example, if a provision which the auditor considered should have been made in the previous period is made in the current period.

4.10 In performing the audit of the current period financial statements, the auditors, in certain unusual circumstances, may become aware of a material misstatement that affects the prior period financial statements on which an unmodified report has been previously issued.

> **ISA 710.15**
>
> In such circumstances, the auditor should consider the guidance in ISA 560 *Subsequent events* and:
>
> (a) if the prior period financial statements have been revised and reissued with a new auditor's report, the auditor should obtain sufficient appropriate audit evidence that the corresponding figures agree with the revised financial statements; or
>
> (b) if the prior period financial statements have not been revised and reissued, and the corresponding figures have not been properly restated and/or appropriate disclosures have not been made, the auditor should issue a modified report on the current period financial statements modified with respect to the corresponding figures included therein.

4.11 In these circumstances, if the prior period financial statements have not been revised and an auditor's report has not been reissued, but the corresponding figures have been properly restated and/or appropriate disclosures have been made in the current period financial statements, the auditors may include an **emphasis of matter paragraph** describing the circumstances and referencing to the appropriate disclosures. In this regard, the auditors also consider the guidance in ISA 560 *Subsequent events*.

Incoming auditors: additional requirements

4.12 The incoming auditor assumes audit responsibility for all the corresponding figures only in the context of the financial statements as a whole.

The incoming auditor reads the preceding period's financial statements and, using the knowledge gained during the current audit, considers whether they have been properly reflected as corresponding figures in the current period's accounts.

4.13 The situation is slightly different if the prior period financial statements were **not audited**.

Part E: Audit completion

> **ISA 710.18**
>
> When the prior period financial statements are not audited, the incoming auditor should state in the auditor's report that the corresponding figures are unaudited.

> **ISA 710.18-1**
>
> If the auditor is not able to obtain sufficient appropriate audit evidence regarding the corresponding figures or if there is not adequate disclosure the auditor considers the implications for the auditor's report.

4.14 The inclusion of such a statement does not, however, relieve the auditors of the requirement to perform appropriate procedures regarding opening balances of the current period. Clear disclosure in the financial statements that the corresponding figures are unaudited is encouraged.

> **ISA 710.19**
>
> In situations where the incoming auditor identifies that the corresponding figures are materially misstated, the auditor should request management to revise the corresponding figures or if management refuses to do so, appropriately modify the report.

Comparative financial statements

The auditors' responsibilities

> **ISA 710.20**
>
> The auditor should obtain sufficient appropriate audit evidence that the comparative financial statements meet the requirements of the applicable financial reporting framework.

4.15 This is effectively involves the auditors following the same procedures on the prior period statements as noted above.

Reporting

> **ISA 710.24**
>
> When the comparatives are presented as comparative financial statements, the auditor should issue a report in which the comparatives are specifically identified because the auditor's opinion is expressed individually on the financial statements of each period presented.

4.16 The auditors may therefore express a **modified opinion** or include an **emphasis of matter** paragraph with respect to one or more financial statements for one or more period, whilst issuing a different report on the other financial statements.

4.17 The auditors may become aware of circumstances or events that materially affect the financial statements of a prior period during the course of the audit for the current period.

15: Forming an audit judgement

> **ISA 710.25**
>
> When reporting on the prior period financial statements in connection with the current year's audit, if the opinion on such prior period financial statements is different from the opinion previously expressed, the auditor should disclose the substantive reasons for the different opinion in an emphasis of matter paragraph.

Incoming auditors: additional requirements

4.18 Again, there are procedures where the prior period financial statements are audited by other auditors.

> **ISA 710.26**
>
> When the financial statement of the prior period were audited by another auditor:
> (a) the predecessor auditor may reissue the audit report on the prior period with the incoming auditor only reporting on the current period; or
> (b) the incoming auditor's report should state that the prior period was audited by another auditor and the incoming auditor's report should indicate:
>   (i) that the financial statements of the prior period were audited by another auditor;
>   (ii) the type of report issued by the predecessor auditor and if the report was modified, the reasons therefor; and
>   (iii) the date of that report.

4.19 In performing the audit on the current period financial statements, the incoming auditors may become aware of a material misstatement that affects the prior period financial statements on which the predecessor auditors had previously reported without modification.

> **ISA 710.28**
>
> In these circumstances, the incoming auditor should discuss the matter with management and, after having obtained management's authorisation, contact the predecessor auditor and propose that the prior period financial statements be restated. if the predecessor agrees to reissue the audit report on the restated financial statements of the prior period, the auditor should follow the guidance in [Paragraph 3.24].

4.20 The predecessor auditors may not agree with the proposed restatement or they may refuse to reissue the audit report for the prior period financial statements. In such cases, the introductory paragraph of the auditor's report may indicate that the predecessor auditors reported on the financial statements of the prior period before restatement.

4.21 In addition, if the incoming auditors are engaged to audit and they perform sufficient procedures to be satisfied as to the appropriateness of the restatement adjustment, they may also include the following paragraph in the report.

> 'We also audited the adjustment described in Note X that were applied to restate the 20X1 financial statements. In our opinion, such adjustments are appropriate and have been properly applied.'

4.22 The other circumstance is that the prior period financial statement may not have been audited.

Part E: Audit completion

> **ISA 710.30**
>
> When the prior period financial statements are not audited, the incoming auditor should state in the auditor's report that the comparative financial statements are unaudited.

4.23 Again, the inclusion of such a statement does not relieve the auditors of the requirement to carry out appropriate procedures regarding opening balances of the current period. Clear disclosure in the financial statements that the comparative financial statements are unaudited is encouraged.

> **ISA 710.31**
>
> In situations where the incoming auditor identifies that the prior year unaudited figures are materially misstated, the auditor should request management to revise the prior year's figures or if management refuses to do so, appropriately modify the report.

Activity 15.1

You have recently been appointed auditor of Lowdham Castings, a limited liability company which has been trading for about thirty years, and are carrying out the audit for the first time for the year ended 30 September 20X6. The company's turnover is about £500,000 and its normal profit before tax is about £30,000. Comparatives are shown as corresponding figures only.

Discuss your responsibilities in relation to the comparatives included in the accounts for the year ended 30 September 20X6. You should also consider the information you would require from the retiring auditors.

5 SUBSEQUENT EVENTS

5.1 'Subsequent events' include:

- Events occurring between the period end and the date of the auditor's report
- Facts discovered after the date of the auditor's report but before the financial statements are issued
- Facts discovered after the financial statements have been issued but before they are laid before the members

> **Exam alert**
>
> Knowledge of the relevant accounting requirements is particularly important when dealing with events after the balance sheet date.

5.2 ISA 560 *Subsequent Events* begins by stating that:

> **ISA 560.2**
>
> The auditor should consider the effect of subsequent events on the financial statements and on the auditor's report.

15: Forming an audit judgement

5.3 You should remember from your Drafting Financial Statements studies that FRS 21 *Events after the balance sheet date* deals with the treatment in financial statement of events, both favourable and unfavourable, occurring after the period end. It identifies two types of event:

- Those that provide further evidence of conditions that existed at the balance sheet date
- Those that are indicative of conditions that arose subsequent to the balance sheet date

Activity 15.2

Give two examples of an event providing evidence of conditions that existed at the balance sheet date and five examples of events that are indicative of conditions that arose subsequent to the balance sheet date.

Events occurring up to the date of the auditor's report

> **ISA 560.5**
>
> The auditor should perform procedures designed to obtain sufficient appropriate audit evidence that all events up to the date of the auditor's report that may require adjustment of, or disclosure in, the financial statements have been identified.

5.4 These procedures should be applied to any matters examined during the audit which may be susceptible to change after the year end. They are in addition to tests on specific transactions after the date of the financial statements, eg cut-off tests.

5.5 The ISA lists procedures to identify subsequent events which may require adjustment or disclosure. They should be performed as near as possible to the date of the auditors' report.

PROCEDURES TESTING SUBSEQUENT EVENTS	
Enquiries of management	Status of items involving **subjective judgement**/ accounted for using preliminary data
	New **commitments**, borrowings or guarantees
	Sales or destruction of **assets**
	Issues of **shares/debentures** or changes in business structure
	Developments involving **risk areas, provisions** and **contingencies**
	Unusual accounting adjustments
	Major events (eg going concern problems) affecting appropriateness of accounting policies for estimates
PROCEDURES TESTING SUBSEQUENT EVENTS	
Other procedures	**Consider procedures** of management for identifying subsequent events
	Read minutes of general board/committee meetings
	Review latest accounting records and financial information

5.6 Reviews and updates of these procedures may be required, depending on the length of the time between the procedures and the signing of the auditors' report and the susceptibility of the items to change over time.

> **ISA 560.8**
>
> When the auditor becomes aware of events which materially affect the financial statements, the auditor should consider whether such events are properly accounted for and adequately disclosed in the financial statements.

Facts discovered after the date of the auditor's report but before the date the financial statements are issued

5.7 The financial statements are the management's responsibility. They should therefore inform the auditors of any material subsequent events between the date of the auditors' report and the date the financial statements are issued. The auditors do *not* have any obligation to perform procedures, or make enquires regarding the financial statements *after* the date of their report.

> **ISA 560.9**
>
> When, after the date of the auditor's report but before the date the financial statements are issued, the auditor becomes aware of a fact which may materially affect the financial statements, the auditor should consider whether the financial statements need amendment, should discuss the matter with those charged with governance and should take action appropriate in the circumstances.

5.8 When the financial statements are amended, the auditors should **extend the procedures** discussed above to the **date of their new report**, carry out any other appropriate procedures and issue a new audit report dated no earlier than the date of approval of the amended financial statements.

5.9 The situation may arise where the statements are not amended but the auditors feel that they should be.

> **ISA 560.11**
>
> When those charged with governance do not amend the financial statements in circumstances where the auditor believes they need to be amended and the auditor's report has not been released to the entity, the auditor should express a qualified opinion or an adverse opinion.

5.10 If the auditors' report has already been issued to the entity then the auditors should notify those who are ultimately responsible for the entity (the management or possibly a holding company in a group), not to issue the financial statements or auditors' reports to third parties. If they have already been so issued, the auditors must take steps to prevent the reliance on the auditors' report. The action taken will depend on the auditors' legal rights and obligations and the advice of the auditors' lawyer.

Facts discovered after the financial statements have been issued but before they are laid before the members

5.11 Auditors have no obligations to perform procedures or make enquiries regarding the financial statements *after* they have been issued.

15: Forming an audit judgement

> **ISA 560.14**
>
> When, after the financial statements have been issued, the auditor becomes aware of a fact which existed at the date of the auditor's report and which, if known at that date, may have caused the auditor to modify the auditor's report, the auditor should consider whether the financial statements need revision, should discuss the matter those charged with governance, and should take the action as appropriate in the circumstances.

5.12 In this situation the auditor may use his statutory right to attend the AGM and make a statement above the facts discovered after the date of the auditor's report.

The auditor would discuss the possibility of withdrawing the financial statements with those charged with governance although there are no statutory provisions for revising financial statements.

It is likely that the auditor would seek legal advice.

5.13 The ISA gives the appropriate procedures which the auditors should undertake when management revises the financial statements.

(a) **Carry out the audit procedures** necessary in the circumstances

(b) **Review the steps taken by management** to ensure that anyone in receipt of the previously issued financial statements together with the auditors' report thereon is informed of the situation

(c) **Issue a new report** on the revised financial statements

> **ISA 560.16**
>
> The new auditor's report should include an emphasis of a matter paragraph referring to a note to the financial statements that more extensively discusses the reason for the revision of the previously issued financial statements and to the earlier report issued by the auditor.

5.14 Where the management does *not* revise the financial statements but the auditors feel they should be revised, or if the management does not intend to take steps to ensure anyone in receipt of the previously issued financial statements is informed of the situation, then the auditors should consider steps to take, on a timely basis, to prevent reliance on their report. The actions taken will depend on the auditors' legal rights and obligations (eg statement at the AGM) and legal advice received.

Activity 15.3

(a) What general procedures should auditors carry out when reviewing subsequent events?

(b) What information relating to after the balance sheet date, might be relevant, and why, in the following audit areas?

  (i) Stock
  (ii) Trade creditors and accruals

(c) How should auditors obtain evidence about legal claims in which clients are involved?

6 GOING CONCERN

> **KEY TERM**
>
> Under the '**going concern assumption**' an entity is ordinarily viewed as continuing in business for the foreseeable future with neither the intention nor the necessity of liquidation, ceasing trading or seeking protection from creditors pursuant to laws or regulations. Accordingly assets and liabilities are recorded on the basis that the entity will be able to realize its assets and discharge its liabilities in the normal course of business'.

> **ISA 570.2**
>
> When planning and performing audit procedures and in evaluating the results thereof, the auditor should consider the appropriateness of management's use of the going concern assumption in the preparation of the financial statements.

> **ISA 570.2-1**
>
> The auditor should consider any relevant disclosures in the financial statements.

6.1 The ISA states that when preparing accounts, management should make an explicit **assessment** of the entity's ability to continue as a going concern. This is also supported by legal requirements and FRS 18. Under these requirements the financial statements are assumed to be prepared on a going concern basis.

6.2 When management are making the assessment, the following factors should be considered.

- The **degree of uncertainty** about the events or conditions being assessed increases significantly the further into the future the assessment is made.
- Judgements are made on the basis of the **information available** at the time.
- Judgements are affected by the **size** and **complexity** of the entity, the **nature** and **condition** of the business and the **degree** to which it is **affected** by **external factors**.

6.3 The following list gives examples of possible indicators of going concern problems.

(a) **Financial indications**

- Net liabilities or net current liability position
- Necessary borrowing facilities have not been agreed
- Fixed-term borrowings approaching maturity without realistic prospects of renewal or repayment, or excessive reliance on short-term borrowings
- Major debt repayment falling due where refinancing is necessary
- Major restructuring of debt
- Indications of withdrawal of financial support by creditors
- Negative operating cash flows indicated by historical or prospective financial statements
- Adverse key financial ratios

15: Forming an audit judgement

- Substantial operating losses or significant deterioration in the value of assets used to generate cash flows
- Major losses or cashflow problems which have arisen since the balance sheet date
- Arrears or discontinuance of dividends
- Inability to pay creditors on due dates
- Inability to comply with terms of loan agreements
- Reduction in normal terms of trade credit by suppliers
- Change from credit to cash-on-delivery transactions with suppliers
- Inability to obtain financing for essential new product development or other essential investments
- Substantial sales of fixed assets not intended to be replaced

(b) **Operating indications**

- Loss of key management without replacement
- Loss of key staff without replacement
- Loss of a major market, franchises, license, or principal supplier
- Labour difficulties or shortages of important supplies
- Fundamental changes in market or technology
- Excessive dependence on a few product lines where the market is depressed
- Technical developments which render a key product obsolete

(c) **Other indications**

- Non-compliance with capital or other statutory requirements
- Pending legal proceedings against the entity that may, if successful, result in judgements that could not be met
- Changes in legislation or government policy
- Issues which involve a range of possible outcomes so wide that an unfavourable result could affect the appropriateness of the going concern basis

> **Exam alert**
>
> Any question on going concern is likely to ask you to identify signs that a particular client may not be a going concern.

6.4 The significance of such indications can often be **mitigated** by other factors.

(a) The effect of an entity being unable to make its normal debt repayments may be counterbalanced by management's plans to maintain **adequate cash flows** by alternative means, such as by disposal of assets, rescheduling of loan repayments, or obtaining additional capital.

(b) The loss of a principal supplier may be mitigated by the availability of a suitable alternative source of supply.

Auditors' responsibilities

6.5 Auditors are responsible for considering:

- The appropriateness of the going concern assumption

Part E: Audit completion

- The existence of **material uncertainties** about the going concern assumption that need to be disclosed in the accounts
- Whether there are adequate disclosures regarding the going concern basis
- The entity's ability to continue for the foreseeable future

> **ISA 570.11/12**
>
> In obtaining an understanding of the entity, the auditor should consider whether there are events or conditions and related business risks which may cast significant doubt on the entity's ability to continue as a going concern.
>
> The auditor should remain alert for audit evidence of events or conditions and related business risks which may cast significant doubt on the entity's ability to continue as a going concern in performing audit procedures throughout the audit. If such events or conditions are identified, the auditor should, in addition to performing the procedures in Paragraph 26, consider whether they affect the auditor's assessments of the risks of material misstatement.

6.6 Management may already have made a preliminary assessment of going concern when performing risk assessment procedures. If so, the auditors would review potential problems management had identified, and management's plans to resolve them. Alternatively auditors may identify problems as a result of discussions with management.

> **ISA 570.17**
>
> The auditor should evaluate those charged with governance's assessment of the entity's ability to continue as a going concern.

> **ISA 570.17-1**
>
> The auditor should assess the adequacy of the means by which those charged with governance have satisfied themselves that:
>
> (a) it is appropriate for them to adopt the going concern basis in preparing the financial statements; and
>
> (b) the financial statements include such disclosures, if any, relating to going concern as are necessary for them to give a true and fair view.

6.7 The auditor should consider:

- the period used by those charged with governance in assessing going concern
- the systems used for identification of future risks and uncertainties
- budget/forecast information and the quality of the systems responsible for producing this information
- assumptions underlying the budgets/forecasts
- sensitivity of budgets/forecasts
- any obligations, undertakings or guarantees arranged with lenders/suppliers
- existence/adequacy/terms of borrowing facilities
- management's plans for future actions

15: Forming an audit judgement

6.8 If management's assessment covers a period of **less than twelve months** from the balance sheet date, the auditor should ask management to extend its assessment period to twelve months from the balance sheet date.

6.9 If the period used by those charged with governance in making their assessment is less than one year from the date of approval of the financial statements, and they have not disclosed that fact in the financial statements, the auditor does so within the audit report.

6.10 Management should not need to make a detailed assessment, and auditors carry out detailed procedures, if the entity has a **history of profitable operations** and **ready access** to **financial resources.**

> **ISA 570.22**
>
> The auditor should inquire of management as to its knowledge of events or conditions and related business risks beyond the period of assessment used by those charged with governance that may cast significant doubt on the entity's ability to continue as a going concern.

6.11 Because the time period is some way into the future, the indications of potential going concern problems would have to be significant. Auditors do not have to carry out specific procedures to identify potential problems which may occur after the period covered by management's assessment. However they should be alert during the course of the audit for any **indications** of future problems.

The auditors' examination of borrowing facilities

6.12 The auditor will usually:

- obtain **confirmations** of the existence and terms of bank facilities
- make their own **assessment** of the **intentions** of the bankers

6.13 If the auditors cannot satisfy themselves they should consider whether the relevant matters need to be:

- disclosed in the financial statements in order that they give a true and fair view, and/or
- referred to in the auditors' report (by an explanatory paragraph or a qualified opinion).

6.14 EXAMPLE

Jo Price is responsible for the audit of going concern at Brown Ltd, although she has asked Jonathan to alert her if he comes across any matters which might suggest that there are going concern problems during the course of his audit work (particularly when he has looked at bank and debtors, for example).

The auditors do not believe that there is any special risk attached to going concern at Brown Ltd. The business is stable, regulations or other market factors which could adversely affect the business and the new competitor has not had a significant impact. Nevertheless, going concern procedures must be carried out.

Jo has had a discussion with the finance director to ascertain the period which the directors have considered in their considerations of going concern. He has been able to provide her with a detailed budget for the next year, as well as strategy projections for the next five years. They have discussed the company's plans for development over future years and Jo is satisfied that the period that the directors have considered with regard to going concern is reasonable. She has asked the finance director if she can borrow the budgets and projections to do some more detailed work on them.

Part E: Audit completion

Jo has now checked the budgets for arithmetical accuracy and has reviewed the assumption made within it to see if they are reasonable. It appears to be a moderate budget which indicates that the directors' belief that the company will continue in the foreseeable future is reasonable. To be sure, Jo has carried out some sensitivity analysis on some of the key balances in the budgets. She has assessed how the picture would look if sales growth were 10% less than predicted, or raw material prices rose 10% more than predicted, and even with such amendments, the budgets indicate that the company would be viable.

Given that the budgets do assume a limited amount of borrowing in terms of the availability of an overdraft facility on occasion, Jo will also consider the borrowing facilities open to the company.

Further audit procedures

> **ISA 570.26**
>
> When events or conditions have been identified which may cast significant doubt on the entity's ability to continue as a going concern, the auditor should:
>
> (a) review management's plans for future actions based on its going concern assessment;
>
> (b) gather sufficient appropriate audit evidence to confirm or dispel whether or not a material uncertainty exists through carrying out audit procedures considered necessary, including considering the effect of any plans of management and other mitigating factors; and
>
> (c) seek written representations from management regarding its plans for future action.

6.15 The auditors should also consider the need to obtain written confirmation regarding:

(a) the assessment of those charged with governance that the company is a going concern
(b) Any relevant disclosure in the financial statements

6.16 When questions arise on the appropriateness of the going concern assumption, some of the normal audit procedures carried out by the auditors may take on an **additional significance**. Auditors may also have to carry out **additional procedures** or to update information obtained earlier. The ISA lists various procedures which the auditors should carry out in this context.

- **Analyse and discuss cash flow**, profit and other relevant forecasts with management
- **Analyse and discuss** the entity's latest available **interim financial statements**
- **Review the terms of debentures and loan agreements** and determine whether they have been breached
- **Read minutes** of the meetings of shareholders, those charged with governance and relevant committees for reference to financing difficulties
- **Enquire** of the entity's lawyer regarding **litigation and claims**
- **Confirm the existence, legality and enforceability** of arrangements to provide or maintain financial support with related and third parties
- **Assess** the **financial ability** of such parties to **provide additional funds**
- **Consider the entity's position** concerning unfulfilled customer orders
- **Review events after the period end** for items affecting the entity's ability to continue as a going concern

6.17 The auditors should discuss with management its **plans** for **future action**, for example plans to liquidate assets, borrow money or restructure debt, reduce or delay expenditure or increase capital, and assess whether these are feasible and are likely to improve the situation.

6.18 When analysis of cash flow is a significant factor, auditors should consider:

- The **reliability** of the **information system** for generating the information
- Whether there is **adequate support** for the assumptions underlying the forecast
- How **recent forecasts** have **differed** from **actual results**

6.19 EXAMPLE

Jo has reviewed the bank letter and ascertained that Brown Ltd has an available overdraft facility which would cover the requirements of the budgets and strategies.

Brown Ltd is currently using the overdraft facility and has on occasion made use of its overdraft facility previously, and has never broken the terms it is offered in accordance with. Jo sees no reason to believe that the bank will not continue to offer this facility in the future.

Jo does not believe that Brown Ltd's intention to make use of an overdraft facility on occasion is in itself an indication of going concern problems, as this is a common business practice, and the budgets clearly show that it is occasional planned use, and there is no sign of the need to borrow increasing overtime.

Audit conclusions

> **ISA 570.30**
>
> Based on the audit evidence obtained, the auditor should determine if, in the auditors' judgement, a material uncertainty exists related to events or conditions that alone or in aggregate, may cast significant doubt on the entity's ability to continue as a going concern.

> **ISA 570.30–1**
>
> The auditor should document the extent of the auditor's concern (if any) about the entity's ability to continue as a going concern.

6.20 An uncertainty will be material if it has so great a potential impact as to require clear disclosure of its nature and implications in the accounts. The accounts should:

(a) **Adequately describe** the **principal events or conditions** that give rise to the uncertainty about continuance as a going concern, and management's plans to deal with the situation

(b) **State clearly** that a **material uncertainty exists** and therefore the entity may be unable to realize its assets and discharge its liabilities in the normal course of business

Part E: Audit completion

> **ISA 570.31-1**
>
> The auditor should consider whether the financial statements are required to include disclosures relating to going concern in order to give a true and fair view.

6.21 As we saw in paragraph 6.9 if the period used by those charged with governance in assessing going concern is less than one year from the date of approval of the financial statements and this has not been disclosed the auditor should do so in his audit report when setting out the basis of the audit opinion.

> **ISA 570.33**
>
> If adequate disclosure is made in the financial statements, the auditor should express an unqualified opinion but modify the auditor's report by adding an emphasis of a matter paragraph that highlights the existence of a material uncertainty relating to an event or condition that may cast significant doubt on the entity's ability to continue as a going concern and draws attention to the note in the financial statements that discloses the matters.

6.22 The auditor's report is considered in detail in Chapter 16. The ISA gives an example of an emphasis of matter paragraph in such circumstances.

> 'Without qualifying our opinion we draw attention to Note X in the financial statements. The company incurred a net loss of ZZZ during the year ended December 31, 20X1 and, as of that date, the company's current liabilities exceeded its total assets by ZZZ. These conditions, along with other matters as set forth in Note X, indicate the existence of a material uncertainty which may cast significant doubt about the company's ability to continue as a going concern.'

6.23 **Adequate disclosure** would include the following:

   (a) A statement that the financial statements have been prepared on the **going concern basis**

   (b) A statement of the pertinent **facts**

   (c) The **nature** of the concern

   (d) A statement of the **assumptions** adopted

   (e) (Where) appropriate and practicable a statement regarding **future plans**

   (f) Details of any **relevant actions** by those charged with governance

6.24 The auditors may express a disclaimer of opinion if for example there are multiple material uncertainties.

> **ISA 570.34**
>
> If adequate disclosure is not made in the financial statements, the auditor should express a qualified or adverse opinion, as appropriate. The report should include explicit reference to the fact that there is a material uncertainty which may cast significant doubt about the company's ability to continue as a going concern.

Adverse opinion

> **ISA 570.35**
>
> If in the auditors' judgement, the entity will not be able to continue as a going concern, the auditor should express an adverse opinion if the financial statements have been prepared on a going concern basis.

6.25 This applies whatever the level of disclosure in the accounts. If a basis other than the going concern basis is used, and the auditors consider it **appropriate**, the auditor should not qualify the auditor's report in this respect.

Limitation on scope

> **ISA 570.37**
>
> If management is unwilling to make or extend its assessment when requested to do so by the auditor, the auditor should consider the need to modify the auditor's report as a result of the limitation on the scope of the auditor's work.

6.26 The auditors may be able to obtain sufficient alternative evidence even if management's assessment is inadequate.

Significant delay

6.27 When there is a significant delay in approving the accounts, auditors should consider whether this is due to doubts about the going concern status of the business. The delay may prompt the auditors to perform additional procedures on going concern.

Activity 15.4

(a) What is meant by the statement 'These accounts have been prepared on a going concern basis'?

(b) What procedures should auditors carry out in order to obtain assurance that a company is a going concern when events have been identified that cast significant doubt on the entity's ability to continue as a going concern?

7 MANAGEMENT REPRESENTATIONS

7.1 The auditors receive many representations during the audit, both unsolicited and in response to specific questions. Some of these representations may be critical to obtaining sufficient appropriate audit evidence. Representations may also be required for general matters, eg full availability of accounting records. ISA 580 *Management representations* covers this area.

> **ISA 580.2**
>
> The auditor should obtain appropriate representations from management.

7.2 These should be obtained before the audit report is issued.

Part E: Audit completion

> **KEY TERM**
>
> **Management** comprises officers and those who also perform senior managerial functions.

Acknowledgement by management of their responsibility for the financial statements

> **ISA 580.3**
>
> The auditor should obtain audit evidence that those charged with governance acknowledges its responsibility for the fair presentation of the financial statements in accordance with the applicable financial reporting framework and has approved the financial statements.

7.3 This is normally done when the auditors receive a signed copy of the financial statements which incorporate a relevant statement of management responsibilities. Alternatively, the auditors may obtain such evidence from:

- **Relevant minutes of meetings** of the board of directors or similar body, or by attending such a meeting
- A **written representation** from management

Representations by management as audit evidence

7.4 In addition to representations relating to responsibility for the financial statements, the auditors may wish to rely on management representations as audit evidence.

> **ISA 580.4**
>
> The auditor should obtain written confirmation of representations from management on matters material to the financial statements when other sufficient appropriate audit evidence cannot be reasonably expected to exist.

7.5 Written confirmation of oral representations avoids confusion and disagreement. Such matters should be discussed with those responsible for giving the written confirmation, to ensure that they understand what they are confirming. Written confirmations are normally required of appropriately senior management. Only matters which are material to the financial statements should be included.

7.6 When the auditors receive such representations they should:

- Seek **corroborative audit evidence** from sources inside or outside the entity
- **Evaluate** whether the **representations** made by management appear reasonable and are consistent with other audit evidence obtained, including other representations
- **Consider whether the individuals** making the representations can be expected to be **well-informed** on the particular matters

7.7 The ISA then makes a very important point.

> 'Representations by management cannot be a substitute for other audit evidence that the auditor could reasonably expect to be available ... if the auditor is unable to obtain sufficient appropriate audit evidence regarding a matter which has, or may have, a material effect on the financial statements and such audit evidence is expected to be available, this will constitute a limitation in the scope of the audit, even if a representation from management has been received on the matter.'

7.8 There are instances where management representations *may* be the only audit evidence available.

- **Knowledge of the facts is confined to management**, eg the facts are a matter of management intention.
- The **matter is principally one of judgement or opinion**, eg the trading position of a particular customer.

7.9 There may be occasions when the representations received do not agree with other audit evidence obtained.

> **ISA 580.9**
>
> If a representation by management is contradicted by other audit evidence, the auditor should investigate the circumstances and, when necessary, consider whether it casts doubt on the reliability of other representations made by management.

7.10 Investigations of such situations will normally begin with further enquires of management; the representations may have been misunderstood or, alternatively, the other evidence misinterpreted. If explanations are insufficient or unforthcoming, then further audit procedures may be required.

Documentation of representations by management

7.11 The auditors should include in audit working papers evidence of management's representations in the form of a summary of oral discussions with management or written representations from management.

7.12 A written representation is ordinarily more reliable audit evidence than an oral representation and can take the form of:

- A **representation letter** from management
- A **letter from the auditors** outlining the auditors' understanding of management's representations, duly acknowledged and confirmed by management
- **Relevant minutes** of meetings of the board of directors or similar body or a signed copy of the financial statements

Basic elements of a management representation letter

7.13 A management representation letter should:

- Be **addressed** to the **auditors**
- **Contain specified information**
- Be **appropriately dated** and **signed** by those with specific relevant knowledge

Part E: Audit completion

7.14 The letter will usually be **dated** on the **day the financial statements are approved**, but if there is any significant delay between the representation letter and the date of the auditors' report, then the auditors should consider the need to obtain further representations.

7.15 A management representation letter should be discussed and agreed by those charged with governance and signed on their behalf by the chairman and secretary, before they approve the financial statements.

Actions if management refuses to provide representations

> **ISA 580.15**
>
> If management refuses to provide written representation that the auditor considers necessary, this constitutes a scope limitation and the auditor should express a qualified opinion or a disclaimer of opinion.

7.16 In these circumstances, the auditors should consider whether it is appropriate to rely on other representations made by management during the audit.

Extract from a management representation letter

7.17 It is **not** a standard letter, and representations do not have to be confirmed in letter form.

(Company letterhead)

(To the auditors)   (Date)

We confirm to the best of our knowledge and belief, and having made appropriate enquiries of other directors and officials of the company, the following representations given to you in connection with your audit of the financial statements for the period ended 31 December 20...

(1) We acknowledge as directors our responsibilities under the Companies Act 1985 for preparing financial statements which give a true and fair view and for making accurate representations to you. All the accounting records have been made available to you for the purpose of your audit and all the transactions undertaken by the company have been properly reflected and recorded in the accounting records. All other records and related information, including minutes of all management and shareholders' meetings, have been made available to you.

(2) The legal claim by ABC Limited has been settled out of court by a payment of £258,000. No further amounts are expected to be paid, and no similar claims have been received.

(3) In connection with deferred tax not provided, the following assumptions reflect the intentions and expectations of the company:

    (a) capital investment of £450,000 is planned over the next three years;

    (b) there are no plans to sell revalued properties; and

    (c) we are not aware of any indications that the situation is likely to change so as to necessitate the inclusion of a provision for tax payable in the financial statements.

(4) The company has not had, or entered into, at any time during the period any arrangement, transaction or agreement to provide credit facilities (including loans, quasi-loans or credit transactions) for directors or to guarantee or provide security for such matters.

(5) There have been no events since the balance sheet date which necessitate revision of the figures included in the financial statements or inclusion of a note thereto.

15: Forming an audit judgement

> **Exam alert**
>
> The most important points to remember about a letter of representation are:
>
> (a) The circumstances in which it can be used
> (b) The auditors' response if the client fails to agree to it
>
> You should also be able to draft appropriate representations if asked.

7.18 The following additional representations are required from those charged with governance.

- acknowledgment of responsibility for the design and implementation of internal control to prevent and detect fraud

- they have disclosed to the auditor the results of their assessment of the risk that the financial statements may be materially misstated as a result of fraud

- they have disclosed to the auditor their knowledge of fraud or suspected fraud involving:

    (i) management and those charged with governance
    (ii) employees who have significant roles in internal control; or
    (iii) others where the fraud could have a material effect on the financial statements

- they have disclosed all known or possible non-compliance with laws and regulations whose effects should be considered when preparing financial statements

Activity 15.5

(a) What are the main purposes of a letter of representation and how far can auditors rely on the audit evidence it provides?

(b) Draft appropriate representations to cover the following circumstances.

(i) A long-term material balance of £200,000 owed by an associated company, Y, has been outstanding for nine months at the year-end. The reason for the delay in repayment has been cash flow problems, but the associate's cash flow has improved since the year-end and the directors are confident the amount can be recovered.

(ii) A major customer has sued the company for £50,000. The directors have disclosed this claim in the accounts, but believe it will be settled in the company's favour. The directors also believe that the reasons why the claim arose are one-off, and do not apply to other customers, or other transactions with this customer.

8 COMPLETION

Summarising errors

8.1 During the course of the audit, errors will be discovered which may be material or immaterial to the financial statements. It is very likely that the client will adjust the financial statements to take account of material and immaterial errors during the course of the audit. At the end of the audit, however, some errors may still be outstanding and the auditors will summarise these **unadjusted errors**.

Part E: Audit completion

8.2 The summary of errors will not only list errors from the current year, but also those in the previous year(s). This will allow errors to be highlighted which are reversals of errors in the previous year, such as in the valuation of closing/opening inventory. Cumulative errors may also be shown, which have increased from year to year. It is normal to show both the balance sheet and the income statement effect, as in the example given here.

SCHEDULE OF UNADJUSTED ERRORS

		20X2				20X1			
		P&L account		Balance sheet		P&L account		Balance sheet	
		Dr £	Cr £	Dr £	Cr £	Dr £	Cr £	Dr £	Cr £
(a)	ABC Co debt unprovided	10,470			10,470	4,523			4,523
(b)	Opening/ closing stock under valued*	21,540			21,540		21,540	21,540	
(c)	Closing stock undervalued		34,105	34,105					
(d)	Opening unaccrued expense								
	Telephone*		453	453		453			453
	Electricity*		905	905		905			905
(e)	Closing unaccrued expenses								
	Telephone	427			427				
	Electricity	1,128			1,128				
(f)	Obsolete stock write off	2,528			2,528	3,211			3,211
	Total	36,093	35,463	35,463	36,093	9,092	21,540	21,540	9,092
	*Cancelling items	21,540			21,540				
			453	453					
			905	905					
		14,553	34,105	34,105	14,553				

Evaluating the effect of misstatements

ISA 320.12

In evaluating whether the financial statements are prepared, in all material respects, in accordance with an applicable financial reporting framework, the auditor should assess whether the aggregate of uncorrected misstatements that have been identified during the audit is material.

ISA 320.12-1

In the UK and Ireland the auditor ordinarily evaluates whether the financial statements give a true and fair view.

8.3 The aggregate of uncorrected misstatements comprises:

(a) **Specific misstatements** identified by the auditors, including the net effect of uncorrected misstatements identified during the audit of the previous period if they affect the current period's financial statements

(b) Their **best estimate** of **other misstatements** which cannot be quantified specifically (ie projected errors)

8.4 If the auditors consider that the aggregate of misstatements may be material, they must consider reducing audit risk by extending audit procedures or requesting management to adjust the financial statements (which management may wish to do anyway).

> **ISA 320.15**
>
> If management refuses to adjust the financial statements and the results of extended audit procedures do not enable the auditor to conclude that the aggregate of uncorrected misstatements is not material, the auditor should consider the appropriate modification to the auditor's report in accordance with ISA 700.

8.5 If the aggregate of the uncorrected misstatements that the auditors have identified approaches the materiality level, the auditors should consider whether it is likely that undetected misstatements, when taken with aggregated uncorrected misstatements, could exceed the materiality level. Thus, as aggregate uncorrected misstatements approach the materiality level the auditors should consider reducing the risk by

- **Performing additional audit procedures** or
- By **requesting management** to adjust the financial statements for identified misstatements

8.6 The schedule will be used by the audit manager and partner to decide whether the client should be requested to make adjustments to the financial statements to correct the errors.

Completion checklists

8.7 Audit firms frequently use checklists which must be signed off to ensure that all final procedures have been carried out, all material amounts are supported by sufficient appropriate evidence, etc.

Key learning points

- Auditors must perform and document an **overall review** of the accounts before reaching an opinion. This review should include a review of **accounting policies** and a review for **consistency** and **reasonableness**.
- Auditors should perform procedures to verify **opening balances** if they themselves did not audit those balances at the end of the previous period.
- Auditor responsibilities on comparatives vary depending on whether they are **corresponding figures** or **comparative financial statements**.
- Auditor responsibilities on **unaudited published information** vary, although auditors should always try and resolve **inconsistencies** or **misstatements of fact**.
- The auditors should consider the effect of **subsequent events** on the accounts, up to the date the accounts are signed.
- Auditors should be alert to indications of **going concern** problems throughout the audit. If there are doubts about the client's survival as a going concern, extra audit work will be required.
- **Bank facilities** may have to be confirmed.
- When reviewing accounts, auditors should consider whether the **going concern basis** is **appropriate**, and whether **disclosures** about going concern problems **are adequate**.
- **Representations from management** should generally be restricted to matters which cannot be verified by other means. They should be confirmed **in writing**.
- Any representations should be **compared** with other evidence and their **sufficiency** assessed.
- Auditors should consider the **cumulative effect of unadjusted errors**.

Part E: Audit completion

Quick quiz

1. What matters should auditors consider when examining accounting policies?
2. What are the principal considerations in a review of the financial statements for consistency and reasonableness?
3. What are the two types of subsequent event?
4. What are the consequences regarding the realisation of assets and liabilities if the going concern basis is not appropriate?
5. What factors affect judgements about the foreseeable future?
6. What criteria should auditors use to judge whether disclosure about going concern problems is sufficient?
7. What forms may written confirmations of representation take?
8. What types of misstatement might be included in the aggregate of uncorrected misstatements?

Answers to quick quiz

1. When examining accounting policies, auditors should consider:

    (a) Policies commonly adopted in particular industries

    (b) Policies for which there is substantial authoritative support

    (c) Whether any departures from applicable accounting standards are necessary for the financial statements to give a true and fair view

    (d) Whether the financial statements reflect the substance of the underlying transactions and not merely their form

2. When reviewing accounts for consistency and reasonableness auditors should consider:

    (a) Whether the accounts reflect the information and explanations and the conclusions reached during the audit

    (b) Whether the review reveals any new factors which may affect the presentation and disclosure of the accounts

    (c) The results of analytical procedures at the end of the audit

    (d) Whether the presentation of the accounts may have been unduly influenced by the directors

    (e) The effect of the aggregate of uncorrected misstatements

3. Some subsequent events provide additional evidence of conditions existing at the balance sheet date. Others concern conditions which did not exist at the balance sheet date.

4. If the going concern basis is not appropriate, the entity may not be able to recover the amounts recorded in respect of assets, and there may be changes in the amounts and dates of maturity of liabilities.

5. Judgements about the foreseeable future are affected by:

    (a) The degree of uncertainty increasing the further into the future consideration is made

    (b) Any judgement being based on information available at the time it is made

6. Auditors should consider whether disclosures about going concern problems include the following:

    (a) A statement that the accounts have been prepared on a going concern basis
    (b) A statement of the pertinent facts
    (c) The nature of the concern
    (d) The directors' assumptions
    (e) The directors' plans
    (f) Relevant actions by the directors

7. Representations may take the form of board minutes or a written representation from directors.

8. Misstatements that may be included in the statement are specific misstatements identified by the auditors, and the auditors' best estimate of other misstatements.

Answers to activities

Answer 15.1

Consideration of the financial statements of the preceding period is necessary in the audit of the current period's financial statements in relation to three main aspects.

(a) *Opening position:* obtaining satisfaction that those amounts which have a direct effect on the current period's results or closing position have been properly brought forward.

(b) *Accounting policies:* determining whether the accounting policies adopted for the current period are consistent with those of the previous period.

(c) *Comparatives:* determining that the comparatives are properly shown in the current period's financial statements.

The auditors' main concern will therefore be to satisfy themselves that there were no material misstatements in the previous year's financial statements which may have a bearing upon their work in the current year.

The new auditors do not have to 're-audit' the previous year's financial statements, but they will have to pay more attention to them than would normally be the case where they had themselves been the auditors in the earlier period. A useful source of audit evidence will clearly be the previous auditors, and, with the client's permission, they should be contacted to see if they are prepared to co-operate. Certainly, any known areas of weakness should be discussed with the previous auditors and it is also possible that they might be prepared to provide copies of their working papers (although there is no legal or ethical provision which requires the previous auditors to co-operate in this way).

Answer 15.2

(a) The following are normally examples of events providing evidence of conditions that existed at the period end.

 (i) Subsequent determination of the price of assets bought or sold before the year-end

 (ii) A property valuation which indicates a permanent diminution in property value which occurred before the year-end

 (iii) Receipt of accounts from a fixed asset investment which indicates a permanent diminution in the value of that investment

 (iv) Indications of the net realisable value of stocks such as the sales prices

 (v) Renegotiation of amounts owed by debtors or the insolvency of a customer

 (vi) Declaration of dividends by investments relating to periods before the balance sheet date

 (vii) Receipt of information regarding rates of tax

 (viii) Amounts received in respect of insurance claims being negotiated prior to the year-end

 (ix) Discoveries of errors or frauds

(b) The following are usually examples of events indicative of conditions arising after the period end.

 (i) Mergers and acquisitions
 (ii) Reconstructions and proposed reconstructions
 (iii) Issues of shares and loans
 (iv) Purchases and sales of fixed assets and investments
 (v) Losses of fixed assets due to fire or flood
 (vi) Opening new trading activities or extending trading activities
 (vii) Closing significant trading activities
 (viii) Post year-end decline in the value of property and investments
 (ix) Changes in the rate of foreign exchange
 (x) Government action
 (xi) Labour disputes
 (xii) Changes in pension benefits

Answer 15.3

(a) Auditors should carry out the following procedures as part of their subsequent events review.

   (i) Consider the procedures management has established in order to ensure subsequent events are correctly treated. Auditors will be concerned with how subsequent events have been identified, considered and properly evaluated as to their effect on the financial statements.

   (ii) Review post year-end accounting records which contain further evidence of conditions existing at the balance sheet date. This review will include review of debtors for evidence of receipt from cash from debtors, and review of bank and cash for evidence of clearance of cheques which were uncleared at the year-end.

   (iii) Review budgets, profit forecasts, cash flow projections and management accounts. These may indicate significant income or expenditure which needs to be disclosed, and will also give general indications about the company's trading position.

   (iv) Search for evidence about known risk areas and contingencies. This includes a review of documentation relating to legal matters (see (c)).

   (v) Read the minutes of directors' meetings which took place after the year-end. These may provide evidence of significant decisions which may need to be disclosed. Auditors should find out details of what has happened at meetings for which minutes are not yet available.

   (vi) Review relevant sources of evidence that are external to the client, such as knowledge of competitors, suppliers and customers and industry trends.

   (vii) Discuss with management whether any events have occurred that may affect the accounts. Examples include new commitments, changes in assets or events which bring into question the accounting policies or estimates used in the accounts.

(b) (i) The main use of after-date evidence in stock is to determine the client's ability to sell its stock and hence to determine what net realisable value should be. The following information may be relevant:

   (1) After-date sales made or orders received
   (2) Details of planned reductions in sales prices
   (3) Industry trends and details, particularly prices and performance of competitors
   (4) Details of increases in average age of stock
   (5) Details of stock scrapped

   (ii) The main uses of information on after-date payables and accruals are to ascertain whether:

   (1) Trade creditors and accruals have been completely recorded.
   (2) Stock cut-off has been correctly applied.

   Relevant information includes:

   (1) Information received after the year-end for goods or services received prior to the year-end
   (2) Credit notes received after the year-end for goods returned before the year-end
   (3) Suppliers' statements received after the year-end relating to periods prior to the year-end
   (4) Payments made after the year-end relating to goods or services received before the year-end

(c) Auditors should carry out the following procedures to obtain evidence about legal actions.

   (i) Discuss with management the arrangements for instructing lawyers.

   (ii) Examine board minutes for indications of legal actions.

   (iii) Examine correspondence with, and bills rendered by, lawyers and obtain confirmation that no bills are outstanding.

   (iv) Obtain a list of matters referred to lawyers.

   (v) Obtain written assurances that directors or other officials are not aware of any outstanding matters other than those disclosed.

   (vi) If appropriate (due to problems with other evidence), obtain confirmation from lawyers about the directors' assessment of likely outcomes of legal actions, and of whether the information provided by the directors is complete.

15: Forming an audit judgement

Answer 15.4

(a) Going concern is one of the fundamental accounting principles which underpin the preparation of accounts. The statement that accounts have been prepared on a going concern basis means that the business will continue to be in operational existence for the foreseeable future. That means assets will be realised in the normal course of business without the necessity for forced sales at knockdown prices, and that no liability will arise other than those incurred in the normal course of business.

(b) When events or conditions have been identified which may cast significant doubt on the entity's ability to continue as a going concern, the auditor should:

   (i) review management's plans for future actions based on its going concern assessment;

   (ii) gather sufficient appropriate audit evidence to confirm or dispel whether or not a material uncertainty exists through carrying out procedures considered necessary, including considering the effects of any plans of management and other mitigating factors; and

   (iii) seek written representations from management regarding its plans for future action, the assessment made and relevant disclosures made.

When questions arise on the appropriateness of the going concern assumption, some of the normal audit procedures carried out by the auditors may take on an **additional significance**. Auditors may also have to carry out **additional procedures** or to update information obtained earlier.

   (i) **Analyse and discuss cash flow**, profit and other relevant forecasts with management

   (ii) **Analyse and discuss** the entity's latest available **interim financial statements**

   (iii) **Review the terms of debentures and loan agreements** and determine whether they have been breached

   (iv) **Read minutes** of the meetings of shareholders, the board of directors and important committees for reference to financing difficulties

   (v) **Enquire** of the entity's lawyer regarding **litigation and claims**

   (vi) **Confirm the existence, legality and enforceability** of arrangements to provide or maintain financial support with related and third parties

   (vii) **Assess** the **financial ability** of such parties to **provide additional funds**

   (viii) **Consider the entity's position** concerning unfulfilled customer orders

   (ix) **Review events after the period end** for items affecting the entity's ability to continue as a going concern

Answer 15.5

(a) The purpose of a letter of representation is to obtain evidence about matters which are critical to the audit where that evidence is not available by other means.

The fundamental weakness of representations is that they are not a substitute for stronger, independent evidence. Therefore representations will be insufficient if other stronger evidence is expected to be available.

If other evidence would not be expected to be available, auditors will consider the following:

   (i) The fact that making misleading representations to auditors is often illegal

   (ii) Whether other evidence that the auditors have sought to corroborate the representations, does do so

   (iii) Whether the representations are consistent with other evidence obtained during the course of audit

   (iv) Whether those making the representations are able to do so knowledgeably

(b) (i) Since the year-end, the cash flows of Y, an associated company, have improved significantly. As a result we believe that amounts of £200,000 which have been owed since WW will be fully recoverable.

   (ii) We are confident that the legal claim made by X for £50,000 will be successfully defended and the disclosures made in the accounts concerning the claim are sufficient. No similar claims from X or other customers have been received or are expected to be received.

Now try Question 15 in the Exam Question Bank

Chapter 16 The external audit opinion

Chapter topic list

1 Introduction
2 Statutory requirements
3 ISA 700 *Auditor's report on financial statements*
4 Modified audit reports

The following study sessions are covered in this Chapter:

Syllabus reference

30(a) Revise the form and content of an auditors' report with an unqualified opinion on the financial statements of an incorporated company (see Sessions 4 and 5)   8

30(b) Outline the circumstances in which an auditor should issue a report with: 8

    (i) A qualified opinion
    (ii) An adverse opinion
    (iii) A disclaimer of opinion

16: The external audit opinion

1 INTRODUCTION

1.1 We deal in detail in this chapter with the audit report, the public product of the auditors' work. An example of a standard, unqualified report was given in Chapter 1.

1.2 We start by restating the matters on which the auditor reports explicitly (truth and fairness, and preparation in accordance with the Companies Act), and those on which the auditor reports by exception.

1.3 We shall then revise the form of the **audit report**. The current version of the audit report is designed to close the public's **expectation gap** between what auditors do and what people think they do by stating the responsibilities of auditors and directors, and setting out the work which auditors perform to obtain a basis for their opinion.

1.4 We shall then examine **modified audit reports**. These are given when the auditors cannot state without reservation that the accounts give a true and fair view.

1.5 An audit report may be modified due to the following circumstances.

- Matters that **do not** affect the auditor's opinion.

    This will result in the addition of an emphasis of matter paragraph.

- Matters that **do** affect the auditor's opinion.

    These may result in a **qualified opinion**, a **disclaimer of opinion** or an **adverse opinion**.

We will look at modified reports in detail in Section 4.

> **Exam alert**
>
> In the exam, you will not be required to reproduce a full audit report; however you may be required to:
> (a) Describe how the audit report in a specific situation differs from an unqualified audit report or
> (b) Give extracts from an audit report dealing with circumstances where the report is modified.

2 STATUTORY REQUIREMENTS

Requirements of the 1985 Act

2.1 The Companies Act requires the auditors to state **explicitly** (s 235) whether in the auditors' opinion the annual accounts have been **properly prepared** in accordance with the Act and **show** a **true and fair view**:

(a) In the balance sheet, of the **state of the company's affairs** at the end of the financial year

(b) In the profit and loss account, of the **company's profit or loss** for the financial year

(c) In the case of **group accounts**, of the state of affairs at the end of the financial year and the profit or loss for the year of the undertakings included in the **consolidation**, so far as concerns members of the company

2.2 In addition certain requirements are reported on by exception; the auditor only has to report if they have not been met. The following are matters with which the auditors **imply** satisfaction in an unqualified report under s 237 of the Companies Act 1985.

Part E: Audit completion

Proper accounting records have been kept and **proper returns adequate** for the audit received from branches not visited.
The **accounts** are in **agreement** with the **accounting records** and returns.
All information and **explanations** have been **received** as the auditors think necessary and they have had access at all times to the company's books, accounts and vouchers.
Details of **directors' emoluments** and other benefits have been correctly **disclosed** in the financial statements.
Particulars of loans and other **transactions** in favour of **directors** and others have been correctly **disclosed** in the financial statements.
The **information** given in the **directors' report** is **consistent** with the **accounts**.

Directors' emoluments

2.3   The auditors should include in their report the required disclosure particulars of directors' emoluments and transactions with directors, if these requirements have not been complied with in the accounts (s 237).

3   ISA 700: AUDITOR'S REPORT ON FINANCIAL STATEMENTS

> **ISA 700.2**
>
> The auditor should review and assess the conclusions drawn from the audit evidence obtained as the basis for the expression of an opinion the financial statements.

3.1   This review and assessment involves considering whether the financial statements have been **prepared** in accordance with an **acceptable financial reporting framework** (being SSAPs/FRSs in the UK). Auditors in the UK also have to consider whether the financial statements comply with statutory requirements.

> **ISA 700.4**
>
> The auditor's report should contain a clear written expression of opinion on the financial statements taken as a whole.

Basic elements of the auditor's report

3.2   The auditor's report includes the following basic elements, usually in the following layout.

(a)   **Title**

(b)   **Addressee**

(c)   **Introductory paragraph** identifying the financial statements audited

(d)   A **statement** of the **responsibility** of the entity's **management** and the **responsibility** of the **auditor**

(e)   **Scope paragraph** (basis of opinion) including a description of the work performed by the auditor

(f)   **Opinion paragraph** containing an expression of opinion on the financial statements

(g)   **Date** of the report

(h) **Auditor's address**

(i) **Auditor's signature**

3.3 *Unqualified auditor's report*

Below is an example of an unqualified audit report.

An unqualified audit opinion should be expressed when the auditor concludes that the financial statements give a true and fair view (or are presented fairly, in all material respects) in accordance with the applicable reporting framework. An unqualified opinion also indicates implicitly that any changes in accounting principles or in the method of their application, and the effects, therefore, have been properly determined and disclosed in the financial statements.

Independent auditors' report to the shareholders of XYZ Limited

We have audited the financial statements of (name of entity) for the year ended ... which comprise (state the primary financial statements such as the profit and loss account, the balance sheet, the cash flow statement, the statements of total recognised gains and losses) and the related notes. These financial statements have been prepared under the historical cost convention (as modified by the revaluation of certain fixed assets) and the accounting policies set out therein.

Respective responsibilities of directors and auditors

The director's responsibilities for preparing the annual report and the financial statements in accordance with applicable law and United Kingdom Accounting Standards are set out in the statement of director's responsibilities.

Our responsibility is to audit the financial statements in accordance with relevant legal and regulatory requirements and United Kingdom Auditing Standards.

We report to you our opinion as to whether the financial statements give a true and fair view and are properly prepared in accordance with the (Companies Act 1985). We also report to you if, in our opinion, the director's report is not consistent with the financial statements, if the company has not kept proper accounting records, if we have not received all the information and explanations we required for our audit, or if information specified by law regarding directors' remuneration and transactions with the company is not disclosed.

We read other information contained in the annual report and consider whether it is consistent with the audited financial statements. This other information comprises only (the Director's Report, the Chairman's Statement, the Operating and Financial Review). We consider the implications for our report if we become aware of any apparent misstatements or material inconsistencies with the financial statements. Our responsibilities do not extend to any other information.

Basis of audit opinion

We conducted our audit in accordance with United Kingdom Auditing Standards issued by the Auditing Practices Board. An audit includes examination, on a test basis, of evidence relevant to the amounts and disclosures in the financial statements. It also includes an assessment of the significant estimates and judgements made by the directors in the preparation of the financial statements, and of whether the accounting policies are appropriates to the company's circumstances, consistently applied and adequately disclosed.

We planned and performed out audit so as to obtain all the information and explanations which we considered necessary in order to provide us with sufficient evidence to give reasonable assurance that the financial statements are free from material misstatement, whether caused by fraud or other irregularity or error. In forming our opinion we also evaluated the overall adequacy of the presentation of information in the financial statements.

Opinion

In our opinion the financial statements give a true and fair view of the statement of the company's affairs as at ... and of its profit (loss) for the year then ended and have been properly prepared in accordance with the (Companies Act 1985).

Registered auditors *Address*

Date

Part E: Audit completion

> **Point to Note**
>
> ISA 700 states that illustrative examples of a UK audit report are to be issued in a **Bulletin**. At present this Bulletin is in **draft** form only and is therefore **not examinable**.
>
> The **examiner** has confirmed that the **above format** of the audit report (based on SAS 600) will be examinable for **December 2005**.
>
> If the Bulletin becomes examinable for **June 2006** candidates it will be covered in the **Practice and Revision Kit**.

Title

3.4   The title could indicate that the report is by an **independent** auditor to affirm that all the relevant ethical standards have been met.

Addressee

3.5   The report should be addressed as required by the circumstances. This is likely to be the **shareholders** or **board of directors**.

Introductory paragraph

3.6   This should:

- Identify the entity being audited
- State that the financial statements have been audited
- Identify the financial statements being audited (for example, profit and loss account, balance sheet, cash flow statement) and the period they cover
- Specify the date and period covered by the financial statements

The auditor may be able to refer to specific page numbers if the financial statements are contained in a larger report.

Management's responsibility

3.7   The report must contain a statement that management is responsible for the presentation of the financial statements. This responsibility includes designing, implementing and maintaining internal controls, selecting appropriate accounting policies and making reasonable accounting estimates. In the UK the reader is referred to the **statement of directors' responsibilities** (see Paragraph 3.8 below).

Auditor's responsibility

3.8   The report must state that the auditor is responsible for **expressing an opinion** on financial statements.

The auditor should distinguish his duties from the relevant responsibilities of those charged with governance, by referring to the summary of the responsibilities of those charged with governance contained elsewhere in the published information. If this information has not been published elsewhere, the auditor should include it in his report.

Scope paragraph (basis of opinion)

3.9 This should explain that the auditor adhered to ISAs and ethical requirements and that the auditor planned and performed the audit so as to obtain reasonable assurance that the financial statements are free from material misstatements. The report should describe the audit as including:

(a) Estimating, on a **test basis**, evidence to support the financial statement amounts and disclosures.

(b) Assessing the **accounting principles** used in the preparation of the financial statements.

(c) Assessing the **significant estimates** made by management in the preparation of the financial statements.

(d) Evaluating the **overall** financial statement **presentation**.

The ISA continues 'In the UK and Ireland, the accounting principles used in the preparation of financial statements are established by legislation. The auditor should consider whether the accounting policies are appropriate to the reporting entity's circumstances, consistently applied and adequately disclosed. Lastly in the scope paragraph, 'the report should include a statement by the auditor that the audit provides a reasonable basis for the opinion'.

Auditor's opinion

3.10 If the auditor concludes that the financial statements give a true and fair view, he should express an **unqualified opinion**.

An unqualified opinion states that the financial statements give a true and fair view or present fairly, in all material respects, in accordance with the **applicable financial reporting framework**. It should clearly indicate the financial reporting framework used, and, if IFRSs are not used, the country of origin of the framework, such as UK accounting standards.

Auditor's signature

3.11 A report must contain a **signature**, whether this is the auditor's own name or the audit firm's name.

Date

3.12 The report must be dated, a date **after all the evidence has been collected**. This date shows the completion date of the audit and should not be before management has approved the financial statements.

Address

3.13 The **location** where the auditor practices must be included. This is usually the city where the auditor has his office.

Part E: Audit completion

Activity 16.1

The following is a series of extracts from an unqualified audit report which has been signed by the auditors of Little Panda Limited.

AUDITORS' REPORT TO THE SHAREHOLDERS OF LITTLE PANDA LIMITED

We have audited *the financial statements on pages .... to ....* which have been prepared under the historical cost convention.

We have conducted our audit *in accordance with Auditing Standards* issued by the Auditing Practices Board. An audit includes examination on a test basis of evidence relevant to the amounts and disclosures in the financial statements.

In our opinion the financial statements give a true and fair view of the state of the company's affairs as at 31 December 20X7 and of its profit for the year then ended and have been properly prepared in accordance with the Companies Act 1985.

Tasks

Explain the purpose and meaning of the following phrases taken from the above extracts of an unqualified audit report.

(a) '... the financial statements of Little Panda Ltd for the year ended 31 December 20X7 which comprise...'
(b) '... in accordance with Auditing Standards.'
(c) 'In our opinion ...'

4 MODIFIED AUDIT REPORTS

4.1 Modified audit reports arise when auditors do not believe that they can state without reservation that the accounts give a true and fair view.

4.2 An auditor's report is considered to be modified in the following situations.

(a) **Matters that do not affect the auditor's opinion:** emphasis of a matter

(b) **Matters that do affect the auditor's opinion**

- Qualified opinion
- Disclaimer of opinion
- Adverse opinion

Matters that do not affect the auditor's opinion

> **KEY TERM**
>
> In certain circumstances, an auditor's report may be modified by adding an **emphasis of matter** to highlight a matter affecting the financial statements which is included in a note to the financial statements that more extensively discusses the matter. The addition of such an emphasis of matter paragraph **does not affect** the auditor's opinion. The auditor may also modify the auditor's report by using an emphasis of matter paragraph(s) to report matters other than those affecting the financial statements.

4.3 The paragraph would preferably be included after the opinion paragraph and would ordinarily refer to the fact that the auditor's opinion is not qualified in this respect.

4.4 The ISA distinguishes between **going concern matters** and other matters.

16: The external audit opinion

> **ISA 700.31/32**
>
> The auditor should modify the auditor's report by adding a paragraph to highlight a material matter regarding a going concern problem.
>
> The auditor should consider modifying the auditor's report by adding a paragraph if there is a significant uncertainty (other than a going concern problem), the resolution of which is dependent upon future events and which may affect the financial statements.

> **KEY TERM**
>
> An **uncertainty** is a matter whose outcome depends on future actions or events not under the direct control of the entity but that may affect the financial statements.

4.5 The following is an example of an emphasis of matter (explanatory) paragraph.

> **Example 4. Unqualified opinion with emphasis of matter paragraph describing a fundamental uncertainty**.
>
> *Fundamental uncertainty* (insert just before opinion paragraph)
>
> In forming our opinion, we have considered the adequacy of the disclosures made in the financial statements concerning the possible outcome to litigation against B Limited, a subsidiary undertaking of the company, for an alleged breach of environmental regulations. The future settlement of this litigation could result in additional liabilities and the closure of B Limited's business, whose net assets included in the consolidated balance sheet total £... and whose profit before tax for the year is £... . Details of the circumstances relating to this fundamental uncertainty are described in note .... . Our opinion is not qualified in this respect.

> **Point to Note**
>
> ISA 700 states that illustrative examples of a UK audit report are to be issued in a **Bulletin**. At present this Bulletin is in **draft** form only and is therefore **not examinable**.
>
> The **examiner** has confirmed that the **above format** of the audit report (based on SAS 600) will be examinable for **December 2005**.
>
> If the Bulletin becomes examinable for **June 2006** candidates it will be covered in the **Practice and Revision Kit**.

4.6 An illustration of an emphasis of matter paragraph relating to going concern is set out in ISA 570 *Going concern*.

> Without qualifying our opinion we draw attention to Note X in the financial statements. The Company incurred a net loss of ZZZ during the year ended December 31, 20X1 and, as of that date, the Company's current liabilities exceeded its total assets by ZZZ. These factors, along with other matters as set forth in Note X, raise substantial doubt that the Company will be able to continue as a going concern.

4.7 This type of paragraph will usually be sufficient to meet the auditor's reporting responsibilities. In extreme cases, however, involving multiple uncertainties that are significant to the financial statements, a **disclaimer of opinion** may be required instead (see below).

Part E: Audit completion

4.8 The auditor may also modify the report by using an emphasis of matter paragraph for matters which do *not* affect the financial statements. This might be the case if amendment is necessary to other information in a document containing audited financial statements and the entity refuses to make the amendment. An emphasis of matter paragraph could also be used for **additional statutory reporting responsibilities**.

Matters that do affect the auditor's opinion

4.9 An auditor may not be able to express an unqualified opinion when either of the following circumstances exist and, in the auditor's judgement, the effect of the matter is or may be **material** to the financial statements:

- There is a **limitation on the scope** of the auditor's work.

- There is a **disagreement** with management regarding the acceptability of the accounting policies selected, the method of their application or the adequacy of financial statement disclosures.

4.10 There are different types and degrees of modified opinion.

- A limitation on scope may lead to a **qualified opinion** or a **disclaimer of opinion**.
- A disagreement may lead to a **qualified opinion** or an **adverse opinion**.

4.11 The ISA describes these different modified opinions and the circumstances leading to them as follows.

> **ISA 700.37-40**
>
> A **qualified opinion** should be expressed when the auditor concludes that an unqualified opinion cannot be expressed but that the effect of any disagreement with management, or limitation on scope is not so material and pervasive at to require an adverse opinion or a disclaimer of opinion. A qualified opinion should be expressed as being 'except for the effects of the matter to which the qualification relates'.
>
> A **disclaimer of opinion** should be expressed when the possible effect of a limitation on scope is so material and pervasive that the auditor has not been able to obtain sufficient appropriate audit evidence and accordingly is unable to express an opinion on the financial statements.
>
> An **adverse opinion** should be expressed when the effect of a disagreement is so material and pervasive to the financial statements that the auditor concludes that a qualification of the report is not adequate to disclose the misleading or incomplete nature of the financial statements.

4.12 The concept of materiality was discussed in Chapter 5 and you can now see its fundamental importance in auditing.

> **ISA 700.40**
>
> Whenever the auditor expresses an opinion that is other than qualified, a clear description of all the substantive reasons should be included in the report and, unless impracticable, a quantification of the possible effect(s) on the financial statements.

4.13 This would usually be set out in a **separate paragraph** preceding the opinion or disclaimer of opinion and may include a reference to a more extensive discussion (if any) in a note to the financial statements.

16: The external audit opinion

Limitation on scope

4.14 There are two circumstances identified by the standard where there might be a limitation on scope.

4.15 Firstly, a limitation on the scope of the auditor's work may sometimes be **imposed by the entity** (eg when the terms of the engagement specify that the auditor will not carry out an audit procedure that the auditor believes is necessary).

4.16 However, when the limitation in the terms of a proposed engagement is such that the auditor believes the need to express a disclaimer of opinion exists, the auditor would usually not accept such a limited audit engagement, unless required by statute. Also, a statutory auditor would not accept such an audit engagement when the limitation infringes on the auditor's statutory duties.

4.17 Secondly, a scope limitation may be **imposed by circumstances** (eg when the timing of the auditor's appointment is such that the auditor is unable to observe the counting of physical inventories). It may also arise when, in the opinion of the auditor, the entity's accounting records are inadequate or when the auditor is unable to carry out an audit procedure believed to be desirable. In these circumstances, the auditor would attempt to carry out reasonable alternative procedures to obtain sufficient appropriate audit evidence to support an unqualified opinion.

> **ISA 700.43**
>
> Where there is a limitation on the scope of the auditor's work that requires expression of a qualified opinion or a disclaimer of opinion, the auditor's report should describe the limitation and indicate the possible adjustments to the financial statement that might have been determined to be necessary had the limitation not existed.

4.18 The following examples are given of reports given under a limitation of scope.

Example 8. Qualified opinion: limitation on the auditors' work

(Basis of opinion: excerpt)

.... or error. However, the evidence available to us was limited because £... of the company's recorded turnover comprises cash sales, over which there was no system of control on which we could rely for the purposes of our audit. There were no other satisfactory audit procedures that we could adopt to confirm that cash sales were properly recorded.

In forming our opinion we also evaluated the overall adequacy of the presentation of information in the financial statements.

Qualified opinion arising from limitation in audit scope

Except for any adjustments that might have been found to be necessary had we been able to obtain sufficient evidence concerning cash sales, in our opinion the financial statements give a true and fair view of the state of the company's affairs as at 31 December 20.. and of its profit (loss) for the year then ended and have been properly prepared in accordance with the Companies Act 1985.

In respect alone of the limitation on our work relating to cash sales:

(a) we have not obtained all the information and explanations that we considered necessary for the purpose of our audit; and

(b) we were unable to determine whether proper accounting records had been maintained.

Part E: Audit completion

> **Example 9. Disclaimer of opinion**
>
> *(Basis of opinion: excerpt)*
>
> .... or error. However, the evidence available to us was limited because we were appointed auditors on (date) and in consequence we were unable to carry out auditing procedures necessary to obtain adequate assurance regarding the quantities and condition of stock and work in progress, appearing in the balance sheet at £.... Any adjustment to this figure would have a consequential significant effect on the profit for the year.
>
> In forming our opinion we also evaluated the overall adequacy of the presentation of information in the financial statements.
>
> *Opinion: disclaimer on view given by financial statements*
>
> Because of the possible effect of the limitation in evidence available to us, we are unable to form an opinion as to whether the financial statements give a true and fair view of the state of the company's affairs as at 31 December 20.. or of its profit (loss) for the year then ended. In all other respects, in our opinion the financial statements have been properly prepared in accordance with the Companies Act 1985.
>
> In respect of the limitation on our work relating to stock and work-in-progress:
>
> (a) we have not obtained all the information and explanations that we considered necessary for the purpose of our audit; and
>
> (b) we were unable to determine whether proper accounting records had been maintained.

Note. Because of the length of the audit report, we have only shown those parts of each modified report which differ from the unqualified report shown in Section 3.

> **Point to Note**
>
> ISA 700 states that illustrative examples of a UK audit report are to be issued in a **Bulletin**. At present this Bulletin is in **draft** form only and is therefore **not examinable**.
>
> The **examiner** has confirmed that the **above format** of the audit report (based on SAS 600) will be examinable for **December 2005**.
>
> If the Bulletin becomes examinable for **June 2006** candidates it will be covered in the **Practice and Revision Kit**.

Disagreement with management

4.19 The auditor may disagree with management about matters such as the acceptability of accounting policies selected, the method of their application, or the adequacy of disclosures in the financial statements.

> **ISA 700.45**
>
> If such disagreements are material to the financial statements, the auditor should express a qualified or an adverse opinion.

4.20 The following examples are given of reports where there is disagreement.

Example 7. Qualified opinion: disagreement

Qualified opinion arising from disagreement about accounting treatment

Included in the debtors shown on the balance sheet is an amount of £Y due from a company which has ceased trading. XYZ plc has no security for this debt. In our opinion the company is unlikely to receive any payment and full provision of £Y should have been made, reducing profit before tax and net assets by that amount.

Except for the absence of this provision, in our opinion the financial statements give a true and fair view of the state of the company's affairs as at 31 December 20.. and of its profit (loss) for the year then ended and have been properly prepared in accordance with the Companies Act 1985.

Example 10. Adverse opinion

Adverse opinion

As more fully explained in note ... no provision has been made for losses expected to arise on certain long-term contracts currently in progress, as the directors consider that such losses should be off-set against amounts recoverable on other long-term contracts. In our opinion, provision should be made for foreseeable losses on individual contracts as required by Statement of Standard Accounting Practice 9. If losses had been so recognised the effect would have been to reduce the profit before and after tax for the year and the contract work in progress at 31 December 20.. by £... .

In view of the effect of the failure to provide for the losses referred to above, in our opinion the financial statements do not give a true and fair view of the state of the company's affairs as at 31 December 20.. and of its profit (loss) for the year then ended. In all other respects, in our opinion the financial statements have been properly prepared in accordance with the Companies Act 1985.

Point to Note

ISA 700 states that illustrative examples of a UK audit report are to be issued in a **Bulletin**. At present this Bulletin is in **draft** form only and is therefore **not examinable**.

The **examiner** has confirmed that the **above format** of the audit report (based on SAS 600) will be examinable for **December 2005**.

If the Bulletin becomes examinable for **June 2006** candidates it will be covered in the **Practice and Revision Kit**.

Activity 16.2

What do the following forms of qualified audit opinion represent?

(a) Disagreement
(b) Adverse opinion
(c) Disclaimer

Activity 16.3

During the course of your audit of the long-term assets of Eastern Engineering, a listed company, at 31 March 20X4 two problems have arisen.

(a) The calculations of the cost of direct labour incurred on assets in course of construction by the company's employees have been accidentally destroyed for the early part of the year. The direct labour cost involved is £10,000.

Part E: Audit completion

(b) The company incurred development expenditure of £25,000 spent on a viable new product which will go into production next year and which is expected to last for ten years. The expenditure has been debited in full to the profit and loss account.

(c) Other relevant financial information is as follows.

	£
Profit before tax	100,000
Long-term asset additions	133,000
Assets constructed by company	34,000
Long-term asset at net book value	666,667

Required

(a) List the general forms of modified report available to auditors in drafting their report and state the circumstances in which each is appropriate.

(b) State whether you feel that a modified audit report would be necessary for each of the two circumstances outlined above, giving reasons in each case.

(c) On the assumption that you decide that a modified audit report is necessary with respect to the treatment of the government grant, draft the section of the report describing the matter (the whole report is not required).

Key learning points

- ISA 700 *The auditor's report on financial statements* gives guidance on both unqualified and modified audit reports.

- The basic elements of the audit report are
    - Title
    - Addressee
    - Introductory paragraph
    - Management's responsibility
    - Auditor's responsibility
    - Scope paragraph (basis of opinion)
    - Opinion paragraph
    - Date
    - Auditor's address
    - Auditor's signature

- An **emphasis of matter** *paragraph* can be used to highlight certain items, without altering he auditor's unqualified opinion.

- There are two types of circumstance which may affect the auditor's opinion:
    - Limitation on scope
    - Disagreement

- You must be able to discuss a **'true and fair view'** (or 'present fairly'), although this is not easy given the lack of a comprehensive definition: refer back to Chapter 1.

- You will not be asked to draft complete unqualified and modified audit reports. However, you should be able to list the basic contents and explain the terms used in the ISA. You may be asked to draft the opinion paragraph of an audit report, including a qualification.

- The **examples of qualification** are given only as an indication of what is required. Each case will be different and will require different disclosures.

Quick quiz

1. How should auditors distinguish between their responsibilities and those of the directors?
2. What are the major elements of the audit process highlighted in the basis of opinion section of the audit report?
3. On what must the auditors conclude in order to be able to give an unqualified opinion?
4. Give two examples of scope limitations on the audit.
5. Why might auditors issue a qualified opinion on the grounds of disagreement?

16: The external audit opinion

Answers to quick quiz

1   Auditors should state that the financial statements are the responsibility of the directors, and state the auditors' responsibility is to express an opinion on the financial statements.

2   The major elements of the audit process are:

   (a) Examine on a test basis, evidence relevant to the amounts and disclosures in the financial statements.

   (b) Assess the significant estimates and judgements made by the directors.

   (c) Consider whether the accounting policies are appropriate, consistently applied and appropriately disclosed.

3   Auditors must conclude that:

   (a) The financial statements have been prepared using appropriate, consistently applied accounting policies.

   (b) The financial statements have been prepared in accordance with relevant legislation, regulations or applicable accounting standards.

   (c) There is adequate disclosure of all relevant information.

4   Scope limitations can arise because of:

   (a) Absence of proper accounting records
   (b) An inability to carry out audit procedures considered necessary

5   Auditors might qualify on the grounds of disagreement because of:

   (a) Inappropriate accounting policies
   (b) Disagreements on the facts and amounts included in the accounts
   (c) Disagreement on the manner and extent of disclosure of facts or amounts
   (d) Failure to comply with relevant legislation or other requirements

Answers to activities

Answer 16.1

(a) '... the financial statements of Little Panda Ltd for the year ended 31 December 20X7 which comprise...'

   Purpose
   The purpose of this phrase is to make it clear to the reader of an audit report the part of a company's annual report upon which the auditors are reporting their opinion.

   Meaning
   An annual report may include documents such as a chairman's report, employee report, five year summary and other voluntary information. However, under the Companies Act, only the profit and loss account, balance sheet and associated notes are required to be audited in true and fair terms. Thus the page references (for instance, 8 to 20) cover only the profit and loss account, balance sheet, notes to the accounts, cash flow statement and statement of total recognised gains and losses. The directors' report, although examined and reported on by exception if it contains inconsistencies, is not included in these page references.

(b) '...in accordance with Auditing Standards...'

   Purpose
   This phrase is included in order to confirm to the reader that best practice, as laid down in Auditing Standards, has been adopted by the auditors in both carrying out their audit and in drafting their audit opinion. This means that the reader can be assured that the audit has been properly conducted, and that should he or she wish to discover what such standards are, or what certain key phrases mean, he or she can have recourse to Auditing Standards to explain such matters.

Part E: Audit completion

Meaning

Auditing Standards are those auditing standards prepared by the Auditing Practices Board.

These prescribe the principles and practices to be followed by auditors in the planning, designing and carrying out various aspects of their audit work, the content of audit reports, both qualified and unqualified and so on. Members are expected to follow all of these standards.

(c) *'In our opinion ...'*

Purpose

Under the Companies Act, auditors are required to report on every balance sheet, profit and loss account or group accounts laid before members. In reporting, they are required to state their *opinion* on those accounts. Thus, the purpose of this phrase is to comply with the statutory requirement to report an opinion.

Meaning

An audit report is an expression of opinion by suitably qualified auditors as to whether the financial statements give a true and fair view, and have been properly prepared in accordance with the Companies Act. *It is not a certificate*; rather it is a statement of whether or not, in the professional judgement of the auditors, the financial statements give a true and fair view.

Answer 16.2

(a) A qualification on the grounds of disagreement may arise for the following reasons.

    (i) Inappropriate accounting policies
    (ii) Disagreements on the facts or amounts included in the accounts
    (iii) Disagreement about the disclosure of the facts or amounts in the accounts
    (iv) Failure to comply with relevant legislation or accounting standards

(b) An adverse opinion is given when the disagreement is not just material but pervasive. The auditors believe that the disputed matters render the accounts misleading. The reasons why this type of matter might arise are listed in paragraph (a).

(c) A disclaimer is a qualification due to a pervasive uncertainty. There will have been a limitation on the scope of the audit and the limitation is such that the auditors feel that they cannot give an opinion on the truth and fairness of the accounts.

Answer 16.3

(a) ISA 700 *The auditor's report on financial statements* suggests that the auditors may need to qualify their audit opinion under one of two main circumstances:

    (i) Limitation on scope of the auditors' examination;
    (ii) Disagreement with the treatment or disclosure of a matter in the financial statements.

For both circumstances there can be two 'levels' of modified opinion:

    (i) *Material but not pervasive,* where the circumstances prompting the uncertainty or disagreement is material but confined to one particular aspect of the financial statements, so that it does not affect their overall value to any potential user;

    (ii) The more serious modified opinion where the extent of the uncertainty or disagreement is such that it will be *pervasive* to the overall view shown by the financial statements, ie the financial statements are or could be misleading.

The general form of modified report appropriate to each potential situation may be seen by the following table.

Circumstance	Material but not pervasive	Pervasive
Limitation on scope	Except for ... might	Disclaimer of opinion
Disagreement	Except for ...	Adverse opinion

(b) Whether a modification of the audit opinion would be required in relation to either of the two circumstances described in the question would depend on whether or not the auditors considered either of them to be material. An item is likely to be considered as material in the context of a company's financial statements if its omission, misstatement or non-disclosure would prevent a proper understanding of those statements on the part of a potential user. Whilst for some audit purposes materiality will be considered in absolute terms, more often than not it will be considered as a relative term.

16: The external audit opinion

(i) *Loss of records relating to direct labour costs for assets in the course of construction*

The loss of records supporting one of the asset figures in the balance sheet would cause a limitation on the scope of the auditors' work. The £10,000, which is the value covered by the lost records, represents 29.4% of the expenditure incurred during the year on assets in course of construction but only 6% of total additions to long-term assets during the year and 1.5% of the year end net book value for long-term assets. The total amount of £10,000 represents 10% of pre-tax profit but, as in relation to asset values, the real consideration by the auditors should be the materiality of any over- or under-statement of assets resulting from error in arriving at the £10,000 rather than the total figure itself.

Provided there are no suspicious circumstances surrounding the loss of these records and the total figure for additions to assets in the course of construction seems reasonable in the light of other audit evidence obtained, then it is unlikely that this matter would be seen as sufficiently material to merit any qualification of the audit opinion. If other records have been lost as well, however, it may be necessary for the auditors to comment on the management's failure to maintain proper books and records.

(ii) *Development costs debited to the income statement*

The situation here is one of disagreement, since best accounting practice, as laid down, requires that development costs should be taken to the income statement over the useful life of the product to which they relate.

This departure from SSAP 13 does not seem to be justifiable and would be material to the reported pre-tax profits for the year, representing as it does 22.5% of that figure.

Whilst this understatement of profit (and corresponding overstatement of undistributable reserves) would be material to the financial statements, it is not likely to be seen as pervasive and therefore an 'except for' qualified opinion would be appropriate.

(c) *Qualified audit report extract*

'As explained in note ... development costs in respect of a potential new product have been deducted in full against profit instead of being spread over the life of the relevant product as required by SSAP 13; the effect of so doing has been to decrease profits before and after tax for the year by £22,500.

Except for ...'

Now try Question 16 in the Exam Question Bank

Question Bank

Question bank

1 INTERNAL AUDIT
45 mins

You are the audit partner responsible for the audit of the accounts of Fastbikes Ltd, a company manufacturing bicycles for the home and overseas markets.

The finance director (Mr Jones) has informed you that the company is to create an internal audit department by appointing an internal audit manager and two assistants. He believes that this should improve internal controls and information received by management but that it will also lead to:

(a) The possibility of your firm auditing the annual accounts of Fastbikes on a fixed fee basis due to a reduced work load

(b) The internal audit manager having unrestricted access to your firm's working papers relating to the audit of the company's accounts.

Required

(a) Identify the principal differences between internal and external (registered) auditors, using the following criteria:

   (i) Eligibility to act

   (ii) Security of tenure

   (iii) Primary objective and the limitations on the scope of the auditor's work in order to achieve this objective. **(9 marks)**

(b) Explain why the appointment of an internal audit department should improve information received by the management of Fastbikes. **(6 marks)**

(c) Explain why the internal audit manager should not report to Mr Jones, stating with reasons to whom she should report. **(5 marks)**

(d) (i) Briefly discuss the problems associated with auditing the accounts of Fastbikes on a fixed fee basis

   and

   (ii) Briefly comment on whether you would allow the internal audit manager to have unrestricted access to your firm's working papers. **(5 marks)**

(25 marks)

2 AUDITOR'S RESPONSIBILITIES
20 mins

(a) Discuss the extent of an auditor's responsibilities to shareholders during the course of their professional engagement.

(b) Outline the auditor's responsibility with regard to detecting fraud in a company.

(c) Outline the reporting requirements of ISA 240.

3 INDEPENDENCE SITUATIONS
45 mins

It is important that an auditor's independence is beyond question, and that he should behave with integrity and objectivity in all professional and business situations. The following are a series of questions which were asked by auditors at a recent update seminar on professional ethics.

Question bank

(a) Can I audit my brother's company? (5 marks)

(b) A B & Co, the previous auditors, will not give my firm professional clearance or the usual handover information because they are still owed fees. Should I accept the client's offer of appointment? (6 marks)

(c) Can I prepare the financial statements of a company and still remain as auditor? (5 marks)

(d) My client has threatened to sue the firm for negligence. Can I still continue to act as auditor? (6 marks)

(e) I am a student of the Association of Chartered Certified Accountants. Am I bound by the ethical guidelines of the Association? (3 marks)

Required

Discuss the answers you would give to the above questions posed by the auditors based on the ACCA Code of Ethics. **(25 marks)**

4 AUDIT ENGAGEMENT (PILOT PAPER) *45 mins*

Houses Limited, a long established, large construction company has recently instructed your firm to act as the company's external auditors. The company has its own internal audit department. Professional clearance has been obtained from the previous auditors and an audit engagement letter has been issued.

It is now 1 March 20X6 and you have been assigned to the audit team who will visit the company in order to obtain as much relevant knowledge as possible for use in planning the audit of the company's financial statements for the year ending 31 July 20X6.

Required

(a) (i) Identify to whom in a company an audit engagement letter should be addressed, and explain how acceptance of the terms of engagement should be conveyed to the auditor. (2 marks)

 (ii) Explain the purpose of an audit engagement letter, state when such a letter should be issued to an audit client and identify the occasions when it may be appropriate to issue a new (replacement) letter. (7 marks)

(b) Give FIVE examples of information your firm would wish to obtain prior to 31 July 20X6 in order to assist in the planning of the audit of the financial statements of Houses. For each example state your reasoning for wishing to obtain the information.

(10 marks)

(c) Identify the principal differences between internal and external auditors, using the following criteria:

 (i) Eligibility to act;

 (ii) Primary objective and the limitations on the scope of the auditor's work in order to achieve this objective. (6 marks)

(25 marks)

5 RISK BASED APPROACH   *45 mins*

The directors of Gocomp Ltd wish to appoint your firm as the company's auditors. At an initial meeting with the audit partner, the directors have provided the following information.

(a) There are three directors each of whom owns one third of the company's share capital. The directors consider themselves to be entrepreneurial and do not have any accountancy experience.

(b) The company's accountant recently resigned and since then the company has employed a temporary accountant.

(c) Gocomp Ltd has been trading for four years selling personal computers and computer software from three retail store outlets to the general public. It purchases in bulk quantities from suppliers and each store carries stock levels equivalent to five months sales on average.

(d) The company accepts payments for goods sold by cash, cheque or credit card only.

(e) Due to an increasingly competitive market, over the past twelve months profit margins have been extremely low and the company's overdraft has been steadily increasing. The overdraft is secured against the assets of the company.

Required

(a) Explain what you understand by the term audit risk, making reference to:

    (i) Inherent risk
    (ii) Control risk
    (iii) Detection risk   (8 marks)

(b) From the information provided by the directors, identify with reasons, *six* factors that would affect your assessment of the inherent risk associated with the audit of the accounts of Gocomp Ltd.   (12 marks)

(c) Briefly explain why in recent years there has been increased use of the risk-based approach to auditing.   (5 marks)

(25 marks)

6 WORKING PAPERS   *45 mins*

You are the audit partner in charge of Watson Manufacturing Limited. The audit senior who conducted the audit presents you with the files on completion of the audit for the year ended 31 March 20X2.

Required

(a) List four reasons why audit working papers are prepared.   (4 marks)

(b) List the main information that is included in:

    (i) Permanent audit files
    (ii) Current audit files   (13 marks)

(c) Briefly state the advantages and disadvantages of following pre-prepared audit programmes.   (8 marks)

(25 marks)

Question bank

7 INTERNAL CONTROL
45 mins

As the auditor in charge of the audit of the accounts of DS Limited you are about to review the internal control of the company.

The company is long established and operates three department stores. Each store has its own warehouse but the administration, buying and accounting operations are centrally located in the largest store. Your review will include a detailed examination of the control environment and of the control activities employed by the company.

Required

(a) Explain in your own words the meaning of the term 'internal control'. (5 marks)

(b) Explain the meaning of the term 'control environment' and identify THREE major factors that will be reflected in the control environment of DS. (8 marks)

(c) Identify SIX different categories of control activity (6 marks)

and

for each category identified give ONE example of a specific procedure you would expect to find in the daily activities of DS. (6 marks)

(25 marks)

8 STOCK AND SALES (PILOT PAPER)
45 mins

You are part of a team auditing the financial statements of Smartbuy Limited. The company sells home decorating and maintenance products from a large retail and warehouse unit. From enquiries into the company's internal control systems you have ascertained the following information.

Stock purchases

New stock is ordered over the telephone by the company buyer who maintains a record of telephone orders. When goods are subsequently received, the buyer has sole responsibility for checking goods received for quantity only, to the record of telephone orders. Invoices from suppliers are sent to the buyer for authorisation, before being forwarded to the accounts department for entry into the accounting records and subsequent payment.

Sales

Customers either pay by cash or cheque and the company operates electronic cash tills. Till receipts are issued to customers but till rolls are not retained. On a daily basis each till operator independently empties their till and takes the day's takings to the company cashier. The cashier counts the total daily takings and makes the appropriate entries in the company's accounting records before depositing the monies with the company's bank.

You are aware from a review of the controls exercised over the company's bank account that the cashier is responsible for reconciling the monthly bank statements to the bank account in the general ledger.

Required

(a) With regard to the stock purchases system of Smartbuy:
   (i) Identify FOUR weaknesses in the system.
   (ii) Describe the implication of each weakness identified.
   (iii) Recommend improvements to address the weaknesses.

You should assume that there is a sufficient number of employees in the company to operate effective controls. (16 marks)

(b) Explain why your team would be concerned about obtaining adequate audit assurances as to the completeness of the sales invoice figure in the financial statements of Smartbuy. Your answer should include brief commentary as to how your team might use analytical review as a substantive procedure. (9 marks)

(25 marks)

9 CONTROLS OVER RECEIPTS *45 mins*

Righton Knitwear Limited sells knitwear products of all types to shops. You are taking part in the audit for the year ended 31 December 20X6 and you have been asked to consider the audit work which should be performed on the company's sales system. Although most sales are on credit, there are some customers who are too small and whose purchases are too infrequent to have a sales ledger account with Righton. They are able therefore to order goods and pay in cash for the goods when they collect them.

You have ascertained the following system for credit sales and cash sales.

Credit sales

(a) Cash and cheques for credit sales are received in the post, which is opened by two people. They make a record of all the cheques and cash received, which are then handed over to the cashier.

(b) The cashier records the moneys received in the cash book, banks them and reports them to the sales accounts department.

(c) The sales accounts department posts the cash and cheques received to the sales ledger.

(d) Credit notes are sent to customers and posted to the sales ledger only after they have been authorised.

Cash sales

(a) The customer places an order with the sales department; the sales department prepares a pre-numbered multi-copy advice note.

(b) The order is put together by the despatch department and this is handed over to the customer along with a copy of the advice note.

(c) The customer submits the advice note to the cashier; the cashier prepares a sales invoice by hand.

(d) The cashier receives payment from the customer by cheque or in cash.

(e) The monies are recorded and banked by the cashier.

Required

(a) (i) Consider why two people should open mail containing cash and cheques from customers.

 (ii) State the audit procedures you would undertake while attending the mail opening and follow up of the cheque banking. (7 marks)

(b) (i) What are the main reasons for the issue of credit notes?

 (ii) How would you go about testing whether all credit notes had been issued for a valid reason and had been authorised? (9 marks)

(c) (i) Point out the weaknesses in the cash sales system described above.

 (ii) In order to check that there is no material fraud or error in operation, what audit tests would you perform on this system? (9 marks)

(25 marks)

Question bank

10 ANALYTICAL PROCEDURES *45 mins*

You are carrying out the audit of Darwin plc, a large manufacturing concern, as at 31 October 20X5 and have obtained the following information in respect of certain aspects of the business prior to preparation of the final accounts.

	20X5 £'000	20X4 £'000
Tangible fixed assets (at net book value)	22,350	22,175
Stock: raw materials	1,100	1,000
work in progress	400	500
finished goods	5,500	4,000
Debtors	4,800	5,200
Creditors	(2,800)	(3,000)
Bank overdraft	(1,900)	(1,400)
Sales	28,000	25,500
Cost of sales *	(20,000)	(18,700)
	8,000	6,800
Distribution cost *	(3,300)	(3,200)
Administrative expenses *	(2,200)	(2,100)
Profit before taxation	2,500	1,500
* Depreciation included in these figures	2,000	1,800

Required

(a) Carry out an analytical review of the above information and list four items you believe would require particular investigation during your final audit, explaining in each case why you believe them to require such investigation. (8 marks)

(b) For each item detailed in your list state two audit enquiries specific to Darwin you would make in order to satisfy yourself that the figure appearing under each heading had been properly stated. (6 marks)

(c) Your audit assistant has asked you to explain the purpose of analytical procedures. Explain briefly, giving examples from Darwin. (6 marks)

(20 marks)

11 JEANS (PILOT PAPER) *45 mins*

Jeans Limited manufactures high fashion jeans for distribution to wholesalers and retailers.

You have been assigned to the audit of stock in the company's financial statements for the year ended 31 July 20X3.

The following points are relevant to the audit.

(i) The company has raw materials, consumables and work in progress stock at its factory base. Finished goods are stored in a separate warehouse located five miles away. The company does not hold stock owned by third parties.

(ii) On 31 July 20X3 employees of the company will physically count the stock at both of the company's sites and members of your audit team will be in attendance.

(iii) The company has significant quantities of finished goods stock held by independent retail stores under its sale or return system. Under this system, stock is displayed for sale at retail shop premises but remains the property of Jeans until it is sold by retailers. Any garments not sold within three months are returned to Jeans for bulk sale at heavily discounted prices.

(iv) Some quantities of finished goods stock were stated at net realisable value in the financial statements of the company for the previous year.

Required

(a) (i) Define inherent risk; (2 marks)

(ii) Explain why the inherent risk associated with stock in the financial statements of Jeans would be assessed as 'high'. (8 marks)

(b) (i) Define net realisable value; (2 marks)

(ii) Identify THREE possible causes for finished goods stock being stated at net realisable value in the financial statements of Jeans for the previous year. (3 marks)

(c) (i) Identify the important tasks that members of your audit team should carry out when attending the company's physical stock count on 31 July 20X3.

(ii) For each task identified explain the purpose of carrying it out. (10 marks)

(25 marks)

12 FIXED ASSETS (PILOT PAPER) *45 mins*

(a) List four controls which would assist in reducing the control risk of non current assets. (4 marks)

(b) State the audit work you would perform to check the completeness and existence of plant and machinery. (6 marks)

(c) State the work you would carry out to check that additions to fixed assets only included capital items, and capital expenditure was not charged in the profit and loss account. (6 marks)

(d) State the methods you would use to verify ownership of:

  (i) Freehold land and buildings and
  (ii) Cars and computers. (5 marks)

(e) Describe the procedures you would carry out to determine the adequacy of a depreciation rate for computer equipment if the computers are being written off over 5 years. (4 marks)

(25 marks)

13 WOODS (PILOT PAPER) *45 mins*

Joy Lee is a very inexperienced member of your audit team and is currently involved in the audit of the financial statements of Woods Limited for the year ended 31 May 20X3. The company is engaged in the manufacture and distribution of garden furniture. Joy is assisting in the audit of the tangible fixed assets and sales and trade debtors of the company. However, given her limited experience, she is puzzled by some areas of the audit plan.

As you are more senior to her she has approached you for guidance on the following issues.

(i) Internal control objectives

(ii) The representations or assertions of the directors of Woods that are embodied in the reported trade debtors figure of £685,000 in the financial statements of Woods for the year ended 31 May 20X3

Question bank

(iii) Testing trade debtors by circularisation and by the examination of post balance sheet date receipts

Required

Prepare guidance notes in any format which:

(a) (i) Give TWO internal control objectives of a tangible fixed assets accounting system, and

(ii) Give THREE internal control objectives of a sales and trade debtors accounting system

For each objective give an example of a control that would help to achieve the objective. *(10 marks)*

(b) Identify and explain the representations or assertions of the directors of Woods that are embodied in the reported trade debtors figure of £685,000. *(7 marks)*

(c) State the primary objective of a trade debtors circularisation test and describe the circumstances in which it would be appropriate to use a positive or negative method of requesting information. Give reasons as to whether this test should be performed in addition to the testing of post balance sheet trade receipts. *(8 marks)*

(25 marks)

14 TOLLERTON *45 mins*

You are the senior in charge of the auditor of Tollerton Limited and you are auditing the company's trade creditors at 30 April 20X6.

A junior member of the audit team has been checking suppliers' statements to the balances on the purchase ledger. He is unable to reconcile a material balance, relating to Carlton, and has asked for your assistance, and your suggestions on the audit work which should be carried out on the differences.

The balance of Carlton on Tollerton purchase ledger, is shown below.

Purchase ledger

Supplier: Carlton

Date	Type	Reference	Status	Dr	Cr	Balance
10.2	Invoice	6004	Paid 1		2,130	
18.2	Invoice	6042	Paid 1		1,525	
23.2	Invoice	6057	Paid 1		2,634	
4.3	Invoice	6080	Paid 2		3,572	
15.3	Invoice	6107	Paid 2		1,632	
26.3	Invoice	6154	Paid 2		924	
31.3	Payment	Cheque	Alloc 1	6,163		
	Discount		Alloc 1	126		
14.4	Invoice	6285			2,156	
21.4	Invoice	6328			3,824	
30.4	Payment	Cheque	Alloc 2	6,005		
	Discount		Alloc 2	123		
30.4	Balance					5,980

Carlton's supplier's statement shows:

Customer: Tollerton

Date	Type	Reference	Status	Dr	Cr	Balance
7.2	Invoice	6004		2,130		
16.2	Invoice	6042		1,525		
22.2	Invoice	6057		2,634		
2.3	Invoice	6080		3,752		
13.3	Invoice	6107		1,632		
22.3	Invoice	6154		924		
4.4	Invoice	6210		4,735		
10.4	Receipt	Cheque			6,163	
12.4	Invoice	6285		2,156		
18.4	Payment	6328		3,824		
28.4	Invoice	6355		6,298		
30.4	Balance					23,447

Carlton's terms of trade with Tollerton allow a 2% cash discount on invoices where Carlton receives a cheque from the customer by the end of the month following the date of the invoice (ie a 2% discount will be given on March invoices paid by 30 April).

On Tollerton's payables ledger, under 'Status' the cash and discount marked 'Alloc 1' pay invoices marked 'Paid 1' (similarly for 'Alloc 2' and 'Paid 2').

Tollerton's goods received department check the goods when they arrive and issue a goods received note (GRN). A copy of the GRN and the supplier's advice note is sent to the purchases accounting department.

Required

(a) Prepare a statement reconciling the balance on Tollerton's purchase ledger to the balance on Carlton's suppliers statement. (6 marks)

(b) Describe the audit work you will carry out on each of the reconciling items you have determined in your answer to part (a) above, in order to determine the balance which should be included in the financial statements. (12 marks)

(c) In relation to verifying trade creditors:

   (i) Consider the basis you will use for selecting suppliers' statements to check to the balances on the creditors ledger

   (ii) Describe what action you will take if you find there is no supplier's statement for a material balance on the purchase ledger. (7 marks)

(25 marks)

15 GOING CONCERN
45 mins

Required

(a) List the factors which may cast doubt about a company's ability to trade as a going concern and describe reasons why these factors may indicate that a company may not be a going concern. (14 marks)

(b) Describe the further investigations you would carry out to decide whether a company is a going concern, and whether it has a reasonable chance of recovering from its going concern problems.

Your answer should include details of checks you would carry out in verifying the company's profit and cash flow forecasts. (11 marks)

(25 marks)

16 AUDIT REPORTING
45 mins

(a) State four types of situation where auditors are required by the Companies Act to report by exception. (4 marks)

(b) In November 20X3, the head office of Theta Limited was damaged by a fire. Many of the company's accounting records were destroyed before the audit for the year ended 31 January 20X4 took place. The company's financial accountant has prepared financial statements for the year ended 31 January 20X4 on the basis of estimates and the information he has been able to salvage. You have completed the audit of these financial statements.

Required

(i) Explain the impact of this information on the auditor's report which you would issue on the financial statements of Theta Limited for the year ended 31 January 20X4. (5 marks)

(ii) Explain the reasons for your audit opinion. (5 marks)

(iii) Explain and distinguish between the following forms of modified audit opinion:

    (1) Disagreement
    (2) Disclaimer
    (3) Adverse opinion. (6 marks)

(20 marks)

Answer Bank

1 INTERNAL AUDIT

> **Helping hand**
>
> (a) You needed to understand the **uncertainties** surrounding internal audit. In theory anyone can act as an internal auditor and internal auditors have no legislative security of tenure. Importantly also internal auditors' work may stretch significantly beyond the areas of accounting records and controls in which the external auditors are primarily interested.
>
> (b) Your answer should expand the point made in (a) that internal audit's work can be focused on the areas of most interest to management.
>
> (c) You should have discussed why there should be a distinction between the **subject of** internal audit's reports, and the **recipient** of those reports.
>
> (d) Note the need for appreciation of ethical considerations. There have been whole questions on ethics in past exams, and therefore the examiner evidently considers ethical matters to be a very important topic.
>
> **What the examiner said.** Generally answers to this question were good, and candidates seemed to have good knowledge of the external audit function, and the functions of an internal audit department. Candidates also demonstrated sufficient awareness of the important practical topics of working papers and fee charging.

(a) **Eligibility to act**

By law, a person is generally **ineligible** to act as **external** auditor if he is an **officer** or **employee** of the company, a **partner** or **employee** of such a person or a **partnership** in which such a person is a partner. An internal auditor is an employee of the company.

External auditors may also be required to belong to a **recognised supervisory body**, and this means they must hold an appropriate qualification, follow technical standards and maintain competence.

By contrast **anyone** can act as an **internal** auditor even if they do not have a formal accounting qualification. It is up to the company's **management** who they appoint.

Security of tenure

Under law, the **external** auditors are **appointed** to hold office until the conclusion of the **next general meeting**. They can be **dismissed** by a majority of **shareholders (or company owners)**, and have the right to make **representations**.

External auditors **cannot** be **dismissed** by **individual directors** or by a vote of the **board**. The only influence directors can have on the removal of external auditors is through their votes as shareholders. The rules on security of tenure are there because of the need for external auditors to protect the interests of shareholders by reporting on directors' stewardship of the business.

By contrast, as **internal** auditors are employees of the company, they can be **dismissed** by the directors or lower level of **management**, subject only to their normal employment rights. The company may have **corporate governance** measures in place to improve the security of internal auditors (for example hiring and firing decisions to be made by an audit committee of non-executive directors) but these are not essential.

Primary objective and limitation on the scope of the audit work

The primary objective of **external** auditors is laid down by legislation, to report on whether the company's accounts **show a true and fair view** of the **state of the company's affairs** at the period-end, and of its **profit or loss** for the period. External auditors are also required to report if certain other criteria have not been met, for example the company **fails** to **keep proper accounting records** or fails to make **proper disclosure** of **transactions** with **directors**.

Internal auditors' objectives are **whatever** the company's **management decide** they should be. Some of the objectives may be similar to those of external audit, for example to confirm the quality of accounting systems. Other objectives might be in areas which have little or no significance to the external auditor, for example recommending improvements in economy, efficiency and effectiveness.

In most countries, legislation says that management **cannot limit** the **scope of external auditors' work**. External auditors have the right of access to all a company's books and records, and can demand all the information and explanations they deem necessary. As the objectives of **internal** audit's work are decided by management, **management** can also decide to **place limitations** on the scope of that work.

(b) The appointment of internal auditors should improve the information flow to management for the following reasons:

    (i) Internal audit work can provide comprehensive information about the **operation** of, and **weaknesses** in a company's **accounting controls,** including the controls over the **reliability** of accounting information. Although external auditors might previously have commented on accounting controls, their review will not have been comprehensive. External auditors' procedures are designed primarily to express an audit opinion on the accounts, and thus may not cover all aspects of the company's systems.

    (ii) Internal audit work can provide information on whatever areas **management** deem **most important** because it is management's decision what internal audit's work should cover. They could for example review the **value for money** of specific departments or **compliance with laws and regulations.**

    (iii) One area internal audit can review is internal management information. Internal auditors can make recommendations about the **detail** and **presentation** of management accounts, budgets and other management information.

(c) The internal audit manager should not report to Mr Jones for the following reasons.

    (i) The recommendations and criticisms made may be about Mr Jones' performance as finance director. Mr Jones therefore may **suppress** or play down **adverse findings** of internal audit.

    (ii) The internal audit manager may feel inhibited about reporting on Mr Jones and the performance of the finance function; his reporting to Mr Jones would thus have undermined his **independence**.

    (iii) If Mr Jones has responsibility, internal audit work may concentrate on the areas of most interest to him, rather than fairly reviewing the organisation as a whole.

The internal audit manager should preferably report to the **managing director** or to an **audit committee** made up mainly or wholly of non-executive directors.

    (i) Non-executive directors are meant to bring an **independent judgement** to bear on the company's affairs. They are thus the right people to raise concerns about the finance director and the other executive directors.

    (ii) The audit committee also acts as a forum for **liaison** between the internal and external auditors.

    (iii) The fact that the audit committee is concerned with the **business as a whole** should mean that internal audit's remit covers equally all areas of the business.

(d) (i) The ACCA's ethical guidance does not forbid auditors accepting work on a fixed fee basis, but does indicate that they should consider the problems involved. These include the following.

Answer bank

(1) The fee may be set **too low** initially. Subsequent developments at the client may mean that the amount of work necessary to gain sufficient assurance increases, and hence the assignment becomes **unprofitable**.

(2) Alternatively, if the fee is set too low, the external auditors may try to stay within fee and budget limits by carrying out **insufficient work.**

(3) A fixed fee may give the impression that the client is dictating conditions to the auditors and hence the auditors **lack independence.**

(4) The fixed fee in this instance is being mooted because of the introduction of the internal audit department. However, even if internal audit is introduced, there is **no guarantee** that external auditors will necessarily **rely** on its work in any way. External auditors are required by ISA 610 to assess the competence and standards of internal audit before relying on its work. In addition the main work carried out by internal auditors may be in areas that are of little relevance to external auditors.

(ii) The internal audit manager should *not* be allowed **unrestricted** access to the external auditors' working papers for the following reasons:

(1) Auditors have a general duty to keep working papers. Working papers may include details of **controversial audit judgements** which it is not desirable that any member of the client's staff sees, such as an assessment of the directors or of senior management.

(2) The working papers will include details of the **assessment of internal audit** mentioned above.

(3) Working papers may contain **information** about the company which the **internal audit manager is not permitted to know** (for example an impending take-over).

However the internal audit manager may be allowed access to certain working papers under the **supervision** of the external auditors in order to assist the work of internal audit.

2 AUDITOR'S RESPONSIBILITIES

(a) **Auditor's responsibilities**

The key responsibility that auditors owe to shareholders directly is to report on the truth and fairness of the financial statements. This means carrying out an audit designed to discover material misstatements in the financial statements, whether caused by fraud or error.

The auditors have other responsibilities imposed on them by law and professional requirements, as follows:

- Ensure the directors' report is consistent with the accounts
- Ensure the company has kept adequate records
- Ensure the underlying records match the financial statements
- Ensure each branch of the business has given sufficient information to the auditor
- Ensure a statement of directors' responsibilities is included with the financial statements

In addition, auditors are required to maintain a professional standard of care towards the client (the shareholders of the client as a whole). This involves, for example, generally adhering to professional standards, such as international standards on auditing.

(b) ISA 240 *The auditors responsibility to consider fraud in an audit of financial statements* requires the auditor to have an awareness that the financial statements might be misstated as a result of fraud and to design procedures to assess the risk of such misstatements and then procedures designed to discover those misstatements if fraud is suspected.

The auditor is not required to prevent and detect fraud in the same way that management are, but must conduct their audit with an attitude of professional scepticism and be alert to factors that indicate that the financial statements might be misstated due to fraud.

(c) There are various reporting requirements in the ISA. Firstly, and importantly, if the auditor suspects or discovers fraud by employees, he should report that to management without delay. If the suspected or discovered fraud involves employees with a key role in internal control or the management of an entity, the auditors should also inform those charged with governance, such as the directors.

In some instances, the auditor may have a statutory duty to report fraud to regulators external to the company. The auditor must not breach their duty of confidentiality unless they have a clear legal duty to make such a report, and should seek legal advice before doing so.

3 INDEPENDENCE SITUATIONS

(a) No. The Code of Ethics state that 'a member's objectivity may be threatened or appear to be threatened as a consequence of a family or other close personal or business relationship'.

Problems arise if an officer or senior employee of an audit client is **closely connected** with the partner or senior staff responsible for the conduct of the audit. In this context, closely connected people include adult children and their spouses, siblings and their spouses and any relative to whom regular financial assistance is given or who is indebted to the staff member or partner. The situation here meets this definition; the audit should not be undertaken.

(b) There are a number of different issues to be considered here. Where the previous auditor has **fees** still owing by the client, the new auditor need not decline appointment solely for this reason. He should decide how far he may go in aiding the former auditor to obtain his fees but should avoid entanglement in any dispute, otherwise he may be asked to give an opinion on whether the fees are reasonable or the work was 'up to standard'.

However the fact that the previous auditors are in dispute over fees may indicate that there could be future problems over charges, and hence lead the prospective auditors to question whether on commercial grounds they should accept the assignment.

Secondly, it is not the place of A B & Co nor is it within their power, to give **professional clearance** to their successors. They are merely required, after obtaining the client's permission and on request from the new auditor, to discuss freely with him all matters relevant to the appointment of which he should be aware and disclose all information which appears to them to be relevant to the client. They cannot refuse to do this because they are owed fees.

(c) There is no objection in principle to a practice providing a client with services in addition to the audit. However, care must be taken not to perform **management functions** or to make **management decisions**. In the case of many audit clients it is common to provide a range of accountancy services, which may include participation in the preparation of accounting records. It is also important that the auditors obtain from the directors an **acknowledgement of their responsibilities** for presenting a set of accounts that give a true and fair view, and maintaining accounting records that comply with the law.

In the case of a **listed company**, however, the auditor should not participate in the preparation of the company's accounts and accounting records save in relation to assistance of a routine clerical nature or in emergency situations.

(d) The Code states that 'a firm's objectivity may be threatened or appear to be threatened when it is involved in, or even threatened with, litigation in relation to a client'.

Litigation of any sort will represent a 'breakdown of the relationship of trust' between auditor and client. This would impair the independence of the auditor or cause the directors of the client to become unwilling to disclose information to the auditor. The point at which the auditor should cease to act as auditor will vary from case to case. The auditor should 'have regard to circumstances where litigation might reasonably be perceived by the public as in contemplation'. The Code applies with particular emphasis here given the nature of the claim, and therefore the practice should cease to act.

(e) Yes. All students are bound by the guidelines of the Association. Incidentally, this includes the period between successful completion of the examinations and admission to membership.

4 AUDIT ENGAGEMENT

> **Helping hand**
>
> (a) Because the engagement letter defines **responsibilities** and **scope** it is a significant safeguard protecting the independence of the auditor.
>
> (b) You should be able to identify plenty of knowledge that auditors would need to carry out the audit. It is crucial to obtain good marks that you explain **why**.
>
> (c) You should be aware of these basic differences between internal and external audit.

(a) (i) The engagement letter should be addressed to the **board of directors** of the company, or the **audit committee**, if the company has one. The reasons for this are that dealing with the auditors is within the directors' general remit to manage the company's affairs.

Acceptance of the engagement letter is evidenced by the **signature** of the **managing director** or another senior official.

(ii) The purposes of the engagement letter are to provide **written confirmation** of the **auditors' acceptance of appointment**, the **scope** of the **audit**, the **form** of the **audit report**, and the basis of **fee charging**. The letter also makes clear the **respective responsibilities** of the **directors** and **auditors**.

The engagement letter should be sent to a new client soon after the appointment as auditors, and, in any event, before the **commencement** of the **first audit assignment**.

A new engagement letter should also be issued in the following circumstances.

Answer bank

(1) The **directors** appear to **misunderstand** the **objectives** and **scope** of the audit.

(2) There are significant changes in:
- **Terms** of the engagement
- The **company's ownership**
- **Senior management** or **those charged with governance**
- The **nature** or **size** of the **company's business**
- **Legal** or **professional requirements**

(b) **Understanding of the business**

There are many examples of information that an auditor will seek:

Timing of accounts preparation

It is important for the auditors to know when the accounts are going to be prepared and published, so that they know **when their audit can begin and when it must be completed by**. It is particularly important that they know this early if the time for the audit to be completed in is short.

Details of stock count

The auditors will want to attend the inventory count to gain **evidence of the existence of stock**. They will therefore need to know when any counts will take place and where, and obtain details of whom to liase with when they attend.

Internal controls

Auditors need to obtain an understanding of internal control operating in the business as part of their assessment of the **risk of misstatement**, and to influence their choice of **audit approach**. This will include an appreciation of any computer systems the company uses.

Company details

The auditors should be aware of the nature of the company, its operations and products and its assets. This will influence their assessment of the risk of misstatement, in particular **inherent risk** and again, their **approach to the audit**.

Complex accounting areas or unusual items

Auditors should be aware of any complex issues or unusual items in the client's financial statements so that they can be **adequately prepared** to audit them. Also, they may need to consider the **involvement of an expert**, for example, an actuary or a specialist valuer to assist them in gaining sufficient audit evidence.

Internal audit department

The auditors should establish whether the company has an internal audit department as this may have an **impact on the control environment**, and also, they may be able to make **use of the work of internal audit**, which may reduce the amount of testing they need to carry out themselves.

Other key personnel, particularly finance personnel

The auditors will work most closely with the finance department, and it will be impossible to carry out their work without getting to know them and being aware of who everyone is, and what they do.

(c) **Differences between internal/external audit**

(i) **Eligibility**

External auditors must meet substantial statutory requirements to act as auditors. There is no such requirement for **internal auditors**. The company may set qualification requirements for persons it wants to employ as internal auditors, but there is no legal requirement.

(ii) **Objectives and scope/limitations**

The primary objective of the **external auditors** is to report on the **truth and fairness** of **financial statements**. If the auditors are limited in their scope, they must give a modified opinion on financial statements.

The objectives of the **internal auditors** are set by management. In general terms they will involve assisting management in safeguarding the investment of shareholders by carrying out work in risk management and in relation to internal control. However, this general scope may be limited by time or finance or any other factors of the organisation. Specific objectives and limitations will vary according to the assignment set.

		Examiner's marking scheme	Marks
(a)	(i)	Identification of addressee of engagement letter	1
		Explanation of conveyance of acceptance of terms	1
	(ii)	Explanation of purpose of an audit engagement letter. Generally **1** mark per point up to a maximum of	3
		Statement as to when such a letter should be sent	1
		Identification of occasions when the issue of a new audit letter may be appropriate Generally **1** mark per point up to a maximum of	3
(b)		Examples of information Generally **1** mark per point up to a maximum of	5
		Reasons for obtaining information Generally **1** mark per point up to a maximum of	5
(c)		Identification of the principle differences between internal and external (registered) auditors: Generally **1** mark per point with a maximum of **3** marks for each single criteria (2 × 3)	6
			25

Answer bank

5 RISK BASED APPROACH

> **Helping hand.** A good example of the type of question that may well come up in future papers, one where you have to know definitions and be able to apply them.
>
> (a) You need to distinguish clearly between the three components, and state that **audit risk** is the **product** of the other risks.
>
> (b) The best approach is to go carefully through the question, **mark anything** that is relevant to the assessment of inherent risk, and then **consider** why these items are **relevant**. In (b) we have listed a number of factors as important under each of the headings, more in most cases than you need to gain the available marks.
>
> (c) Note how **legal and commercial pressures** have both influenced the increased use of risk analysis.
>
> **What the examiner said.** Most answers to (a) and (b) were very good, but answers to (c) were significantly poorer.

(a) **Audit risk** is the risk that auditors may give an inappropriate opinion on the financial statements. It is the risk of failing to modify the audit opinion when it should be modified, and modifying the audit opinion when it should not be modified.

Audit risk is the product of two components: the risk of material misstatement in the financial statements (inherent and control risks) and the risk that the auditor will fail to discover material misstatements (detection risk).

   (i) **Inherent risk**

   Inherent risk is the likelihood that a specific **item** in the accounts will be **misstated** due to **characteristics** of that item or of the organisation as a whole. **Organisational factors** include the nature of its business or whether the directors are under pressure to produce favourable results. Factors affecting **individual items** include the complexities of the accounting involved, such as whether a significant degree of estimation is involved.

   (ii) **Control risk**

   Control risk is the risk that an organisation's internal **controls fail** to **prevent,** or **detect and correct material misstatements**. Control risk depends on whether the controls that have been **designed** are appropriate for the business, and whether the controls in place are **operating** properly.

   (iii) **Detection risk**

   Detection risk is the risk that **audit procedures fail** to **identify material misstatements. Sampling risk**, the risk that the auditors' conclusion differs from what would be the conclusion if the whole population was tested, is a component of detection risk. Other elements of detection risk are the risk that auditors might use **inappropriate procedures** or **fail to recognise** an **error**.

(b) Factors affecting the assessment of inherent risk are as follows:

Ownership

The company's continuation in business may depend upon the **continued involvement** of all of the directors, as each director is a major shareholder. If the directors fall out amongst themselves, the company may not be able to continue.

Involvement of directors

The fact that the directors are major shareholders may mean that they **confuse** the **business's assets** with their own **personal assets**, and hence there may be a risk to security of assets.

The directors' lack of accountancy experience may mean that they do not understand the importance of keeping **proper accounting records** or maintaining proper accounting systems.

The directors may be unwilling as distinct from unable to introduce proper accounting systems. Their **entrepreneurial focus** may mean that they are unwilling to devote sufficient resources to the company's accounting function.

Change of accountant

Auditors should consider the **reasons** for the change. If the accountant left because he disagreed with the directors' approach to the accounts, this may indicate high inherent risk. The accountant might alternatively have left in suspicious circumstances, which may indicate a high risk of fraud.

The temporary accountant **lacks experience** of the company, and may lack experience of the industry. The fact that he is employed on a temporary basis means that he lacks incentive to learn.

The fact that the accountant is employed on a temporary basis will mean he **lacks the authority** to stand up to the directors if they should propose dubious accounting practices.

Stock

Because the stock is being held in bulk for long periods of time, it may be difficult to assess whether the stock is **slow-moving** and needs to be written down.

The long period of stock-holding also means that a significant amount of stock may suddenly become **obsolete** owing to developments in the fast-moving computer industry.

The fast-moving nature of the industry may also mean that **comparisons** with previous years' stock levels and other companies in the industry may be of **limited value.**

The fact that a lot of stock is held in the shops may mean that the company could lose significant amounts through **theft**, particularly as a lot of the equipment will be very portable.

Payments

The shops may hold **large amounts of cash**, which may be vulnerable to theft. However most expenditure in the shops is likely to be for large amounts by cheque or credit card, and therefore less vulnerable to theft.

The fact that the company does not operate a system of payment by instalments means that it **does not face** the **risk** of **bad debts**.

Going concern problems

The company faces a number of pressures that cast doubt on its going concern status. This has very serious implications for the assessment of inherent risk, since the accounts may be prepared on a misleading basis.

The pressures include the following.

(i) The company is in a high-technology, changing business, and the company may **not** be able to **adjust easily to changes** owing to its inventory-holding policies.

(ii) All three directors have entrepreneurial natures, and may invest heavily in **risky new developments**.

(iii) The company appears to be **significantly dependent** on **short-term finance** which the bank could in theory call in at any time.

Answer bank

The **competitive nature** of the industry may also mean that the company's accounts need to show a favourable position, and hence there may be pressure on the directors to **overstate profits.**

However there are other factors which may suggest the risk of going concern problems is lower. The fact that it operates three shops implies that it has been able to **maintain a certain level of business**. If the company owns its three shops, the **bank** may be **less concerned** about overdraft levels, as it may consider the business offers a high level of security.

(c) The reasons for the increase in risk-based auditing are as follows.

(i) The growing complexity of the business environment increases the **danger of fraud or misstatement**. Risk-based auditing provides a framework for assessing business risks such as computerisation developments or complexities of accounting.

(ii) **Pressures** are increasingly being exerted by **audit clients** on auditors to keep fee levels down while providing an improved level of service. Using risk-based auditing that auditors can spend most of the time available on the most important audit areas, whilst spending less time on the areas that are less risky, and hence keeping fees down.

(iii) The increased threats of **legal action** have increased the pressures on auditors to identify problems.

(iv) The introduction of the **supervisory regime** mean that it is more important for auditors to be able to demonstrate that they have followed a formal system that is in accordance with current best professional practice. Risk analysis has over recent years become recognised as **best professional practice**, and has now been formally incorporated into auditing standards.

(v) Risk analysis involves reducing audit risk to a level low enough to be tolerable. The assessment of audit risk will therefore readily determine the audit areas on which testing will be concentrated (those areas with high inherent/control risk), and also the amount of testing done (number of items in samples).

Examiner's marking scheme

		Marks
(a)	Explanation of audit risk	2
	Explanation of inherent risk, control risk, detection risk	
	Generally 1 mark for each point raised with maximum 2 marks for each component, up to a maximum of	6
(b)	Identification of six factors affecting the assessment of inherent risk associated with the audit of the accounts of Gocomp Ltd	
	Generally 1 mark per point up to a maximum of	6
	Reasoning underlying above factors	
	Generally 1 mark per point up to a maximum of	6
(c)	Explanation for increased reliance on a risk based auditing approach in recent years	
	Generally 1 mark per point up to a maximum of	5
		25

6 WORKING PAPERS

(a) Audit working papers are prepared:

(i) To provide **tangible evidence** of the **work done** in support of the audit opinion

(ii) To give evidence to the reporting partner that the **work** delegated by him has been **properly performed**

(iii) To provide for **future reference** details of **problems** encountered

(iv) To encourage the auditor to adopt a **methodical approach**.

(b) (i) Permanent audit files contain information of **continuing importance** to the audit such as the following.

(1) Engagement letters
(2) New client questionnaire
(3) The company's constitution
(4) Other legal documents such as prospectuses, leases, sales agreements
(5) Details of the history of the client's business
(6) Board minutes of continuing relevance
(7) Previous years' signed accounts, analytical review and management letters
(8) Accounting systems notes, previous years' control questionnaires

(ii) Current audit files **contain information of** relevance **to the** current year's audit, such as the following.

(1) Financial statements

(2) Accounts checklists

(3) Management accounts details, and reconciliations of management and financial accounts

(4) A summary of unadjusted errors

(5) Report to partner including details of significant events and errors

(6) Review notes

(7) Audit planning memorandum

(8) Time budgets and summaries

(9) Letter of representation

(10) Management letter

(11) Notes of board minutes

(12) Communications with third parties such as experts or other auditors

They also contain working papers covering each audit area. These should include the following.

(1) A lead schedule which should include details of the figures to be included in the accounts, problems encountered and conclusions drawn. It should be cross-referenced to schedules that give more details of the make-up of the individual figures.

(2) Audit plan

(3) Risk assessments

(4) Sampling plans

Answer bank

(5) Results of analytical procedures

(6) Details of substantive procedures and tests of controls

(c) (i) **Advantages**

(1) They may **improve efficiency** as individual audit plans do not then need to be prepared for each client, when many of the procedures required will be common to all audits.

(2) They **assist** in the **instruction and training** of audit staff.

(3) They **facilitate the delegation** of work.

(4) They **provide a means of controlling the quality** of the audit work.

(ii) **Disadvantages**

(1) They are **not specifically adapted to special client situations** and hence may lead to the omission of important audit procedures.

(2) Staff may be **tempted to follow pre-prepared programmes** automatically without considering whether the procedure is appropriate or necessary.

(3) They may encourage the **use of more junior staff** to perform the audit work who may **not have sufficient experience** to identify problem areas.

(4) They may result in **insufficient emphasis** being placed on areas of **high audit risk**.

7 INTERNAL CONTROL

> **Helping hand**
>
> (a) A number of marks on this paper are available for knowing the key terms highlighted in the text. Note here that the system is not only concerned with the accounting records, but also whether **assets** are **safeguarded** and **internal policies** are **implemented**.
>
> (b) Remember the control environment is not to do with specific controls, but is concerned with the **ethos** of the business, and how well the business is **organised**. For DS Stores, you needed to do more than repeat the definition you had just given. The key element in this answer is the fact that the business operates on a number of sites with some, but not full, central control.
>
> (c) Our answer ranges over the whole organisation; a good way to tackle this question is to think of the general procedures, and then how these might be used in the central departments, stores and warehouse. That should give you enough good controls. Note that a number of the procedures that we suggest (bank reconciliations, comparison of suppliers' statements) would also be carried out on the external audit. We have given more than the required number of procedures and there are many controls that you could have listed under the various general headings. Some controls could be listed under more than one heading, for example passwords are a computerised control, and also as a safeguard for the accounting records.

(a) The main elements of internal control are:

- The control environment
- The entity's risk assessment process
- The information system
- Control activities
- Monitoring of controls

Internal control includes everything that helps directors run the business efficiently and effectively, and which ensures:

(i) **Internal policies** are **followed**
(ii) **Assets** are **safeguarded**
(iii) **Fraud and error** are **prevented**, or, if they do occur, **detected**
(iv) **Accounting records** are **accurate** and **complete**
(v) The **published accounts** show a **true** and **fair view**.

The internal control system may be **computerised** and should incorporate **financial** and **non-financial** controls.

(b) The **control environment** provides the **foundation** for the **other internal controls** to operate. It represents how concerned directors and managers are about controls, how much they know about controls, and what they do to ensure controls operate effectively. Other elements include how the business is managed and operated, and the values and culture that all employees share.

Factors that will influence the control environment for DS include the following.

(i) The degree of **central control** over the **stores** and **warehouse**. The auditors will consider whether the degree of control exercised is appropriate; controls may work for example more effectively if some administration was devolved to the other stores.

(ii) The **attitudes** and **knowledge** of the **managers** of the **stores and warehouses**. The role of the directors will still be important, but the local managers will have a significant role in setting the 'tone' of individual sites.

(iii) The **criteria** against which the **performance** of stores is judged. This will influence how much attention is paid to controls; if for example turnover is the main criteria, controls that do not affect turnover may be neglected.

(c) **Control activities** include the following.

(i) **Approval and control of documents.** An example would be **approval** of **overtime sheets** of store staff by the store manager.

(ii) **Controls over computerised applications.** A control might be checking the reasonableness of stock codes entered by means of a **check digit.**

(iii) **Checking the arithmetical accuracy of records.** An example would be the buying department checking that **invoices received** from suppliers **added up.**

(iv) **Maintaining control accounts.** A **sales ledger control account** should be maintained in the general ledger.

(v) **Reconciliations.** An example would be **reconciling** the **amount shown** on the **bank statement** with the **cash book balance**.

(vi) **Comparing the results of cash, security and stock counts with the accounting records.** Regular counts should take place of **stock held** in the **warehouses**; the results should be compared with the computer stock records and the differences investigated.

(vii) **Comparing internal data with external sources of information.** An example would be **comparing purchase ledger balances** with **suppliers' statements,** and investigating differences.

(viii) Limiting **access** to **assets** and **accounting records.** Till operators might have to key in an entry code before being able to operate the tills.

Answer bank

	Examiner's marking scheme	Marks
(a)	Detailed explanation of the term 'internal control' Generally 1 mark per point up to a maximum of	5
(b)	Explanation of the term 'control environment' Generally 1 mark per point up to a maximum of	5
	Identification of three major factors that will be reflected in the control environment of DS Ltd Generally 1 mark per point up to a maximum of	3
(c)	Identification of categories of control activities and specific examples of each 1 mark for each category given up to a maximum of	6
	1 mark for one example per category of control activities up to a maximum of	6
		25

8 STOCK AND SALES

Helping hand

(a) The most important aspect of part a is the fact that it has three elements. You must ensure that you answer all the elements of the question. What the control weaknesses are should be no problem. Why they are a problem and how they should be solved are the harder parts, but you should try to answer them. Remember to always use your common sense.

(b) This question is also about control problems. The auditors cannot hope to get sufficient audit evidence, because they cannot trust the financial records (very few are maintained.

(c) It is the lack of records which presents the problem here also. The auditors cannot check everything, because they have no record of what everything is.

(a) **Weaknesses in the stock purchase system**

Segregation of duties

Weakness

There is currently no segregation of duties in the stock purchase system. All aspects of stock purchase are handled by the buyer.

Implication

The fact that no one else is involved in the purchase of stock means that no one acts as a check to the buyer. This means that he could make mistakes or purposely defraud the company, and no one would know, because no one else has any involvement with the records.

Recommendation

Some of the duties within the stock purchase system should be segregated. For example:

- A director should authorise purchases (particularly those above a certain cost limit) rather than the buyer
- The goods should be checked into stock by a stores person. This person could check that the goods received matched the original order made by the buyer.

Checking of goods into stock

Weakness

The buyer only checks the goods received to ensure that the quantities are the same as was ordered.

Implication

Smartbuy could accept poor quality goods into stock, or could accept goods which are not exactly the right spec.

Recommendation

The checking should be done by someone other than the buyer (as mentioned above). The check should be more comprehensive, certainly including a check for quality.

Authorisation

Weakness

The buyer appears to have complete control over what is purchased by Smartbuy. There does not appear to be any kind of purchase limit placed upon him, or any reference made to the sales department for what they want to sell.

Implication

The buyer does not appear to have liaison with anyone in deciding what is purchased, and so could purchase stock which is not saleable (out of fashion/season) or could fail to order sufficient stock to coincide with the plans and promotions of the marketing department.

Recommendation

Purchases should be authorised by a director, or requisitioned by someone in sales and marketing, or there should be a formal system of planning purchases with a committee made up of such people (sales director/marketing department/buyer.)

(b) **Completeness of sales**

The auditors will be concerned about obtaining sufficient assurance about the completeness of sales because the client does not maintain sufficient records for the auditors to find evidence of completeness of sales. There are three ways which the auditors could find evidence about sales:

- Sales records (that is, continuous till receipts)
- Cash receipts
- Stock purchases less stock on hand

These ways have some inherent problems, and also some problems specific to Smartbuy, which are outlined below.

Sales records

Smartbuy does not retain sales records. They do not keep till receipts, which are the only evidence of sales made.

Customers are given receipts (which are likely to be a duplicate of the till roll), but as the **business** is a **consumer based, cash** business, the auditors are going to be **unable to contact customers** to make enquiries about sales, as they might be able to in a business to business situation (although, even in that situation, obtaining information about sales rather than current debts might also be difficult).

If Smartbuy only made sales to customers using credit cards, the auditor might be able to obtain records from the credit card company, but sales are made in cash as well.

Smartbuy therefore maintain no record whatsoever of sales made.

Answer bank

Cash receipts

As the business is cash based, Smartbuy receive cash or cash equivalents (credit/debit card purchases) at the time of sale, so these equate to sales and could be used to obtain evidence about the completeness of sales.

However, **controls over cash recording are also poor** in the absence of till rolls. The till operators empty tills **independently** (and so have opportunity to misappropriate cash) and give the cash to the cashier who records and banks it (and who also therefore has opportunity to misappropriate cash and still make her books balance to the bank records).

As there is no direct, independent reconciliation of till records to the bank records, there is no assurance available about the completeness of cash receipts either, and so this method cannot be used to gain assurance about sales completeness.

Stock

If desperate, the auditors could try and perform a reconciliation between stock purchased and stock remaining in the shop at year end to identify what has been sold.

This would be a complicated reconciliation even if the records were perfect, because the auditors would have to account for stock written off or thrown away and it would only provide evidence for what had been sold, not at what price it had been sold.

However, given the poor controls over stock in the business (discussed above), in this case, it is unlikely even that the auditors could reconcile the physical stock sold, let alone have any idea about the value of sales.

Examiner's marking scheme	**Marks**
(a) Stock purchase system. Generally 1 mark for identifying a weakness in the system up to a maximum of	3
Generally 1½ marks for describing the implications of the weakness up to a maximum of	6
Generally 1½ marks for recommending an improvement to address the weakness up to a maximum of	6
(b) Explanation of why there would be concerns about obtaining adequate audit assurance as to the completeness of the sales income figure.	
Recognition that a high inherent risk factor should be attached to the sales income figure and reasoning for this. Generally 1 mark per point up to a maximum of	2
Recognition of inadequate controls. Generally 1 mark per point up to a maximum of	4
Other relevant points. Generally 1 mark per point up to a maximum of	3
	25

9 CONTROLS OVER RECEIPTS

(a) (i) This control is designed to ensure that all **receipts** are **banked** in the **company's account**. This presence of two employees when mail is opened makes it unlikely that there will be theft of receipts, as this would require collusion between them. Compilation of a list of receipts provides an **agreed record** which can be used as a check that receipts are not misappropriated before they are banked. Neither of

Answer bank

these people should be the cashier as this too would be a breakdown of internal control in terms of segregation of duties.

(ii) Audit procedures on the **opening of mail** and the subsequent **banking of cheques** might include the following.

(1) **Observation** (by surprise) of the routine for opening mail and discussion with management and with the staff involved of the way in which it is conducted. In particular, discuss routine in case of staff absences or holidays.

(2) **Select** a representative sample of **listing of receipts** and **agree** the amounts to the **cash book, paying-in slips** and **bank statements**. Ensure that each day's receipts are banked intact and promptly (ie that day to the next).

(3) Check that the **banking appears** on the bank statements **within two working days**. If there is any delay I should investigate as a teeming and lading fraud may be taking place.

(4) **Compare receipts per listings** with **other evidence** of the amount sent, for example customer remittance advice.

(5) **Circularise** a **representative sample** of customers. This will provide evidence, among other things, that customer receipts are banked intact.

(6) **Check** the **bank reconciliations** performed during the year and ensure there are no long-outstanding lodgements or unexplained differences.

(b) (i) Credit notes will be issued for a number of reasons.

(1) **Goods are returned** by customers for a variety of reasons and the credit note 'reimburses' them, cancelling all or part of the relevant invoice.

(2) An **error** of some kind on the **customer's account requires correction**. This could involve posting an invoice to the customer's account which does not apply to that customer, etc.

(3) **Errors** in the **calculations on an invoice require correction**, eg wrong prices charged, sales tax errors, errors in arithmetic etc.

(4) **Short delivery** has been made on an invoice, ie the customer has received fewer items than specified on the invoice.

(5) **Compensation** is given to the customer, perhaps because goods were faulty (but they were not returned) or goods were delivered late, etc.

(ii) I would carry out the following audit work to test whether credit notes were authorised and issued for a valid reason.

(1) **Select a sample** of **credit notes** issued during the year (from the complete sequence of numbers issued) and **check authorisation** and **supporting documentation** (returns note from customer and GRNs, copy of invoice marked up for errors, confirmation from the production department that the goods were faulty etc).

(2) **Select** a further sample of **credit notes** from customer accounts in the sales ledger and **check** that they are **valid, supported by documentation** and **authorised**.

(3) It may be worth **checking** a larger sample of **high value credit notes** from during the year as these present an opportunity for fraud. Once again, validity, documentation and authorisation should be checked.

Answer bank

(4) Any **provision** for credit notes **at the year end** should be **checked in detail**, particularly for high value items, as these present an opportunity for window dressing (ie reversing sales which are then put through again after the year end).

Any weaknesses discovered in the system should be reported to management.

(c) (i) The weaknesses in the cash system are as follows.

(1) The physical location of the despatch department and the cashier are not mentioned here, but there is a **risk of the customer taking the goods without paying**. The customer should pay the cashier on the advice note and return for the goods, which should only be released on sight of the paid invoice.

(2) There is a **failure in segregation of duties** in allowing the cashier to both complete the sales invoice and receive the cash as he could perpetrate a fraud by replacing the original invoice with one of lower value and keeping the difference.

(3) No-one **checks** the **invoices** to make sure that the cashier has **completed** them **correctly**, for example by using the correct prices and performing calculations correctly.

(4) The completeness of the **sequence** of sales invoices **cannot be checked** unless they are pre-numbered sequentially and the presence of all the invoices is checked by another person. The advice notes should also be pre-numbered sequentially.

(5) There is also **no check** that the **cashier banks all cash received**, ie this is a further failure of segregation of duties.

(6) If the sales department prepared and posted the invoices and also posted the cash for cash sales to a **sundry sales account**, this would solve some of the internal control problems mentioned above. In addition, the sales department could run a **weekly check** on the account to look for invoices for which no cash had been received. These could then be investigated. All of these weaknesses, and possible remedies, should be reported to management.

(ii) After confirming the cash sales system was operating as described (by walk-through test) I would carry out the following tests in order to ensure that there was no material fraud or error in the operation.

(1) **Select** a sample of **advice notes** issued to customers during the year. **Trace** the **related sales invoice** and **check** that the **details correlate** (date, unit amounts etc). The customer should have signed for the goods and this copy should be retained by the despatch department.

(2) For the sales invoices discovered in the above test, I would **check** that the **correct advice note** number is **recorded on the invoice**, that the **prices used** are **correct** (by reference to the prevailing price list) and that the **castings** and **cross-castings** (ie arithmetic) are **correct**.

(3) I will then **trace** the **value** of the **sales invoices** to the **cash book** and from the cash book **check** that the **total receipts** for the day have been **banked** and **appear promptly** on the bank statement.

(4) I would check that the **sales invoices** have been correctly **posted** to a cash or **sundry sales** account. For any sales invoices missing from this account

(assuming they are sequentially numbered), I will **trace** the **cancelled invoice** and check that the cancelled invoice was initialled by the customer and replaced by the next invoice in sequence.

(5) Because of the weaknesses in the system I would carry out the following sequence checks on large blocks of advice notes/invoices, eg four blocks of 100 advice notes/invoices.

- **Check all advice notes present**; investigate those missing.
- **Check sales invoices raised** for all advice notes.
- **Check all sales invoices** in a sequence have been **used**; investigate any missing.

Using the results of the above tests I would decide whether the system for cash sales has operated without material fraud or error. If I am not satisfied that it has then I will consider qualifying my audit report on the grounds of limitation of scope.

10 ANALYTICAL PROCEDURES

(a) Four financial statement headings which should be considered by the auditors, as part of their analytical procedures, are as follows.

(i) **Liquidity**

It would seem that the liquidity position of the company has declined over the last year. The **'acid test' ratio** has reduced from 1.24: 1 (5,200,000: 4,200,000) to just 0:98: 1 (4,800,000: 4,900,000). In the absence of more detailed information, it is impossible to say just how serious this decline in the company's liquidity position is likely to be. The **level of bank overdraft** has **gone up considerably** and it appears that a major part of the increase results from the **increase** in the **stock levels** held, although this would need to be confirmed by other audit work.

(ii) **Tangible fixed assets and activity**

It is obvious that the tangible fixed assets are a major item in the accounts and that the depreciation charged thereon is a material factor in the determination of profits and losses. The turnover has increased in the current year by some 10%, and there has also been an upturn in the level of stock held, with finished goods stock up by 12.5%. If it transpires that a major part of these increases is the result of inflation, then, especially given the decrease in the level of work in progress, there may well be signs that the plant is **not being worked** at a **full level** of **capacity**.

If this is so, the auditors would need to review carefully management's assessment of asset lives and whether the **level of depreciation** currently being charged is **adequate**.

(iii) **Sales and debtors**

Given that revenue has increased, the fact that receivables have declined seems to be worthy of further investigation. The average number of days sales in debtors at the end of the current year is 63 days as compared with 74 days twelve months earlier. The auditors should consider the possibility that debtors (and therefore possibly sales as well) have been understated because of **inadequate**

Answer bank

cut-off procedures (this could also have a bearing on the stock figure) or that they might have been reduced as a result of a **significant level** of **bad debts**.

It might also be noted that **distribution costs** (which are clearly related to sales) are **lower this year** as a percentage of sales (11.8% compared to 12.5%) and the significance of this can only be seen after further investigation has taken place.

(iv) **Stock and activity**

It is possible that the **increase in raw materials** stock and the **decrease in work in progress** are an indication of a **reduction** in the level of **activity** (see (ii) above), whilst the increase in the level of finished goods stock may be the result of **sales falling short** of budget.

The gross profit rate has actually increased from 26.7% to 28.6%, possibly suggesting that increased selling prices have resulted in a lower volume of sales. In this connection, the average number of times that finished stock is turned over in the year has decreased from 4.7 times to 3.6 times. The **lower stock turnover** should also cause the auditors to consider much more carefully the possibility of a provision for stock obsolescence or deterioration being required.

(b) (i) **Liquidity**

(1) **Check** the terms of the **bank overdraft** and ensure that they are being complied with, since if the bank were to call in the overdraft the company would be in a very difficult situation indeed.

(2) **Enquire** into the **forecast overdraft requirements** and the likelihood of the bank being prepared to continue providing the company with the borrowing facility it requires.

(ii) **Tangible fixed assets**

(1) **Test** the calculation of **depreciation charges** to ensure that they are appropriate to the company's circumstances.

(2) **Enquire** into the present and anticipated level of **production capacity** and consider the implications of a prolonged period of working at less than full capacity.

(iii) **Debtors**

(1) **Consider** the need to **circularise debtors** at the year end in order to provide some assurance as to the reliability of the debtors figure.

(2) **Review** the **recoverability** of the **outstanding debtors** by considering an aged analysis.

(iv) **Stock**

(1) **Carry out** tests on the **stock records** and **note** carefully any **slow moving items**, giving careful consideration to their valuation.

(2) **Carry out** a full series of **tests** into the adequacy of the company's **cut-off procedures** at the year end.

(c) **Analytical procedures**

Analytical review involves studying **significant ratios, trends** and other **statistics** and investigating any unusual or expected variations. The precise nature of these procedures and the manner in which they are documented will depend on the circumstances of each audit.

What determines comparisons made

The comparisons which can be made will depend on the **nature**, **accessibility** and **relevance** of the data available. Once the auditors have decided on the comparisons which they intend to make in performing analytical procedures, they should determine what **variations** they expect to be disclosed by them.

Investigation and evaluation of results

Unusual or **unexpected variations**, and expected variations which fail to occur, should be **investigated**. **Explanations** obtained should be **verified** and **evaluated** by the auditor to determine whether they are consistent with his understanding of the business and his general knowledge. Explanations may indicate a change in the business of which the auditors were previously unaware in which case they should reconsider the adequacy of their audit approach. Alternatively, they may indicate the possibility of misstatements in the financial statements; in these circumstances the auditors will need to **extend** their **testing** to determine whether the financial statements do contain **material misstatements**.

In the case of Darwin, for example, the auditors might ask, 'Knowing the company as we do, does a 10% increase in sales, accompanied by an increase in the gross profit percentage and in the level of stock held, make sense?'

11 JEANS

> **Helping hand**
>
> In (a), define inherent risk briefly and then work through the information given in the question, identifying areas that make the risk high and explaining to the examiner why they make inherent risk high.
>
> In (b), make sure you state that if NRV is lower than cost, NRV is used. One reason why this may be the case is given in the question. For the other two, consider common reasons why NRV is lower than cost and try to apply those reasons to a retail context.
>
> You might want to do (c) in two columns, so that you put the reason for the task next to the task and do not confuse your answers to (i) and (ii).

(a) **Inherent risk**

  (i) **Definition**

  Inherent risk is part of the risk of material misstatement. It is the risk that items will be misstated due to the **characteristics** of the item. In some cases this may be the fact that the item is an **estimate**, or very **important** in the accounts, or particularly **complex**.

  (ii) **Reasons for high inherent risk associated with Jeans Limited's stock**

  Finished goods warehouse

  The warehouse is located five miles away from the factory.

  This increases the risk of there being goods not included in the count because they are in transit or loaded onto a lorry and forgotten about.

  Work in Progress

  The company has work in progress.

  This can be difficult to value correctly, as the value often depends on judgmental issues, such as degree of completion or apportionment of overheads.

Stock held at retail stores

There is a significant amount of stock maintained at various third party premises, which may be spread around the country.

The stock at the retailers may come from various sources and they may not give an accurate return of the stock that belongs to Jeans.

This also increases the risk that stock will not be included in the count.

Three-month returns

There is a policy that unsold stock is returned to Jeans after three months when the price is then heavily discounted.

This has two risks attached to it. The first is that goods will be in transit on the date of the count and will therefore not be included. The second is that the valuation may become complex if the discounted price drops below cost, as stock must be valued at the lower of cost and NRV.

(b) **Net Realisable Value**

   (i) **Definition**

   Net realisable value is the value than can reasonably be expected to be realised on the sale of the goods. In other words, it is the selling price. This may sometimes be as low as zero, but is usually higher than cost.

   (ii) **Causes of goods being valued at net realisable value**

   Goods must be valued at net realisable value if that value is lower than original cost. The three reasons why this might be the case in Jeans are:

   (1) **Goods have not been sold in three months**

   The heavily discounted price of old stock may be lower than original cost.

   (2) **Goods have been damaged**

   There may be stock that has been slightly damaged in transit or at the warehouse or factory that cannot be sold for the retail price.

   However, there may still be a market for these goods at a reduced price. This reduced price may be lower than cost.

   (3) **Marketing strategy**

   It is possible that in a competitive industry such as the clothing industry, the marketing department may have taken a decision to sell clothes at a loss for a specified period for various reasons, for example, to establish their brand, or to undercut competitors.

   In this case, certain blocks of stock might have a lower retail price than cost, so the net realisable value will be lower.

(c)

(i) Tasks to undertake	(ii) Purpose
(1) Check the staff are following instructions	Failure to follow the instructions may jeopardise the reliability of the count.
(2) Make test counts, checking from the records to the physical inventory and vice versa	To confirm the accuracy of the count records.

Tasks to undertake	Purpose
(3) Observe whether procedures for identifying damaged or obsolete stock are working properly	This is to ensure that items that are in poor condition are separately identified, as they will need to be valued specially.
(4) Ask how stock held at third parties is accounted for and checking there are returns from all retail outlets	This is to ensure that all stock is included in the count.
(5) Observe whether there are appropriate controls in place over the movement of stock during the stock count, and make note of details of last goods in and out	To ensure that stock is not counted twice, or left out, and to facilitate cut off testing at the final audit.
(6) Conclude whether the stock count has been carried out properly and is reliable	Because the auditor will rely on the stock count as evidence for the existence and quantity of stock, and as the basis for valuation.

Examiner's marking scheme		Marks
(a)	Definition of inherent risk	2
	Explanation as to why inherent risk associated with auditing the area of inventories would be high	
	- Generally 1 mark per point up to a maximum of	8
(b)	Definition of net realisable value	2
	Identification of three causes for finished goods stock being stated at net realisable value	
	- Generally 1 mark per point up to a maximum of	3
(c)	Identification of important tasks to be carried out by audit team members and purpose of each task	
	- Generally 1 mark for each point up to a maximum of	10
		25

12 FIXED ASSETS

> **Helping hand**
>
> (a) Your answer should show that the main emphasis on fixed asset control should be on ensuring **custody of fixed assets**, and that any **dealings in fixed assets** are **authorised** and for a **fair price**.
>
> (b) Possible sources of evidence include **asset inspection** by the client and auditor and also **review of records**. **Reconciliation** of different sources of evidence is a key test for completeness.
>
> (c) Your answer should include tests to ensure that **no capital items** should be treated as **revenue**, and **no revenue items** should be treated as **capital**. You should also specifically mention checking for compliance with legal and statutory requirements.
>
> (d) For part (i) you need to consider **who** might **hold deeds**, and how the various **legal requirements** that affect deeds provide sources of audit evidence. For (ii) again your answer needs to discuss the legal documentation connected with motor ownership.
>
> N.B. You should note carefully the distinction which this question brings out between testing for **existence** and testing for **ownership**.
>
> (e) Five years does seem a long period for computer equipment, and if auditors are to be satisfied that the client's rate is reasonable, they will need to carry out successfully the tests mentioned.

Answer bank

(a) Controls which would assist in reducing the control risk associated with tangible fixed assets are as follows.

   (i) Procedures are in place to ensure the **physical safeguarding** of assets.

   (ii) A **fixed asset register** is used, combined with tagging of assets or identification codes on assets.

   (iii) The **purchase of fixed assets is controlled by authorised capital expenditure budgets.**

   (iv) Procedures to **control disposal/scrapping** of fixed assets are in existence.

(b) I would carry out the following tests on **existence** of fixed assets in the fixed asset register.

   (i) **Confirm** that the **company inspects** all items in the fixed asset register.

   (ii) **Inspect assets** concentrating on high value items and additions.

   (iii) **Review records of income yielding assets** for confirmation that income was yielded during the year.

   (iv) For some assets, for example motor vehicles, I would **reconcile the opening** and **closing balances** by number of assets as well as amounts.

   To check **completeness** of assets in the fixed asset register, I would carry out the following tests.

   (i) Compare the fixed asset register with the general ledger and obtain explanation for differences.

   (ii) Check whether fixed assets which physically exist have been recorded in the fixed asset register.

(c) I would confirm the correctness of capital/revenue items as follows.

   (i) **Consider** whether the company's **capitalisation policy complies** with the law and accounting standards, and is consistently applied.

   (ii) For **additions in** the year, **assess** whether the item should be treated as an **expense**.

   (iii) **Check** whether items with **small monetary values** have been **capitalised**. Most often there will be a *de minimis* limit (assets costing less < £500 are not capitalised).

   (iv) **Confirm** whether **any expenditure** on repairs, motor expense or sundry expenses **should have been capitalised**. I would do this by **checking documentation** for individual items (mostly high value items) and carrying out an overall **analytical review**, investigating any significant increases in any of the expense categories.

(d) (i) **Ownership of freehold land and buildings**

   I would test this by carrying out the following.

   (1) **Check the latest conveyance,** which should be in the client's name.

   (2) **Verify title to land and buildings by inspection of title deeds and land registry certificates. Check** that **all deeds link up** with the draft balance sheet. Confirmation can be received from the land registry and this would be even stronger evidence than inspection of the certificate. The plan of the land and buildings in the registry should agree to those owned by the company and this should by checked.

(3) **Obtain a certificate from solicitors** temporarily holding deeds, stating the **purpose** for which they are being held and that they hold them **free from any mortgage or lien**. Where deeds are held by bankers, obtain a similar certificate stating also that the deeds are held for safe custody only.

(ii) **Ownership of cars**

In the case of cars I would carry out the following.

(1) **Inspect registration documents** to ensure that they are in the client's name.

(2) **Check** that the **cars** are **insured** by the client (you should not be able to insure a car you do not own).

(3) **Inspect purchase invoices** (made out to the client) and **vouch** the **payment** to the cash book. This is usually done only for current year additions as documentation for previous years will be archived/dumped and it is assumed that the auditors will have checked material additions on previous audits.

(4) Checking all the cars on the non current asset register by **physical inspection** will not prove ownership (although it does prove *existence*) but at least it shows that the company is still in *possession* of them.

(5) **Check** the cash book for sundry **large receipts** which might indicate that cars have been sold.

Ownership of computers

Many of the same tests apply for the computer equipment, the main one being to **agree description**, serial number etc to **purchase invoices** (only for new additions this year if necessary). **Vouch payments** to the cash book and bank statements. Invoices should be made out to the company. Insurance is not compulsory for computers (whereas it is for cars), nor are registration documents required. However, **warranty certificates**, made out to the company, should be available for the computers.

(e) Five years is a long life for computers. Most companies write off computer equipment over three years, or even less. Others may depreciate over longer periods, but 'front load' depreciation by charging it on the reducing balance. This means that more of the cost is written off while the computer is being used a great deal. I would carry out the following to check for depreciation policy on computers.

(i) **Discuss** with **management** the buying cycle for computers. If there are plans to buy new computers in the near future (eg two or three years) then obviously the depreciation rate is too low. If the purchase of computers is some way off, this may have an adverse impact on the business, because of using out of date software, slow hardware, capacity too small etc.

(ii) I would **select the computers** on the fixed asset register which are **three years old or older** and I would look for them in the offices to see if they were being used, and to what extent. Computers in bits (because they have been cannibalised) or stuffed into store/rooms and cupboards have definitely outlived their useful lives. This would indicate that the depreciation rate was too low as a value is still being assigned to something that has no value to the business. These computers are obsolete and their cost should be written off.

(iii) I would **check sales and scrappings** of computers over the last year (or more). If it is usual for large losses to be made on disposal (when comparing sales price to carrying value) then depreciation must be too low.

Answer bank

(iv) I would consider **current technological developments** in order to determine whether the present hardware and software will soon be out of date.

I would use the evidence found from the above procedures to determine the true useful lives of the computers and related equipment.

13 WOODS

> **Helping hand**
>
> (a) Note the focus on *objectives* of controls. Controls over **transactions** and **other changes** (especially authorisation) are important, but **ongoing controls** such as maintenance of a fixed asset register and review and pursuit of bad debts are also very important. (Note in (a) that our answer gives more objectives than were required; you were only asked for two objectives relating to fixed assets, and three relating to debtors.)
>
> (b) This demonstrates the importance of being able to explain the **financial statement assertions** that relate to balance sheet items.
>
> (c) This illustrates the importance of understanding the specific requirements of the question. You were asked for certain information relating to the debtors' circularisation but were *not* asked for a detailed description of the procedures required.

(a) (i) **Maintenance and use**

One of the most important control objectives is that fixed assets are **maintained properly, and used on the company's business** rather than for private purposes.

The client should ensure proper maintenance by **regularly inspecting** fixed assets.

Authorisation of purchases

It is important that fixed asset purchases are **authorised properly**, since they represent a substantial commitment of resources.

The client should have formal procedures in place for **authorisation** by **senior management**, and authorisation for the most significant expenditure by the **board**.

Security

Non current assets should be **held securely**.

There should be appropriate arrangements for keeping fixed assets, particularly portable fixed assets, in **secure accommodation**, and identifying the company's property by means of an **identification code** printed on assets. Additional arrangements, such as **passwords**, should be in place over computers.

Recording

Fixed assets should be **completely recorded** in the company's accounting records.

The company should maintain a **fixed asset register,** which is regularly **reconciled** to the **general ledger**. The fixed asset register is also an important **security control**. Moreover there should be regular **physical inspection** of a sample of items in the fixed asset register, and the company should regularly also check that **fixed assets** that are **in use** are **recorded** in the fixed asset register.

Depreciation

Fixed assets should be **depreciated** at a **reasonable rate**.

Management should **review annually** the **depreciation rates** used.

Disposals

The **best possible price** should be obtained for **fixed assets** that are **sold**.

Disposals should be **authorised** by **senior management**, and the authoriser should be given **evidence** about the price, for example a published business guide on motor cars or rival offers on property.

Income producing assets

All **income** that is **due** to the company should be **collected** from income-producing assets.

There should be **regular review** of all assets that produce income to ensure all **income owed** is **identified**, and all **cash due received**.

(ii) **References for new customers**

Credit sales should only be made to customers who are **good credit risks**.

Information should be sought from **credit agencies**, and **references obtained**, before customers are given credit for the first time.

Credit limits

The level of **bad debts** should be **minimised**.

Credit limits should be given to each customer which limit the maximum amount they can owe, and the maximum debt they can have outstanding. Slow paying customers should be **pursued** for payment, and credit terms **suspended** if they continue to fail to pay. **Write-off of bad debts** should only be authorised when there is conclusive evidence that the receivable will not be paid.

Authorisation of despatch of goods

An important objective is that goods are only **despatched** to **bona-fide customers** for proper orders.

Despatch of goods should be **authorised**, and authority only given for despatches to authorised customers when a **sales order** has been made.

Invoicing

All **despatches** to customers should be **followed** by a subsequent **invoice**.

Despatch notes should be **prenumbered** and **matched to invoices**. There should be a regular review to identify any old despatch notes that have not yet been matched by invoices.

Pricing

Customers should be **charged correctly**.

Prices charged on sales invoices should follow a **price list,** and authorisation be required for anything other than standard prices.

Accounting

Procedures must be in place for ensuring that trade debtors and sales are **accounted** for **accurately and correctly.**

An important control is maintenance of a **sales ledger control account** in the general ledger showing total sales and total amounts received. The **balance** on this account should be **reconciled** to the **total of balances** in the sales ledger on a regular basis.

Completeness

All sales should be **recorded** in the accounting records of the company.

All documentation should be **numbered sequentially**, and missing items investigated.

(b) The representations (known as the **financial statement assertions**) are as follows:

(i) The debtors **exist**. All customers who have balances included in total debtors are real entities.

(ii) The debtors balance represent legitimate **rights** that the company has. All debts included in the balance are amounts on which the company has a legitimate claim.

(iii) Debtors are **valued** at an appropriate valuation. The amounts in debtors are monies that the client will be able to collect, and no extra provision is needed against debts which may be bad.

(iv) Debtors are stated **completely** in the accounts. No debts to which the client has title have been omitted from the accounts.

(v) Debtors are **presented** and **disclosed** correctly. The presentation and disclosure of debtors are in accordance with the law and accounting standards.

(c) **Primary objective of the debtors' circularisation**

The primary objective of the debtors' circularisation is to obtain evidence that debtor balances represent monies that are owed to the client (checking the assertions of **existence** and **rights**.)

Positive versus negative circularisation

Under a **positive** circularisation, the customer is requested to confirm the accuracy of the balance shown or state the amount by which he disagrees with the client, giving reasons if possible. Under a **negative** circularisation, the customer is required to reply only if the amount stated is disputed.

Auditors generally use a **positive circularisation** because it is designed to encourage responses. They should use a positive circularisation if there are **weak internal controls, poor accounting records**, or **evidence of irregularities.**

Auditors are likely to use a **negative circularisation** when the client has **good internal controls** and the debtors figure in the accounts is made up of a large number of small amounts owed.

The debtors circularisation and testing of after-date cash

The debtors' circularisation should generally be used to test debtors as well as the **testing of after-date cash**. The prime objective of testing after-date cash is to provide evidence that debtors are **valued correctly,** and represent amounts that the **company** will be **able to collect**. It is not to confirm that amounts owed are valid, although it provides some evidence of this.

Answer bank

Examiner's marking scheme	Marks
(a) Identification of control objectives	
Generally 1 mark for each objective up to a maximum of	5
Example of a control that would help to achieve the objective	
Generally 1 mark up to a maximum of	5
(b) Identification of the following assertions or representations:	
Existence	
Rights/Ownership	
Completeness	
Valuation	
Presentation and Disclosure	
Generally 1 mark per point up to a maximum of	4
Explanation of the above as applied to Woods	
Generally 1 mark per point up to a maximum of	3
(c) Identification of primary objective of receivables circularisation	1
Explanation of positive and negative methods of circularisation	2
Explanation of when to use either method	3
Explanation of test of post balance sheet events	1
Recognition that both tests should be carried out	1
	25

14 TOLLERTON

(a) Reconciliation of Tollerton's purchase ledger account to supplier statement from Carlton.

	£	£
Balance per purchase ledger		5,980
Reconciling items		
4/3 Transposition invoice DZ169	180	
31/3 Discount disallowed by supplier	126	
4/4 Invoice 6210 not on purchase ledger	4,735	
28/4 Invoice 6355 not on purchase ledger	6,298	
30/4 Cash in transit	6,005	
30/4 Discount not allowed	123	
		17,467
Balance on supplier's statement		23,447

(b) The audit work carried out on the reconciling items should be as follows.

Transposition error

The correct position should be checked to the invoices. Creditors would be increased if Tollerton had made the error(s); no adjustment would be required if Carlton had been wrong.

Invoices omitted

Invoice 6210 was sent sometime before the year-end. I would therefore **check** whether the **goods** had been **received**, by checking whether there were any unmatched goods in notes/delivery notes to which the invoice might relate. If I could find no evidence of the goods been received I would ask Carlton to confirm that Tollerton had received the goods. If Carlton could not confirm this, no purchase accrual would be made.

If the goods had been received, I would check whether Tollerton had had a copy of the purchase invoice. If the company had received a copy, I would check why it had not been posted. If it was due to a dispute between the two companies, I would examine correspondence etc to assess whether an accrual should be made.

Answer bank

Invoice 6355 was not sent out until just before the year end. The key check would therefore be to see whether the **goods** had been **received** by the **year-end**. The date on the goods in note should provide strong evidence. If the goods were received before the year end, a purchase accrual would be required.

Discounts

I would **inspect correspondence** with Carlton, and **discuss** the **discounts** with the purchase ledger manager. It is quite likely that a similar problem has arisen in the past; the discounts are likely to be written back or allowed to stand depending on whether in the past Tollerton has ultimately had to pay the amounts of the discount or has had the discounts allowed.

If it is likely that the discounts will be disputed, we should **investigate** when the monies were received by Carlton.

The fact that the payments were dated with the month-end date on Tollerton's purchase ledger suggests that Carlton may well not have received the cheques until after the month-end. If the date the cheques are cleared by the bank is **early** in the next month and this is consistent with the clearance of other cheques written at the same time, then the discount may be valid. Bank clearance of the cheque after the end of the first week of the next month will suggest Carlton received the cheque after the month-end and hence Tollerton will not be entitled to the discount.

Cash in transit

I would **check when the cheque** to Carlton was **cleared**. If the cheque was cleared within a week or so of the year-end, it will be cash in transit and should be recorded as an unpresented cheque on the bank reconciliation. If the cheque took more than a week to clear, further investigations would be required, particularly as the earlier cheque to Carlton took ten days to clear. I would examine the length of time other cheques written around the year-end took to clear. If most of them took more than ten days, then Tollerton will most likely have sent them out after the year-end. Therefore adjustments would be required to reduce payments (as the payments were not made till after the year-end) and increase creditors.

(c) (i) The primary purpose of testing balances on the purchase ledger is to look for **understatement of liabilities**. Hence directional testing should be used, with suppliers' statements being the starting point for the test, with those selected being reconciled to the purchase ledger balances. Audit tests should cover **suppliers** with **large year-end balances** and suppliers from whom **significant purchases** have been made in the year as these are key items. Other suppliers' statements should be selected on a random basis.

(ii) The action to be taken would be dependent on whether:

(1) **Internal controls are poor**

(2) **Tests of suppliers' statements** on other balances have revealed **material errors**

(3) **Suppliers' statements are available** after the year-end (it may be possible to work back to the year end balance).

It may be necessary to **circularise** the **suppliers** for a positive confirmation of the outstanding balance at the year end.

Otherwise the following alternative tests could be carried out.

(1) **Review invoices processed after the year-end** to ensure none relate to the previous year.

(2) **Review cut-off** to ensure all goods received before the year-end from this supplier have been accrued for.

(3) **Carry out analytical review** of the monthly outstanding balance for the year under review and previous year to highlight whether the year-end balance is abnormally low.

(4) **Investigate** any **discounts taken**/adjustments made on the account to ensure these are valid.

15 GOING CONCERN

> **Helping hand**
>
> (a) Your answer should have included **signs** that the company is trying to cut **costs**, is overtrading or appears to be in a **weak bargaining position** (shown by suppliers taking extended credit).
>
> (b) Work will be needed on **every element** of the forecast. For sources of finance, you should have considered the consequences of the company not being able to obtain the necessary finance, the likelihood of alternative sources being obtained and whether any curtailment would undermine the business's ability to continue as a going concern.

(a) There are many factors which could indicate that a particular company was not a going concern, of which some of the most important are as follows.

(i) **Failure to generate sufficient profits**. Obviously any company which proves unable to operate at a profit will not be a going concern since the losses which it makes serve to drain existing capital from the business. However, where a previously successful company begins to trade at a loss this may be a symptom of other problems.

(ii) **Reductions in liquidity**, as shown by increasing overdraft levels, worsening gearing and current asset ratios and a growing level of payables. If payables exceed inventories, this could suggest that a company must sell its goods before it can pay for them. As with trading losses, liquidity problems are likely to be a symptom of going concern difficulties as much as they are their cause.

(iii) **Loss of important customers**. If these had previously accounted for a major part of turnover, there could be serious implications unless alternative outlets are found. The company will have insufficient revenue while fixed costs will remain the same. A manufacturing company may continue to produce goods which cannot be sold.

(iv) **Shortage of materials** essential to a company's manufacturing process. This could happen through the failure of a major supplier or simply because of a general shortage of raw materials in the industry. Clearly if a company cannot produce the goods it needs to sell its future must be in doubt.

(v) **Taking of extended credit by customers**. The most likely cause of this would be poor credit control on the part of the company. Excess credit would reduce working capital and might have a 'knock on' effect if the company found itself unable to meet its own bills as they fell due. In these circumstances, the company could be at risk of being put into receivership or going into liquidation.

(vi) **Overtrading by the company**. If sales are increasing too rapidly, the company may encounter an equally rapid increase in the amount invested in stock and debtors. A manufacturing company may also find itself buying more plant and equipment in an effort to meet demand. All these factors will have the effect of draining liquid funds from the company, with the result that it may be unable to pay for the goods and services it requires to carry on.

(vii) **Redemption of loan capital**. This may originally have been part of long term borrowings and redemption is at a time when a company is unable to finance this from its own resources. If alternative sources of finance are not readily available, the company may come under quite severe financial pressure.

(viii) **Replacement of fixed assets** which are nearing the end of their useful lives might be necessary at a time when finance is tight. This may have a serious impact upon the company's ability to maintain capacity levels or even to continue in business at all.

(ix) **Adverse movements in exchange rates.** These would affect companies with substantial imports where the national currency was weak against other currencies and would affect exporting companies where the national currency was strong against other currencies.

(x) **Reductions in research and development expenditure**. Liquidity problems may encourage a company to cut back on its research and development expenditure. However, the savings are likely to be very short term. In the longer term, the company may become less and less competitive as it fails to produce new products to meet changes in demand.

(xi) **Changes in policy**, such as a decision to lease rather than buy new fixed assets. These may indicate going concern difficulties, particularly where, as is frequently the case, the finance charges for such lease arrangements are higher than they would have been using a conventional bank loan.

(b) If after a preliminary review, the auditors feel that a more thorough investigation is called for in order to decide whether the company is a going concern and whether it has a reasonable chance of recovering from going concern problems, they should consider the following points.

(i) **Work on forecasts**

A detailed examination of cash flow and other forecasts for the next twelve months (at the very least) will be necessary. Particular attention should be paid to the following matters.

(1) **Forecast sales**. The auditors can determine whether past predictions have been accurate by comparing previous forecasts with the actual sales achieved. The level of current orders may also assist in deciding on whether future targets are likely to be met.

(2) **Forecast profitability rates and trends**, particularly if these are declining. Gross profit margins are obviously important, but so too are the various categories of expense, which should be adequately controlled.

(3) **Levels of stock, debtors and creditors**. These should also be consistent with the anticipated future activity of the business. Points to watch for include the average age of debtors and creditors balances, which should be in line with past experience. It is unlikely that creditors will agree to any postponement without prior consultation. On the other hand, a decision to increase sales by allowing more credit to customers or to obtain faster settlement by granting larger discounts may be acceptable in some circumstances.

(4) **Projected capital expenditure** must be adequate to support the future activity of the business.

(5) **Receipts from any sales of fixed assets.** Care must be taken to ensure that anticipated receipts are not overly optimistic and that the selling of fixed assets will not jeopardise the future operation of the business.

(6) **Plans for the repayment of any borrowings.** Cash receipts must be adequate to support the repayment of any overdrafts or loan capital, unless there are clear indications that other finance will be available. Where it is not intended to repay overdrafts or other borrowings, the auditors must ensure that the bank or other lending institution is prepared to accept such an arrangement.

(7) **Interest payable on borrowings** may be affected by the company's other plans.

(8) **Projections for taxation** may be affected by recent or proposed legislative changes.

(9) **Proposed dividends.** Consideration should be made of whether the company will have the profits available to pay dividends and what the shareholders' reaction will be if dividends are not paid.

(10) **The margin available for error** should be estimated, having regard to the client's overall financial position.

(11) **The estimated effect of inflation** on each of the above should be considered.

Where no forecasts are available, the auditors should ask the directors to have them prepared. In extreme cases they may attempt to assess the business's future cash flows himself.

(ii) **Future finances**

The auditors may discover that the company has already made firm arrangements to continue or expand existing overdraft facilities. In these circumstances, they would expect to see written confirmation of the fact. Alternatively, they may find that the directors are in the process of negotiating further finance. In this case, they will have to use their judgement in assessing the likelihood of success in obtaining it. Whether they are in any doubt regarding the availability of finance, they should consider the following questions.

(1) Can the company keep within its **available resources** by curtailing its activities?

(2) Will this lead to the **sale of assets** no longer required as a result of the curtailment?

(3) Is it reasonable to assume that the **curtailment of the business** and/or the sale of assets no longer required may be made in good time?

(4) Is any part of the business which could be closed or curtailed under such an arrangement likely to be of such a size as to **jeopardise the application of the going concern concept**?

Answer bank

16 AUDIT REPORTING

> **Helping hand**
>
> (a) This should be a straightforward test of memory
>
> (b) Note in (i) the different paragraphs that are modified. You also need to state that the report will need to mention explicitly the failure to **obtain** all the **necessary information** and **explanations**, but that the **section** of the opinion dealing with **proper preparation** would be unqualified. The key point in (ii) is that the loss of records affects **most** areas.
>
> In (iii) you must be able to distinguish clearly the different types of report qualification.

(a) The auditor would report by exception if any of the following conditions were not fulfilled.

    (i) **Proper accounting records** have been kept and proper returns adequate for the audit received from branches not visited

    (ii) The **accounts** agree with the **accounting records** and **returns**

    (iii) **All information and explanations** have been **received** as the auditors think necessary and they have had access at all times to the company's books, accounts and vouchers

    (iv) **Details** of **directors' emoluments** and **other benefits** have been correctly **disclosed** in the financial statements

    (v) Particulars of **loans** and **other transactions** in favour of **directors** and others have been correctly disclosed in the financial statements

    (vi) The **information** given in the **directors' report** is **consistent** with the **accounts**

(b) (i) The situation described would give rise to a limitation on the scope of the auditor's work. Therefore the audit report would be amended as follows.

    We would include an explanatory paragraph stating that, as a majority of the company's books and records were destroyed by fire, the **evidence** available to us was **limited**. In this case it would be **difficult to quantify** the financial impact.

    Our audit **opinion** would be a **disclaimer** on the grounds that the limitation was so material and pervasive. We would have to state that due to the **limitation** in **scope** of our work we were **unable to form an opinion** regarding the truth and fairness of the information. **Proper preparation** in accordance with the law would be **unqualified**.

    We would also have to report by exception that we had **not obtained all the information and explanations** which we considered necessary, and that we were **unable to determine** whether **proper accounting records** had been **maintained**.

    These points would be included in an additional paragraph after the opinion paragraph.

    (ii) A lack of accounting records results in a **limitation in scope**; the auditors cannot obtain all the evidence which they would normally expect to collect, and will therefore have difficulty in forming an opinion.

    This **limitation** may be **material or pervasive**. In this situation it would seem more likely that a pervasive qualification would be appropriate as the destruction of the records will have had a significant impact on most of the balances rather than one particular item.

I am also assuming that destruction of the information is such that it is not possible to obtain any other satisfactory information to support the estimates made by the accountant.

The work that we have been able to do has been inconclusive.

(iii) (1) The auditor may modify the audit report due to **disagreement** with any of the following:

- **Non-compliance** with **law**
- **Non-compliance** with **accounting standards**
- **Disagreement** due to known facts
- **Inadequate disclosure** by the directors of inherent uncertainties and/or the assumptions made.

If the disagreement is material but does not render the accounts as a whole meaningless an **'except for'** qualification would be used. The opinion would state that the accounts give a true and fair view overall apart from this one specific item.

The opinion paragraph would be headed up as qualified on these grounds and would include an explanation of the disagreement.

(2) A **disclaimer** by contrast is a qualification due to a **pervasive limitation of scope**. This would arise due to a limitation in scope of the auditors' work which has such a severe impact that the auditors are not able to form an opinion on the truth and fairness of the accounts at all.

The audit opinion would be headed up as a disclaimer.

Normally the audit report would not be qualified in respect of proper preparation of the accounts.

(3) An **adverse opinion** would be given where a **disagreement** is not just material as in (1) but has such an impact on the **accounts** that they are rendered **meaningless** as a whole. The basis for such disagreements are listed in part (1).

Here the audit opinion would be headed up as an adverse opinion and would state that the accounts do **not give a true and fair view**. Depending on the nature of the disagreement the proper preparation opinion may also require qualification.

List of key terms and Index

List of key terms

These are the terms which we have identified throughout the text as being KEY TERMS. You should make sure that you can define what these terms mean; go back to the pages highlighted here if you need to check.

Accounting estimate, 200
Analytical procedures, 79, 192
Anomalous error, 104
Application controls, 129
Audit, 10
Audit evidence, 70
Audit plan, 92
Audit risk, 81
Audit sampling, 104
Audit strategy, 92

Closely connected, 43
Comparative financial statements, 283
Contingent asset, 269
Contingent liability, 269
Control activities, 127
Control environment, 125
Control procedures, 127
Control risk, 82
Corresponding figures, 283
Cost, 209

Detection risk, 82
Direct verification approach, 72

Emphasis of matter, 316
Error, 104
Expected error, 104
Expert, 95

Fair, 11
Final audit, 86

General IT controls, 129
Going concern assumption, 292

Inherent risk, 81
Interim audit, 86
Internal control, 124

Management, 300
Materiality, 76

Net realisable value, 209
Non-sampling risk, 104

Opening balances, 280

Population, 104
Provision, 269

Sampling risk, 104
Sampling units, 104
Statistical sampling, 104
Stratification, 104
Substantive procedures, 72
Systems-based approach, 72

Tests of control, 72, 136
Tolerable error, 104
True, 11

Uncertainty, 317

Working papers, 110

Index

Ability to perform the work, 55
Acceptance procedures, 52
Accounting estimate, 200
Accounting records, 5
Accounting standards, 12
Accruals listing, 262
Analysis of errors, 109
Analytical procedures, 192
Analytical review, 334
Application controls, 130
Approval, 56
Audit, 6, 10
Audit appointment, 7
Audit evidence, 70
Audit exemptions, 6
Audit interrogation software, 100
Audit opinion, 338
Audit programmes, 331
Audit requirement, 6
Audit risk, 331
Audit sampling, 103, 104
Auditing profession, 30
Auditing standards, 12, 32
Auditor rights, 8
Auditors' report, 7
Automated working papers, 114

Bad debts, 248
Bank, 251
Bank balances, 251
Bank letter, 251
Before accepting nomination, 52
Beneficial interests, 44
Business risk, 24

Cash balances, 255
Cash system, 175
Changes in nature of engagement, 58
Charges and commitments, 232
Chartered Association of Certified Accountants (ACCA), 30
Chronology of audit, 12
Client screening, 55
Client staff, 95
Combined approach, 72
Communications between auditors and management, 143
Communications on internal control, 144
Companies Act 1985, 4, 30, 54, 209, 311
Companies Act 1989, 4
Comparative financial statements, 283
Comparatives, 283
Compliance with accounting regulations, 278
Confidence, 47
Confidentiality, 47, 113
Contingent asset, 269

Contingent liability, 269
Contract law, 24
Control assessment, 135
Control environment, 125
Control procedures, 127, 353
Control risk, 331
Corresponding figures, 283
Cost, 209, 217
Cost of conversion, 209
Creditors audit, 336
Current liabilities, 262

Debtors' circularisation, 243
Debtors' listing, 242
Decision support systems, 102
Dependence on an audit client, 42
Detection risk, 331
Direct verification approach, 72
Disagreement with management, 320
Disclaimer of opinion, 318
Dormant companies, 6
Duty of reasonable care, 25

Embedded audit facilities, 101
Emphasis of matter, 316
Engagement economics, 55
Engagement letter, 56, 345
Error, 104
Evaluating the effect of misstatements, 304
Evaluation of sample results, 109
Expected error, 104, 108
Expert, 95

Fair, 11
Financial records, 5
Financial statements, 6
Finished goods, 209, 217
First in first out (FIFO), 209
Fixed asset register, 229
Fixed assets, 182, 335
Flowcharts, 137
Fraud and error, 22
FRS 12 Provisions, contingent liabilities and contingent assets, 269
Fundamental principles, 41

General computer controls, 131
Going concern, 316, 338
Goods on sale or return, 250
Goods subject to reservation of title clauses, 265

Haphazard selection, 105
Hospitality, 45

Index

IAS 10 Contingencies and events occurring after the balance sheet date, 289
Incoming auditors, 287
Independence, 41, 329
Independent estimate, 202
Ineligible for appointment, 30, 49
Inherent risk, 331, 361
Initial audit engagements, 280
Integrity, 41
Inter-company indebtedness, 250, 266
Interim audit, 137
Internal audit, 14, 97, 329
Internal auditors, 24
Internal Control Evaluation Questionnaires (ICEQs), 139
Internal Control Questionnaires (ICQs), 138
Internal control systems, 22
    practical issues, 137
Investment income, 236
Investments, 234
ISA 210 *Terms of audit engagements*, 56
ISA 230 *Documentation*, 110
ISA 240 *Fraud and error*, 22
ISA 300 *Planning*, 92
ISA 320 *Audit Materiality*, 76
ISA 500 *Audit evidence*, 70
ISA 510 *Initial engagement - opening balances*, 280
ISA 520 *Analytical procedures*, 192
ISA 530 *Audit sampling*, 103
ISA 540 *Audit of accounting estimates*, 200
ISA 560 *Subsequent events*, 285, 288
ISA 580 *Management representations*, 299
ISA 610 *Considering the work of internal auditing*, 97
ISA 620 *Using the work of an expert*, 95
ISA 700 *The auditor's report on financial statements*, 312
ISA 710 *Comparatives*, 282

Judgmental sampling, 108

Knowledge-based systems, 102

Last in last out (LILO), 209
Letter on internal control, 145
Limitation on scope, 318, 319
Limitations, 132
Litigation, 43
Loans, 45
Long term liabilities, 268

Management, 300
Management integrity, 55
Management representation letter, 302
Modified reports, 316

Narrative notes, 137
Negligence, 25
Net Realisable Value (NRV), 209, 362

Objectivity, 41
Opening balances, 280
Other services, 45
Overall review of financial statements, 278
Overdue fees, 43
Overhead absorption, 219

Parallel simulation, 102
Payments on account, 209
Personal computers (PCs), 133
Personal relationships, 43
Planning meeting, 94
Population, 104
Prepayments, 251
Procedures, 72
Procedures after accepting nomination, 54
Provision, 269
Purchases, 264
Purchases cut-off, 265
Purchases system, 160

Qualified opinion, 316, 318
Qualitative aspects of errors, 109

Random selection, 105
Raw materials, 209
Re Bond Worth, 265
Reasonable care, 24
Receipts controls, 333
Recognised Supervisory Bodies (RSBs), 31
Recording control systems, 137
Registrar of Companies, 5
Reliability of evidence, 74
Removal, 9
Reservation of title, 265
Resignation, 9
Review procedures, 46
Romalpa, 265
Rules of professional conduct, 41

Sales, 249
Sales system, 156
Sample selection, 244
Sample size, 106
Sampling risk, 104, 107
Sampling units, 104

Index

SAS 010 *The scope and authority of APB pronouncements*, 32
Schedule of unadjusted errors, 304
Selection of the sample, 105
Significant fluctuations or unexpected relationships, 195
Simulation, 102
Small charities, 6
Small companies, 6
Small computer systems, 133
Specimen letter on internal control, 145
SSAP 9 *Stocks and long term contracts*, 209, 217, 218
Statement of directors' responsibilities, 21
Statistical sampling, 108
Stock count, 363
Stock cut-off, 215
Stock system, 180
Stocktake, 210
Stratification, 104
Subsequent events, 202, 288
Substantive approach, 72
Substantive procedures, 72, 192

Summarising errors, 303
Sundry accruals, 266
Suppliers' statements, 337
Systematic selection, 105
Systems-based approach, 72

Tangible fixed assets, 229
Test data, 101
Tests of controls, 72, 136, 158, 162, 166, 178, 181, 184, 333
Tolerable error, 104, 108
Trade creditors listing, 262
True, 11
True and fair, 11

Uncertainty, 317

Wages and salaries, 266
Wages system, 164
Work in progress, 209, 217
Working papers, 110, 331

CAT Paper 8 – Implementing Audit Procedures (UK) (6/05)

REVIEW FORM & FREE PRIZE DRAW

All original review forms from the entire BPP range, completed with genuine comments, will be entered into one of two draws on 31 January 2006 and 31 July 2006. The names on the first four forms picked out on each occasion will be sent a cheque for £50.

Name: _____ Address: _____
                                          _____
                                          _____

How have you used this Interactive Text?
(Tick one box only)

☐ Home study (book only)
☐ On a course: college _____
☐ With 'correspondence' package
☐ Other _____

Why did you decide to purchase this Interactive Text? *(Tick one box only)*

☐ Have used BPP Texts in the past
☐ Recommendation by friend/colleague
☐ Recommendation by a lecturer at college
☐ Saw advertising
☐ Other _____

Which BPP products have you used?

☑ Text   ☐ Kit   ☐ i-Pass   ☐ i-Learn

During the past six months do you recall seeing/receiving any of the following?
(Tick as many boxes as are relevant)

☐ Our advertisement in *ACCA Student Accountant*
☐ Other advertisement _____
☐ Our brochure with a letter through the post
☐ Our website www.bpp.com

Which (if any) aspects of our advertising do you find useful?
(Tick as many boxes as are relevant)

☐ Prices and publication dates of new editions
☐ Information on Interactive Text content
☐ Facility to order books off-the-page
☐ None of the above

Your ratings, comments and suggestions would be appreciated on the following areas

	Very useful	Useful	Not useful
Introductory section (How to use this Interactive Text)	☐	☐	☐
Key terms	☐	☐	☐
Examples	☐	☐	☐
Activities and answers	☐	☐	☐
Key learning points	☐	☐	☐
Quick quizzes	☐	☐	☐
Exam alerts	☐	☐	☐
Question Bank	☐	☐	☐
Answer Bank	☐	☐	☐
List of key terms and index	☐	☐	☐
Structure and presentation	☐	☐	☐
Icons	☐	☐	☐

	Excellent	Good	Adequate	Poor
Overall opinion of this Interactive Text	☐	☐	☐	☐

Do you intend to continue using BPP products?   ☐ Yes   ☐ No

Please note any further comments and suggestions/errors on the reverse of this page. The BPP author of this edition can be emailed at catherinewatton@bpp.com

Please return this form to: Mary Maclean, CAT Range Manager, BPP Professional Education, FREEPOST, London, W12 8BR

CAT Paper 8 – Implementing Audit Procedures (UK) (6/05)

REVIEW FORM & FREE PRIZE DRAW (continued)

Please note any further comments and suggestions/errors below

FREE PRIZE DRAW RULES

1. Closing date for 31 January 2006 draw is 31 December 2005. Closing date for 31 July 2006 draw is 30 June 2006.

2. No purchase necessary. Entry forms are available upon request from BPP Professional Education. No more than 8 one entry per title, per person. Draw restricted to persons aged 16 and over.

3. Winners will be notified by post and receive their cheques not later than 6 weeks after the relevant draw date.

4. The decision of the promoter in all matters is final and binding. No correspondence will be entered into.

CAT Order

To BPP Professional Education, Aldine Place, London W12 8AW
Tel: 020 8740 2211   Fax: 020 8740 1184
email: publishing@bpp.com   website: www.bpp.com
Order online www.bpp.com/mybpp

Mr/Mrs/Ms (Full name) _____

Daytime delivery address _____

_____ Postcode _____

Daytime Tel _____ Email _____

Date of exam (month/year) _____

Occasionally we may wish to email you relevant offers and information about courses and products. Please tick to opt into this service. ☐

POSTAGE & PACKING

Study Texts/Kits
	First	Each extra	Online
UK	£5.00	£2.00	£2.00
EU**	£6.00	£4.00	£4.00
Non EU	£20.00	£10.00	£10.00

Passcards/Success CDs/i-Learn/i-Pass
	First	Each extra	Online
UK	£2.00	£1.00	£1.00
EU**	£3.00	£2.00	£2.00
Non EU	£8.00	£8.00	£8.00

Learning to Learn Accountancy/Business Maths and English
	Each	Online
UK	£3.00	£2.00
EU**	£6.00	£4.00
Non EU	£20.00	£10.00

Order Table

		6/05 Texts	2/05 Kits	2/05 Passcards	2/05 i-Learn CD	2/05 i-Pass CD	Learn Online
INTRODUCTORY							
Paper 1	Recording Financial Transactions	£19.00 ☐	£10.95 ☐	£6.95 ☐	£29.95 ☐	£19.95 ☐	£100.00 ☐
Paper 2	Information for Management Control	£19.00 ☐	£10.95 ☐	£6.95 ☐	£29.95 ☐	£19.95 ☐	£100.00 ☐
INTERMEDIATE							
Paper 3	Maintaining Financial Records	£19.00 ☐	£10.95 ☐	£6.95 ☐	£30.95 ☐	£19.95 ☐	£100.00 ☐
Paper 4	Accounting for Costs	£19.00 ☐	£10.95 ☐	£6.95 ☐	£30.95 ☐	£19.95 ☐	£100.00 ☐
ADVANCED CORE							
Paper 5	Managing People and Systems	£19.00 ☐	£10.95 ☐	£6.95 ☐	£30.95 ☐	£21.95 ☐	£100.00 ☐
Paper 6	Drafting Financial Statements	£19.00 ☐	£10.95 ☐	£6.95 ☐	£30.95 ☐	£21.95 ☐	£100.00 ☐
Paper 7	Planning, Control & Performance Management	£19.00 ☐	£10.95 ☐	£6.95 ☐	£30.95 ☐	£21.95 ☐	£100.00 ☐
ADVANCED OPTION							
Paper 8	Implementing Audit Procedures	£19.00 ☐	£10.95 ☐	£6.95 ☐	£30.95 ☐	£21.95 ☐	£100.00 ☐
Paper 9	Preparing Taxation Computations (FA2005)	£19.00 ☐†	£10.95 ☐	£6.95 ☐	£30.95 ☐	£21.95 ☐	£100.00 ☐
Paper 10	Managing Finances	£19.00 ☐	£10.95 ☐	£6.95 ☐	£30.95 ☐	£21.95 ☐	£100.00 ☐
INTERNATIONAL STREAM						3/05*	
Paper 1	Recording Financial Transactions	£19.00 ☐	£10.95 ☐	£6.95 ☐		£21.95 ☐	
Paper 3	Maintaining Financial Records	£19.00 ☐	£10.95 ☐	£6.95 ☐		£21.95 ☐	
Paper 6	Drafting Financial Statements	£19.00 ☐	£10.95 ☐	£6.95 ☐		£21.95 ☐	
Paper 8	Implementing Audit Procedures	£19.00 ☐	£10.95 ☐	£6.95 ☐		£21.95 ☐	
Learning to Learn Accountancy (7/02)		£9.95 ☐					
Business Maths and English (6/04)		£9.95 ☐					

SUBTOTAL £ _____

*Available in March 2005
†Published in October 2005

Grand Total (incl. Postage)

I enclose a cheque for £ _____
(Cheques to BPP Professional Education)

Or charge to Visa/Mastercard/Switch

Card Number ☐☐☐☐☐☐☐☐☐☐☐☐☐☐☐☐

Expiry date _____ Start Date _____

Issue Number (Switch Only) _____

Signature _____

We aim to deliver to all UK addresses inside 5 working days; a signature will be required. Orders to all EU addresses should be delivered within 6 working days. All other orders to overseas addresses should be delivered within 8 working days. **EU includes the Republic of Ireland and the Channel Islands.

CAT Order

To BPP Professional Education, Aldine Place, London W12 8AW

Tel: 020 8740 2211   Fax: 020 8740 1184
email: publishing@bpp.com   website: www.bpp.com
Order online www.bpp.com/mybpp

Mr/Mrs/Ms (Full name)

Daytime delivery address

Postcode

Daytime Tel   Date of exam (month/year)   Scots law variant Y / N

Occasionally we may wish to email you relevant offers and information about courses and products. Please tick to opt into this service. ☐

	Home Study Package*	Home Study PLUS*	2/05 i-Learn CD	Learn Online
INTRODUCTORY				
Paper 1 Recording Financial Transactions	£100.00 ☐	£180.00 ☐	£29.95 ☐	£100.00 ☐
Paper 2 Information for Management Control	£100.00 ☐	£180.00 ☐	£29.95 ☐	£100.00 ☐
INTERMEDIATE				
Paper 3 Maintaining Financial Records	£100.00 ☐	£180.00 ☐	£30.95 ☐	£100.00 ☐
Paper 4 Accounting for Costs	£100.00 ☐	£180.00 ☐	£30.95 ☐	£100.00 ☐
ADVANCED CORE				
Paper 5 Managing People and Systems	£100.00 ☐	£180.00 ☐	£30.95 ☐	£100.00 ☐
Paper 6 Drafting Financial Statements	£100.00 ☐	£180.00 ☐	£30.95 ☐	£100.00 ☐
Paper 7 Planning, Control & Performance Management	£100.00 ☐	£180.00 ☐	£30.95 ☐	£100.00 ☐
ADVANCED OPTION				
Paper 8 Implementing Audit Procedures	£100.00 ☐	£180.00 ☐	£30.95 ☐	£100.00 ☐
Paper 9 Preparing Taxation Computations (FA2005)	£100.00 ☐	£180.00 ☐	£30.95 ☐	£100.00 ☐
Paper 10 Managing Finances	£100.00 ☐	£180.00 ☐	£30.95 ☐	£100.00 ☐
INTERNATIONAL STREAM				
Paper 1 Recording Financial Transactions	£100.00 ☐	£180.00 ☐		
Paper 3 Maintaining Financial Records	£100.00 ☐	£180.00 ☐		
Paper 6 Drafting Financial Statements	£100.00 ☐	£180.00 ☐		
Paper 8 Implementing Audit Procedures	£100.00 ☐	£180.00 ☐		
Learning to Learn Accountancy (7/02)	Free/£9.95 ☐			
Business Maths and English (6/04)	Free/£9.95 ☐			

SUBTOTAL £ ☐

POSTAGE & PACKING

Home Study Packages

	First	Each extra	Each
UK	£6.00	£6.00	-
EU**	-	-	£15.00
Non EU	-	-	£50.00

i-Learn

	First	Each extra	Online
UK	£2.00	£1.00	£1.00
EU**	£3.00	£2.00	£2.00
Non EU	£8.00	£8.00	£8.00

Learning to Learn Accountancy/Business Maths and English

	Each		Online
UK	£3.00		£2.00
EU**	£6.00		£4.00
Non EU	£20.00		£10.00

Postage and packing not charged on free copy ordered with Home Study Course.

Grand Total (incl. Postage) £ ☐☐☐☐☐☐

I enclose a cheque for
(Cheques to *BPP Professional Education*)

Or charge to Visa/Mastercard/Switch

Card Number ☐☐☐☐☐☐☐☐☐☐☐☐☐☐☐☐

Expiry date ☐☐☐☐   Start Date ☐☐☐☐

Issue Number (Switch Only) ☐☐

Signature

We aim to deliver to all UK addresses inside 5 working days; a signature will be required. Orders to all EU addresses should be delivered within 6 working days. All other orders to overseas addresses should be delivered within 8 working days. *Home Study Courses include Texts, Kits, Passcards and i-Pass. You can also order one free copy of either Learning to Learn Accountancy or Business Maths and English per Home Study Package, to a maximum of one of each per person. Please indicate your choice on the form. **EU includes the Republic of Ireland and the Channel Islands.